GUIDELINES FOR PROJECT EVALUATION

UNITED NATIONS INDUSTRIAL DEVELOPMENT ORGANIZATION
VIENNA

PROJECT FORMULATION AND EVALUATION SERIES, No. 2

GUIDELINES

FOR

PROJECT EVALUATION

UNITED NATIONS
New York, 1972

ID/SER.H/2

UNITED NATIONS PUBLICATION

Sales No.: E.72.II.B.11

Price: $U.S. 6.00 (or equivalent in other currencies)

Manufactured in Austria

Preface

This publication represents the cumulative experience of UNIDO in the methodology and practice of national benefit-cost analysis for industrial project preparation and evaluation. UNIDO's work in this field began with the Interregional Symposium on Project Preparation and Evaluation held in Prague in 1965. On the basis of the recommendations of this symposium, UNIDO undertook to develop a set of guidelines which the developing countries could use for incorporating the evaluation and approval of new industrial projects into their over-all industrial planning mechanism.

The work has gone through a number of stages since then. The first set of background papers was written in 1966/1967. These papers were extensively used in national training workshops in Mexico, Ceylon, India, and Iran. On the basis of the practical experience gained in analysing projects in these countries and in training local cadres to apply the techniques, the work was revised to make it more operational and to reflect better the diversity of the needs of the developing countries. It is hoped that these Guidelines will be used for drawing up detailed instruction manuals in individual countries.

The views and opinions expressed are those of the authors and do not necessarily reflect the views of the secretariat of UNIDO.

Authors' Foreword

We, the authors, have consulted together with the UNIDO secretariat on all substantive aspects of this publication and, therefore, consider ourselves to be jointly responsible for the final publication as a whole. However, not all of us worked equally on all chapters. Partha Dasgupta is primarily responsible for chapters 6, 7, 10, 19 and 20; Amartya Sen for chapters 1 through 5, 8 and 9; and Stephen Marglin for chapters 11 through 18. Chapter 21 is adapted from a case study prepared by Thomas Weisskopf of Harvard University, and chapter 22 was prepared by the UNIDO secretariat. In addition to the case study, Professor Weisskopf contributed to the writing of chapters 4 through 7, as well as to the groundwork of the formulation of these Guidelines. Mrinal Datta-Chaudhuri of the Delhi School of Economics also contributed significantly to the development of the ideas reflected in this volume. In addition to UNIDO sponsorship, the secretariat has provided continuing intellectual as well as material and moral support from the inception of this project at the Prague Symposium in 1965 to the present.

We are grateful to Professors Weisskopf and Datta-Chaudhuri, to several members of the UNIDO secretariat and to workshop participants, too numerous to mention individually, who have left their imprint on the present work.

PARTHA DASGUPTA and AMARTYA SEN,
London School of Economics,

STEPHEN MARGLIN, Harvard University.

CONTENTS

Part I

INTRODUCTION TO THE METHODOLOGY OF NATIONAL BENEFIT-COST ANALYSIS

Chapter 1

THE RATIONALE FOR SOCIAL BENEFIT-COST ANALYSIS

Chapter 2

COMMERCIAL PROFITABILITY AND ITS LIMITATIONS

Chapter 3

NATIONAL ECONOMIC PROFITABILITY

CONTENTS *(continued)*

Part II

APPLICATION OF METHODOLOGY AT THE PROJECT LEVEL

Chapter 4

AGGREGATE-CONSUMPTION OBJECTIVE: MEASUREMENT OF DIRECT BENEFITS

Chapter 5

AGGREGATE-CONSUMPTION OBJECTIVE: MEASUREMENT OF DIRECT COSTS

Chapter 6

MEASUREMENT OF INDIRECT BENEFITS AND COSTS

Chapter 7

THE REDISTRIBUTION OBJECTIVE

Chapter 8

THE EMPLOYMENT OBJECTIVE

CONTENTS *(continued)*

Chapter 9
TOTAL NET BENEFIT OF THE PROJECT: A SUMMING UP

Chapter 10
PROJECT EVALUATION UNDER UNCERTAINTY

Part III
APPLICATION OF METHODOLOGY AT THE ACTIVE PLANNING LEVEL

Chapter 11
THE ROLE OF NATIONAL PLANNING IN PROJECT FORMULATION AND EVALUATION

Chapter 12
NATIONAL PARAMETERS: MEANING, SIGNIFICANCE AND DERIVATION

Chapter 13

INTERTEMPORAL CHOICE: THE SOCIAL RATE OF DISCOUNT

Chapter 14

INTERTEMPORAL CHOICE: THE SOCIAL VALUE OF INVESTMENT

CONTENTS *(continued)*

Chapter 15
THE SHADOW WAGE IN A SURPLUS-LABOUR ECONOMY

Chapter 16
THE VALUE OF FOREIGN EXCHANGE

Chapter 17
CO-ORDINATION OF INVESTMENT DECISIONS

Chapter 18
CONFLICT AND CHOICE: A SUMMING UP

CONTENTS *(continued)*

Part IV
CASE STUDIES

Chapter 19
SOCIAL BENEFIT-COST ANALYSIS OF A PULP AND PAPER MILL IN SARANIA

Chapter 20
SOCIAL BENEFIT-COST ANALYSIS OF A CHEMICAL PLANT IN PALAVIA

Chapter 21
SOCIAL BENEFIT-COST ANALYSIS OF THE MANAGUA WATER PROJECT

CONTENTS *(continued)*

Chapter 22
FIBREBOARD PLANT IN OASIS

LIST OF FIGURES

INTRODUCTION TO THE GUIDELINES

In almost all developing countries the national Government plays an important role in formulating and evaluating investment projects, although of course, the mix of private and public-sector investment varies from one country to another. Either by direct investment in the public sector or by imposing controls on private investment, or by the use of domestic taxes, tariffs, subsidies and the rationing of scarce investment resources the Government is generally in a position to guide development in the country.

Concomitant with this authority of the Government to control new investments is the responsibility to pursue policies that are in the national interest. Projects should, therefore, be formulated and evaluated in such a way as to single out for implementation those that contribute most to the ultimate objectives of the country. It follows that the Government requires a methodology for comparing and evaluating alternative projects in terms of their contributions to these objectives. This volume is concerned with the formulation of such a methodology.

GOVERNMENT PROJECT EVALUATORS AND THE REST OF THE ECONOMY

The search for public-investment criteria is an important part, but nonetheless only a part, of the investigations involved in the study of public finance. And what makes matters awkward is that what is appropriate as a criterion by which to assess public-sector projects depends rather sensitively on the extent to which the Government is able to wield the other instruments at its disposal. For it is clear that public investment is only one of several instruments that are normally at the disposal of the Government to enable it to pursue one policy rather than another. To the extent that the Government has at its disposal a larger number of instruments and a greater flexibility in their use it can presumably choose a more desirable programme for the economy. But what we are focusing on at this point is the rather obvious (but often neglected) fact that the rules that ought to govern the selection of public-sector projects depend on what policies the Government is actually following (or is likely to follow) in the use of its other instruments of control.

A simple example may help to illustrate this point. Suppose that the return from investing in a project if located in region A is higher than what

1

it would be if the project were located in region B. But suppose that B is a particularly impoverished region, and that the Government is concerned about regional income distribution. If it were possible for the Government to enable income to be redistributed between the two regions through inter-regional income transfers, then it might well be appropriate to install the project in A. That is to say, it would be right to generate more national income by the Government's production policy and to handle its distribution through such transfers. But it may well be that for a variety of political and social reasons the Government is unable (or even unwilling) to employ such transfers as a means of income redistribution. It may then make sense to install the project in B. In this latter situation the burden of achieving income redistribution also falls on public investment.

Now it may, on first thought, be supposed that commercial profitability is a reasonable criterion by which to assess public-sector projects. The *raison-d'être* of this volume is the clear recognition that the prices that obtain in the market in developing countries are not necessarily the prices that ought to be used in public-sector project evaluation. Many reasons can be advanced in favour of this view, and we consider them in chapter 2. The problem then is to obtain notional prices that the Government ought to use instead. These prices, which we shall call "shadow prices", are the values that we would want to attach to specific commodities (e.g. steel, bulldozers, fertilizers and machine tools); or to services (e.g. unskilled labour); or to the "act of waiting" (the rate of discount). The problem, therefore, is to obtain appropriate shadow prices. But the nub of the matter is that, apart from depending on the purely technological possibilities facing an economy, these shadow prices depend also on the objectives of the Government and the variety of instruments of policy that the Government possesses: in particular the shadow prices depend on the extent to which the Government does in fact wield these instruments of policy.

In a very broad sense taxes, tariffs, quotas, licences and public investment are all instruments of the Government as a whole. And since in any planning exercise all these instruments hang together, so to speak, the reader may be tempted to think that one cannot really obtain clear-cut rules for public investment unless at the same time one obtains rules for the rest of the fiscal and monetary system. And he would be right. What is ideally required is a treatise on "planning". It is, nevertheless, our view that a good understanding can be obtained of the considerations that matter when a planner is choosing among public-sector projects even if he leaves somewhat in the background the working of the rest of the fiscal system.

These Guidelines are addressed primarily to government project evaluators. As we have emphasized already, it is extremely important for such an agent of the Government to know how the other agencies of the Government are (and are likely to be) wielding their instruments. He will need to know whether regional transfers through taxation are possible, and whether they will be forthcoming when he is confronted with the problem of the location of a

public-sector project. He will need to know the extent to which the Government is able to regulate the monopolies that exist in the economy. He will need to know the Government's import policy with regard to a commodity when he is evaluating a project that requires this commodity as an input. And so on.

As we have already remarked, taxes, tariffs, licences etc. are also instruments of the Government as a whole. But the extent to which these instruments are (and can be) controlled is constrained by a variety of social and political considerations. These considerations vary from country to country and from time to time. And even though the public-sector project evaluator is a part of the government machinery, he may not necessarily approve of the way certain other government instruments are wielded. He may think that they can be wielded in a more appropriate fashion. But he may not wish to suppose that he can necessarily influence the other government agencies responsible for policies that he thinks can be improved upon. What is important for our purpose here is that it is a recognition of whether or not he can influence these other agencies that will in general determine what rule he ought to follow in evaluating public-sector projects. Public-sector project evaluation should, therefore, reflect what will (or more realistically, what is likely to) happen, and not what ought to happen in the wielding of the other government instruments of control. ←

To take another simple example, suppose that it appears that project **X** would be a good investment if a certain intermediate input **R** needed for it were to be imported but not if **R** is manufactured domestically (assuming that **R** is not economically produced in the country). But suppose that the project evaluator knows that if he were to choose project **X**, thus creating a domestic demand for **R** (or augmenting the demand that existed earlier), certain pressure groups would emerge—for example, those who would like to produce **R** under the protection of a quota, or an enhanced tariff, or some other restriction. It would follow that the criterion by which he would want to evaluate **X** (specifically, the shadow price of **R**) will depend crucially on whether he thinks the pressures for the domestic production of **R** will be successfully crushed by the government agencies responsible for policies on tariffs, quotas etc.

It follows that the project evaluator's reading of the constraints that bind the decisions of the various government agencies is of immense importance to the criterion by which he evaluates the projects that come to him for assessment. But, as we have mentioned earlier, these constraints vary from place to place and from time to time. For this reason what we have written is more a guideline than a manual on project evaluation. Indeed, it is our belief that a manual cannot be written if one is to address it, as in the present case, to nearly 100 developing countries. What emerges in the present volume are rules for evaluating projects under a variety of circumstances. The particular set of rules the project evaluator would wish to follow will depend, naturally, on the circumstances that he finds prevailing in his country. The guide has been written in terms general enough to allow the project evaluator a good

deal of freedom in choosing his assumptions and to enable him nevertheless to obtain rules for evaluating projects. Indeed, it is our hope that this volume will be of use in the writing of manuals in individual countries. In this sense the guide is open-ended.

PLAN OF THE GUIDELINES

This volume is divided into four parts. Part I, consisting of chapters 1 to 3, is introductory in nature. It reviews the reasons for the need for project evaluation (chapters 1 and 2). It discusses in some detail the various objectives that Governments typically consider in their national plans (chapter 3), and what role public investment is likely to play in the realization of such objectives. It is then clearly of importance to have some account of the exchange of information between the project evaluators and the central planning organization. This is touched on in chapter 1.

For the purposes of these Guidelines, we have found it convenient to divide the set of shadow prices into two classes. One consists of those prices that pertain to specific commodities (such as the price of a lathe or of a ton of cement) and that, roughly speaking, the project evaluator can assess for himself; the second consists of those parameters that pertain, roughly speaking, to the economy as a whole and are to be used uniformly in all projects. The latter class, which consists of such prices as those of unskilled labour and foreign exchange, we call the set of "national parameters". These national parameters consist also of a variety of national weights whose logic consists in their being a reflection of the Government's various goals. By their very nature we take it that in the first instance these national weights are unknowns to the project evaluator.

Part II of these Guidelines contains a detailed discussion of the shadow prices in the first class of our division. In a crude sense, for the project evaluator, the chapters in this Part go to the core of the matter. Here we consider the net contribution of a project towards the national objective of improving the time profile of aggregate consumption (chapters 4, 5 and 6); the project's impact on the national objective of improving the distribution of income (chapter 7); and its impact on such objectives as increasing employment (chapter 8). In chapter 9 we summarize the impact of a project on the various objectives of the Government and present the logic of the final calculation that has to be done by the project evaluator. Throughout these chapters we make the conventional assumption that the project evaluator faces a world shorn of risk. In chapter 10, therefore, we give an account of what the evaluator needs to do in the face of uncertainty.

We have already mentioned that we regard the national parameters as those that in the first instance are unknowns for the project evaluator. By their very nature they are parameters that one cannot normally expect the project evaluator to evaluate and to assess by himself. Such quantities as national weights (discussed briefly in chapters 1 and 3) reflect national policy

and as such are not normally within the purview of the project evaluator's office. It is in a discussion of national parameters that one faces in its pristine form the problem of the grafting of project planning to a national plan and, in turn, the interaction between the project evaluator's office and the central planners. Part III of the Guidelines is concerned precisely with this basket of problems. In chapters 11 and 12 we discuss in detail the meaning and significance of national parameters. Chapter 13 contains a detailed discussion of one set of national weights, namely, the social rates of discounting. In chapters 14 and 15 we derive various formulae for such derived national parameters as the social values of investment and the shadow price of unskilled labour. Chapter 16 contains a discussion of the shadow price of foreign exchange. Chapters 17 and 18, which conclude Part III, go in detail into the role of national planning in project formulation and evaluation.

In Part IV we present four case studies. All have been taken from actual feasibility reports, but we have adapted these studies to accommodate a number of circumstances that project evaluators are likely to find in practice. For this reason we have placed the projects in mythical countries. The purpose of presenting the case studies is to illustrate the nature of the calculations described in Part II. Our idea was to make the case studies as self-contained as possible, since it is our belief that the methods of evaluating projects that are advanced in these Guidelines can best be understood in the actual process of evaluating projects. We have, therefore, made the case studies unusually detailed. Many of the arguments presented in chapters 4 to 9 are repeated in the studies so that the reader is not compelled too often to go back and forth between Parts II and IV.

Taken as a whole, this volume, though not a treatise on planning, is concerned with the integration of project planning and national planning. As such the volume is not addressed exclusively to government project evaluators. Indeed, as we have emphasized repeatedly in the body of the text, the methods we are advocating for project evaluation cannot properly be set into use if there is not a good deal of feedback between the project planners and the central planners. This, we would like to stress, is not a feature unique to our methods, but is in the nature of national economic planning itself.

How to read the Guidelines

The reader may, of course, wish to read the Guidelines from cover to cover. We would certainly hope so. But the practical project evaluator may become impatient at first with the detailed discussions in the chapters of Part II. There we discuss such issues as consumers' surplus and the possible inefficacy of the tax system. These are important matters for the project evaluator. He might, nevertheless, find the issues somewhat dry at first reading. If so, we would encourage him to go directly to the case studies. Only occasional glances back at the preceding chapters (there are ample cross references in the case studies) are required for the reader to get a very broad

idea of the mechanics of it all. We would hope that the reader would by then be persuaded that such a system of social benefit-cost analysis is workable. He should then carefully read through the chapters in Parts II and III.

A FINAL WORD

This volume can be read by non-economists. Indeed, it was written with this aim in mind. We have, therefore, avoided technicalities as far as possible. Terms have been defined all along the way, even those that are very familiar to economists. We have avoided mathematics as well, except for some simple algebra that was inescapable in Part III. For a more formal description of the underlying model upon which the Guidelines have been based, the interested reader may consult the selected bibliography that follows. See in particular Marglin [2], Sen [4] and [6] and Dasgupta and Stiglitz [1].

SELECTED BIBLIOGRAPHY

There is by now extensive literature on the subject of social benefit-cost analysis. The following list is a selection of books and articles that discuss the methods presented in this publication.

1. DASGUPTA, P. and J. E. STIGLITZ: *Benefit-Cost Analysis and Trade Policies*, Cowles Foundation discussion paper, Yale University, October 1971 (mimeo.).

2. MARGLIN, S. A.: *Industrial Development in the Labour Surplus Economy*, Harvard University, 1966 (mimeo.).

3. MARGLIN, S. A.: *Public Investment Criteria*, George Allen and Unwin Ltd., London and Massachusetts Institute of Technology, Cambridge, Mass., 1967.

4. SEN, A. K.: *Choice of Techniques*, 3rd ed., Blackwell, Oxford, 1960.

5. SEN, A. K.: "General criteria of industrial project evaluation", in *Evaluation of Industrial Projects*, United Nations, 1967 (Sales No.: 67.II.B.23).

6. SEN, A. K.: "Accounting prices and control areas: An approach to project evaluation", *Economic Journal*, March 1972.

An alternative approach to project evaluation is to be obtained in the following:

7. LITTLE, I. M. D. and J. A. MIRRLEES: *Manual of Industrial Project Analysis in Developing Countries*, Vol. II, Organisation for Economic Co-operation and Development, Paris, 1969.

The emphases in the Little-Mirrlees *Manual* are considerably different from those brought out in these Guidelines. A comparison of the two approaches can be found in the following publication:

8. DASGUPTA, P.: "An analysis of two approaches to project evaluation in developing countries", *Industrialization and Productivity*, Bulletin No. 15, UNIDO (Sales No.: E.70.II.B.10), and republished in the *Oxford Bulletin*, February 1972.

Other discussions pertaining to project evaluation include:

9. Arrow, K. J. and M. Kurz: *Public Investment, the Rate of Return and Optimal Fiscal Policy*, The Johns Hopkins Press, Baltimore, 1970.

10. Bruno, M.: "The Optimal Selection of Export Promoting and Import Substituting Projects", Paper presented to First United International Seminar on Development Planning, Ankara, Turkey, 1965 (ISDP I/AKR.3).

11. Chenery, H. B.: "Comparative advantage and development policy", *American Economic Review*, March 1961.

12. Diamond, P. A. and J. A. Mirrlees: "Optimal taxation and public production", *American Economic Review*, March and June 1971.

13. Stiglitz, J. E. and P. Dasgupta: "The theory of differential taxation, public goods and economic efficiency", in Symposium on Public Economics, *Review of Economic Studies*, April 1971.

14. Prou, C. and M. Chevel: *Etablissement des programmes en economie sous-développée, tome 3: L'étude de grappes de projects*.

PART I

Introduction to the Methodology of National Benefit-Cost Analysis

Chapter 1

THE RATIONALE FOR SOCIAL BENEFIT-COST ANALYSIS

1.1 PROJECT CHOICE AND NATIONAL PLANNING

For a private commercial entrepreneur project choice is a rather simple exercise. If he knows his own objectives, which seems to be a reasonable assumption, all he has to do is to ascertain which projects satisfy his objectives best. For a planner the picture is somewhat more complex. In choosing projects he has to ascertain which ones best satisfy the interests and objectives of the nation. His personal objectives are fairly unimportant; he must choose the best thing for the society. This is complex not merely because the national interests are not easy to define, but also because the reading of these interests by different planners may well be different. If different planners pursue different national objectives, the result may be unsatisfactory and conceivably disastrous.

The main reason for doing social benefit-cost analysis in project choice is to subject project choice to a consistent set of general objectives of national policy. The choice of one project rather than another must be viewed in the context of their total national impact, and this total impact has to be evaluated in terms of a consistent and appropriate set of objectives.

The avoidance of a complete dichotomy between project choice and national planning is one of the main reasons for doing social benefit-cost analysis. When one project is chosen rather than another, the choice has consequences for employment, output, consumption, savings, foreign exchange earning, income distribution and other things of relevance to national objectives. The purpose of social benefit-cost analysis is to see whether these consequences taken together are desirable in the light of the objectives of national planning.

1.2 BASIC DIFFERENCES BETWEEN COMMERCIAL CALCULATIONS AND SOCIAL BENEFIT-COST ANALYSIS

A commercial firm faces specific prices (or demand and supply conditions) and does not need to go into the question of what these prices represent for

11

the nation as a whole. If a specific soap costs 1 shilling a bar, or if a particular type of cigarette sells at 2 shillings a packet, the manufacturer of the soap or cigarettes gets some hard information from this. For a planner, however, this information is really very "soft", and he needs to go deeper to ascertain what these prices mean. Does the price of cigarettes take account of the smokers' higher probability of heart disease or cancer? Does the price of soap take note of the benefits that others receive from people's use of soap, e.g., the reduced risk of spread of disease, or the advantage of not having to travel with dirty fellow passengers? For the commercial entrepreneur these questions may be interesting as a pastime, but for a public-project planner they are crucial questions that should influence his decisions.

By the very nature of his work a commercial entrepreneur can confine his thoughts to a rather limited range of effects, but a planner on behalf of the country must, of necessity, take a wider view. This point is simple enough, but it is often overlooked when one contrasts the quick and clear-cut decisions of private entrepreneurs with the rather slow and cumbersome exercises of public-project evaluation. The two jobs are not really comparable.

This is not to say that multiplicity of objectives is an exclusive characteristic of public-project evaluation. Most economic agents have many objectives. An entrepreneur may try to get more profits, but may also be interested in being big and having a large volume of sales. A worker may wish to earn more, but may also desire more leisure. While the reconciliation of these different objectives does involve problems, the job is likely to be much more complex for a planner who has to seek an appropriate compromise between the various divergent objectives and goals of national planning. These objectives may severely conflict with each other, since the nation is a collection of diverse groups with different interests. The problem cannot be casually dismissed, and social benefit-cost analysis must face the problem of multiple objectives of diverse types.

Even the choice of a rate of interest to discount future social benefits reflects a particular compromise of the conflicting interests of different generations. For a commercial firm the rates of interest may simply reflect the rates at which it can lend or borrow. But to a planner interest rates must be viewed as a method of apportioning benefits and costs to different time periods, and possibly between different generations. He has to compare the value of benefits today with that of benefits in the future.

Thus, the contrast between commercial decision making and the planning of projects on behalf of the nation is simple but important. The latter would appear usually to be a much more complex exercise than the former, and the techniques used in the former exercise may be unhelpful in the latter. The approach of social benefit-cost analysis is aimed precisely at systematizing the complex problems of project planning from the point of view of the society or the nation.

1.3 NATIONAL PARAMETERS

It is important to recognize that for choosing between projects it is not sufficient to know all the impacts of the choices on all economic and social magnitudes, since the planner must also have some method of evaluating this total impact. Suppose the choice of project A rather than project B involves losing consumption worth $1 million this year for getting additional consumption worth $1.1 million next year. Is this worth doing? This is not a question of ascertaining the facts but of obtaining values to evaluate facts. At a rate of interest of 5 per cent used to discount future consumption, it will be better to choose A, but at a discount of 15 per cent, B will be better; 10 per cent is the break-even point. The choice of the appropriate rate of discount is a problem that will be faced not merely by this project planner, but by all project planners. It is therefore a matter of national policy, and it would be incorrect to expect the government project evaluator to be able to decide on the rate of discount.[1] The rate of discount is, thus, a national parameter.

There are other types of national parameters as well. Each project will affect employment and wage payments. It may be important for each project evaluator to know how much of the wage bill is consumed and how much is saved; also to know whether there exists a pool of unemployed people from which unskilled labour can be obtained without having to cut down employment elsewhere. These are matters on which the evaluators of particular projects may not have direct information. Furthermore, the same set of information may be relevant for different evaluators, so that there is a case for gathering information centrally and communicating it to the project evaluators. These magnitudes can also be viewed as national parameters.

The set of national parameters is, thus, not merely concerned with value judgements and national objectives, but also with systematic information on facts that are relevant to all (or many) project-selection exercises. There are calculations that the project evaluator must make himself (e.g. how much output a particular plant in the project will produce), but there are others that one cannot justifiably expect the evaluator to make.

The effectiveness of social benefit-cost analysis depends much upon how national parameters are derived and used. In Part II of these Guidelines the use of national parameters will be discussed. The derivation of these national parameters will be investigated in Part III.

1.4 SIGNIFICANCE OF SOCIAL BENEFIT-COST ANALYSIS

The inability of commercial profitability to reflect national gains is discussed in chapter 2. It is quite common nowadays to reject commercial profitability as a basis of planned choice, but this causes a gap that social

---

[1] The national level is designated as the CPO (Central Planning Organization). We discuss the role of the CPO in Part III. See in particular chapter 11.

benefit-cost analysis has to fill. First, it has to provide a basis for evaluation by providing prices that will be appropriate for social calculations ("shadow prices" as opposed to market prices). Second, it has to serve as substitute for pure *ad hoc* decision making. A project evaluator may be able to justify practically any project by making appropriate assumptions, e.g. about interest rates, or consumption habits, or the value of the earnings of foreign exchange. If the project evaluators are not required to use a given set of social parameters and values, bias may well be an important factor in project choice (which would open the door to chaos).

It is worth remembering that social benefit-cost analysis is not a technique but an approach. It provides a rational framework for project choice using national objectives and values. Projects are judged in terms of their precise impact on the economy, and this impact is evaluated by using parameters reflecting national goals, social objectives and global facts. This is relevant not merely for the evaluation of given projects but also for formulating new ones and implementing the chosen projects. There are always a very large number of elements one can vary in formulating new projects. Which of these are important and worth pursuing will depend on the guidance provided by social benefit-cost analysis. Similarly, in implementation there are always small choices between variants that are not fully specified in the plan and are left to the implementors, and it helps to have a clear picture of the social benefits and costs of these choices.

1.5 INSTITUTIONAL FRAMEWORK

The institutional pattern of governmental decision making is usually rather complex. We shall examine this in some detail in Part III. For the purpose of this chapter, however, it is important to catch the essence of a system in order to be able to analyse precisely the appropriate procedures for project formulation and evaluation. On the basis of the reasoning that has been put forward above, it seems necessary to have information flows going in several directions. A simple representation of the basic framework is given in figure 1.

Project evaluators evaluate projects on the basis of factual information on the projects and the national parameters. These national parameters consist of (1) value parameters (like the social rate of discount and regional distribution weights),[2] which we shall also call "national weights"; and (2) factual parameters (like the Government's propensity to reinvest or the marginal propensity to invest in the private sector).[3] Part II of these Guidelines reviews the procedures that the project evaluator should pursue in the use of the factual information on projects. But as we have already mentioned, the choice of national parameters does not fall within the purview of the individual project evaluator.

---

[2] See chapter 3.
[3] See in particular chapters 11 and 12.

Figure 1   A four-unit view of formulation, evaluation, and planning

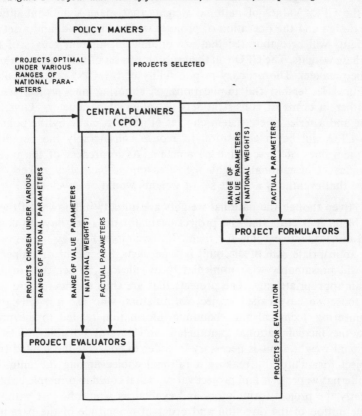

The CPO will have some notion of the factual national parameters on the basis of data supplied in a well-formulated national plan, since these parameters are basic characteristics of the pattern of development of the country[4] and are needed to provide an over-all check on the consistency of the development plans of the various sectors of the economy. However, the value parameters, which reflect ethical judgement, cannot be readily inferred from even the best of national plans currently in existence.[5] In the long run it may be possible for the CPO to be able to inform the project formulators and evaluators of the values of the national parameters that are chosen by the policy makers for the economy. But for reasons that are spelled out in chapter 12, we do not believe that this is possible as yet. What is envisaged instead is that the CPO will inform the individual project evaluators only of the values of the national parameters that are factual in nature. For the immediate future those national parameters that are ethical in nature should be regarded as unknown by the project formulators and evaluators. The project evaluator will carry out a sensitivity analysis on projects on the

4 See Part III, especially chapters 11, 12 and 17.
5 See chapter 12.

basis of a range of values of these national weights and submit this analysis to the CPO. Values of national weights that make significant differences in the design and the operation of projects will be identified, and a set of project variants will be elaborated that are optimal in different ranges of the values of these weights. The CPO will then submit this set of variants to the responsible policy makers. The primary responsibility of the CPO is to articulate to the political leadership the implications of choosing one project variant over another in terms of consistent sets of values of parameters. Given sufficient time and a series of consistent choices of projects made by the policy makers, the CPO will be in a position to reduce considerably the potential ranges of the values of these value parameters. As awareness of the meaning and significance of national weights increases among the policy makers, one would hope that eventually a single set of weights would be developed.

Even though the national weights are initially unknowns of the planning problem, it is clear that the project evaluator does not have to consider any and every possible value for them. For example, he may not know whether the appropriate rate of discount is 5 per cent, 8 per cent or 10 per cent, but he will presumably wish immediately to rule out 50 per cent or 1 per cent as an appropriate rate. The projects that are thus considered are formulated by those we have called project formulators, who use not only the specific engineering, technical and economic information related to the project, but also the factual national parameters and several possible values for each national weight. This is necessary in order to conserve the limited time of the project formulator by making a rational choice among the infinite number of alternative projects and project variants that could in principle be considered. Clearly the project formulators and evaluators would be lost without having some notion of the direction and order of magnitude of the parameters that the policy makers consider to be of national importance.

Thus, we envision project evaluators and project formulators conducting a dialogue. As the ranges in values of national parameters are gradually narrowed, the evaluation of the projects formulated may reveal some bias in formulation, e.g. a tendency to draw on too much imported equipment or too little domestic labour; the evaluators should then call this to the attention of the formulators. One way of viewing this is to have arrows of information going in both directions between formulators and evaluators. This is, however, rather mechanical, and it is difficult to view formulation and evaluation as separate processes. Basically, formulation involves some evaluation, and the two have to be jointly performed. Formulation is an expensive process in terms of both money and time, so that the idea of doing successively many complete formulations in the light of respective evaluations is not very practical.

Thus, it may be more convenient to think of the process as a two-unit one with formulation and evaluation completely merged. This is presented in figure 2. The point at issue is not merely how we visualize the process of project choice but also how we analyse it and suggest appropriate techniques

Figure 2   A three-unit view of formulation, evaluation and planning

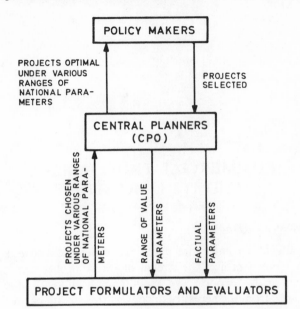

for the best results. It is therefore essential for the Guidelines to assume a realistic structure rather than one based on hypothetical dichotomies that cannot work in practice.

One point is especially important to note in this context. The Guidelines' chief concern will be with evaluation, since formulation is crucially dependent on techniques of evaluation. Indeed, it is not possible to say much at a general level about the non-evaluational aspects of formulation that would apply to formulating all types of projects. The formulation of chemical projects as opposed to the manufacture of machine tools involves different types of technical and engineering knowledge. What is common to all projects, however, is the use of parameters in making an over-all evaluation, and it is on this that the Guidelines can concentrate most fruitfully.

Chapter 2

COMMERCIAL PROFITABILITY
AND ITS LIMITATIONS

2.1 COMMERCIAL PROFITABILITY

The profits of an enterprise equal the difference between its earnings and its costs.[6] For a project the stream of future profits and losses may be calculated period by period. The main complications in the concept of profitability arise from the necessity to convert this stream of profits and losses into some simple measure expressed as a number, e.g. the "rate of return" or "the present value" of the project.

If the stream of profits is $P_0, P_1, P_2, \ldots, P_n$, with a positive figure standing for net profits and a negative figure for a net loss, or the net expenditure, the "present value" of the stream is simply the discounted sum of this stream, the discounting being done at the appropriate rate of interest, i. Representing the present value of the project at interest rate i as $V(i)$, we get:

$$V(i) = \sum_{t=0}^{n} \frac{P_t}{(1+i)^t} \tag{2.1}$$

What kind of measure of profitability is the present value? It is a fairly good measure, since it converts the entire stream of profits into one number representing the total amount of profits today that would be equivalent to the entire stream of profits. The equivalence is defined as that given by the appropriate rate of interest. For the evaluation of commercial profitability, the appropriate rate of interest is the rate that rules in the market for borrowing and lending. If a person can lend and borrow at 10 per cent, he would have no reason to choose a project that costs £100 today and yields only £109 next year. Similarly, he would have no reason to reject a project that yields £111 one year from now and costs only £100 today. Even if he does not have the money, he can borrow it at 10 per cent and make a net profit of £1 by next year.

---

[6] Costs, of course, include real investment costs rather than bookkeeping depreciation costs.

18

What, it may be asked, if the person in question has a personal rate of discount that is different from 10 per cent? What if he finds £115 next year to be equivalent to £100 today? Would he then not be justified in rejecting a project that yields £111 next year and costs £100 this year? He would be, but the question that arises in this case is: Why does he have a personal rate of discount of 15 per cent when he can borrow and lend at 10 per cent? If there were this difference, should he not proceed to borrow a large quantity of money, since he pays only £110 next year for £100 this year while he considers £115 next year to be just as satisfactory as £100 this year? He should thus make use of the market by borrowing, and this he should continue to do until his personal rate of discount comes down to the level of the market rate of interest of 10 per cent. (Another possibility is that the market rate of interest will rise, thanks to his borrowing, but this would be unlikely in a large market, since any individual would tend to be a small operator compared with the enormity of the entire market.) Similarly, if the person initially has a personal rate of discount lower than the market rate (e.g. if he thinks that £100 this year is equivalent to £108 next year), then he should use the market as a lender. He can get £110 by lending £100 this year, and clearly it is worth his while to do this, since he regards £108 to be enough compensation for losing £100 this year. As he lends more and more he will have more and more money later and less and less now, so that he will tend to shift his preference in favour of money now; this rise in the rate of discount will continue until it equals the market rate of interest.

Thus, for a private operator, the correct discount rate is the market rate of interest, at least if we accept the conventional assumptions of economic rationality.[7] And this he can use for calculating the present value of a project. It is, of course, possible that the interest rate would vary from period to period, and the calculation of the present value need not be based on the assumption of an unchanging interest rate. Suppose that the interest rate between year 0 and year 1 is i_1, and that between year 1 and year 2 is i_2 (and so on), then the present value of the project is given as:

$$V(i_1, i_2, \ldots, i_n) = \sum_{t=0}^{n} \frac{P_t}{(1+i_1)\ldots(1+i_t)} \qquad (2.2)$$

It is clear that (2.1) is a special case of (2.2) when $i_1 = i_2 = \ldots = i_n$.

A relevant question to ask is the following: At what rate of interest, constant over time, would the present value of a project be exactly zero, i.e. for what i would we have $V(i) = 0$? This is not unduly complicated to calculate. An interest rate for which the present value of a project is zero is called the "internal rate of return" of the project. It is perfectly possible in principle that the present value of a project may become zero at more than one rate of interest, e.g. the stream (100, —500, 600) has two internal

---

[7] See section 13.3 for further discussion of "rationality" in the context of intertemporal decisions.

rates of return, namely, 100 per cent and 200 per cent. This problem, while somewhat intriguing, is perhaps not very important for a variety of reasons. For one thing, this multiplicity of the internal rate of return would never occur if a project yielded losses up to a certain point in time and thereafter yielded profits (e.g. after it comes into operation). In such a case, the higher the interest rate the lower will be the present value (as in figure 3), and the internal rate of return must be unique (0A in figure 3).

Figure 3   Present value at alternative discount rates

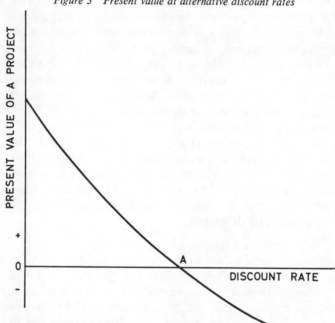

While we cannot spend time on the question of multiplicity of the internal rate of return, the question of the relative significance of the internal rate of return and of the present value is an important one and should engage our attention. The present value at the market rate of interest and the internal rate of return are both measures which convert the stream of profits into one number, and it is relevant to know which one is a better guide. Do they, in fact, conflict? In choosing projects we may follow the rule that all projects with an internal rate of return higher than the market rate of interest should be chosen. Alternatively, we may recommend that all projects with a positive present value should be selected. Does it make any difference which of the two rules we follow? The answer is "No, not at all", so long as the present value always goes down as the discount rate is raised, as in figure 3. If the market rate of interest is less than 0A, the project represented in figure 3 should definitely be chosen according to both criteria, while if it is more than 0A it should be rejected by both tests. There is no conflict whatever in all this.

The real conflict arises when the rule of choosing all projects satisfying either of these criteria cannot be followed. There may be certain specific constraints. For example, the choice of one project may rule out another, e.g. projects A and B may be two variants of a dam on a certain river, and the construction of one would eliminate the possibility of having the other. Suppose that A yields a higher internal rate of return (say, 20 per cent rather than 10 per cent) and a lower present value at the market rate of interest of 5 per cent (say, £1 million rather than £2 million), which should we choose? The conflict arises with the question of ranking the two projects in terms of their relative desirability. Figure 4 represents this and also illustrates that

Figure 4   Conflict between present value and discount rate

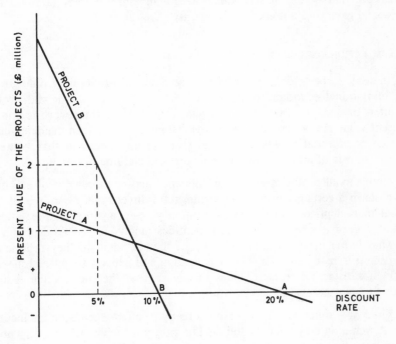

such a conflict can arise even though the present value of each project declines with the discount rate.

One can say that, in a significant sense, the present value is a better guide than the internal rate. It yields a measure of total gains which the latter does not. If 5 per cent is the market rate (and also the rate at which a person is ready to discount future earnings), project B yields twice as much return as project A, and clearly this is a good thing for B. The fact that the rate of return is higher with A than with B is not very compelling so long as the choice is between having project A and having project B. To take an extreme case, a person may get a return of 500 per cent on a penny and a return of only 20 per cent on $1,000. The latter is likely to be more attractive if the

market rate of interest and the person's rate of discount are 10 per cent. The present value gives a measure of total gains, which the internal rate does not. In what follows, the present value of the commercial returns of a project at the market rate of interest will be taken as a measure of the profitability of a project.

The present value is a good framework also for public choice even though the rate of discount to be used should not necessarily be the market rate of interest but the appropriate social rate of discount; also, the profits should be social profits as measured from the point of view of the society and not commercial profits as normally defined. The reason for preferring the present-value formulation in this case is the same as in the case of a commercial evaluation, that is, the present value gives a measure of total gains (in this case social gains and not commercial gains).

2.2 LIMITATIONS OF COMMERCIAL PROFITABILITY

In what respects does a measure of commercial profitability differ from that of national economic profitability? Why is it that commercial profits are often treated as a bad guide to social gains? If the framework is one of "present value" in both cases, clearly the distinction must lie in the divergence between commercial profits and social gains in any year and that between the market rate of interest and the appropriate social rate of discount.

Commercial profits measure the difference between the value of earnings and costs in a certain period. The earnings are direct money earnings of the firm at market prices and the costs are money costs, again at market prices. As was argued in chapter 1, social benefit-cost analysis must go deeper and ask what is the meaning of market prices, that is, what do they represent? If a person is ready to offer £1 for something, he expects to get at least £1 worth of satisfaction from it. Does this mean that the social value is also worth £1? Not necessarily.

First, how much money a person is ready to offer depends on his income level. A rich man may offer a good deal of money for trivia, while a very poor person may find it difficult to spend even very small amounts of money on essentials. The price offered in the market is, thus, not a good guide to social welfare, for it includes the influence of income distribution on the prices offered.

One could, of course, retort by asking why, if the guardians of public policy do not like the income distribution (e.g. if they disapprove of the existing inequality), they do not reform it directly. Once the distribution is reformed, the project evaluator can simply treat the money prices offered as guides to welfare without worrying about income distribution. This retort, while not uncommon, is somewhat hollow, since there are constraints—political, economic and social—that prevent such reforms of income distribution, and given these limitations the exercise of project evaluation cannot be based

on the notion that all appropriate income redistributions have already been carried out.

Further, one of the simpler means of income redistribution may, in fact, be project selection. For example, the choice may be between project A to be located in a poor region or project B to be placed in a rich area, or between project X, which uses a large amount of poor, unskilled labour, which might otherwise be unemployed, and project Y, which uses factors of production supplied by rich people. Project choice has distributional implications, and sometimes it may be politically or socially more feasible to redistribute income this way rather than through taxes or other direct means. We have, therefore, quite a legitimate reason to consider distributional questions in evaluating social gains from a project. This immediately takes one beyond commercial profitability.

Second, a project may have influences that work outside the market rather than through it. For example, a particular industrial project may produce a great deal of smoke and foul air in the town in which it is located. Or a firm may train the labour force in the region. While the first impact may be undesirable and the second laudable, the firm's profits may not reflect either. The cost of bad health or the unpleasant life of neighbours may not depress commercial profits, and the reward for training may not go to the firm, since, after training, the workers are free to leave.

The effects that work outside the market are called "externalities". These do not enter calculations of commercial profits, since these are made at market prices. Externalities are obviously relevant for social choice and provide a sufficient argument for rejecting commercial profitability as a guide to public policy. Externalities can arise in the process of production (e.g. industries causing water pollution), in the process of consumption (e.g. additional private cars adding to the crowding of the roads), and also in the process of sales and distribution (e.g. garish shop display or advertising affecting the tranquillity of the community). Externalities are often most pervasive.

Third, even in the absence of externalities and considerations of income distribution, commercial profitability may still be misleading. If a consumer is ready to pay £1 for a good, he expects to get at least £1 worth of satisfaction from that particular good; but he could expect to get more, conceivably much more. If we look at the market value of a good produced by a project, we get a measure of a floor, to expected satisfaction. But in fact the consumer may expect more and get more. If we try to go into the question of total satisfaction from a project, we would have to examine the excess of what consumers are willing to pay for its products and what they actually pay. This difference is sometimes called the "consumers' surplus". In figure 5, the line AB represents the maximum a consumer is ready to pay for each unit of a good. If the market price is BC, he will then buy 0C units of it. The total expenditure he will make on it is 0DBC, which will represent the earnings of the producer from him. But the value of the satisfaction that he anticipates is more, namely,

Figure 5   Consumers' surplus

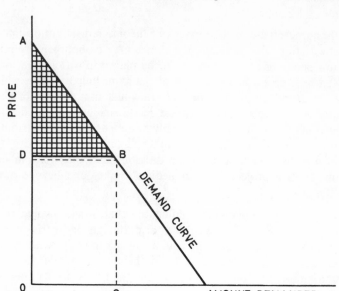

0ABC. The difference, ABD, represents the surplus that he enjoys. While commercial profitability takes no account of it, it is clearly a relevant consideration for public-project evaluation.

It is worth noting that for the last unit purchased there is no surplus, since the price paid, BC, is no lower than the price the buyer is ready to pay. Thus, the question arises not for variations near point B, but for the choice between bulky projects. In ascertaining the social gains from one sizable project rather than another, it is relevant to know the respective magnitudes of the consumers' surplus.

Considerations of income distribution, externalities and consumers' surplus are among the factors that distort commercial profits as a measure of national gains. There are other factors also, but the considerations discussed should have been sufficient to illustrate the difference between social and private gains.

Another ingredient of present-value estimates is the social rate of discount. Given any series of profits (private or social) the size of present value depends on the rates of discount. The social rates of discount may differ from commercial rates of interest for many reasons. An individual may expect to live only a certain number of years and the discounting of future that springs from this limitation may not be appropriate for social choice, since the planners may wish to take a longer view and give greater importance to the welfare levels of future generations. Even the general public of today (as distinct from policy makers) may feel that for public projects, where all are forced to save simultaneously, a lower rate of discount may be appropriate than

would be reflected in the market behaviour of individuals. Individuals may be ready to sacrifice for the future only if others are ready to do the same, and while such a joint action is possible through public policy, there is no way of bringing it about in individualistic market behaviour. Deep problems are involved here, and this question will be taken up more thoroughly in Part III. Suffice it to note now that there are no compelling reasons to believe that the market rate of interest must be the appropriate rate at which to discount future benefits. This is still another reason for commercial profitability to differ from measures of social gain.

2.3 PROFIT MAXIMIZATION AND EFFICIENCY

The usual defence of commercial profit maximization as a criterion is based on the implicit assumption of "perfect competition". Perfect competition is a case where there are many sellers and many buyers so that no one has any monopoly power; each person has perfect knowledge; there are free entries into the market; the product is homogeneous, i.e. there are no variations in quality. It can be proved that if there are no externalities (and a few other relatively minor conditions are satisfied), an equilibrium in a perfectly competitive market must achieve "economic efficiency", which is defined as a state where no one can be made better off without making someone else worse off. Economic efficiency is also sometimes called "Pareto optimality" after the economist Pareto. Each firm maximizing its profits at given prices helps to achieve this type of optimality for the society.

Is this result—which is made much of in the formal economic literature—a compelling reason for recommending that public-project evaluation be guided by profit maximization at given market prices? The answer is a decided "no". First, the absence of externalities is a very dubious assumption, since they are quite widespread. In the presence of externalities, even perfect competition may not achieve economic efficiency. Second, economic efficiency is a very limited requirement. It tells us nothing whatever about income distribution. Some people may be terribly poor and others extremely rich, and still if no poor person can be made better off without making someone else worse off, the situation will still be called economically efficient. As a criterion it does not go very deep.

A no less disturbing consideration is the recognition that the result is based on all markets being perfect. Suppose some are and some are not. There will then be no reason for believing that one would move closer to economic efficiency by maximizing profit at given market prices, and indeed such a policy might conceivably take one further away from economic efficiency. The rule in question works only if all units are in competitive equilibrium. It does not give much guidance to an individual enterprise if imperfections exist in the rest of the economy.

Thus, it should be clear that the relationship between efficiency and profit maximization under competitive conditions does not really establish any

very strong reason for basing project selection on commercial profit maximization at given market prices. The arguments outlined in section 2.2 stand even when the relationship between profit maximization under perfect competition and economic efficiency is noted. In the next chapter we turn away from commercial profitability to national economic profitability as a guide to project choice.

Chapter 3

NATIONAL ECONOMIC PROFITABILITY

3.1 SOCIAL BENEFIT-COST ANALYSIS AND NATIONAL ECONOMIC PROFITABILITY

The object of social choice is to maximize social gains, and the concept of social gains is clearly a basic constituent of rational public policy, including the selection of public projects. How do we measure the over-all gains of the society? Clearly, we seem to need some concept of benefits and costs that would permit us to identify net gains as the difference between aggregate social benefits and aggregate social costs. This difference may usefully be called national profits, when the society is identified with the nation.

From national profits to national economic profits, the translation is not a simple one. It may be thought that benefits (and costs) can be classified into economic and non-economic types, and national economic profitability is concerned with the difference between economic benefits and economic costs. This view would not, however, take us very far, since economic benefits and costs are not easy to distinguish from other types of benefits and costs. Is the increase in longevity an economic benefit or a non-economic one? Is the self-reliance of a nation an economic gain? There are many other ambiguities. Further, even if the distinction is somehow carried through, it would not be at all clear why the choice between projects should be guided by considerations of national economic profits and not by national profits as such. If a project yields a low value of economic benefits but an immense amount of non-economic benefits, why should the latter fact not be relevant for the selection or rejection of it?

Efforts to distinguish between economic and non-economic benefits would, therefore, appear to be a rather unpromising approach. What then is the reason for the usual concentration on the so-called "national economic profitability"? Two lines of reasoning may be relevant here. First, the national profits of an economic project may be called its national economic profits, so that the relevant distinction may be between different types of projects and not between different types of benefits and costs. This is not really a satisfactory approach, since the distinction between economic and non-

27

economic projects is also somewhat arbitrary. The second line is to consider national economic profits as national profits measured in some economic units. Benefits and costs are of different kinds. For ranking projects in terms of their over-all profitability, some method has to be found to convert different types of benefits and costs into a common measure. For this common measure some relevant economic units may be used, e.g. a unit of aggregate consumption or a unit of foreign exchange. With this interpretation national economic profits are national profits measured in some economic terms.

How we define the term "national economic profitability" (NEP) is, ultimately, not very important. What is very important, however, is the recognition that project selection cannot be fruitfully done by concentrating only on the so-called "economic" benefits and costs. The benefits and costs must include all relevant factors that in our view affect national welfare, because the object of project selection is welfare maximization and not maximization of purely economic gains. In what follows, therefore, we would take "national economic profitability", which is to be maximized, simply as a measure of total national profitability, expressed in economic units. While the units that we choose are purely a matter of convenience and need not affect our decisions, there are some clear computational and other advantages of measuring all benefits and costs in corresponding units of some standard economic magnitude.

We may fruitfully begin with discussing some of the more important objectives of public policy that are thought to be relevant for project selection. This we do in section 3.2, where we also consider the relationship between objectives and measures of benefits. In section 3.3 we consider the general problem of getting one measure of national economic profitability from the diverse measures of different types of benefits and costs corresponding to different goals and objectives.

3.2 GOALS, OBJECTIVES, BENEFITS AND COSTS

We might begin by noting that the distinction between benefits and costs is simply one of the sign. A cost is a sacrificed benefit. If project A yields an additional £1 million of aggregate consumption, it is one of the benefits of project A. If project B is now chosen at the expense of project A, using exactly the same resources, then the £1 million of aggregate consumption is a relevant cost for project B. The benefits that are sacrificed by the choice of a project are, in a very real sense, its costs, so that there is no clear-cut analytical distinction between measuring benefits and measuring costs. In the text that follows, therefore, we shall concentrate on relating benefits to objectives, and this will also demonstrate the relation between costs and objectives.

We discuss now some of the more important objectives and the corresponding measures of benefits.

(1) *Aggregate consumption*

The raising of the standard of living is a fundamental goal of national planning, and this naturally includes project selection. One important measure of the standard of living is the level of aggregate consumption per head. The raising of this level may be called the aggregate-consumption objective, which is clearly a crucial objective for project choice. By its very nature aggregate consumption raises certain measurement problems.

First, there are different types of goods that people buy; somehow a heterogeneous bundle of goods has to be converted into one homogeneous measure. The usual way of making this conversion is to weight each good by its price. If p_1, p_2, ..., p_n are the respective prices of goods 1, 2, ..., n, and x_1, x_2, ..., x_n are the corresponding amounts of consumption of each good, then an aggregate measure of consumption is given by C, where:

$$C = \sum_{i=1}^{n} p_i x_i \qquad (3.1)$$

In this procedure of aggregation, the relative weight on each commodity reflects the prices that the consumers pay for it. If necessary, these prices may be corrected to take externalities into account, but it may be more convenient to introduce these considerations separately. Precisely how those corrections are to be worked in is not a matter of principle but one of convenience.

Second, aggregate consumption also involves adding the consumption level of different persons. Should these be simply added in given money terms, or should they be added after taking due note of income differences, with a lower weight attached to the money of the richer man? There are analytical advantages in the latter way, but for operational convenience there may be a good case for introducing considerations of income distribution into a separate category of benefits. In fact, it is very difficult to get information on precisely who buys what, so that the actual sums may have to be done with rather more rough information. We shall discuss the objective of income redistribution presently.

Third, there is also the question of aggregating consumption over time, and this involves problems of discounting. The appropriate social rate of discount is the rate at which the decision makers believe that the future benefits must be discounted to bring them in line with present benefits. If a_0 is the value of a unit of consumption today (year 0), and a_1 is that for the next year (year 1), according to the planners, then a_0 units of consumption next year is equivalent to a_1 units today. Thus, next year's consumption levels have to be discounted at the rate:

$$i_1 \equiv \frac{a_0 - a_1}{a_1}, \qquad (3.2)$$

which represents the proportionate decline in the value of a marginal unit of consumption between this period and the next. Likewise, if a_2, according

to the planners, is the value of a unit of consumption in the following year (year 2), then this following year's consumption level has to be discounted at the rate

$$i_2 \equiv \frac{a_1 - a_2}{a_2}, \tag{3.3}$$

to bring the consumption level of year 2 in line with that of year 1. This has to be discounted once again, at the rate i_1, to bring it in line with consumption benefits of year 0. In general, if a_t is judged by the planners as the value of a unit of aggregate consumption in year t, then we have to discount the consumption level of year t at the rate

$$i_t \equiv \frac{a_{t-1} - a_t}{a_t} \tag{3.4}$$

in order to bring the consumption level of year t in line with that of year $t-1$.

Formally, if Q_t is the contribution to aggregate consumption from a hypothetical project in year t, then we can write down the over-all contribution by this project to aggregate consumption as the weighted sum

a_t = VALUE OF UNIT OF CONSUMPTION IN YEAR t

$$a_0 Q_t + a_1 Q_1 + \ldots + a_t Q_t + \ldots = \sum_t a_t Q_t \tag{3.5}$$

By the definition of the social rate of discount (as expressed in 3.4), expression (3.5) is identical to the weighted sum

$$\sum_t \frac{Q_t}{(1 + i_1) \ldots (1 + i_t)} \tag{3.6}$$

As a special case, if the planners judge that the proportionate decline in the value of a unit of consumption from one year to the next is constant—which is equivalent to judging that the social rate of discount is constant—expression (3.6) reduces to the simpler form

$$\sum_t \frac{Q_t}{(1 + i)^t} \tag{3.7}$$

where $i_1 = i_2 = \ldots = i_t = \ldots = i$.

Thus, the greater the value of expression (3.5) [or the equivalent expression (3.6)] the greater is the project's contribution to aggregate-consumption benefits weighted according to its marginal value at different times. If, therefore, one is asked to choose between two or more variants of a proposed project, with the criteria of choice being solely aggregate consumption, then the variant for which the value of expression (3.6) is highest will be the preferred one. Thus, given the social rates of discount, the project evaluator may simply calculate the present value of all consumption—present and future—by discounting at these rates of discount, in accordance with formulae (3.6) and (3.7).

(2) *Income redistribution*

While we must be interested in the size of aggregate consumption, the considerations of distribution are clearly important for estimating national profits. Strictly speaking, considerations of distribution cannot really be separated from questions of aggregate consumption. For one thing, the relative prices used in equation (3.1) to estimate aggregate consumption depend on income distribution, since prices are influenced by demand and demand is influenced by income distribution. Further, the idea of a given total of real consumption being parcelled out among various persons is unreal, since the composition of the output will be influenced by demand and therefore by distribution of money income. Also, there are no clear measures of income distribution that can easily be abstracted from the structure and aggregate consumption, both of which are heterogeneous.

As we argued earlier, it is, in principle, possible to correct the prices offered by each purchaser by using considerations of income distribution, namely, by attaching a lower weight to a richer man's money expenditure. The weight on income accruing to a rich man may also be taken to be less than that accruing to a poor person. Such detailed corrections are, however, not easy to make, and refuge may be taken by the project evaluator in the use of some rough methods that may be practicable.

One such measure is to attach an additional weight to income accruing to, or consumption enjoyed by, the poorest group, e.g. the lowest 10 per cent. More crudely, a certain poor region may be separated out and any consumption generated in that region may be given an additional weight. Similarly, the assumption of a certain class, e.g. unskilled workers, may be given an additional weight in the estimation of total benefits on distributional grounds.

In this approach, the measure of redistribution benefit is the amount of consumption that is generated in the poorest region or is enjoyed by the poorest class. In combining this objective with other objectives, e.g. with the aggregate-consumption objective, a precise weight would have to be chosen for attaching an additional value to the consumption of the poor. The choice of this weight is, of course, ideally a preliminary to policy decisions. But for reasons articulated at length in Part III the value of the weight can, in our view, emerge only from the process of project choice.

(3) *Growth rates of national income*

It is common these days to treat the raising of the rate of growth of national income as an important policy objective. The rationale of this may lie in the fact that, given other things, in particular given the present levels of consumption and income, a higher growth rate is undoubtedly better. It is an indicator of future consumption possibilities.

However, it is somewhat redundant to take the growth rate as a separate objective when the entire future consumption stream has already been considered and aggregated in the measure of aggregate-consumption benefit. As a provider

of information about future consumption, the growth rates may go into our estimation procedures, but the goal is already subsumed by the aggregate-consumption objective, unless of course a high growth rate is desired for its own sake, irrespective of its influence on future consumption. Such a judgement is, however, uncommon.

(4) *Employment level*

An expansion of the employment level, or, more specifically, a reduction of unemployment, is usually treated as a good thing. It is worth asking, however, whether less unemployment is desirable for its own sake, or for its impact on aggregate income and consumption or on income distribution. The last is often a major consideration, since unemployment makes it difficult for some people to have an income, thereby contributing to the ill-distribution of income and consumption.

One particular argument for avoiding unemployment is that the unemployed tend to lose their skills and expertise through lack of practice. This consideration is bound up with the measure of aggregate consumption, since the loss of future output and consumption will be reflected in the figure of aggregate consumption if properly estimated. This process of "unlearning" is, however, not an easy thing to quantify, and the calculation of the impact on future consumption may well be rather imprecise.

There may, however, be reasons for liking employment for its own sake. Unemployment may be thought to be a denial of human dignity, and its reduction may be preferred irrespective of considerations of total consumption and its distribution. Then the size of unemployment may be a measure of costs, i.e. of negative benefits. The reduction of unemployment can then be taken as a separate objective.

(5) *Self-reliance*

Many developing countries are severely dependent on the richer countries for their economic development efforts because of chronic shortages of savings or of foreign exchange. To reduce dependence on foreign countries and to develop self-reliance may be treated as a goal. One project may help to achieve self-reliance while another may increase the country's dependence on other countries, and in the choice between the two projects this contrast may be taken to be relevant.

It is not easy to measure dependence on other countries. A crude but simple measure is the deficit in the balance of payments, leaving out the obviously "balancing" transactions, which brings it into *ex post facto* balance. A cruder but simpler indicator is the measure of trade deficit, i.e. the gap between imports and exports. This leaves out normal capital transfers, but it can be a first approximate indicator of the dependence of one country on others. In recent years, self-reliance has come to be much discussed. Very often it is measured by the deficit in the balance of trade, and sometimes as the deficit in balance of payments, excluding the "balancing" transactions.

(6) *Merit wants*

Employment and self-reliance are examples of goals whose national importance is not determined by individuals in their capacity as consumers. In general we call these goals "merit wants". Other attributes of projects, including specific consumer goods, may be singled out as a subject for special attention on the grounds that their national importance is greater than what consumers think it is. In a backward rural society, people may be reluctant to spend money on education (especially girls' education), but public policy may aim to foster this notwithstanding the reluctance of the recipients to spend for this service. Education may be thought to be a specially meritorious want.

"Merit wants" are often important in public policy. These tend to be more commonly associated with social projects than with industrial projects, which are the subject of concern of these Guidelines, but even in industries merit wants have been identified. A modern factory may be located in a backward area to bring the people in that primitive area into "contact with the twentieth century"; this may be treated as a merit want. There are other examples also, even though they may not be so numerous as in the field of social projects.

It is possible to list many other objectives, but most of the important ones have already been touched on. There remains the question of converting these measures of different types of benefits into one aggregate measure. This is discussed in the next section.

3.3 AGGREGATE NATIONAL ECONOMIC PROFITABILITY

Suppose B_1 is a measure of benefit of type 1, B_2 that of type 2, and so on to type n. These indicate the structure of benefits. But how can we convert this picture into one simple measure of aggregate benefits? It will not do to add them, for they are in different units, and it is not possible to add, say, £1 million of aggregate consumption to 2,000 of additional employment and get a single meaningful figure. Clearly, some method must be found to convert the different measures of benefit into one set of units. The precise procedures for doing this are complex, but at this stage we may be interested only in the principle, namely, what should this conversion aim at? What does it mean to say that 10 units of benefit of type 1 are exactly equivalent to 1 unit of benefit of type 2? The answer is not really very difficult: it must mean that the decision taken is to assume that 10 units of benefit of the first kind are as important for the country as 1 unit of benefit of the second kind. Thus, what is involved is a measure of the amount of one kind of benefit that must be obtained to compensate for the loss of one unit of benefit of the other kind. The exercise is concerned with establishing such equivalences between different types of benefits.

Suppose that a planner considers that v_1 units of B_1 are equivalent to v_2 units of B_2, and also to v_3 units of B_3. Then the aggregate measure of benefits from B_1, B_2, and B_3 can be represented as:

$$\overline{B} = v_1 B_1 + v_2 B_2 + v_3 B_3 \tag{3.8}$$

We can easily choose one of these benefits as our "unit of account" and express total benefits in those units. If we wish to express total benefits in units of B_1, then we can divide everything by v_1.

$$B = B_1 + w_2 B_2 + w_3 B_3 \tag{3.9}$$

where w_2 equals v_2/v_1 and w_3 equals v_3/v_1. It is obvious that w_2 and w_3 represent, respectively, the amounts of B_2 and B_3 that are equivalent to one unit of B_1 in the judgement of planners.

More generally, when there are many types of benefits, say n types, we define total benefits as:

$$B = \sum_{i=1}^{n} w_i B_i \tag{3.10}$$

Total benefits, in this view, are simply weighted sums of specific benefits, the weights representing the rates at which we are ready to substitute one kind of benefit for another.

But should these weights be constant? Clearly not, since the relative importance of a particular type of benefit will depend on the amount the country has of it. If considerable investment is going to a "poor" region, this region will tend to get richer, and the high value that we might have otherwise wished to apply to the income or consumption of the region may now be reduced. In general the set of w_i depends on the set of B_i.

In spite of this, the formulation given in (3.10) may be usable in project planning in many cases. This is because a project may be too small to affect radically the over-all distribution of benefits for the country as a whole. A small project in a poor region may be beneficial to it, but still may not be able to raise its income per head so substantially that the ratio of its *per capita* income to that of the country rises remarkably. Similarly, a project may reduce unemployment in the country, but unless it is a gigantic project, it may still leave the proportion of unemployment about the same.

Of course, many projects taken together may precisely reduce the proportion of unemployment, or raise the ratio of *per capita* income in a poor region to that in the country as a whole, but this calls for integration and co-ordination, which cannot be achieved by the individual project selector and must be carried out at the national level. Indeed, the selection of the weights w_i, which can be viewed as national parameters, must take full account of such effects. This problem will be examined in Part III of the Guidelines.

As far as the individual project evaluator is concerned, the exercise may look very much like that represented in (3.10). The project may contribute

to benefits of different kinds (e.g. consumption today, consumption next year, consumption of the poorest group this year, and so on), but these effects may well be too small to warrant an immediate change in weights.

There is a clear analogy between this operation and that of the choices made by an individual firm in a big, competitive market. For example, a fisherman may sell his catch at the pre-existing market price, since the volume of his output will be too small to affect the price in the market. However, for all fishermen taken together, the volume of output will affect the prices fundamentally. The role of the individual fisherman may be compared with that of the individual project evaluator, while the role of the market corresponds to that of central planning.

The analogy breaks down, however, at one crucial point: whereas each fisherman can be assumed to know the market price before he sets out in the morning, the national weights will not, for some time to come, be known in advance of project selection.

Finally, it may be noted that the discount rate between one period and another corresponds closely to weights on benefits. In the last section we discussed the relationship between weights on consumption levels in different periods and the appropriate rates for discounting future consumption, and the exact relationship was spelled out in (3.4). To recapitulate, if we treat consumption in different periods as separate benefits, than the value of weight w_1 on consumption next year (given a weight of unity on consumption this year) corresponds to $1/(1+i)$, where i is the social rate of discount between the next period and this one. This is obvious, since multiplying consumption next year by w_1 is the same as discounting it by i. A similar correspondence holds for later periods, e.g. w_2 (being the weight on consumption two years hence, given a weight of 1 on consumption today) must correspond to $1/(1+i)^2$, if i is also the social rate of discount between period 1 and period 2 and so on.

However, once future consumption levels have been thus converted into equivalent values of present consumption, we can treat a unit of such aggregate consumption in the same way as a unit of present consumption. We can then proceed to weight other benefits in terms of aggregate consumption if we wish to take present consumption as our general unit of account. What we choose as our unit of account is purely a matter of convenience, but there does seem to be some advantage in taking present, or aggregate, consumption as our unit of account. By now we are coming to concrete problems of calculations, leaving behind general principles, and this is a sign that Part I, which is introductory, may fruitfully end here, and problems of detailed calculations can be explored, keeping in mind the general background provided in Part I.

PART II

Application of Methodology at the Project Level

Chapter 4

AGGREGATE-CONSUMPTION OBJECTIVE: MEASUREMENT OF DIRECT BENEFITS

4.1 AGGREGATE CONSUMPTION

When commenting on the prosperity or poverty of a country, it is quite conventional to refer to the real *per capita* income or to the real *per capita* consumption. International comparisons of consumer expenditures *per capita*, or calories per man, or the value of the output of consumer goods per head are all attempts at reflecting some measure of the current welfare of the country through consumption benefits. It cannot escape a shrewd observer that these are all questionable indices of welfare. Indeed, average consumption in the country is an inadequate basis for the estimation of welfare, because, among other reasons, the precise distribution of the consumption—among classes, regions, groups and individuals—is relevant. Other considerations were listed in chapter 3.

In spite of this plethora of objectives, aggregate consumption is very often taken as a rough measure of current welfare. Indeed, in common judgement, *per capita* consumption is one of the main determinants (often, the most important determinant) of welfare. The practice of treating consumption as the unit of account is largely a result of the practical importance of aggregate consumption vis-à-vis other objectives, even though analytically any type of benefit—important or unimportant—can be treated as the unit of account.

However, aggregate consumption is an inherently slippery concept. It is not easy to get a real number to represent a heterogeneous set of consumer goods, e.g. bread, shirts, apples, travel and movies. The aggregation is usually performed in terms of the consumers' willingness to pay. If someone is ready to pay 1 shilling for a unit of a product and 2 shillings for a unit of another, then the latter is taken as twice as valuable as the former in estimating the "aggregate-consumption" benefit.

It may appear odd that consumers' valuations should form the basis of combining disparate items into a single index of aggregate consumption. This would seem to suggest that if consumers place the same marginal

valuation on a packet of cigarettes that they place on a performance of a classical dance, the Government ought to attach equal priorities to marginal increments of the two, notwithstanding the deleterious effects of cigarettes on health and the cultural enrichment provided by the dance performance. Actually, reliance on consumers' valuation to measure aggregate consumption does not suggest this. It is diametrically opposed to the purpose of these Guidelines to suggest that aggregate consumption is the sole objective of public investment, and contributions to it the sole test of the national economic profitability of an investment. Nevertheless, consumers' valuations are important in general; it seems sensible to consider departures from consumers' valuations as the result of additional social objectives and to reserve the term "aggregate consumption" to measure the value of consumption as consumers see it. Valuations different from those made by the consumers themselves are not ruled out from our benefit-cost analysis but only from the measure of that particular objective which we shall call the "aggregate-consumption objective".

This approach is merely a matter of convenience, and it matters little how we bring in the corrections of consumers' personal evaluations, whether through the consideration of separate objectives (e.g. "merit wants"), or through a correction of the measure of aggregate consumption itself. The choice of the former system in these Guidelines is based on the belief that this is a simpler way of making the calculation.

In fact, even within the general area of measuring "aggregate consumption", there is one place in which it seems convenient to depart directly from the consumers' evaluation; this is with respect to valuation over time. There are many reasons for treating this as a special area in which the market is notoriously unreliable—even without counting the quite widely held belief that the consumers are particularly "irrational" in choices over time, in the sense that the individual frequently wants to "kick himself" for his own past decisions.

Quite apart from the question of "irrationality", which may or may not be accepted, there is the overriding problem that the composition of consumers changes over time, i.e. some die, some are born, and children become adults. Decisions over time involve a shifting body of consumers with the consequent problem of possible inconsistency of values and objectives as revealed by the market. There are also other more complex problems that we do not wish to consider here. As stated in chapter 3, we shall treat the rates of discount as national parameters, the determination of which will be discussed in Part III.

Leaving out the question of choice over time and discounting, we shall try to evaluate aggregate consumption in terms of the consumers' willingness to pay. We now turn to the problem of measuring this willingness.

4.2 NET OUTPUT OF THE PROJECT

The basic problem involved in calculating the aggregate-consumption benefits of a project is to measure the consumers' "willingness to pay" for

the "net output" of the project. By the "net output" of the project, we mean the goods and services made available to the economy that would not have been available in the absence of the project. If the goods and services physically produced by the project [add to the supply] in the economy, they may appropriately be regarded as the net output for the purposes of our analysis. However, if the goods and services produced by the project do not add to the supply available in the economy, but instead [substitute] for an alternative source of supply, leaving the total supply constant, then the net output of the project is really reflected by the resources released from the alternative source of supply. Clearly, as far as the economy as a whole is concerned, the net effect of the project is not the output of the project, since this output would be available anyway. The net benefits created by the project are the newly available resources that have been released by the discontinuation of the old, displaced activity. One good example is the recognition that the real output of an import-substitution project is the net foreign exchange saved by the project.

In every instance one must ascertain whether the physical output of a project adds to supply or substitutes for supply. In the first case, we identify the net output of the project as the actual physical output, and we proceed to measure the corresponding project benefits according to consumer willingness to pay for the goods and services produced. In the second case, we identify the net output of the project as being the resources previously used in the alternative source of supply of the same amount of physical output. In this case, the value of the benefits depends on the saving in the alternative costs of supply of the goods and services. Here we measure the corresponding project benefits according to consumer willingness to pay for the goods and services released—or saved—by the project.

Once the project benefits have been identified, the problem is to find a suitable measure of consumer willingness to pay for the relevant net output. Here it is useful to distinguish several categories of net output. On the one hand, the net output may consist of final consumer goods for domestic consumption. This can occur only when the project itself produces consumer goods and these represent an addition to the supply available to the economy. On the other hand, the relevant net output may consist of intermediate producer goods which are either produced by the project—resulting in an increase in domestic availability—or are released by the project from an alternative source of supply, resulting also in a net increase in their availability to the domestic economy. Finally, we must consider the important case in which the relevant net output of the project consists of foreign exchange. This will occur when the project output is exported, directly or indirectly, or when it substitutes for imports, directly or indirectly.

It is also possible that part of the net output of a project will be labour or land, if these primary resources are released from an alternative source of supply. Since labour and land figure much more conspicuously as project inputs, a discussion of their measurement will be deferred until the next chapter, on the measurement of costs. The same comments apply equally

to the measurement of benefits and costs; benefits in this case are simply costs that are saved.

4.3 BENEFITS FROM CONSUMER GOODS

Suppose that the project under consideration is a sugar manufacturing plant which will sell sugar on the domestic market for home consumption. This sugar will not substitute for imported sugar, nor for any alternative domestic sugar production, but will simply add to the supplies available on the domestic market. It is expected that the sugar will sell for 2 shillings a kilogram.

What is the best measure of consumer willingness to pay for the sugar? The first measure that may be suggested is the market price itself, for when a consumer pays a given price for a good, the satisfaction he derives from that good must be at least as great as the sacrifice he makes in cash. In other words, his willingness to pay must be at least as great as the market price of the good, or else he would not engage in the transaction. Under certain conditions it can also be shown that consumer willingness to pay cannot be greater than the market price. Then we can be sure that the consumer willingness to pay—and hence the appropriate value to attach to the sugar—is precisely equal to its market price.

The conditions which guarantee that consumer willingness to pay for the sugar project does not exceed its market price are threefold: (1) the sugar is freely available to any potential customer willing to pay the market price, i.e. the absence of rationing and other restrictions; (2) no consumer is big enough to exercise "monopsony" power, i.e. monopoly buying power, to influence through his own purchases the market price level; and (3) the addition to the total supply of sugar brought about by the project is not large enough to change the market price.

Conditions (1) and (2) are the conditions of competitive buying. Wherever buying is competitive we should expect that the price paid by each consumer for his last kilogram of sugar reflects precisely his expectation of satisfaction from that kilogram, and therefore, also his willingness to pay for it. For if his willingness to pay exceeded the market price, he would buy more sugar at that price—provided that he was free to do so—and that his own purchases would not push up the price. Indeed, he would continue to buy more sugar up to the point where his willingness to pay for an extra kilogram would be brought down to the market price. This argument holds irrespective of whether the sugar is taxed or subsidized, and irrespective of whether the sellers—as distinct from the buyers—are in a position to influence the market price level through their actions (thereby exercising "monopoly" power). All that is required is that the conditions of purchase be competitive.

Condition (3) is also required to ensure that the anticipated market price of the project of sugar manufacture reflects the willingness to pay for all the additional kilograms of sugar supplied by the project. If the willingness to

pay for an extra kilogram—as reflected by the market price—is the same both before and after the project takes effect, we can be sure that no consumer of the additional output was willing to pay any more than the market price for it.

If one of the three conditions is not satisfied, we can no longer say that consumer willingness to pay is limited to the market price. Suppose, for example, that the project output of sugar is large enough relative to the total supply so that the market price is expected to fall from a previously prevailing level of 3 shillings to 2 shillings a kilogram. Before the plant begins to operate, consumer willingness to pay for the last kilogram of sugar is 3 shillings; when the plant begins production, consumer willingness to pay for the last unit falls to 2 shillings. Under these circumstances, neither the old nor the new price is an adequate measure of consumer willingness to pay for a unit of the project output.

This situation is illustrated in figure 6, in which DD' is a demand curve indicating the total annual demand for sugar (on the horizontal axis) at a range of possible prices (on the vertical axis). Suppose that the current annual production and supply of sugar is 10 million kg; the demand curve shows that the market will just be cleared at a price of 3 shillings per kg, and this is the price that would prevail in a free market. If our projected sugar plant

Figure 6   Willingness to pay for a commodity

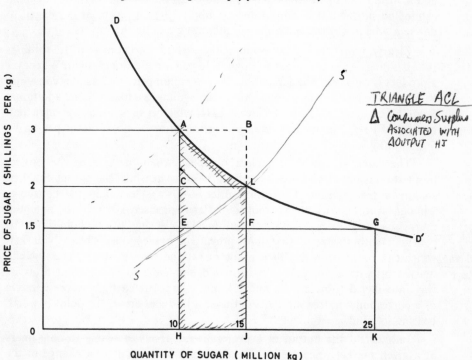

QUANTITY OF SUGAR (MILLION kg)

were to produce another 5 million kg a year, bringing the total annual supply to 15 million kg, we observe from the demand curve that the new market-clearing price would fall to 2 shillings per kg. The consumer willingness to pay for an extra kg of sugar is measured by the height of the demand curve at the given supply level.

Inspection of figure 6 will show that the correct measure of the total willingness to pay of the consumers for the new sugar plant output is neither the actual market payment of 2 shillings per kg times 5 million kg (represented by the area CLJH) nor the old market price of 3 shillings per kg times 5 million kg (the area ABJH). Instead, the correct measure is the area ALJH under the demand curve between the old and the new supply levels. The excess ACL of consumer willingness to pay over the actual market payments (CLJH) for the new plant's sugar is the "consumers' surplus" from the output JH (see chapter 2).

Now, let us suppose that the first condition is violated, i.e. sugar is not freely bought and sold on the domestic market, but is rationed according to a quota system. The need for rationing arises only if the sugar is being sold at a price lower than required to bring the demand into equality with the supply. For example, in figure 6, with the current rate of supply of sugar equal to 10 million kg per year, suppose that the Government decides to fix the price of sugar at 1.5 shillings per kg in order to benefit low-income consumers. This is well below the market-clearing price of 3 shillings per kg, and it would call forth an annual demand of 25 million kg. Since this demand cannot be satisfied at existing rates of supply, the Government is obliged to devise a scheme for rationing the 10 million kg among the buyers.

Clearly, under such circumstances, the current market price of 1.5 shillings per kg is no guide to consumer willingness to pay for additional sugar. Whenever a product is rationed, one can be sure that its ration price understates consumer willingness to pay. In our example, the actual willingness to pay for an additional 5 million kg of sugar is still the area ALJH, which is substantially greater than the area EFJH, obtained by multiplying the price of 1.5 shillings per kg by 5 million kg.

The same argument also clearly applies when the size of the project in question is not large enough to affect the price at which the output could be sold in a free market. The ration price is always less than the consumer willingness to pay, whether or not the latter is precisely equal to the potential market-clearing price. The potential market-clearing price should not be confused with the price that may prevail in a secondary "black" market, which can result from the illicit resale of rationed commodities. The "black" market price is a function of the limited demand and supply that finds its way into illegal transactions, and it cannot be assumed to be representative of a corresponding free market. As this is a frequent error, the point is worth bearing in mind.

BLACK MARKET

A SEGMENTED MARKET

In short, if the output of a project is not freely available to consumers at a given market price, or if it is large enough to result in a change in the

corresponding price, the measurement of consumer willingness to pay has to depart from the value of the consumers' actual payment, which it will exceed. An estimation of willingness to pay will then require investigation into the shape of the demand curve for the product. This is a more difficult task than simply applying a market price, but it cannot be avoided if a realistic appraisal of the project is to be made. While we do not wish to go into the exact methods of demand estimation here, which is a general technical problem and not special to project evaluation, we should note that there are some fairly well-developed techniques for this purpose.

A more difficult task arises when the output of the project is not purchased at all in the market, so that there is not even a first approximation in the form of a market price. Part of the consumer good output of a project may involve educational or medical facilities, and housing or welfare programmes, which often carry no meaningful market price. To evaluate such benefits of public investment is a challenging task; but the problems that arise will not be considered here in detail, for they are unlikely to figure prominently in the formulation and evaluation of industrial projects, the area of our concern. We should, however, note that in these cases the planners will have to do their own evaluation directly, and such an evaluation should be based on an estimation of the importance of these free facilities to the community in comparison with the consumer goods that are purchased. Is a unit of free medical service twice as valuable as a dollar's worth of purchased commodities? The planner may get some guidance in answering this question by trying to consider the price the consumers would have been ready to pay for these services if these were not free. But such a task is not easy, and the planners may be forced to make their own evaluation of the importance of these benefits to the community. This is not a unique problem, since such judgements are needed in other areas as well, e.g. in establishing the national parameters.

4.4 BENEFITS FROM PRODUCER GOODS

Let us now consider a project in which the relevant net output involves a producer good such as steel, which may be used either as an intermediate good or as a capital good in the production of other goods. For convenience, we shall assume that the project itself is designed to turn out a million tons of steel and adds the same amount to over-all domestic supplies. The same kind of analysis, however, would apply if the project output merely substituted for an alternative source of supply, and steel was among the resources thereby saved and increased in net domestic availability.

When the relevant net output of a project is used in the production of other goods and services, the principle of measurement according to consumer willingness to pay still applies. The only difference is that the ultimate increase in consumption made possible by the increased availability of the producer good may be many stages of production removed from the project output, and this tends to make the problem of measurement more complex. Thus, the extra steel made available by the projected steel plant may be used to fabricate

bicycles that will be sold directly to final consumers. Or it may be used to build rails that will enable the railways to provide both final and intermediate transportation services. Or it may be used to fabricate machines that will turn out both consumer goods and more producer goods. The value of the steel from the point of view of the aggregate-consumption objective is the final consumers' willingness to pay for all the ultimate consumption attributable to the steel.

As a first approximation, the manufacturers' willingness to pay for the steel may be taken as a measure of its value to the ultimate consumers. As in the case of consumer goods, there are certain conditions under which the market price actually paid by the producers reflects their true willingness to pay. These conditions include first of all the three mentioned earlier: (1) anyone can purchase as much steel as he wants at the prevailing market price; (2) the purchasers of steel do not exercise any power of monopsony (monopoly power of buyers); and (3) the augmented supply of steel does not bring about a change in its market price. A fourth condition is also necessary: the purchasers of steel do not exercise any monopoly power in the markets where they sell their product. This fourth condition did not apply in the case of purchasers of consumer goods, for the consumer goods purchased are directly consumed. But a producer who can command a higher price for his bicycles if he limits his production will make monopoly profits, and his willingness to pay for steel will exceed what he actually pays by the amount of monopoly profits he can make.

Thus, if the additional steel made available by the project is not bought under competitive conditions, if the product for which it is used is not sold under competitive conditions, or if the price of steel is lowered by the extra supply due to the project, the would-be market price of steel will understate the purchasers' willingness to pay. In such cases it may be necessary to look into the demand conditions for steel just as one would examine the demand curve for sugar, with the difference that the demand for steel is a "derived" demand rather than a demand based directly on consumer preferences.

In certain instances it may be possible to measure indirectly the willingness to pay of purchasers of producer goods by calculating the net profit the producer realizes on the purchased input. For example, if the market for steel is hopelessly non-competitive, we may still estimate the willingness of a given producer to pay for steel by calculating the residual after deducting the costs of all inputs other than steel from the sales value of the producers' output. This residual is a measure of how much the producer would be willing to pay to get the steel: if he paid more, he would make losses; if he paid less, he would make profits on his enterprise. So far we have tacitly assumed that the willingness to pay for the steel of the producer who purchases it is in fact the appropriate measure of its ultimate consumption value. This assumption is valid only if the same four conditions listed above apply to all the markets between the purchaser of steel and the ultimate consumer of the steel-based final good or service. In other words, there must be no departures from

competition in the further processing of the project steel, and the increased supply of steel due to the project must not be significant enough to lower any prices further along the line.

If there are monopoly or monopsony elements in the further processing of the project output, or if the relevant markets are subject to rationing or other interference with free market exchange, the immediate purchaser of the project output does not capture the full consumption benefits of that output when he resells it after processing. The price he receives is artificially lowered from what it would be under competitive conditions, and hence his willingness to pay for project output is also reduced. In principle, to measure the full value of project benefits, the immediate purchaser's willingness to pay must be supplemented by the excess in subsequent purchasers' willingness to pay over and above their actual payments.

✡ RULE

MARKET VALU
+ Σ Consum
Surplus
Down Th
Line

Exactly the same rule holds when—under competitive conditions—the increment in the supply of the good produced by the project results in a lower price of that good in processed form at a later stage. The aggregate-consumption benefits include not only the immediate purchaser's willingness to pay, but also the extra benefits enjoyed further along the line by those people whose willingness to pay for the processed good exceeds the market price. These extra benefits correspond exactly to the "consumers' surplus" defined earlier.

4.5 Benefits in Earning Foreign Exchange

In developing and newly industrializing economies, it happens frequently that the ultimate net impact of a project is not on the domestic availability of goods and services, but on the market for foreign exchange. This is obviously the case when the project involves the production of goods for increasing exports; the net effect of the project is to increase the supply of foreign exchange available to the economy rather than the availability of any particular good or service. The same is true when the project involves the production of goods that will substitute for imports. Provided these goods actually can be expected to replace previous imports, rather than augment total supplies, the net effect is to release a sum of foreign exchange equivalent in value to the foreign exchange cost of the previous imports. Exports and import substitution may also be promoted indirectly if a project releases goods from an alternative source of supply, and these goods are then used to increase exports or save on imports. In either case, the relevant net output is foreign exchange to the extent that exports are increased or imports decreased.

PURELY EXPORT
OR IMP. SUBSTI
PROJECTS

It is sometimes argued that when a project provides goods of a kind that were previously imported, the net output of the project should be treated as foreign exchange whether the goods are actually used to replace imports or whether they simply add to the total supply on the domestic market. This argument can be analysed with reference to figure 7. Let DD' represent the demand curve—and the willingness to pay—for nitrogen fertilizer on the domestic market, with the price of the fertilizer measured on the vertical

axis and the quantity demanded on the horizontal axis. Suppose that the current fertilizer supply consists of 1 million tons, of which half is produced domestically and half is imported. The foreign exchange cost of the imported fertilizer is the equivalent of £150 per ton, but the domestic production cost is higher. To protect the domestic manufacturers, the Government applies an import tariff amounting to £50 per ton, and all the fertilizer is sold at the market-clearing price of £200 per ton.

A new plant is now proposed to manufacture 200,000 additional tons of fertilizer. If this is added to domestic supplies, it can be seen from figure 7

Figure 7   Willingness to pay, availability and foreign exchange

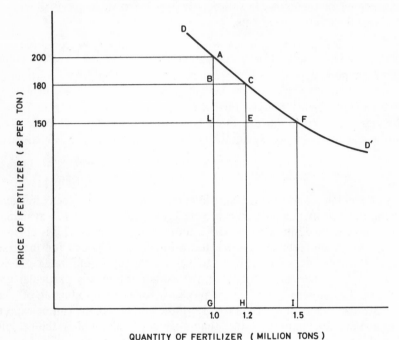

that the market-clearing price will fall to £180 per ton. If it substitutes for previously imported supplies, the price will, of course, remain at £200 per ton. Now if the total supply of fertilizer to the domestic market is held constant when the project goes into operation, the net effect of the project will be to substitute for 200,000 tons of previously imported fertilizer, and the net output of the project will be the £30 million (£150 per ton times 200,000 tons) worth of foreign exchange that is saved (corresponding to the area LEHG).

If the effect of the project is to increase the total supply of fertilizer from 1.0 to 1.2 million tons, then according to the principle of willingness to pay, the benefits of the project should be measured as the area ACHG under the demand curve between the supply levels of 1.0 and 1.2 million tons. The

argument to the contrary suggests that, even under these circumstances, the benefits should be measured as the area LEHG, because the Government could capture the additional benefits ACEL in any event simply by increasing imports by 200,000 tons. Benefits that could be obtained by a mere change in import policy, so the argument goes, should not be attributed to any particular project. So long as the Government can reap benefits by increasing imports (which it can do by importing up to the point where the total supply of fertilizer reaches 1.5 million tons), it should be advised to do so. Once the import level has become optimal it should then consider whether a new domestic plant is justified—and the import-substituting criterion will then lead to a measure of benefits at the foreign exchange saving value of £150 ton.

The above argument is perfectly valid provided the Government can and does raise imports to the optimal level when advised to do so. It is certainly proper to recommend that it improve its import policy, and to measure the net benefits attributable to increased imports by the area between the demand curve and the foreign exchange cost curve. But if, for good or bad reasons, the Government does not in fact change its import policy—if imports of fertilizer are actually kept constant at a level of 500,000 tons—it is quite misleading to pretend that the Government is pursuing an optimal trade policy. The issue is really an empirical one, to be decided on the merits of each case. If the Government does pursue an optimal trade policy or can be persuaded to do so, this should be taken into account. But if the Government seems to be acting otherwise, the evaluation of project benefits must proceed on the basis of what is most likely to happen.

Having established in a particular case that a certain saving of foreign exchange is the relevant net output of a project, it is still necessary to find a measure of the value of foreign exchange. Up to now we have been measuring all benefits in terms of consumer goods measured in domestic currency, while foreign exchange as an output is expressed in some foreign currency. The principle to be applied is the same as with any material output—we must determine what is the willingness to pay (in terms of domestic currency) for the extra foreign currency made available by a given project.

As a first approximation, we may again consider the market price as a measure of willingness to pay. The market price of any given foreign currency is nothing but the official rate of exchange between that currency and the domestic currency. If this market price is to be appropriate, the same conditions listed earlier in the case of producers' goods must apply to foreign currencies, which are purchased not by final consumers but by intermediate traders or producers. Condition (3) is in fact likely to be satisfied in most foreign exchange markets: the changes in supply due to individual projects will be negligible in comparison with the total supply of foreign exchange. If, in addition, the foreign exchange market (and all related markets) is perfectly competitive, so that foreign currency can be bought and sold without limit at the official exchange rate, the domestic willingness to pay is presumably accurately reflected by the domestic currency equivalent at the official rate.

In fact, however, it is much more common to find in developing economies a strictly controlled foreign exchange market, where the supply of foreign exchange is rationed in one way or another over the much greater demand that arises at official rates of exchange. Under these circumstances, the official market rates quite clearly understate the domestic willingness to pay for foreign currencies, and it becomes necessary to estimate by other means the true aggregate-consumption value, expressed in domestic currency, of a unit of foreign currency.

If we assume for the moment that all foreign currencies may be exchanged among themselves at an official set of exchange rates, the problem of valuing foreign currencies is reduced to finding a single price for a common unit of foreign exchange. We first convert all foreign currency values into their domestic currency equivalents, using the official rates of exchange. Then we have only to ask: what is the domestic willingness to pay for an amount of foreign exchange officially equivalent to a unit of domestic currency? The required number we call "the shadow price of foreign exchange".[8]

Because of the importance of the foreign exchange impact of most projects in developing countries, the estimation of the shadow price of foreign exchange is of great significance for social benefit-cost analyses. It should be noted, however, that if not all foreign currencies are freely convertible among themselves, the shadow price of foreign exchange will not be unique. For each non-convertible currency, a distinct shadow price will have to be evaluated reflecting domestic willingness to pay for that currency, and the currency must be kept separate in the accounting of foreign exchange benefits and costs.

It should be obvious, however, that the "shadow prices" of foreign exchange are best evaluated at the central level, and these indeed should fall under the category of national parameters. The important thing to note at this stage is not how these shadow prices should be arrived at, which will be discussed in detail in Part III, but how to use these prices. For that purpose the question of the precise impact of a project on the availability of foreign exchange and goods is crucial, and we have tried to clarify the relevant questions involved in this, including the question of what the project evaluator has to assume about the nature of government policy in general.

[margin handwritten note: FX TREATED AS A CONSUMPTION BENEFIT ONLY UNDER ASSUMPTION THAT FX RELEASED WILL BE USED AS CONSUMPTION]

4.6 STEPS IN THE ESTIMATION

Although the structure of the evaluation of direct benefits of aggregate consumption has been outlined above, it will be convenient to describe the procedure step by step. In the light of the preceding discussion we can split up the exercise into the following steps:

(a) Ascertain the "net output" of the project, and split it up into adding to supply and saving resources.

(b) Estimate the amount that the consumers will actually pay for the additional supply of goods.

---

[8] As might be expected, the shadow price of foreign exchange will vary from year to year.

(c) For additional supply of consumer goods, check whether the consumers are free to buy as much as they like; if there are restrictions (e.g. rationing), try to estimate what the consumers will be willing to pay for the additional supply, which will in general exceed the market price.

(d) For additional supply of consumer goods, check whether any consumer has buyers' monopoly power, and if so, correct the price of the commodity upwards to reflect the difference between the consumers' willingness to pay and what they actually pay. (This is unlikely to be a very important consideration.)

(e) For additional supply of consumer goods, check whether the size of it is so large compared with other sources of supply that the prices would be perceptibly lowered by the additional supply. If so, try to estimate, approximately at any rate, the shape of the demand curve to estimate the consumers' willingness to pay, which would exceed what they actually have to pay.

(f) For producer goods, complete (c), (d) and (e). The same exercises must be done and supplemented by considerations of monopoly power for the subsequent stages of production, e.g. for steel consider the question of the rationing of steel-using products, response of the prices of steel-using products to additional supply, existence of monopoly in later stages and so on. This should be extended to as many stages as practicable.

(g) For goods that substitute for imports or add to exports, estimate the impact on foreign exchange availability by making explicit assumptions about foreign markets etc., and also about the policies of the Government. Use the shadow prices of foreign exchange, supplied by the central planners, to convert foreign exchange benefits into units of aggregate consumption in domestic currency.

(h) In any estimation where future benefits of consumption are directly involved, convert them into present value by using the social rates of discount supplied by the central planners.

(i) For goods that are not sold in the market but are supplied free instead, try to estimate, if possible, what the purchasers would have been ready to pay for these facilities if they were to be purchased. If this is impossible, simply use some estimation of the relative importance of the facilities in terms of general aggregate consumption. This would involve judgements, and while they must be made, it may be helpful for rational discussion on project choice to state these explicitly.

(j) For each project add up all these direct benefits of aggregate consumption to arrive at the total. The total figure is in units of current aggregate consumption; the benefits are homogeneous thanks to the use of appropriate shadow prices (including the shadow rates of discount and the shadow prices of foreign exchange).

Chapter 5

AGGREGATE-CONSUMPTION OBJECTIVE: MEASUREMENT OF DIRECT COSTS

5.1 OPPORTUNITY COST

The concept of cost is amenable to various interpretations, and it is useful to begin with a clear understanding of what costs stand for in the context of benefit-cost analysis. If a person goes to a movie and spends two hours there and has to pay 5 shillings, it can be said that his relevant cost is 5 shillings plus the value of two hours which he might have spent otherwise. Suppose an alternative would have been to stay at home and listen to music on the gramophone. It could then be thought that the cost was the loss of 5 shillings and the sacrifice of the opportunity of listening to music that evening. However, he could have gone to another movie, and from that point of view the sacrifice or cost involved is the loss of the opportunity to see a different movie that evening, or the opportunity of being at home and doing nothing. The person can list other alternatives. Each of these represents an opportunity forgone. What then is his relevant cost? It is, clearly, the best of the opportunities that he is sacrificing, i.e. the maximum benefit from a feasible alternative course of action. Thus, the appropriate concept of costs is that of the *maximum alternative benefits forgone*.

The same concept is relevant for project choice. If by choosing project A we forgo the opportunity of having either project B or project C or project D, the maximum of the respective benefits involved in these three projects is the relevant cost. By not having A, we could have had B or C or D, and if rational we would have chosen the best of these three, so that the best opportunity sacrificed is really what we are losing.

In practice, choices are usually not offered to us between whole projects. But the same considerations hold in the choice of using up resources for the purpose of having this project rather than letting these be used in the best alternative way. If we absorb 10,000 tons of steel in our project, the relevant question is: What would have been the best alternative use of this steel? It could have been exported, or used domestically to make consumer goods A, or to make producer goods B, and so on, and we have to identify the relevant

cost as the maximum benefit that is lost by using up this amount of steel in our project. The same considerations will apply to the use of other resources.

In the identification of costs as the maximum benefits sacrificed, we must be careful to define the alternative opportunities realistically, bearing in mind the real feasibility and not merely technical possibilities. Suppose that it would be best to export those 10,000 tons of steel, but the political forces (e.g. the lobby of steel-using industries) would cause the steel not to be exported but to be sold at a subsidized price to the domestic steel-using firms. Then the fact that technically the steel could be exported is irrelevant, since that is not really feasible given the social and political structure of the country. The maximum benefit that has to be identified with cost will be from the list of feasible alternatives. The technical opportunities that cannot be made use of, given social constraints, are not real opportunities, and the identification of costs as maximum benefits sacrificed must be based on real feasibility.

This last point is analytically simple, but quite difficult to handle from the point of view of empirical estimation. The project evaluator has to make judgements on political and social constraints, and asks: What would really happen if we did not use up x amount of steel, or y amount of labour? Is the alternative to employment here unemployment, or employment in the best technical alternative use, or employment in some use but not the best that is technically possible? To identify feasible opportunities (as opposed to technical possibilities) requires a considerable depth of understanding of the political and social structure, which will take project evaluation beyond pure economics. This is inevitable, given the nature of the task in question, and it is best to recognize explicitly that the framework involves more than technical and economic considerations. The starting point of all project evaluation is to ask the question: If we did not choose the project, what difference would it make? And the assessment of the differences that would result depends on a clear identification of political and social constraints that limit economic opportunities.

5.2 WILLINGNESS TO PAY

Since costs are the (maximum) benefits forgone, we measure costs in much the same way as we measure benefits. As with aggregate-consumption benefits, we measure aggregate-consumption costs according to the criterion of the consumers' willingness to pay. We have seen that the benefits of a project consist of its "net output", defined as the goods and services made available to the economy that would not have been available in the absence of the project. By the same token, the costs of a project consist of its "net input", which may be defined as the goods and services withdrawn from the rest of the economy that would not have been withdrawn in the absence of the project.

DEF. OF NET INPUT

As in the case of measuring benefits, the first step in measuring costs is to identify correctly the relevant net input to the project. Here again we

must distinguish between alternative possibilities. On the one hand, the use of various physical inputs for a project may result in a decline in the total availability of those inputs exactly equal to their consumption by the project. To the extent that this is true, the net input to the project consists of the actual physical inputs.

On the other hand, in response to the demand made by the project for these inputs, their supply may be correspondingly increased in the rest of the economy. In that event, there may be no change in the total availability of the goods and services actually used as inputs to the project. The net input to the project will then consist of those goods and services whose availability to the rest of the economy is reduced because they are used up in producing inputs for the project. In effect, we include within the scope of the project any ancillary production that takes place only because of the demands raised by the project.

In every case, the problem is to identify which goods and services suffer a net decline in availability because of the project. The distinction drawn earlier between the demand and the supply margin may be carried over from benefits to costs. If the actual physical inputs to the project suffer a decline in total availability, we must look to the demand for these goods and services by other potential purchasers in order to measure their aggregate-consumption costs. Here the relevant margin for measurement is the demand margin. If, on the other hand, the project requirement of inputs is met by increased supply from other sources, we are concerned with the supply margin. Given the variety of inputs that are required by any single project, it is most likely that some inputs will have to be measured on the demand margin and others on the supply margin.

Once the project costs have been properly identified, the problem of finding a suitable measure of willingness to pay is precisely the same as in the measurement of benefits. Consumer goods will not figure as relevant project inputs, but producer goods will. Foreign exchange is also an important net input. In addition, we must consider the two primary factor inputs which are not produced: land and labour. In the following pages, we consider separately the special problems that arise in connexion with each category of project input, i.e. (a) producer goods, (b) foreign exchange, (c) land and (d) labour. The relevant methods of estimation of cost will vary from case to case.

5.3 PRODUCER GOODS

Let us suppose that the project in question involves the construction of a large, concrete-filled dam. One of the important inputs is cement, the cost of aggregate consumption of which we seek to measure. If the total availability of cement to the rest of the economy is reduced by the amount of cement used in the project, we seek to evaluate the willingness to pay for the cement that is no longer available. The calculation is very similar to the

measurement of the aggregate-consumption benefits owing to an increase in the availability of cement (e.g. as a result of a new project for manufacturing cement).

Producer willingness to pay for the cement is the first approximation to its aggregate-consumption benefits (if the availability is decreased). If the market price of cement is to serve as an appropriate measure of producer willingness to pay, the same four conditions noted earlier (chapter 4) in the discussion of producer-good benefits must apply. If there are no controls and competitive conditions prevail, the market price reflects producer willingness to pay, provided that the demand for cement by the project is not so great as to push up its market price. In the case where the cement project is large, producer willingness to pay is understated by the original (lower) market price and overstated by the final (higher) market price. This situation is represented in figure 8.

Figure 8   Willingness to pay and withdrawal of a producer good

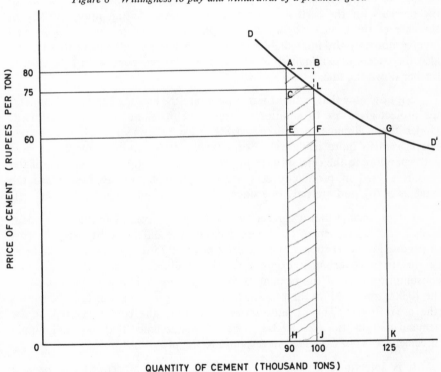

QUANTITY OF CEMENT (THOUSAND TONS)

Before the dam is begun, let the annual rate of supply of cement be 100,000 tons, and suppose that it sells at a market-clearing price of 75 rupees per ton. If the annual demand raised by the dam is 10,000 tons, and if no additional supplies of cement are forthcoming in response to the construction of the dam, the supply available to the rest of the economy is reduced to

90,000 tons. This most limited supply clears the market at the higher price of 80 rupees per ton. The willingness to pay for the 10,000 tons of cement used by the dam is clearly neither the new market price of 80 rupees times 10,000 tons (the area ABJH) nor the old market price of 75 rupees times 10,000 tons (the area CLJH); it is precisely equal to the area ALJH under the demand curve. The correct measure involves the addition of the "consumers' surplus" ACL, enjoyed by the previous purchasers of the last 10,000 tons of cement, to the value of the cement obtained by using the original market price.

If the cement were rationed, or if the cement purchasers exercised monopsony power in the relevant markets, the market price of cement would understate the willingness of purchasers to pay for it, and a more careful study of the demand conditions would be required. In this event, one could attempt to measure producer willingness to pay according to the net profits realized on cement—as suggested earlier (chapter 4, section 4.4) in the case of the steel output. The same qualifications raised earlier with respect to the markets for the further processing of the steel output apply equally in the case of the cement input. In principle, the aggregate-consumption costs involve not only the immediate would-be purchaser's willingness to pay, but also the excess of willingness to pay over actual payment for all purchasers further down the line.

Suppose now that, rather than cutting into the existing supplies of cement, the project gives rise to additional supplies in the same amount as required. Under these circumstances, the market price of cement does not change, but it is also quite irrelevant. For now we must evaluate the input cost corresponding to the cement in terms of the cost of supply, i.e. the cost of the resources used in producing cement. The principles involved here are the same as above and are only one stage further removed from the dam project.

Let us assume that a careful evaluation of the cost of producing cement leads to an assessment of 60 rupees per ton. The difference between the cost of production of 60 rupees and the sales price of 75 rupees may, for example, be due to a government excise tax. We should now value the aggregate-consumption cost of the cement at 60 rupees per ton, which, multiplied by the 10,000 tons used on the project, leads to an over-all cost of 600,000 rupees (the area EFJH). This is substantially less than the cost measured at the demand margin (the area ALJH), when it was assumed that the total supply of cement was not expanded in response to the project.

It is sometimes argued that even if the supply of cement can be and is expanded at a real cost (viz. 60 rupees per ton) lower than the willingness to pay for it (viz. 75—80 rupees per ton), it is the latter figure that is relevant for the benefit-cost analysis. The point here is akin to the one raised earlier in connexion with import substitution. It is argued that benefits in the amount of ALFE can be obtained in any event by expanding cement production independently of the dam project, so that these benefits should not be implicitly

attributed to the dam project by lowering the cement input costs from ALJH to EFJH.

Once again, the argument is valid if in fact there will be an independent expansion in cement production. Such an expansion would reap net benefits equal to the area between the demand curve and the 60 rupees cost curve, and these net benefits would be positive up to a total supply of 125,000 tons of cement. Certainly the Government should be advised to undertake such a project, if there are no other good reasons for doing without it. But unless the production of cement is actually expanded by an independent project, it is wrong to pretend that it is. The evaluation of the dam project must proceed on the basis of the most likely occurrences, which need not turn out to be the optimal ones. This relates to the point we discussed in section 5.1.

5.4 FOREIGN EXCHANGE

Cases in which foreign exchange proves to be the relevant net input to a project are perhaps more common than one might initially suspect. To begin with, directly imported inputs on current or capital account are likely to involve a net drain of foreign exchange equivalent to the foreign exchange cost of the inputs. As long as the availability of these particular inputs to the cost of the economy is not affected, it is the availability of foreign exchange in general that is reduced by the project, and the relevant net input is precisely the foreign exchange used up.

There are only two rather unlikely circumstances under which the foreign exchange used for directly imported inputs to a project would not be obtained at the expense of the availability of foreign exchange to the rest of the economy. First, if there is a fixed quota of imports of a product used as a project input, the result of using such imported products for the project is to reduce the availability of the product to the rest of the economy. In this event, the effective net input is not foreign exchange but the product itself, and its cost should be measured in terms of willingness to pay for that product (rather than for foreign exchange in general), along the same lines as in section 5.3. Second, it may happen that a project does not draw from free foreign exchange for its imported inputs, but uses instead a foreign exchange loan or grant that is tied exclusively to the project. If the loan or grant made to this one project in no way reduces the chances of additional loans or grants to other projects in the country nor the total availability of foreign economic assistance, the imported input results in no immediate drain on the supply of foreign exchange available to the economy. In the case of a grant, the imported input is costless, except for its possible political costs, if any. In the case of a loan, the relevant costs must be determined according to the loan repayment obligations, for it is only when these repayments are made that foreign exchange will have to be diverted from other uses.

Apart from directly imported inputs, foreign exchange may appear as the relevant net input in a variety of indirect ways. Suppose, for example,

that rubber is to be used as an input to a projected tire manufacturing plant in a country producing large quantities of rubber for export. The project demand for rubber might lead to additional rubber production, in which case the rubber input should be valued at its cost of production. The project might also draw rubber away from other domestic uses, in which case the rubber input should be measured according to the other purchasers' willingness to pay for it. But another likely result of the project would be to direct rubber away from the export market, where most of it was previously going. In this event, what the economy loses is the foreign exchange that would have been earned by the exportable product, and the relevant net input is simply foreign exchange.

INDIRECT FX EFFECTS
REDUCE EXPORTS OF INPUT

The same kind of situation may arise with respect to import substitutes. Let us consider the same tire plant in a different country in which there are no rubber plantations, but a domestic synthetic rubber plant has begun to substitute for some previously imported rubber. If the tire plant uses domestic synthetic rubber as an input, it may appear that there is no drain on foreign exchange. However, unless the supply of rubber to other domestic users is curtailed, the net effect of the project will be to raise the requirements of rubber in the economy as a whole. And unless there is idle capacity in the synthetic rubber plant or a new plant is installed right away, the only source from which the additional requirements can be raised is the world market. Once again, the relevant net input would turn out to be foreign exchange.

INCREASE IMPORT OF INPUT

This line of reasoning may be carried even further. Any input whose supply is increased in response to a project must be valued according to the resources used up in its production. If these resources include foreign exchange—via directly imported inputs, via exportables, or via import substitutes—then to that extent the relevant net input consists of foreign exchange. Whenever the measurement of an input takes place on the supply margin, according to production costs rather than immediate willingness to pay for the input, foreign exchange is likely to figure among the relevant net inputs.

FX REQUIRE-MENT OF INPUTS OF INPUT

Once the relevant foreign exchange inputs to a project have been identified, it only remains to measure them according to the principle of willingness to pay. Here the procedure becomes identical to the measurement of foreign exchange benefits, and the earlier discussion of benefits can be carried over entirely to costs. As noted already, unless the market for foreign exchange is sufficiently competitive for one to accept the official rates of exchange as measures of willingness to pay for foreign currencies, one must introduce shadow prices of foreign exchange to value the domestic currency equivalent of the foreign exchange inputs. The estimation of the shadow prices of foreign exchange will be discussed in chapter 16.

5.5 LABOUR COSTS

Production of any type obviously requires the input of labour. From manual workers to highly skilled operatives, from errand boys to top executives,

labour of different grades and in different proportions figures prominently in the cost accounting of any major enterprise. To identify the relevant net input to a project that corresponds to the hiring of any given man, one must as usual ask the question: What does the rest of the economy ultimately lose when this man joins the project? To begin with, what productive resources—human or material—decline in availability as a result of the input of labour to a project?

The immediate effect of engaging a man's services on a project is to deprive the rest of the economy of those services. Unlike steel, cement, or (indirectly) foreign exchange, the supply of human beings cannot be increased by judicious investment in response to the demand of any particular project. Here—and elsewhere—it is important to distinguish between unskilled and skilled labour. Unskilled labour is defined to represent only the most primary labour, of a kind that can be supplied by a man without any special education or training. Skilled labour is defined to include all grades of labour that involve some degree of education or training above the minimum established in the society. The supply of unskilled labour cannot be varied in the short-run; it is a function of long-run demographic trends. The supply of skilled labour of any given type, however, can be increased (at the expense of the supply of less skilled labour) by suitable investment in education and training. Such investment represents what is often called "human capital formation".

Often a project requiring certain specialized services includes a training programme to upgrade the quality of part or all of the labour force. Just like the costs of housing, transport, welfare etc. that may also fall within the scope of the project, the costs of a training programme must be reckoned as net inputs to the project. (Note that the net benefits of housing, training etc.—to the extent that they are not reflected in the direct project output—must be reckoned as part of the over-all net output of the project.) Irrespective of the amount of training a man may get on the project itself, his cost as an input to the project depends on his skill at the time of joining the project, for that is what the rest of the economy is deprived of.

When an unskilled worker is hired for a project, the availability of unskilled labour to the rest of the economy declines, and the relevant net input for a given year is one man-year of unskilled labour services. When a skilled worker joins a project, a man-year of labour services of that particular skill represents the relevant net input—unless, in response to the requirements of the project, training programmes elsewhere in the economy are stepped up so as to prevent the net availability of this kind of skilled labour from declining. In the latter event, we must look at the supply margin for skilled labour: the relevant net input to the project becomes the input required for the training programme to turn out more skilled labour, including the input of an equivalent amount of labour at a lower skill level. Thus, whatever the nature of the case, the use of labour on a project involves a decline in the availability of the same amount of labour—although not necessarily of the same skill—to the rest of the economy.

Having identified the relevant labour component of the inputs to a project, it remains to determine the ultimate consumer willingness to pay for a unit of labour services of each particular kind. Once again, if the necessary conditions involving competitive markets and relatively small changes in supply can be assumed to hold, the market price, or wage rate, of a particular grade of labour may be taken as an appropriate measure of willingness to pay. In many developing countries, however, such a guideline will be of little practical value, for labour markets tend to be notoriously uncompetitive. In certain developing economies, significant amounts of disguised or overt unemployment of labour may coexist with a positive market wage.

To the extent that labour services are drawn (directly or indirectly) from previously unemployed labour, the net loss of productive services to the rest of the economy is clearly nil, even if a conventionally determined positive market wage must be paid. Thus, under the conditions of a "labour surplus", the appropriate cost of labour inputs (sometimes called "the shadow price of labour") may be zero. X - Cost leisure

However, before proceeding to evaluate all labour costs at a price of zero one must note several words of caution.

First, it is essential to distinguish carefully between the different types of labour. While the real cost of unskilled labour may well be zero—if the jobs in question can be adequately filled at all times by workers otherwise unemployed—the same is not necessarily true for skilled labour. It is more than likely that where population is in surplus, skills are in short supply, with the result that the willingness to pay for skilled labour may not only be greater than zero, but perhaps even greater than the market wage.

A second consideration to be borne in mind is the regional dimension of labour supply. Even if there is a labour surplus in the economy as a whole, it may well be unevenly distributed between regions and, in particular, between urban and rural areas. If the project in question is located in an area where the immediate supply of surplus labour does not match the project demand for unskilled workers, the net cost to the economy of bringing in unemployed labour from elsewhere must include the costs of transfer. These costs include not only the immediate costs of transportation, which are not likely to be high, but the extra cost of providing basic social amenities to the workers on the project site that they would not have required in their original location. Usually such expenses must be incurred when an industrial project draws unskilled labour from one place to another, especially from rural to urban areas, where the cost of essential public services is likely to be higher. If these transfer costs are incurred by the project, they can be considered separately as project net input. But to the extent that they are borne by the workers, they must be included in the over-all social cost of labour input.

A final word of caution on the cost of labour applies even when the costs of skills and of transfer may be ignored. The payment of a market wage

to an unskilled worker (whose cost is measured at zero because he is otherwise idle) results in a transfer of income from the Government or private employer to the extent of the wage rate. If the Government or the private employer has a greater propensity to invest out of income than the worker, and if the ultimate consumption value of funds invested exceeds the corresponding value of immediate consumption, there will be a net aggregate-consumption loss arising from the transfer. Taking this argument into account, the "shadow price of labour" should be positive rather than zero. This is, of course, related to the determination of national parameters. In any case, this final correction involves precisely the category of "indirect" benefits and costs that will be discussed in the next chapter.[9]

[Margin annotation: DISTRIBUTIO EFFECT DESPITE USe OF SHADOW WAGE = 0]

5.6 COSTS OF LAND AND NATURAL RESOURCES

Land as an input is naturally associated with every project requiring a site, but specifically for industrial projects it is likely to form a negligible fraction of total costs. For that reason, no elaborate discussion is called for here. As a factor of production that is by definition in constant supply, land as an input must always be measured on the demand margin. When land is used up by the project, that land is denied to the rest of the economy and cannot be substituted for from any other source of supply. The appropriate measure of the cost of land as an input is the ultimate consumer willingness to pay for the aggregate-consumption benefits made possible by the use of the land.

[Margin annotation: RULE]

Where land markets are competitive, and where the project demand for land does not appreciably bid up its price, it may be thought at first glance that the market price of land (or the market rental rate) may be taken as the measure of the willingness to pay for the land (or its use). This would not be quite correct, since the interest rate one would wish to use is not the market rate but the social rate of discount.[10] If the land required by a project has no other potential use, the market-clearing price of the land is zero, and irrespective of the actual cost that must be paid for it, the land must be measured at zero cost as an input to the project. If the land does have an alternative use, but if the market price does not provide an appropriate measure of its value, it may be possible to measure the cost of the land by the net benefits forgone because the land can no longer be devoted to the alternative use.

It is obvious that much the same analysis applies to all natural resources, e.g. water flowing down a river. The building of a dam at one place and its use in the neighbouring areas may affect water supply farther down the stream, and the valuation of this impact is, in principle, similar to that of land. However, while private markets exist for land, they may be absent for river water, and the users' willingness to pay for water may have to be guessed rather than observed in the market.

---

[9] See also chapter 15 for a detailed discussion of this point.
[10] For a similar argument in the measurement of rentals of machinery see section 19.7.

In this case, as in the case of land, there is no prospect of increasing the total flow of water. Hence the relevant alternative is demand reduction rather than supply expansion; so that should be the relevant cost to examine. We have already discussed the methodology involved.

5.7 MARKET PRICES AS FIRST APPROXIMATION

While we have noted several reasons why costs as evaluated by the market would have to be corrected in measuring the social costs in terms of the objective of aggregate consumption, market costs may still provide a good first step in the estimation. Whether or not we use market costs as the first approximation is not a matter of principle, but there are certain operational conveniences in beginning with market prices and costs and then introducing the corrections systematically. This we discussed also in the case of benefit estimation in the last chapter.

Some of the corrections are fairly easy to make. Once the impact of foreign exchange has been evaluated, the correction that the project evaluator has to do is simple, since he just uses the shadow prices of foreign exchange provided by the central planners. To determine these shadow prices is a complex exercise (see chapter 16), but that is a problem faced at the central level and not by individual project evaluators. In contrast, the correction for "consumers' surplus" may involve more detailed calculations, e.g. of the shape of the demand curves. This is especially so when the demand relations in question are a few stages removed. For example, the price of bicycles is affected by a reduction in the supply of bicycles caused by a decline in the availability of tubular steel, which itself may have resulted from an expansion of other categories of steel production to meet the steel demand of the project in question. In estimating these various rounds of impact the standard techniques of input-output analysis may be useful. This is not a problem of evaluation but of correct calculation, and we shall not go into this further. Needless to say, which techniques the project planners will use is a matter of convenience and will depend on the technical sophistication of the planning machinery. In some cases, the estimates would have to be rough and approximate, while in others detailed and fine calculations may be possible. However, in every case the further problem of evaluation will remain.

It is worth bearing in mind that occasionally the subsequent stages may not merely be distant in terms of production processes but also in time. Investment in project A may be partly financed through a reduction in investment in the economy (e.g. through a tax system that would reduce private investment). The impact of that reduction of investment will be on the consumption in the future, and may be for a long time in the future. In evaluating the aggregate-consumption benefits forgone in the future, we shall have to use the appropriate social discount rates to estimate the social present value of the loss. The value of investment in terms of market costs, however, reflects—at best—an evaluation of future benefits discounted at the market

rates of interest. Clearly, some corrections will be needed on the investment costs. Since several indirect relations are involved, we shall postpone a further exploration of this problem to the next chapter, where indirect benefits and costs will be considered. The point to note here is the diversity of considerations requiring a correction of costs (and benefits) as evaluated by the market. Some are obvious and some quite subtle.

5.8 STEPS IN THE ESTIMATION

We now provide a step-by-step breakdown of the estimation procedures for direct costs related to the aggregate-consumption benefits:

(a) Ascertain the "net input" of the project, and split it up into reducing the total supply of inputs and absorbing resources to keep the input supply constant through expanded production.

(b) Check the market cost of the inputs.

(c) In the case of reduction of total supply, estimate the willingness to pay for these inputs through several corrections. The first correction is related to the value of rationed inputs at some stage or other.

(d) The second correction is concerned with the monopoly power in buying or selling at the immediate stage or at a later stage.

(e) The third correction is concerned with the size of the input-supply reduction and its impact on price. If there is a real impact on price, the demand curves would have to be estimated—finely or roughly—to correct for the willingness to pay. This, too, should be carried to later stages in production involving the products made by these inputs.

(f) If the absorption of producer goods in this project is to be compensated by an expansion of supply of these resources from other sources (e.g. an expansion of domestic production), calculate the actual costs involved in that expansion.

(g) If some of the resources are imported, or are obtained at the expense of potential exports, calculate the sacrifice of foreign exchange involved, and correct by the shadow prices of foreign exchange.

(h) Direct future costs are discounted at the appropriate social rates of discount.

(i) Corrections for labour and land must be in terms of reduction of supply, as they cannot be met by expansion of production. Appropriate corrections will include all considerations of willingness to pay discussed in (c), (d) and (e).

(j) For each project add up all these direct costs related to the aggregate-consumption objective. Note that indirect costs, e.g. future benefits sacrificed through absorbing some investment in the project partly (or wholly) at the expense of other investment, are yet to be corrected.

Chapter 6

MEASUREMENT OF INDIRECT BENEFITS AND COSTS

6.1 INDIRECT BENEFITS

So far the discussion of the measurement of aggregate-consumption benefits (chapter 4) has been limited to the willingness to pay of the immediate users of the project output, which might be labelled a measure of the "direct" consumption benefits. (Project output is understood here in the wide sense of all output produced by the project and its ancillary activities, which would not have been produced in the absence of the project.) In this section we examine the possibilities of "indirect" consumption benefits that a project may yield and that are not reflected by immediate willingness to pay. It must be admitted that, to an extent, the distinction between "direct" and "indirect" benefits is arbitrary. For example, suppose that the output of a project is not directly consumed, but is purchased for use in further processing. Moreover, suppose that there are monopoly or monopsony elements in the further processing. We have seen that the immediate purchaser of the project output then does not capture the full consumption benefit of that output when he resells it after processing. It was argued in chapter 4 that in such a situation, to measure the full value of the output benefits the immediate purchaser's willingness to pay must be supplemented by the excess in the subsequent purchasers' willingness to pay over and above their actual payments. It is largely a matter of convenience to incorporate such an output within "direct" benefits, which is what has been done in these Guidelines.

When the existence or operation of a project results in a net gain to society, but not a direct gain to those who acquire the project output, this gain will not be reflected in the willingness to pay for this output. This category of indirect benefits is generally encompassed by the term "external effects", although the term should probably be avoided because of the confusion surrounding its definition. Here we are not concerned with those indirect benefits that are thought likely to be common to all industrial projects of similar size and that are so vague as to defy measurability. Typical of such indirect benefits is that industrialization leads to a rejection of traditional modes of thought and creates an enterprising spirit among the population.

Such claims are an argument for undertaking a plan for industrialization and a reason for encouraging industry vis-à-vis, say, agriculture. But in these Guidelines we are taking for granted that the Government has decided to embark on a plan for industrialization. We are concerned with evaluating industrial projects that compete for available funds. At our present stage of knowledge it appears to be impossible to prove decisively that one project is superior to another in terms of its contribution to the indirect benefits mentioned above.

It must, nevertheless, be admitted that projects often yield a net gain to society that is not wholly captured by those that acquire the project output. In such a case the "additional" benefits ought ideally to be added to the over-all contribution of the project to the aggregate-consumption objective. Such a situation typically occurs when an ancillary good or service produced in connexion with the project contributes not only (internally) to the value of the project output, but also (externally) to the supply of output from other enterprises, or to the satisfaction of consumers other than those who receive the project output. For example, suppose that in the construction of a steel project a system of access roads is included for the purpose of transporting materials required by the project. The benefits provided by the roads are not limited to the service of the project; they will also improve communications and lower transport costs for the whole area, and this is likely to result in lower costs for local industry and hence net consumption benefits for the community as a whole.

The foregoing example represents externalities that result in lower production costs for other producers owing to their ability to use a project by-product free of charge. Somewhat similar indirect benefits are provided by a project that involves the training of its labour force. This, in particular, has received a good deal of attention in development literature. The new skills acquired by the workers contribute to the output of the project, but if the workers eventually move on to other jobs, they bring with them opportunities for greater production than they could have without their acquired skill. These skills then result in a contribution to aggregate consumption made possible by the project, but not included among its direct benefits. Formally speaking, such a by-product could be included with the main project output and evaluated according to the willingness to pay of the beneficiaries. For example, as an unskilled worker gradually acquires new skills on the job his higher productivity will be reflected in the estimated output of the project. The indirect benefits arise only when this newly trained worker moves to another project. If he is paid a higher wage by his new employer because of his newly acquired skills, then even though the production cost borne by the new employer will not be any lower than what he would have had to bear in the absence of the first project, there is still an indirect benefit, namely, the higher wage benefit going to the worker. Therefore, in the evaluation of the benefits due to the first project one would have to include the excess of higher wages that the worker will command over the wage that he would have received had he not

been trained in the first project. The question is whether such evaluations are always worth doing. It is plausible to suggest that one is often inclined to exaggerate the magnitude of such indirect benefits. If workers, having acquired new skills, leave a project site after ten years, the indirect benefits, viewed from the present, may well be quite small (owing to the discounting of these future indirect benefits). Put another way, in the calculation of the present value of a project the errors that are likely to arise as a result of inaccurate forecast of future outputs and inputs and prices is often likely to be much greater than the errors that will result from neglecting such an indirect benefit.

Beyond this it is difficult to generalize. One has to look rather carefully at the nature of the externality before passing judgement. For example, a somewhat different kind of externality is provided when the consumption of project output is enjoyed not only by the purchaser, whose willingness to pay is measured as a direct benefit, but also by other consumers who benefit indirectly from the increased consumption of the purchaser. For some types of industrial projects, such as those producing telephones or vaccines, the measurement of consumption benefits will be seriously distorted if only the purchaser's valuation is considered.

6.2 INDIRECT COSTS

In the discussion of chapter 5 it was pointed out that the basic principle in calculating costs with respect to any objective is that costs are simply equivalent to maximum benefits forgone. Consequently, to the category of indirect aggregate-consumption benefits discussed in section 5.2 there corresponds indirect aggregate-consumption costs—the negative counterpart of the corresponding indirect benefits—and it is this that we discuss briefly here. What we wish to do is to assess the external effects that result in a net loss to society. A typical example is the pollution of air or water by industrial plants. The discharge is a by-product of the industrial process which results in net disbenefits to the surrounding population, although the people affected are not generally compensated for their discomfort by those responsible for the plant. In such cases there is a consumption cost to society which ought ideally to be included in the assessment of a project. Society may justifiably regard the pollution of the atmosphere or water as extremely undesirable. But this would appear to be a reason for questioning a programme for industrialization without adequate precautions against the arbitrary disposal of industrial waste. To repeat the argument of the last section, we are concerned here in the main with competing industrial projects. At our present state of knowledge it appears to be impossible to prove decisively that one project is inferior to another in terms of its contribution to indirect disbenefits.

6.3 LIMITATIONS ON MEASURING INDIRECT BENEFITS AND COSTS

The discussion in the foregoing two sections has, we hope, been sufficient to suggest that at our present state of knowledge, it appears to be practically

impossible to quantify many externalities. We cannot emphasize too strongly that this is not a good reason for ignoring externality. Rather, we should recognize it as one of the most serious limitations of social benefit-cost analysis.

The approach to social benefit-cost analysis presented in these Guidelines consists in attempting to measure as many of the impacts of a project on an economy as possible. Along the way we shall obviously be forced to miss many such impacts—external effects being one of them. One will often be able to assess whether the inability to measure certain impacts very accurately (owing, say, to limited data) will make much of a difference to the measurement of the present value of the net social benefit of a project. But for certain other impacts, specifically externalities, one simply cannot tell how seriously a project is overvalued or undervalued; and it is misleading to suggest otherwise. The impossibility of measuring externalities has led some economists to justify ignoring them by the use of a variant of the "principle of insufficient reason". The argument is roughly that since there are as many reasons for supposing that a given project yields external benefits as there are for supposing that it yields external disbenefits, it is not misleading to suppose that they add up to zero. This argument will simply not do. Even though for most projects it may prove impossible to quantify external effects, their direction may be obvious. Instead of rationalizing away present ignorance, it is far better, in our view, to acknowledge that external effects may well be important even though we may not be able to quantify them. The project evaluator should clearly be aware of these aspects of a project. He should certainly take into account the qualitative descriptions of these effects. In certain situations such qualitative judgements about externalities may well prove decisive in the choice of a project. At any event, such broad descriptions may facilitate decisions by putting the quantified net benefits of a project into perspective.

6.4 SAVINGS AND INVESTMENT

We turn now to the last category of indirect benefits and costs. It will be convenient to treat savings and investment simultaneously. The economic feature that leads to such benefits and costs is essentially this: an individual who benefits from a project may respond to his improved position not by increasing his present consumption but by increasing his savings; and an individual who incurs costs on a project may respond not by cutting down his consumption but by reducing his savings. Such changes in savings may be translated into changes in investment, which in turn will have consequences for future production, consumption and savings. To the extent that a project influences current investment rather than current consumption, it will provide not direct current consumption benefits but indirect future consumption benefits.

If the Government judges the level of savings of the whole economy to be "just right", in that there is no need to attempt special measures to increase (or decrease) aggregate savings and investment, the value of the indirect future consumption benefits due to a unit of funds devoted to investment would be regarded as being equal to the value of the direct current

consumption benefits due to a unit of funds devoted to consumption. In such a situation it would make no difference to our social benefit-cost analysis whether benefits (or costs) are consumed or saved, since, after all, a rupee is just as valuable to consume as it is to save. If, however, the Government judges that the level of savings of the whole economy is insufficient, society would be judged to gain in the long run by some increase in savings and investment at the expense of consumption. To put it in another way, future benefits (in the form of future consumption) due to investment could be judged to exceed the corresponding present benefits due to consumption. When such a situation exists it becomes essential to evaluate the over-all effect of a project on the mix of consumption and investment in the economy for every year in which the project is in operation. It is, moreover, necessary to estimate the ultimate aggregate-consumption benefits due to a unit of current investment, so as to make these comparable with the benefits due to a unit of current consumption. To do this we require a measure of the value of a unit of current investment relative to the value of a unit of current consumption. This measure we shall call the "shadow price of investment". Like the shadow price of foreign exchange, the shadow price of investment is one of those parameters that describe conditions relating to the economy as a whole, rather than characteristics of particular projects. It is, therefore, regarded as a national parameter.

One may well ask at this point why any individual project should be expected to help in attaining an optimal rate of saving and investment for the economy as a whole. After all, it may be asked, is not the rate of saving and investment a macroeconomic problem that should be resolved by an appropriate fiscal and monetary policy? The answer is that if in fact a Government is able to achieve its desired rate of saving and investment via fiscal and monetary measures, there is no reason to confront the problem at the project level, and no need to inquire into the use of benefits realized or forgone on account of any individual project. If there are no constraints on the fiscal powers of the finance minister, there should be no indirect future benefits and costs attributable to a particular project.

If, on the other hand, the Government is not in a position to achieve its desired rate of saving and investment via fiscal and monetary policy, or if there are significant costs associated with the required policy measures, it becomes perfectly legitimate to use individual projects as another instrument to achieve the same goals. The fact that almost all developing countries are striving for higher rates of saving and investment than they are currently able to obtain is a convincing argument for the need to consider the saving and investment implications of individual projects. In most of these countries, political and institutional constraints limit the ability of finance ministers to raise rates of saving and investment to their desired level.

Once this proposition is accepted, we must first inquire into the effect of project benefits and costs on the rate of investment in the economy, and then evaluate the indirect benefits or costs due to any change in the rate of investment. During the period of project construction, resources are drawn

away from the rest of the economy, and funds to pay for these resources must be raised at the expense of the rest of the economy. How much of the sacrifice made by the rest of the economy is a sacrifice of consumption, and how much is a sacrifice of investment? Later, during the period of project operation, benefits are returned to various sectors of the economy in the form of goods and services or cash flows. How much of the gains made by these sectors of the economy result in increased consumption, and how much result in increased investment?

Two ways of approaching the issue are suggested here. One might link the consumption-investment effect of the project to the technological nature of the goods and services used as inputs or produced as outputs. Thus, if an investment good is diverted from elsewhere in the economy to be used in project construction, this would be regarded as a sacrifice of investment. Similarly, if the project benefits are associated with the production of an investment good, this would be regarded as a gain for investment. And the converse would hold for consumption goods.

The alternative approach would link the consumption-investment effect of the project to the expenditure patterns of the groups who gain and lose by the project. Thus, if the project construction costs are ultimately paid for by group A, the fraction representing a sacrifice of investment is given by the marginal propensity to save of group A, and the fraction representing a sacrifice of consumption is given by their marginal propensity to consume. Similarly, if the beneficiaries of the project are group B, the division of the gains between consumption and investment is determined according to the marginal propensities to consume and to save of group B.

The choice between the two approaches should depend upon how one judges the factors that limit investment in the economy. The first approach is appropriate to a situation in which the effective constraint on investment is the supply of certain investment goods. In this case, the net effect of the project on the supply of these goods is what determines its effect on the over-all consumption-investment mix in the economy; any other good or service should be regarded as a consumption good for the purposes of the evaluation. The second approach is appropriate to a situation in which the effective constraint on investment is the availability of savings. Under these circumstances, any required investment good can be obtained through domestic or international transformation—by a sacrifice in consumption. It should be noted that one approach may be appropriate in some years, and the second approach in others. In particular, the supply of certain investment goods may be regarded as relatively inelastic for the immediate future, but more elastic in the long run, so that the first approach would apply initially and the second approach later.

The most plausible example of binding supply constraint on investment would probably be the case of an economy dependent upon imported capital goods for investment, where essentially all available foreign exchange is already being directed into investment in one form or another, and where the opportunities for increasing foreign exchange earnings are sharply limited by

an inelastic world demand for the country's exports. Under circumstances such as these, there would still be a substantial fraction of investment inputs not subject to a supply constraint. Hence the amount of investment forgone by using up a unit of foreign exchange (the constrained input)—or the amount of investment made possible by earning or saving a unit of foreign exchange— would actually be a multiple of the consumption value of that unit of foreign exchange. Thus, to assess the quantitative effect of project input or output on the over-all consumption-investment mix of the economy according to the first approach, it is necessary to evaluate in each year of the project the net claim on the constrained input(s), and to multiply this net claim by the reciprocal of the fraction of total investment which, on average, consists of the constrained input(s).

On balance, it appears to us that the effective constraint is more like y to be on demand than on supply.[11] If so, then it becomes relevant to inquire into the distribution of project benefits and costs among different economic groups or sectors, and to examine the savings behaviour of each. The net gain to a particular group or sector is equal to the value of the net aggregate-consumption benefits it receives, minus the value of any net cash payments it has to make. Thus, the evaluation of the ultimate distributional effects of a project must take into account both the initial distributional effect of the aggregate-consumption benefits and costs and the further redistributional effects of the cash flows brought about by the project.

From the conceptual point of view, it is desirable to distinguish the immediate impact of the project benefits and costs from the accompanying monetary transfers, for the two may not correspond. The first step in assessing the distributional effects of a project is to associate a sector of the society as an immediate gainer and loser with each aggregate-consumption benefit and cost. Thus, when a government agency undertakes the construction and operation of a project, it diverts resources away from use elsewhere in the economy; to the extent that these resources are drawn from the private sector, the private sector as a whole sustains the immediate cost, and to the extent that the resources come from government stocks, the Government is the immediate loser. If the project output is made available to a given set of consumers, these consumers enjoy the corresponding immediate benefits.

The ultimate loss of the private sector depends on the extent to which it is compensated for the resources it gives up, and the ultimate gain of the consumers depends on the amount they are required to pay for their benefits. Thus, the second step in assessing the distributional effects of a project is to distinguish and examine all the cash flows to which it gives rise. If the Government increases taxes in direct response to the project, there is a transfer from the taxed public to the government coffers which increases government gains and increases public losses by exactly the same amount—the aggregate-consumption value of the cash flow. If the Government finances its outlays by

---

[11] See section 14.9 for a more detailed discussion of this.

borrowing, there is a transfer from lenders to Government in the initial stage, and a series of transfers from Government to lenders in a later stage when the loan is being repaid. If the consumers of the project output must pay for that output, there is a transfer of cash—and hence consumption benefits—from the consumers to the producers of the output in the amount of the actual cash payments.

Three basic points should be emphasized: (1) cash flows must be considered only if they would not have arisen in the absence of the project; (2) for every cash flow the indirect benefits and costs sustained by the parties involved are necessarily equal; and (3) the sum of the net benefits (gains minus losses) to each group must add up to the net direct aggregate-consumption benefits of the project as a whole.

Following this approach, let B_t^D be the direct aggregate-consumption benefit of a given project in year t. Let C_t^D be the direct aggregate-consumption costs; and let ΔB_t^D be the corresponding net benefits. Then

$$\Delta B_t^D = B_t^D - C_t^D \qquad (6.1)$$

We now distinguish N different groups or sectors affected by the project: $n = 1, 2, \ldots, N$. For example, one group may consist of wage earners ($n = 1$), a second group of profit earners ($n = 2$), and a third group might be represented by the government sector ($n = 3$). The classification of groups should be made according to their consumption and savings behaviour, as far as available data will permit. Denote the marginal propensity to save (out of net benefits or their cash equivalent) by $s_n(t)$ for group n in year t. If we further denote the direct benefits, direct costs and direct net benefits realized by each group on account of the project by $B_n(t)$, $C_n(t)$, and $\Delta B_n(t)$, then

$$\Delta B_n(t) = B_n(t) - C_n(t) : n = 1, \ldots, N \qquad (6.2)$$

Moreover, since the groups include everyone affected by the project,

$$\sum_{n=1}^{N} B_n(t) = B^D(t) \qquad (6.3)$$

$$\sum_{n=1}^{N} C_n(t) = C^D(t) \qquad (6.4)$$

$$\sum_{n=1}^{N} \Delta B_n(t) = \Delta B^D(t) \qquad (6.5)$$

In chapter 14, it will be argued that if different groups in the economy have different propensities to save, and/or if the returns to the investment from the savings of different groups are different, we cannot associate a unique shadow price of investment with all the net investment generated by a project in a given year. Instead of a global shadow price of investment $P^{inv}(t)$ we shall require a separate shadow price $P_n^{inv}(t)$ to be applied to the net change in investment due to each group n in year t. If we define the "social value" $V_n(t)$

of a unit of net benefits to group n in year t according to the proportion in which the group divides its net benefits between consumption and saving, and the social value of each part, we get

$$V_n(t) = [(1 - s_n(t)) \times 1 + s_n(t) \times P_n^{inv}(t)] \qquad (6.6)$$

It will be shown in the appendix to this section that the total net benefits (which is a sum of the direct net benefits and the indirect net benefits) in year t is:

$$\Delta B^T(t) = \sum_{n=1}^{N} V_n(t) \, \Delta B_n(t) \qquad (6.7)$$

That is, the total net benefits can be expressed simply as the sum of the net benefits realized by each group multiplied by the social value of benefits to that group.

If in year t savings are judged insufficient, we shall wish to assume that $P_n^{inv}(t)$ is greater than unity. From equation (6.6) it is seen that the numerical value of $V_n(t)$ lies between 1 and $P_n^{inv}(t)$. For a group that consumes its entire marginal income (which might be approximately true of wage earners), $s_n(t) = 0$ and so $V_n(t) = 1$. For a group that saves its entire marginal income (possibly the Government), $s_n(t) = 1$ and $V_n(t) = P_n^{inv}(t)$. It follows then that any transfer from a group with a relatively high marginal savings rate (and, therefore, a relatively high social value of net benefits) to a group with a relatively low marginal savings rate (and therefore a relatively low social value of net benefits) results in indirect future costs. This point lies behind the argument raised in section 5.5, that the employment of unskilled labour that is otherwise idle might still be regarded as having a cost. For, whenever a positive market wage is paid by an employer to a previously unemployed worker, there is a money transfer from a group with a higher $V_n(t)$ to one with a lower $V_n(t)$. The result is "an indirect future cost" equal to the difference in the values of the $V_n(t)$ times the cash amount of transfer. Having said all this, let us emphasize that in the foreseeable future it is most unlikely that countries to whom these Guidelines are addressed will possess data sufficiently detailed to justify dividing the economy into more than two classes (for example, capitalists and workers). Thus, while the arguments of this section are perfectly general, the application to the case studies in Part IV reflects the crude kind of division that we believe is at present relevant.

APPENDIX TO CHAPTER 6

Using the notation developed in section 6.3 we see that the net increase in saving on the part of group n in year t as a result of a project is

$$\Delta S_n(t) = s_n(t) \, \Delta B_n(t) : n = 1, \ldots, N \qquad (A.6.1)$$

and the corresponding net increase in consumption is

$$\Delta C_n(t) = [1 - s_n(t)] \, \Delta B_n(t) : n = 1, \ldots, N \qquad (A.6.2)$$

The total net contribution of the project to investment $(\Delta I(t))$ and to consumption $(\Delta C(t))$ in year t may be obtained by summing the net increases due to each group

$$\Delta I(t) = \sum_{n=1}^{N} \Delta S_n(t) \qquad (A.6.3)$$

$$\Delta C(t) = \sum_{n=1}^{N} \Delta C_n(t) \qquad (A.6.4)$$

Since we are dealing with benefits net of costs, any of the magnitudes $\Delta I(t)$, $\Delta C(t)$, $\Delta S_n(t)$, and $\Delta C_n(t)$ may be negative or positive. Summing equations A.6.1 and A.6.2 over all groups and using equations 6.5, A.6.3 and A.6.4 we see that

$$\Delta B^D(t) = \Delta C(t) + \Delta I(t) \qquad (A.6.5)$$

What is the net direct aggregate-consumption benefits of a project in year t can be divided into two components representing the net increase in consumption and the net increase in investment, respectively. It remains now to evaluate the net indirect aggregate-consumption benefits due to the inadequacy of over-all saving.

If we are in a position to distinguish among different groups in the economy, the measurement of indirect benefits should proceed separately group by group. Thus, the measurement of indirect benefits due to group n will involve simply the multiplication of the net change in savings by group n in year t by the excess in the social value of investment due to that group over the social value of consumption. In other words

$$\Delta B_n^I(t) = (P_n^{\text{inv}}(t) - 1)\,\Delta S_n(t) \qquad (A.6.6)$$

where we are assuming that the nth group's investment is equal to the group's saving. The indirect net benefits from the project as a whole are then obtained by summing over the separate groups:

$$\Delta B^I(t) = \sum_{n=1}^{N} \Delta B_n^I(t) = \sum_{n=1}^{N} (P_n^{\text{inv}}(t) - 1)\,\Delta S_n(t) \qquad (A.6.7)$$

Using equations (A.6.3)—(A.6.5) we find

$$\Delta B^T(t) = \Delta B^D(t) + \Delta B^I(t) = \sum_{n=1}^{N} [\Delta C_n(t) + P_n^{\text{inv}}(t)\,\Delta S_n(t)] \qquad (A.6.8)$$

Defining $V_n(t)$ as in expression (6.6) and substituting equations (6.6), (A.6.1) and (A.6.2) into equation (A.6.8) we obtain

$$\Delta B^T(t) = \sum_{n=1}^{N} V_n(t)\,\Delta B_n(t) \qquad (A.6.9)$$

If, as is likely, data limitations force us to accept a single global shadow price of investment $P^{inv}(t)$ based on some average propensity to save and rate of return to investment, equation (A.6.6) then reduces to

$$\Delta B_n^I(t) = (P^{inv}(t) - 1) \, \Delta S_n(t) \tag{A.6.10}$$

Moreover, equation (A.6.7) becomes

$$\Delta B^I(t) = \sum_{n=1}^{N} \Delta B_n^I(t) = [P^{inv}(t) - 1] \sum_{n=1}^{N} \Delta S_n(t) =$$
$$= (P^{inv}(t) - 1) \, \Delta I(t) \tag{A.6.11}$$

Furthermore, equation (A.6.8) simplifies to

$$\Delta B^T(t) = \Delta B^D(t) + \Delta B^I(t) = \sum_{n=1}^{N} \Delta C_n(t) + P^{inv}(t) \sum_{n=1}^{N} \Delta S_n(t) =$$
$$= \Delta C(t) + P^{inv}(t) \, \Delta I(t) \tag{A.6.12}$$

We could, of course, express the total aggregate-consumption benefits due to the project also in the form of equation (6.7), the only difference being that $V_n(t)$ would be

$$V_n(t) = [(1 - s_n(t)) \times 1 + s_n(t) \, P^{inv}(t)] \tag{A.6.13}$$

The remarks made at the end of section 6.3 hold: if over-all savings are judged insufficient in year t, one would presumably want $P^{inv}(t)$ greater than 1. It follows that to the extent that the net benefits of a project accrue to a group (or groups) having a high propensity to save, the net indirect benefits are high and the project is given credit. Likewise, to the extent that the project draws resources from a group that has a high propensity to save and distributes benefits to those that save little, the project is penalized.

Chapter 7

THE REDISTRIBUTION OBJECTIVE

7.1 REDISTRIBUTION OF INCOME AS A SEPARATE OBJECTIVE

In the discussion of "direct" aggregate-consumption benefits and costs (chapters 4 and 5), we consistently used the criterion of willingness to pay to measure project benefits and costs. In chapter 6 we took into consideration one respect in which the immediate willingness to pay of an individual consumer may fail to reflect the value of a good or service to society as a whole. When the value of the future consumption made possible by saving and investing a unit of benefits exceeds the value of the present consumption of that unit, we cannot be satisfied with immediate willingness to pay as a measure of benefits and costs, and we must inquire also into the distribution of project benefits and costs between consumption and investment. The point was to correct the valuation of those net benefits that result in increases in investment in such a way as to take into account the "social value" of the investment relative to consumption.

What is meant by the "social value" of investment? The social value of a unit of investment, measured by the "shadow price of investment", is simply the present value of the future consumption made possible by a unit of investment, evaluated according to the principle of consumer willingness to pay for that consumption. In other words, the use of a shadow price (or several shadow prices) of investment to calculate indirect future consumption benefits is required to account for future benefits on the same willingness-to-pay basis as present consumption benefits. For this reason we spoke of indirect aggregate-consumption benefits: there was no departure from the principle of willingness to pay, but it was necessary to adjust immediate willingness to pay wherever it failed to reflect the ultimate willingness to pay for present and future benefits on a comparable basis.

It was noted earlier that the aggregate-consumption objective makes no distinction among the recipients of benefits or the bearers of cost. It is completely neutral with respect to the wealth, the nature or the habits of the person who enjoys the benefits or incurs the costs. A rich man's consumption counts as much as a poor man's. As long as someone is willing to pay for another

unit of a good or service, that good or service is valued according to his willingness to pay. No questions are asked about the value of a good or service to society as a whole as distinct from its value to the individual.

In this chapter, therefore, we go on to consider another important respect in which the immediate willingness to pay of an individual consumer fails to reflect benefits and costs to society as a whole. This time we depart from the objective of increasing aggregate consumption—present or future—and consider instead the possible social objective of redistributing income from more favoured to less favoured groups within the society. This was just touched upon in section 3.2. This objective involves a clear rejection of the principle that willingness to pay is considered irrespective of the individual and requires instead that a distinction be made between different groups enjoying different levels of well-being. As long as we wish to redistribute income (in the form of net benefits) from one group to another, we cannot be indifferent as to who are the gainers and who are the losers from a project.

In connexion with the redistribution objective, the same question raised earlier in the context of savings and investment may be posed: Why must redistribution goals be achieved via individual projects? Should not the Government seek to bring about the desired distribution of income through taxation, transfers and other instruments of national fiscal policy and let projects be judged on the basis of their contribution to aggregate consumption alone? Once again, the answer is an empirical one. To the extent that it can use other means of redistributing incomes without great cost, any Government is well-advised to do so. But to assume that the desired redistribution of consumption is to be achieved independently of projects is to place undue reliance on fiscal policy—taxes and subsidies—and on the pricing policies used in the distribution of the outputs of public enterprises. In the first place, tax systems in most developing countries are weak. Political, institutional and administrative obstacles prevent taxation of the rich to the point necessary to reduce consumption inequalities substantially. And the other side of the coin is the widespread objection to increasing the consumption of the poor through direct subsidies. Critics of subsidies, ranging from conservative to radical in their politics, argue that the enhancement of the self-respect that accompanies active participation in the process of increasing one's standard of living is worth some sacrifice of aggregate consumption even if direct subsidies would be less costly.

To sum up: given the concern with mitigating inequalities professed by most of the developing countries, disregard of the distribution of benefits and costs from a project can be justified only if it is assumed that the desired distribution of consumption is to be achieved independently of the mix of public investment. Otherwise, a Government that means what it says when it professes a concern for mitigating inequalities should be prepared to sacrifice some potential aggregate consumption realizable from public projects in order to improve its distribution.

7.2 IDENTIFICATION OF FAVOURED GROUPS OR REGIONS

To turn to the measurement of project benefits and costs with respect to redistribution, it is important to consider the sense in which the objective is to be understood. In principle, we might consider every individual or family a separate "group", for the value attached to extra consumption may be different for each individual. This is obviously impractical, first, because we could never hope to calculate the benefits and costs so finely, and, second, because we could never hope to determine the value of marginal consumption individual by individual, or family by family.

Clearly, some compromise between theoretical rigour and operational feasibility is required, and necessarily the compromise will be rather far in the direction of the second pole. One possibility (discussed in section 3.2) is to draw a "poverty line" at, say, the tenth percentile of the population ranked in terms of consumption. That is, the poorest 10 per cent of the population would be singled out as a group to whom income is to be redistributed; within this group all would be treated equally. (Conceivably the richest 5 or 10 per cent of the population might be designated a separate group from the middle class, a separate group from which it is relatively desirable to take away income.) Alternatively, classification might be on a regional basis, the poorest regions (in terms of *per capita* consumption) being treated as "groups" to whom redistribution is desired. The drawback with regional classification is that it precludes consideration of the distribution of benefits and costs within the region; it is possible that the rich in a poor region will be the beneficiaries of the redistribution of consumption. Thus, the regional classification makes sense only if one has confidence that benefits and costs in poor regions will, at the very least, be distributed uniformly among the population.

It was argued in section 3.3 that a Government may give expression to its redistribution objectives by attaching some extra positive weight to the net benefits accruing to the more deserving group(s) and/or by attaching some extra negative weight to the net benefits accruing to the less deserving group(s). A discussion of the choice of a numerical value—positive or negative—for the weight associated with any given group is beyond the scope of this chapter.[12] Here we are concerned only with the measurement of the amount of net benefits realized by any particular group singled out for special treatment.

A redistributional benefit (or cost) must be defined with respect to the particular group in question: it is nothing but an aggregate-consumption benefit (or cost) that accrues to that group. Thus, the measurement of redistributional benefits and costs involves exactly the same principles used in the previous three chapters to determine the ultimate allocation of project benefits and costs among different economic groups or sectors. The redistributional benefits to a group are equal to the immediate aggregate-consumption benefits it receives minus any offsetting payments made to other groups, and the redistributional costs to the group are equal to the immediate aggregate-consumption costs it incurs minus any compensating receipts from other

---

[12] See chapter 12 for a detailed discussion of the distributional weight.

groups. To measure the net redistributional benefits realized by a particular group, we must examine all the aggregate-consumption benefits and costs—direct and indirect—of a project, as well as all the accompanying cash transfers, and determine to what extent each item affects the group in question.

7.3 REDISTRIBUTED BENEFIT

Let us consider first the redistributional effect of the direct aggregate-consumption benefits of a project. Whether the net output of the project consists of the particular goods and services it produces, or of goods and services it releases from alternative sources of supply, the immediate beneficiaries may be identified as the persons who make use of the additional supply, and whose willingness to pay for it measures the corresponding direct aggregate-consumption benefits. To the extent that the immediate beneficiaries must pay for their use of the project net output, their redistributional gains are reduced and those of the group receiving the payment are increased. Depending upon the associated cash transfers, the direct aggregate-consumption benefits of a project may be spread over a number of different groups other than the immediate beneficiaries.

Suppose, for example, that we are considering a multipurpose water project that will add to the availability of both irrigation water and power. The immediate beneficiaries of the project are the farmers who receive water for their fields and the domestic and industrial electricity consumers who make use of the additional power. Thus, in the first instance the farmers as a group gain aggregate-consumption benefits equivalent to their willingness to pay for the water, and the power consumers gain benefits equal to their willingness to pay for the electricity. However, both the water and power consumers will have to pay something for their benefits. Irrigation and power charges will be levied by the government authority operating the project. The payments for these charges represent cash transfers back to the Government, and these add up to the share of total benefits captured by the Government. Typically, the irrigation and power charges will amount to less than the original willingness to pay for the water and electricity, so that the farmers and the power consumers still emerge with net redistributional benefits in their favour. The calculation of the benefits derived by a given group is thus independent of whether the aggregate consumption or the redistribution objective is at issue. What differs in benefit calculations with respect to the two objectives is the weights assigned to the benefits.[13]

Suppose now that the net output of the project consists of foreign exchange: Who is the immediate beneficiary? This depends on the way in which foreign exchange is allocated in the economy. The immediate beneficiaries will be those persons in the public or private sector who are able to use the extra foreign exchange for marginal increases in imports. Whether these importers themselves realize any benefits depends on how much they have to pay for the

---

[13] See chapters 2 and 12 for a more detailed discussion of this point.

foreign exchange they use for importing. If the foreign exchange is auctioned off in a free market, the importer may part with domestic currency equivalent to his full willingness to pay. If the foreign exchange is allocated via some quota system, the importer may buy his foreign exchange at an officially determined rate substantially less than his willingness to pay, in which case he directly benefits. The rest of the direct aggregate-consumption benefits may be returned in the form of domestic currency to the enterprise that operates the project earning or saving foreign exchange.

7.4 REDISTRIBUTED COST

The analysis of the redistributional effect of the direct aggregate-consumption costs of a project is similar to that of the benefits. The net input to a project may be associated at first with the persons who forgo the use of the good or service whose supply is reduced, and whose willingness to pay for it measures the corresponding direct aggregate-consumption costs. To the extent that those who give up the goods and services are compensated by others, or reduce their own payments to others, the cost is shifted to other groups. Via such cash transfers, the ultimate costs may be borne by groups quite distant from those who are most immediately affected by the project.

Let us consider some examples. When a worker is withdrawn from employment elsewhere in the economy to work on a public project, the cost is usually passed on to the government employer. A private-sector employer loses one man but saves his wage and, assuming the wage reflected the employer's willingness to pay for a marginal worker, comes out even. The worker himself changes employers, but presumably gets the same wage as before and thus realizes no net gain. But the government employer pays a wage that would not be paid in the absence of the project and therefore suffers a loss. It should be noted that although the income group to which the worker belongs is unaffected by his new job, the regional group may well be affected. If the worker came from another region to work on the public project, the region into which he has immigrated gains benefits equal to his earnings and the region he left loses the same amount.

Suppose now that the worker in question was unemployed before getting a job with the project. (The same argument would hold if he held a job earlier, but his previous position was filled by an otherwise unemployed man.) In this case there may be no direct aggregate-consumption costs to the economy when the man is put to work on the project. As before, the Government suffers a loss in the amount of the wage it pays. However, in this case there is also a gain in the same amount, which accrues to the worker. From the point of view of direct aggregate consumption, the direct cost is zero, because the worker's gain cancels the Government's loss. But from the point of view of redistribution, the result of the transfer depends on the weight attached to workers and to the Government.[14]

---

[14] See chapter 15 for further discussion of this.

When the net input to a project consists of a material good withdrawn from alternative use elsewhere in the economy, the cost is generally passed on to the Government in the same way as for employed labour. A private-sector firm loses the input but saves the costs it otherwise would have incurred and, except for any excess of willingness to pay over purchase cost, comes out even. The Government, on the other hand, pays for an input it would not otherwise have bought and suffers a loss. Unlike the case of labour inputs, there are no redistributional effects involving income for regional groups, except to the extent that discrepancies arise between willingness to pay and actual market payments.

The same is true for inputs of foreign exchange. When such inputs are used on public projects in one region rather than in another, there are non-governmental income or regional group gains and losses only to the extent that actual payments for foreign exchange differ from willingness to pay. As we noted earlier, this may well be the case when foreign exchange is rationed. When a Government licenses foreign currency to private firms who are allowed to pay for it at the official (undervalued) rate, these firms are in effect receiving a government subsidy. If the Government subsequently embarks on a public project and cuts down on the foreign exchange available to the private sector in order to allocate it to the project, there is a loss to the group and region of the marginal private-sector firm that forgoes its implicit subsidy. If the Government makes any of this foreign exchange available to private firms or individuals in the project region, there is a corresponding group and regional gain in the amount of the accompanying implicit subsidy.

It has so far been assumed that the input costs of a public project will be paid by the Government. They may also be passed on in part or in full to the tax-paying or the lending public, in which case new cash flows arise with redistributional implications. To the extent that taxation is increased, there are net losses to each income and regional group that pays the taxes. In the case of borrowing, there is redistribution against the lenders at the initial stage and in their favour when the loan is repaid.

7.5 THE REGIONAL-INCOME MULTIPLIER

After the ultimate net redistributional impact of a project on any given group has been calculated as outlined above, there remains one further adjustment, which is of importance primarily in the case of regional group redistribution. Whether the net benefits accruing to a particular region are consumed or invested, a part of them will be respent within that region. To the extent that they result in a net transfer of wage or profit income from elsewhere in the economy to the project region, they will result in a new round of benefits to the region. For example, the expenditure arising from incomes earned on the project may draw small business and ancillary services into the area. The income of these enterprises is now earned in the project region and contributes

to the redistribution of benefits in its favour. Such a chain of "indirect" benefits can in principle continue indefinitely, with the benefits on each successive round progressively declining.

If γ represents the marginal proportion of the "direct" net redistributional benefits, R^D, which—when respent—results in additional net benefits to the region, then the value of the "indirect" net redistributional benefits, R^I, can be expressed as:

$$R^I = \gamma R^D + \gamma\,(\gamma R^D) + \gamma\,(\gamma^2 R^D) + \ldots = R^D\,(\gamma + \gamma^2 + \gamma^3 + \ldots) \quad (7.1)$$

and the total net redistributional benefits to the region, R^T, is given by:

$$R^T = R^D + R^I = R^D\,(1 + \gamma + \gamma^2 + \gamma^3 + \ldots) = R^D\left[\frac{1}{1-\gamma}\right] \quad (7.2)$$

The expression $\left[\dfrac{1}{1-\gamma}\right]$ is called the "regional-income multiplier".

It is applied to the "direct" net redistributional benefits $R^D(t)$ in a given year t to yield the total net redistributional benefits $R^T(t)$ to a particular region in that year. The use of equation (7.2) for the regional-income multiplier is subject to one qualification: the successive rounds of benefits γR^D, $\gamma^2 R^D$, $\gamma^3 R^D$ etc. actually occur only after an interval of time, whereas the formula assumes that they all take place instantaneously. To be precise, one should distinguish the successive rounds of benefits according to the time at which they occur. In practice, however, the calculations are likely to be sufficiently rough so that no such careful distinctions will be called for.

In the case of redistribution among groups defined according to income class, the counterpart to the regional-income multiplier is a "class-income multiplier" based upon respent benefits that return in future rounds to the same group. It would appear highly unlikely, however, that such a phenomenon could be significant enough either to warrant or to make possible its inclusion in the redistribution calculus. Thus, for all practical purposes we may dispense with any such adjustment of the net redistributional benefits according to particular income groups.

In retrospect, one might raise the question why no multiplier effect is applicable to aggregate-consumption benefits for the entire economy. These benefits, too, are respent in successive rounds and might be considered income-creating for the economy as a whole. The objection is that unless there are idle resources to be activated in such a process, no additional net national income can be created. With resources fully employed, it is possible to shift income from one region to another (whence the regional-multiplier effect) but not to add to national income in any given year. What we are assuming at this stage, then, is an absence of an over-all deficiency in effective demand that results in underutilized resources. A project cannot, therefore, generate

additional income for the economy as a whole. What it can lead to is a shift in income from one region to another. To illustrate this point a simple example may help. The location of a fertilizer plant in a particularly impoverished region A may (through the income earned on the project) lead to the creation of new services, e.g. a movie hall. The point to recognize now is that this movie hall would have been established in region B had the project been located in region B. That is to say, if extra income earned in a region owing to the location of the project in that region results in a service there, this same service would have been created elsewhere had the project been located elsewhere. There are no idle resources to be activated for the economy as a whole. The location of the fertilizer plant in A rather than in B leads to the creation of the movie hall in A rather than in B. If B is relatively prosperous, so that A is earmarked for extra consideration, the indirect benefit to A reflected through the multiplier for A is caught via the redistributional weight associated with the income of A.

On the other hand, if there are idle resources that can be activated in response to a given project—and not otherwise—any additional income generated on this account should be credited as aggregate-consumption benefits to the project.

It is clear from the foregoing discussion that certain kinds of redistributional effects of a project are fairly easy to evaluate, while others are almost impossibly difficult. In particular, it is usually possible to assess fairly accurately the consequences of consumption benefits and costs, or cash transfers, which are confined to the project region and affect solely a well-defined group within that region. Thus, the employment of labour on a project or the consumption of project output by local consumers involves readily measurable redistributional effects. But it is generally very difficult to isolate such benefits and costs, or cash transfers, which affect "the rest of the economy" or the economy as a whole. Which regions or groups gain or lose when the rate of investment is increased in the economy as a whole, with a resultant gain in future consumption that exceeds the value of the alternative present consumption? In practice, one may well have to abandon the attempt to measure the economy-wide redistributional consequences of a given project and concentrate simply on its major impact on the local region and various local groups.

7.6 GOVERNMENT PRICING POLICY

The detailed discussion of the redistributional effects of a project—as between investors and consumers, between regions and between groups—serves to bring out clearly one aspect of the role pricing policy plays in public projects. The price charged by the Government to the consumers of the output of a public project determines directly the distribution of the corresponding benefits. The consumers gain to the extent that their willingness to pay exceeds their actual payments, and their actual payments are determined by the price set by the Government. By setting a (relatively) high price, the Government can capture the bulk of project benefits for itself; by setting a (relatively) low

price, it passes them on to consumers. If these consumers live in a region or belong to a group to which the Government wishes to redistribute income, there would appear to be a good case for a low price to serve these objectives. On the other hand, if the consumers have a much lower marginal propensity to save than the Government, and if the social value of investment exceeds the social value of consumption, a greater contribution to consumption benefits for the nation as a whole would be obtained by setting a high price to keep most of the benefits in government hands. The same set of potentially conflicting goals apply to all the prices in the project over which the Government has some control, for every price has some distributional consequences. The determination of an optimal pricing policy—just as the evaluation of the project itself—can be made only with knowledge of the relative importance attached to conflicting objectives.

The distributional effects described above are only one aspect of the pricing problem. A second aspect is that the price charged for a good or service has an important bearing on how the good or service is used, and, in particular, on whether it is put to use in such a way as to provide a maximum of aggregate-consumption benefits to the economy as a whole. Prices that are below "what the traffic will bear" call for a system of rationing to determine who will get the good or service in question at the favourable rate. Rationing may result in careless allocation of resources by the beneficiaries, and it may also entail significant administrative costs. Against this argument for relatively high prices—to aid in allocating scarce resources in accordance with their most productive uses—must be placed an argument for concessional prices to ensure the quick response of potential users to a new and profitable good of which they are initially sceptical. The case for such promotional pricing clearly becomes less compelling over time; once the users of the resource in question have become familiar with it, a subsidy cannot be justified by the aggregate-consumption objective.

All these issues may be illustrated by the following example. Suppose that the Government undertakes to provide fertilizers to the small farmers of a certain region. The issue is to decide what price to charge. The farmers' willingness to pay for the fertilizer may be measured by subtracting the cost of all inputs in cultivation other than fertilizers from the receipt for the sale of their agricultural output. If this willingness to pay exceeds the price actually charged by the Government, this excess represents benefits that the Government could in principle capture through a higher price for fertilizer, whereas in fact the Government has chosen to place these benefits in the hands of the farmers. Thus, by charging a concessional price for fertilizer, the Government has increased the yearly net benefits to this region and the yearly net benefits to the farmers. Now, it is most likely that the marginal propensity to save by the small farmers is lower than that of the Government. It follows then that the Government's social value of income (as defined in section 6.4) exceeds the small farmers' social value of income. Thus, the concessional pricing leads to a decrease in the aggregate-consumption benefits. Of course, apart

from the contribution to redistribution objectives, the Government may defend its concessional pricing on the grounds that the incentive of substantial profit from using fertilizer is necessary in order to encourage the farmer to use the fertilizer. If a higher price were charged the farmer might prefer not to use fertilizer at all: there would then be an aggregate-consumption loss, as well as a redistribution of the remaining benefits from the farmers to the Government.

The main point emerging from this discussion is that pricing in public-investment projects affects different national objectives in different ways. It is therefore necessary in formulating a pricing policy to examine the implications of a given price for each separate objective and to consider the relative importance of the conflicting objectives to the nation as a whole. The need to recover cost through revenues—however crucial in the investment decisions of private enterprise—should play a decisive role neither in the allocation of public-investment funds nor in the pricing policy of public projects.

Chapter 8

THE EMPLOYMENT OBJECTIVE

8.1 Value of employment

Among the objectives of economic policy that tend to attract attention is the objective of employment creation. Indeed, in many ways, this objective has occupied as important a place in the literature on policy making as any other. Since different projects have different employment implications, it is particularly important to have a clear idea about the relevance of employment creation as a goal to be pursued by planners. For this, the first step is to understand the reasons why additional employment is regarded as valuable.

Perhaps the simplest reason for wanting more employment relates to viewing manpower as an important economic resource. Indeed, for many developing countries it is the most important of all economic resources. It is common to regard the existence of unemployment as a sign that important economic resources are being wasted. Thus, the objective of employment creation may be related to the goal of a fuller exploitation of the production potential.

We have to regard this point of view critically to appreciate its importance for project formulation and evaluation. First of all, it should be noted that employment is not desired for its own sake in this argument, but entirely as a means to the objective of production: if additional employment generates more output, employment is desirable, but otherwise not. Employment is completely subservient to output creation in this system. Indeed, it could well be that if we tried to spread a given amount of capital investment too thinly over a great many workers, the output might be less than if the same amount of investment were made for equipping fewer workers. The opportunities of productive labour, given the stock of capital, might well be restricted, so that additional employment might conceivably generate no additional output and might even lead to a decline in production. If employment is desired not for its own sake but for the output it would generate, employment becomes an objective not to be pursued beyond a certain point.

The contribution of more employment, if any, in this view, will be covered by calculations that take aggregate consumption as an objective. Additional

85

output, if any, will either take the form of additional immediate consumption or of additional investment, which will reflect itself in additional future consumption. Both will be reflected in the value of aggregate consumption. There is no need under this approach for taking employment as a separate objective at all.

However, the contribution to production is only one of several reasons why more employment may be desired. Unemployment has a deep and distressing psychological impact on society. Indeed, most countries regard large-scale unemployment as a disaster. Lawlessness, vagrancy, crime and social disorder are closely associated with widespread unemployment. It could, therefore, be argued that employment is valuable in itself, quite apart from the contributions it makes to output creation. The distress of unemployed families is well known, and problems of poverty, undernourishment, disease and chaos for families without work cannot be ignored in project selection. — better put under distrib. of income

This line of reasoning should be examined more thoroughly to appreciate its precise role in the exercises with which we are concerned. It is important to distinguish between those benefits of employment that are generated from work as such and those that are generated from the income-distributional implications of employment. An unemployed family is also a poor family, and in a society with widespread unemployment there will tend to be great inequality. Problems of undernourishment and acute economic suffering related to unemployment are basically problems of income distribution. As such we have already considered this factor in the last chapter under the redistribution objective. In a later section in this chapter (section 8.3) the relation between the employment objective and the redistribution objective will be examined more thoroughly. For the moment we simply separate the output and distributional considerations underlying the employment objective from other reasons for desiring employment.

It is, of course, not easy in practice to distinguish between social problems associated with unemployment as such and those that arise from the loss of income to the unemployed families. There is, however, little doubt that psychologically unemployment is a very disturbing phenomenon; quite apart from the income-creating implications of more employment there are also considerations of self-respect and self-confidence that relate to unemployment. The precise content of these considerations will depend on the nature of the society and the values associated with work. It is important in this context to distinguish between "open unemployment", meaning that people are visibly out of work, and "disguised unemployment", meaning that many people are doing the work a few could do. This latter kind of unemployment may be more important in a number of developing countries where the agricultural sector is characterized by pre-capitalist modes of production. In a peasant economy a family with, say, four working members but land enough to provide fruitful opportunities of work for only three will not keep one member completely unemployed. Work will be divided among all the working members and no one will be visibly unemployed. When unemployment takes this

disguised form, the psychological impact on self-respect, self-confidence and such things may indeed by less acute than it is when unemployment is open. Further, social problems of lawlessness and chaos are likely to be much larger in urban areas with a sizable number of unemployed people than in rural areas having an equal number of disguised unemployed.

The social problems of unemployment that have been discussed most in the literature in the industrialized countries have been related to severe open unemployment, especially in urban centres, arising from periodic slumps, e.g. in the 1930s. The analysis cannot be applied easily to unemployment in the pre-capitalist developing countries. This is not to say that employment as such is an unimportant objective for the developing countries, but only to argue that the desirability of employment in the context of such countries may be due mainly to its redistributional impact.

We have not yet considered some types of impact of employment. Having work is a good way of learning, and being out of work is an efficient method of forgetting productive skills; unemployment makes labour rusty. One impact of additional employment, therefore, is an improvement in the quality of the labour force. How relevant is this as an additional consideration? That will depend on several things.

First, the consideration will be important only for specific types of jobs. In particular, in the introduction of modern technology learning may be very important, whereas for certain traditional techniques there may be so much practice in any case that the impact on learning and forgetting may be very little. This is particularly so when unemployment takes the form of under-employment, with people working for a smaller number of hours rather than not at all.

Second, the impact of learning and forgetting is on future productive abilities. If we do our calculations correctly, this will be reflected in the aggregate-consumption benefit. That is, additional employment leading to the acquisition of skills may increase future output, but if it does so we should raise the value of aggregate consumption to take note of this. Thus, it is also related to the aggregate-consumption objective even though the impact comes only in the long run. Indeed, it is common to assume that when modern technology is introduced in the developing countries productivity will be low to start with, but will rise with practice. This is, of course, largely a reflection of the considerations that we have been discussing. If we do the calculations realistically, the value of employment as reflected through greater productive ability will indeed be incorporated in our estimates of benefits and costs of the projects.

Finally, it can be argued that a larger volume of employment in an under-developed country may mean a greater participation of the female population in the productive processes and may thus be an indicator of modernization. Indeed, the employment ratio varies noticeably from country to country, partly

as a reflection of the extent to which society permits women to work outside the household. There is no doubt that this may be a very important consideration for the development of a primitive economy, and in the calculations of project selection it may be important to reflect this consideration. A project that employs many workers, particularly female workers, may be regarded as having a quality that is important for ushering the country into the twentieth century; while these values are vaguely definable they are nonetheless extremely important.

The fact remains, however, that this important consideration is once again best tackled through some means other than attaching a specific weight to employment as such. For one thing, this is not an argument for attaching weight to every kind of employment but to specific types of employment. The best thing may be to attach a specific weight to female employment in modern centres of production. If the problem is viewed thus, employment of women in the modern sector can be treated as a "merit want". A specific weight may be assigned to female employment along the lines that we have already discussed. The purpose will not be very well served by attaching a general weight to total employment.

Everything considered, it would appear that employment may be valued essentially as a means rather than as an end, and as such it is best tackled through a proper accounting of more basic benefits for which employment creation is an efficient means. This is obviously so for the output-creating impact of employment. Although a little less transparent, much of the distress of unemployment is really related to problems of income distribution, and the value of employment may be most conveniently related to the redistribution objective. The impact on learning and forgetting comes once again, under the aggregate-consumption benefit. And the value of employment as an indicator of modernization can be tackled, it would appear, more efficiently by choosing more precise indices of modernization, such as the employment of women in the modern sector, and treating them as merit wants. There is, of course, no harm in treating employment as an objective on its own, but then in determining what value to attach to employment we would have to go into the ends for which employment serves as a means. The procedure adopted in these Guidelines is perhaps more convenient; employment is treated not as an objective in itself but merely as a means for generating benefits under other objectives ("aggregate consumption", "redistribution objective" and "merit wants").

8.2 LABOUR-INTENSIVE TECHNIQUES

Whether we treat employment as a means or as an end, investigation of variability of employment, given the technological facts, is an important consideration for project selection. In the literature on project selection, it is quite common to encourage decision makers to choose labour-intensive techniques in economies where labour is plentiful. This advice makes sense

up to a point, but we have to examine the problem a little more closely. In particular, it is important to distinguish between employment creation that conflicts with output expansion and employment creation that does not. If, for example, employing 100 people with a given amount of capital investment produces an output of $1,000 and employing 101 people will produce an output of $1,001, there is no conflict between output creation and employment expansion. If, on the other hand, employing 101 people makes the output equal $999, then employment could be expanded only at the cost of output. The two cases are important to distinguish, since in the first case employment does not conflict with the objective of aggregate consumption, whereas in the second it does.

The problem can also be discussed in the terminology of "efficiency", i.e. in the second case additional employment will be inefficient, whereas in the first case it is efficient. But even when a technique is efficient it may still not be desirable. In the example given above, the employment of an additional person increases output by only one dollar. If the wage rate is more than this, a private entrepreneur may have no incentive to hire the additional person. However, we have already rejected commercial profitability as a guide for project choice from the national point of view. Thus, the fact that with a wage rate of $5 the additional person will lead to a marginal commercial loss is not a compelling reason for deciding against the more labour-intensive technique. However, even from a social point of view the costs of employment have to be taken into account. In particular, the fact that additional employment generates additional immediate consumption through an increase in the purchasing power is an important consideration. A diversion of resources from investment to immediate consumption may be socially costly if we hold investment to be more valuable than consumption at the margin. We shall discuss this point in a separate section later in this chapter.

From what we have discussed already, it should be clear that some employment expansion may conflict with efficiency and some expansion that does not conflict with efficiency may nevertheless be undesirable on the ground that the social costs of employment may be greater than the social benefits. In the search for labour-intensive techniques these limitations must be borne in mind, since even in economies with plentiful labour, labour-intensive techniques may not be desirable. Much depends on the precise facts of the various projects and the importance of alternative objectives.

A great deal of research has been carried out in recent years on what is described as "intermediate technology". Intermediate technology is supposed to include techniques that are neither very primitive (as the techniques commonly used in the developing economies tend to be), nor very capital intensive (as those commonly used in the industrialized countries are prone to be). It is argued that very often the developing countries do not have the research and development apparatus to evolve techniques that are appropriate to their economic conditions, and the industrialized countries have, of course, little incentive to develop techniques that are not suitable to their own

economic conditions. As a consequence "intermediate technologies" may be neglected. There have been attempts to develop possible technology to fill this gap, and several organs of the United Nations and other bodies have been concerned with this. When these intermediate technologies are really developed, they may be relevant for developing countries, but as yet the list of achievements is not very impressive. In any case, in these Guidelines we are not concerned with whether such intermediate technologies will be found, but with how to evaluate them when such technologies are proposed for adoption. The general approach to this problem is not different from that we have been taking throughout: these intermediate techniques would have to be judged in terms of social costs and benefits in precisely the same way as any other project. The output-creating impact of employment, the income-redistributional consequences, the implication in terms of merit wants etc. would all have to be balanced against the social costs, including the costs of shifting resources from investment to consumption as a consequence of an additional wage bill.

It may be relevant in this context to clarify one problem of project selection that tends to be overlooked. In choosing a particular project the employment generated in that project is often looked at with a great deal of care, but the project's indirect impact on employment is neglected. The indirect impact may, however, be very important. In some cases the indirect effects are obvious. For example, if a certain project induces other complementary projects to be set up that would generate employment, the total employment impact must take this totality into account. What may not, however, be so obvious is that the over-all opportunities of employment expansion are integrally connected with the availability of consumer goods, and greater employment generated through one project may reduce the opportunities to generate employment in other fields by using up the limited resources of consumer goods. This aspect of the problem deserves some discussion.

Suppose the total amount of consumer goods is valued at $10,000 and to absorb a worker we have to pay him a wage equal to $10, which he would spend entirely on consumption. In such a situation the total employment that we can generate is 1,000 workers. If we employ fewer, we would be left with a surplus of consumer goods, and if we employ more we would be running short of consumer goods. Given the total supply of consumer goods, if a certain project employs many workers the amount that will be left for meeting demands arising from employment elsewhere will be less. That is, in being concerned with the creation of employment we must look not merely at the employment generated in the project but also at the impact on opportunities to expand employment elsewhere. Very often a very labour-intensive technique that makes a very small contribution to output may not be desirable even though employment is regarded as a good thing, since more employment here may cut down employment opportunities elsewhere. Viewing the problem this way, the total employment opportunity is really closely connected with the total availability of consumer goods, since an attempt to expand employment beyond the limit set by the supply of consumer goods would lead only

to shortages and social problems. From this viewpoint, employment may not be taken separately into our calculations, since it will be fully reflected in the volume of consumer goods.

To the extent that the wages can be pushed down and more workers can be employed with the same volume of consumer goods, the picture will not be so rigid. For example, in the previous cases, with a supply of consumer goods worth $10,000 it may be possible to employ 2,000 rather than 1,000 workers if the wage rate is pushed down to $5, and from a distributional point of view this may be better because a larger number of families would then share the income and the consumer goods. On the other hand, there tend to be various institutional limitations to variations in the wage rate, and given the structure of the economy and the society, it may not be possible to push the wage rate below a certain limit. Under these circumstances the opportunities for employment will be very closely related to the total supply of consumer goods.

The total supply of consumer goods is not in itself constant, and it is not being suggested that employment variations are not possible. But what is being argued is that employment opportunities are themselves very closely related to the present supply of consumer goods, so that in the evaluation of present consumer goods some indirect valuation of employment may already be included. It is not easy to treat employment and present consumption as two unrelated objectives, not merely because employment creates output but mainly because output of consumer goods permits employment for the economy as a whole. Since a project evaluator is specifically concerned with only one project, he may be misled into thinking that employment maximization means maximization of employment in that project. Clearly, however, he has to be concerned with the opportunity for over-all employment, and this does not depend only on how labour-intensive a project he chooses.

8.3 EMPLOYMENT AND THE REDISTRIBUTION OBJECTIVE

It was noted earlier that one reason why employment is valued is because of its impact on income distribution. An unemployed person does not have a source of income; although it is possible to give him some income through a dole, this practice may be difficult to follow. In most developing countries a dole for the unemployed is not provided. Undoubtedly part of the reason is that with a large volume of surplus labour a poor country can ill-afford a dole system, and productive employment even with low output is preferable. Partly also, with disguised unemployment it is not very easy to identify those to whom a dole should be paid. Under these circumstances, an expansion of employment in spreading the real income very widely may contribute efficiently to the redistribution objective. As was noted earlier, many of the desirable aspects of employment creation, its impact on nourishment, on education etc. really relate to the fact that employment creates a source of livelihood for the family.

This being the case, it is worth considering whether employment should be valued separately in project selection in the light of its impact on income distribution, or whether income distribution should be given a specific value and employment treated as a means to it. Fundamentally, this is not a crucial question, since which way we do the calculation makes little difference so long as the link between employment and redistribution is clearly recognized and realistically calculated. However, from the point of view of the convenience of calculation this is a question of some importance.

If, on the one hand, we treat the income level of the poorer classes as the relevant item to which value is attached, that value will simply reflect the planners' idea of the relative importance of channelling consumption to the poor. The planners' evaluation need not be concerned with the precise calculation of the impact of employment on the consumption of the poor classes; this would be left to the project evaluator. If, on the other hand, the central policy makers attach precise value to employment, in estimating this value the policy makers will have to take into account the impact of employment on the consumption of the poor classes, and the value will have to be determined by considering this in conjunction with the innate importance of giving consumption opportunities to the poor. The second procedure is less direct than the first, and there are obvious advantages in following the first procedure. The project evaluator himself is in a better position to judge the precise impact of employment and other factors on income distribution, and it seems best to do this calculation directly and to leave the central policy makers in fixing social weights unencumbered by this complex detail. By valuing redistribution the division of labour between the project evaluator and the over-all policy maker will be more appropriate, and this is the procedure we follow in these Guidelines.

A more fundamental issue is why employment should be regarded as a vehicle of income distribution and why income cannot be redistributed more directly through taxation and fiscal policy. In principle there is no difficulty in paying a person a certain amount of money even without employing him in a project. Employment may be quite extraneous to the act of payment. The objection that paying someone without employing him will be unethical need not detain us; since we are considering the role of employment in income distribution, our real concern is with getting income to the poor person, whether or not he is employed. In fact, to the extent that work is regarded as unpleasant and leisure is regarded as valuable, paying people without making them work may well be considered a superior means of income redistribution than employment.

The picture is, however, not so simple. Payment without work may have important political and social repercussions. If the Government decides to give a number of people some income without work, the question would naturally be raised why these people rather than others are selected for such support. This question of selection arises even for employment when unemployment is widespread, and charges of favouritism in job giving are not uncommon. However,

in the case of employment creation, there are at any rate some possible criteria for suitability for jobs and also some definite procedure for giving employment. Also, getting paid for one's job is considered a compensation for one's effort, even though the institutional wage rate may be regarded as very much in excess of the unpleasantness of work in a country with unemployment. However that may be, politically the question of arbitrariness in job distribution, while important, is not likely to be such an explosive issue as the giving out of income without work.

In some situations income may be redistributed better through a direct payment than through giving employment. In dealing with people with some crying need, e.g. medical facilities, it may be simpler to give income than to give jobs. It is not being suggested that employment giving is always the best means of redistributing income. It need not be so at all. But often employment will be an important vehicle of income redistribution and the fact that its political feasibility is somewhat greater than pure distribution of money, except in very special situations, cannot be overlooked.

It might be mentioned in this context that the possibility of corruption is perhaps also less when income is redistributed through employment rather than through subsidies. It has been found, for example, that in giving famine relief in countries like India, the system of paying wages to labour in specially devised work programmes is less open to misuse than the system of a direct dole. There are clearer records of employment and also less possibility of distributing money to nonexistent persons, which is not uncommon in the context of a pure dole in a country with a defective administrative system. This is another reason why employment may be an important means of redistribution.

Be that as it may, in considering project selection we should have to see the redistributional impact of employment creation as a possible part of the objectives of some projects. There is nothing strange about this. Basically, this is another reflection of a phenomenon we have outlined in several places in these Guidelines: the best economic possibilities are not the same as political feasibilities. The redistribution of income through employment may be feasible when pure redistribution without employment may not be, even when the latter may be economically perfectly possible.

What we are mainly concerned with is an understanding of how employment may affect income distribution. This will vary from project to project. One has to see to what extent additional employment will provide income to particularly depressed groups. We have already discussed earlier (chapter 7) how the redistribution objective can be formulated in a variety of ways. One of the ways is to attach an additional weight to the consumption of depressed groups or classes. Sometimes when a whole region is known to be economically depressed, income generating in that region may be given a special weight. Quite clearly this will include the impact of employment because in estimating the income generated in that region, note must be taken of employment and

wages paid out. If we are concerned with such broad considerations, no special efforts need be made to see that the effects of employment are reflected in the income-distribution objective; the procedure already suggested will do it very well. However, sometimes we may wish to attach a special importance to income accruing to depressed groups within a specific region, and we may then wish to attach a special weight to the wages paid to that group. Regions very often are internally unhomogeneous, and it may be important to distinguish between the depressed and the not-so-depressed classes in a certain region.

While such a distinction requires a fairly detailed calculation, it does not really affect the principles. On the one hand, the work should consist of making precise estimates of the income generated that will be enjoyed by these specific depressed groups. On the other hand, the policy makers must indicate the additional value to be attached to the income thus generated. For most of these really depressed groups, income and consumption are practically identical, so that we shall not be far wrong if we treat the accrued income of these groups as equivalent to their present consumption. In determining the value to be attached to the present consumption of these poorer groups, the policy makers must note that consumption to these groups will, on redistributional grounds, be regarded as more important than the consumption of the average citizen of the country. As part of aggregate consumption, consumption of these depressed groups will receive a weight in any case in the system of evaluating benefits of the projects. The additional weight to be attached to the consumption of these groups may be reflected through putting a positive value on the consumption of this group over and above the value of aggregate consumption. The procedures for this were discussed in detail in the last chapter in the context of broader categories, e.g. regional distribution, but the principle is the same.

For assessing the impact on employment and sectional income, the precise pattern of disbursement between different categories of expenditures would have to be examined. Very often project data are provided in such an aggregate manner that the expenditures on wages are not separated, nor is it specified where the additional people to be employed would be found. In the context of the objective of redistribution in relation to employment it would be important to obtain this breakdown, and to check what part of the disbursement reflects the additional wage bill and also to whom these wages are to be paid, i.e. whether the workers come from particularly depressed classes on whose income we would like to place an additional weight.

Compromises in project evaluation would, of course, have to be struck between the demands of perfection and the constraints of practicability. In principle it would be best to determine the precise income level of each employed person and attach a variable weight to his respective consumption; the weight will go up as the average income level goes down. This will not, however, be possible to do in any detail. The calculation would have to be done in terms of broad categories.

8.4 SOCIAL COST OF LABOUR

So far we have concentrated on the benefit side of employment, making only passing references to costs. In a country with full employment the cost of employment of labour is fairly easy to calculate. A person can be employed in a certain project only if he is withdrawn from employment somewhere else. From the point of view of this project, therefore, the cost of employing him may be thought to be equal to what he would have produced had he been employed elsewhere. This measure of what he would have alternatively produced is sometimes called "the social opportunity cost" of labour, a term that is often used in project-evaluation literature. By employing the person here the society is forgoing the opportunity of employing him elsewhere, and thus the social opportunity cost measures the value of the alternative opportunity that the society is losing by putting him to work in the project under discussion.

Defined this way, the opportunity cost of labour will be positive when there is full employment, but if there is unemployed labour it should be possible to employ labour in this project without having to withdraw it from elsewhere. Thus, the opportunity cost of labour as defined above may well be zero in the context of an economy with unemployment, and it is for such economies that the objective of employment creation is important. Does this mean that employment of labour is costless for an economy with unemployment? The answer is "not at all", since along with employment come other changes in the economy that may or may not involve specific costs from the social point of view.

A few of the simpler considerations may be mentioned first, followed by a more complex problem. Although labour may be unemployed, it does not follow that there is no unpleasantness of work, especially since working conditions in developing countries often tend to be extraordinarily bad. The unpleasantness of work for those who would have otherwise been idle cannot be dismissed. This point assumes particular importance when there is a transfer of labour from the rural areas to the harsh living conditions of the growing towns and cities in the poor countries. The conditions of living, including the sanitary facilities and other social amenities in some of the urban areas of the developing countries, are often miserable, and it must be assumed that there is some loss in making people work under such conditions. It is possible to feel that this is an unimportant consideration, since the worker in question prefers to take the job rather than be unemployed. However, this is not a convincing argument. The worker prefers this job because he is paid a certain wage, and while this wage may overcompensate him for the inconvenience of bad working and living conditions, this does not mean that the working and living conditions do not involve some suffering. Therefore, just as we must calculate the benefits from employment in terms of output creation as well as of income redistribution and other objectives, we must also take into account the social costs, if any, of additional employment, especially when it involves migration.

From the social point of view, a further consideration may arise because the Government may have to construct housing and other facilities in an area to which the workers may be moving, and these costs may not be borne, at any rate not fully, by the workers themselves. Because a large proportion of the capital expenditure of a project lies in the cost of townships, this could be an important cost related to employment. If the benefits from new houses and good working conditions are provided, they may be included among the benefits of the project, but the cost of townships and housing must be counted as part of the cost of employment creation of the project.

A more complex consideration relates to the impact of employment on the distribution of the current income between consumption and investment. When an additional person is employed, drawn from the pool of the unemployed, and he is paid wages, some additional purchasing power is generated, and this will reflect itself in an increase in consumption. Of course, increased consumption is desirable, and, indeed, aggregate consumption is the first objective that we examined in the context of cost-benefit calculation. However, an increase in immediate consumption may be achieved, under most circumstances, only through a reduction in investment. If the policy makers feel that, on balance at the margin, consumption and investment are equally attractive from the point of view of the society, it makes no difference whether investment is cut a little to increase immediate consumption correspondingly or whether immediate consumption is somewhat reduced for the sake of expansion of a corresponding amount of investment. If, however, we are dealing with an economy where the policy makers feel that the over-all rate of investment is deficient, a reduction in investment for the sake of an expansion of immediate consumption may be regarded as a loss. One way of viewing this problem is to regard the price of investment in terms of immediate consumption to be greater than one. This problem was discussed in chapter 6 and in the appendix to the chapter. The shadow price of investment, $P^{inv}(t)$, is a crucial factor in assessing the social cost of employment, since the expansion of employment means a shift from investment to consumption, and the loss involved in this per unit is equivalent to the value of $[P^{inv}(t) — 1]$. If investment and consumption are already optimally distributed, i.e. there is neither underinvestment nor overinvestment, then the value of $P^{inv}(t)$ should be equal to 1 and the loss involved would be precisely 0. However, as is common in most developing countries, if the planners believe that the level of investment is too low, there will be a loss, since $P^{inv}(t)$ exceeds 1. The social cost of labour depends not merely on the social opportunity cost of labour but also on the shadow price of investment. How precisely the shadow price of investment should be determined will be explored in detail in chapter 14, and in that context the shadow price of labour will become calculable.[15]

We may seem to be contradicting ourselves in some ways by regarding additional consumption generated through additional employment (a) to be a

---

[15] In chapter 15 we shall present an expression for the shadow wage rate.

good thing because it leads to a better distribution of income, and (b) to be a bad thing because it leads to a shift from investment to consumption. This is, however, not a contradiction, and both facts are correct and relevant, though they work in opposite directions. A unit of income that accrues to a worker in a project rather than accruing to the project authorities can be viewed in one of two ways. To the extent that it reflects workers' consumption as opposed to average consumption of the community, it can be regarded as more valuable; to the extent that it reflects consumption rather than invest-ment it must be regarded as less valuable if the country is suffering from a shortage of investment vis-à-vis consumption. The latter is the comparison of consumption with investment and the former is the comparison of consump-tion by a poorer group vis-à-vis that by a richer group. In making a detailed calculation of benefits and costs of a project both these considerations are relevant, but they will come into our estimation under different objectives and will work in different directions.

Under the broad hat of aggregate consumption would come the question of the relative weight of investment vis-à-vis average consumption today, since the impact of investment on future consumption is fully reflected in our estimation of the aggregate-consumption benefit. On the other hand, the special weight to be attached to the consumption of the poorer groups vis-à-vis average consumption today must come under the heading of the redistribution objective. Employment creation will, therefore, come in both the benefit and the cost side under these two sets of objectives; additional employment will involve a cost through the "aggregate-consumption objective" and a benefit through the "redistribution objective".

8.5 ENDS AND MEANS

The question of the social importance of employment creation is one of the more intricate aspects of project evaluation. This is partly because the problem itself is complex, and, as we have seen, employment has various implications for a number of disparate objectives of planning. The complexity arises partly because the subject of employment is charged with emotion. In various official and unofficial studies singular emphasis is placed on the expansion of employment, and it is indeed quite common for practical project selectors to consider employment a major objective in itself. While we have outlined what appears to be the relevant economic considerations in this field, it would be worth while to emphasize precisely where we differ, if at all, with what might appear to be the more usual approach.

In the common approach, employment is taken as an objective in itself and thus given a certain weight, usually implicitly, in the evaluation of projects. This weight reflects the planners' opinion of the importance of employment, with the various factors that have been outlined in this chapter presumably taken into consideration. In contrast, in these Guidelines we do not take employment as an objective in itself, and among the various factors to be

valued directly employment is not one. This, however, does not at all mean that an expansion of employment will not receive any value in the system outlined here. On the contrary, a great deal of weight could be placed on employment, but it will come through the weights attached to other objectives, especially the redistribution objective. Greater employment, especially of people from depressed classes or regions, will increase a component of aggregate consumption to which additional weight is to be attached for the sake of redistribution, and thus employment will have its impact on the benefit figure of the project.

The difference, thus, does not lie in whether employment is regarded as good or bad, but lies in whether the weighting of employment as something good should be direct or indirect. In these Guidelines the position is taken that employment is basically desired not for its own sake, but for what it generates, namely, output for the productive system, income to certain people, opportunities for learning, increased modernization and so on. These objectives are valued, and employment is viewed as a means to achieving them.

We have, of course, also emphasized some negative aspects of employment, e.g. employment may lead to a shift from investment to consumption, which could be undesirable if investment should be in short supply vis-à-vis consumption. Once again, no negative value has been attached to employment directly, and its possible negative impact on investment comes into the calculation through the shadow price of investment if it should exceed unity. Thus, employment could also have undesirable consequences, but in either capacity the effects of employment are estimated in connexion with other objectives and not directly.

Chapter 9

TOTAL NET BENEFIT OF THE PROJECT:
A SUMMING UP

9.1 REVIEW OF MULTIPLE OBJECTIVES

Project selection has to be done in terms of benefits and costs reflecting several alternative objectives of economic decision. As our basis of computation we have taken the objective of aggregate consumption, and our unit of account is a unit of average present consumption today. The consumption stream of the future is measured in terms of the amount of present consumption to which this time stream will be equivalent. The process was discussed in detail in chapters 4, 5 and 6.

While aggregate consumption was taken to be our unit of account, other objectives have also been explored in some detail. In particular, the objective of income redistribution, reflecting the planners' judgements on inequality and related questions, was discussed in chapter 7. The objective of employment creation, studied in the last chapter, was shown to be important but essentially related to other objectives. For the purpose of these Guidelines, the employment objective will be reflected mainly through the aggregate-consumption objective and the redistribution objective, and the reasons for this have already been discussed in detail.

The case of "merit wants" was outlined in chapter 3. In the context of industrial project evaluation, merit wants will not usually be so important. There are, however, some things that can conveniently be looked at as merit wants, e.g. the importance of employing female workers in a backward economy, as discussed in chapter 8. Since modernization of the society is frequently viewed as an objective that cannot, by its very nature, be well reflected by the value of transactions in the market, there is a good case for taking certain indicators of modernization as merit wants in the evaluation of benefits and costs of industrial projects.

There is not much point in discussing these specific considerations, since what would be treated as merit wants would largely depend on the particular nature of the society and the particular approach of the planners in the country in question. Therefore, we shall not go into this question further

here. It might just be indicated that after a certain measure of achievement of merit want is chosen, e.g. the number of women employed, some value would have to be assigned to this achievement to put it in terms comparable to aggregate consumption. This value, then, is a national weight. For example, the CPO may eventually infer from the policy makers' choice of projects that the policy makers regard the employment of one female worker in a certain underdeveloped society as equal to, say, a quarter of the prevailing wage rate. This will be over and above the value of aggregate output produced by the worker who is employed. As with other national weights, we assume that the weight on this merit want is in the first instance an unknown of the planning process.

It might be noted that we have left out a number of specific objectives that are often thought to be important in the context of planning in general and project selection in particular. Chief among them are the objective of maximization of growth and the objective of self-reliance in foreign trade. Since these are complicated considerations and since a discussion of how they relate to what has already been done will take some time, we shall devote the next two sections to these two problems.

The multiple objectives that are relevant to project selection have to be reconciled with each other in terms of national parameters reflecting relative weights. We have already discussed this quite a bit, but perhaps a further look at it in the context of the summing up may be relevant. In section 9.4 this will be re-examined.

9.2 THE OBJECTIVE OF ECONOMIC GROWTH

In the context of development planning in recent years the objective of generating economic growth has received a remarkable amount of attention. In our calculation so far this has not, however, figured explicitly. Does this mean that in the approach of these Guidelines the objective of economic growth is not taken seriously? The answer is: it is taken very seriously indeed, but it is already reflected in the aggregate-consumption objective.

The growth rate of income between one period and the next is a reflection of the difference in the income level in the two periods in relative terms. Thus, if we have a measure of income levels at each period of time within the planning horizon we already have a complete measure of all the growth rates between periods. In our aggregate-consumption objective, we have based our measure of benefits on the totality of consumption during each period suitably weighted so that in some sense growth from period to period has already come into our picture. In assessing whether this is appropriate the following questions would have to be discussed:

    (1) Instead of reflecting the growth rate from year to year in our calculation, we have reflected the value of consumption during each period in our estimation. A direct indication of growth rates, given the level

of the first year's consumption level, would have indirectly indicated all the future years' consumption, just as by directly indicating the consumption level of each year we have indirectly indicated growth rates relevant between each period. For the purpose of project choice, is it more convenient to take growth rates as the direct measure or the consumption levels?

(2) We have concentrated on the year-to-year figures for consumption rather than on those for income, so that we have measures of growth rates of consumption rather than of growth rates of income. Since much discussion on growth tends to deal with income rather than with consumption, does this mean that we have left out something significant?

In answering the first question we have to note that these Guidelines hold that one of the main objectives of planning is to raise the standard of living. To demand a high standard of living at a certain date in the future is, of course, equivalent to demanding a high growth rate starting from today's standard of living. Fundamentally, it makes no difference whether we wed ourselves to a high standard of living in the future or to a high growth rate, since they are equivalent. However, we have chosen the former rather than the latter as the more convenient basis for reflecting our values. Since our ultimate concern is with the levels of standard of living, this seems perfectly legitimate.

However, one could have taken the view that the level of well-being of a community depends not merely on the absolute standard of living it enjoys but on the relative standard of living in comparison with what it enjoyed in the past. If this view is taken, the growth rates will become important considerations on their own, since the growth rates will reflect the extent to which the standard of living at a certain date will exceed those of the past. There is little point in going into this question further, since, at the level of practical decision making with which project selection is concerned, the difference between these two approaches may not be very important. If it is thought that the future standard of living and the social value of it should be judged specifically in the context of the extent to which it exceeds the present standard of living, this can also be done perfectly easily within our framework. The equivalence of growth rate information and the information concerning the absolute levels that we noted earlier makes this an elementary idea. The only question is one of convenience.

In the Guidelines we have preferred the approach of directly weighing the contribution to consumption at each period of time (thereby taking into account the growth rates indirectly) rather than directly attaching weights to growth rates (thereby indirectly taking into account the actual levels of consumption).

The answer to the second question should be clear from what has already been said. If the standard of living (and therefore the level of consumption)

in each period is thought to be relevant rather than the value of output produced or income earned, there is an obvious case for being concerned with the time series of consumption rather than of output or income. National income or national output consists of consumption and investment, and the question here is whether investment is desired for its own sake, or for the sake of the consumption it will generate in the future. In the approach of the Guidelines we have taken the latter position, and it was this position that has been elaborately studied in chapter 6. This seems to be a reasonable position to take, for investment goods do not usually add directly to enjoyment and their contribution to national welfare seems to lie in their role in making future consumption possible. However, the view may be taken that national pride in a developing economy may easily depend, to a large extent, on the presence of modern machinery and other types of productive capital goods and if so, the value of these capital goods may exceed their contribution to future consumption. This is an intricate issue because the question of national pride and related matters is a complex psychological one. In particular, it has to be determined whether this national pride arises from a recognition that these capital goods will raise the level of consumption in the future; if so, the national pride in certain capital goods may be really a reflection of the future consumption prospects arising from them. On the other hand, if national pride takes the form of simply enjoying the possession of capital goods, the position will be quite different. If such a view is taken, the presence of modern capital goods may even be considered a merit want, but this would be a rather odd view to assume. In any case we shall not go into this problem further and shall proceed with the assumption that the estimation of benefits and costs from aggregate consumption will be done along the lines already specified in these Guidelines.

Finally, the growth rate of an economy may not be very sensitive to the presence or absence of one project. As a measure, the actual contribution of the project to total consumption is a much more sensitive indicator, and this is an important reason why choosing the aggregate-consumption objective is the more convenient way of reflecting the impact of a project on the national standard of living than doing it through the more summary measure of growth rates for the country as a whole.

9.3 BALANCE OF PAYMENTS AND SELF-RELIANCE

The contribution of a project to the balance of payments may be an extremely important part of its impact. Some projects will substantially improve the balance of payments whereas others may lead to a deterioration. Although we have discussed the methods of estimating the impact of a project on foreign exchange in some detail in chapters 4 and 5, we have not treated the balance-of-payments position as a separate objective. It is relevant to examine the reasons for this.

We have to ask, first of all, why it is that we want a more favourable balance-of-payments situation. One obvious reason is that an improvement in the balance of payments would permit a country to do several things to improve its standard of living that it could not do otherwise (e.g. to import more machinery). If that is so, the availability of foreign exchange is desired not for its own sake but for the sake of other objectives, e.g. aggregate consumption, to which it contributes. In this view, foreign exchange is not something that makes people happier directly; it is a means to other ends. In contrast, however, it is possible to take the view that the possession of foreign exchange may be a source of delight in itself, and if such a view were taken, the benefit-cost calculation for projects should reflect this aspect of the impact on foreign exchange.

The question assumes great importance for those developing countries that suffer from a chronic shortage of foreign exchange. Persistent balance-of-payments difficulties have made many of these countries thoroughly dependent on foreign aid, and the value of self-reliance has often been articulated in that context in highly moving terms. Indeed, in looking at the literature on economic development, one would tend to feel that it is more usual to regard self-reliance as a value in itself than to regard it merely as a means to some other end. However, the picture is somewhat deceptive, since very often the argument takes the form of pointing out that a chronic balance-of-payment difficulty reduces the freedom of action of a country and thereby restricts possibilities of pursuing certain policies that may be conducive to economic growth and betterment of the standard of living in the future. And in this case, while self-reliance remains important, it is ultimately related to aggregate consumption and other objectives.

The whole question is expressed in the determination of the appropriate shadow price for foreign exchange, and in chapter 16 this problem will be discussed in detail. We simply note here that if earning foreign exchange and being self-reliant are desired for their own sake, the benefits and costs of the project should reflect this value. On the other hand, if earning foreign exchange is considered desirable precisely because it permits the country to import economic resources from abroad or permits the country to abstain from exporting certain other goods abroad that may be needed at home, the shadow price of foreign exchange would have to be derived in terms of other objectives, especially aggregate consumption. In the context of project evaluation the problem of collecting all the relevant information on a project's impact on exports, imports, loans and loan repayments has to be distinguished from the problem of evaluating the net foreign exchange earned using a shadow price. The latter exercise can be done only after the methodology outlined in chapter 4 for the use of shadow prices has been fully pursued; here we concentrate merely on drawing attention to the relevant motivation of the exercise. In chapters 4 and 5 the methods of estimating the impact on foreign exchange have been discussed in some detail. The methodology outlined is also illustrated later in terms of the case studies in Part IV.

9.4 NATIONAL PARAMETERS

In summing up the total impact of a project from the point of view of benefit-cost evaluation, the benefits and costs of achieving different objectives have to be estimated in terms of their respective units. After this estimation, however, there remains the further problem of putting them all into one aggregate measure of net benefits. In chapter 3 of these Guidelines we have already discussed the relevance of national weights reflecting the relative weights to be attached to different objectives. It may be convenient at this stage to deal with this subject a little more concretely than was possible in chapter 3.

As has been made clear, if a project contributes a certain number of units of present consumption today for the country as a whole, these units are incorporated in the calculations as base units. Units of future consumption are all discounted at the appropriate social discount rates reflecting the relative value of future consumption vis-à-vis present consumption. For example, a social rate of discount of 10 per cent would indicate that 110 units of future consumption one year hence is equivalent to 100 units of consumption today and so on.

However, in estimating how much future consumption a certain project will generate, we have to take into account what proportion of the value of the output of that project will be immediately consumed and what proportion will be reinvested for the sake of further production and consumption at dates still further in the future. This requires detailed calculation of proportions of reinvestment and related magnitudes, as well as a measure of the productivity of investment in terms of the flow of future output. It was discussed in chapter 6 how these considerations must come into the shadow prices of investment in terms of present consumption.[16] This is a set of national parameters that has to be taken into account on top of the social rates of discount in order to do the estimation of future consumption benefits.

While all these considerations are aggregate considerations, we are also deeply involved in the distribution of this consumption among different classes, income groups and regions. That being so, the redistribution objective is an important one for project evaluation. While this objective can be measured in several ways, the measure we are using in these Guidelines consists mainly of separating out certain depressed classes or groups and attaching special additional weights to the consumption they enjoy. The additional weights to be attached to the consumption of these poorer classes or groups are also a set of national parameters reflecting the relative weights on the redistribution objective vis-à-vis the objective of pursuing aggregate consumption.

The employment objective leads to a different set of considerations. The view was taken that additional employment in a country with surplus labour is desirable, but not for the sake of just employing people. Rather, it is desired

---

[16] For a more detailed discussion see chapter 14.

for the sake of other objectives, such as income distribution and the efficient use of national resources. Thus, the employment goal is not directly reflected in our calculations. A special weight on employment is, therefore, not being taken as a value on its own. Instead, this consideration is reflected through the weights on the additional value of income of depressed groups, which depend on their employment opportunities, as well as through other weights related to the impact of employment on consumption and distribution. If additional employment leads to learning and improvement in the quality of labour, this will also be reflected in the output calculations of projects and will be incorporated in the measure of aggregate consumption.

The objective of self-reliance was also taken to be a derived objective. It is, of course, convenient to specify the shadow price of foreign exchange, which may be used conveniently in the estimation of net benefits of projects. The shadow price will essentially reflect the contribution that a unit of foreign exchange will make to aggregate consumption. A unit of foreign exchange may permit us to expand our imports or to contract our exports, and whichever is the more desirable of the two will be the relevant reward for earning an additional unit of foreign exchange. This desirability, however, will be judged not for its own sake, but through its impact on consumption opportunities today and in the future. It was noted, however, that if the view is taken that the earning of foreign exchange is to be regarded as desirable for its own sake over and above its contribution to the consumption opportunities, this can also very well be done through the shadow price of foreign exchange.

The objective of maximization of the growth rate does not figure at all explicitly in our calculation. The approach of these Guidelines takes the growth rates to be merely a reflection of the sequence of consumption levels over time, and these are already fully reflected in the aggregate-consumption objective.

We are at this stage concerned entirely with the logic of national weights and not their derivation. What relative weight we attach to present consumption vis-à-vis future consumption is, of course, a reflection of our moral judgements concerning the distribution of consumption over time. One extreme may be to concentrate entirely on present consumption, forgetting about future consumption altogether. It is conventional to regard the other extreme to be the situation where no discrimination is made between present consumption and future consumption, no matter how distant is the future in question. The latter view is based on the idea that consumption whenever it occurs is equally valuable, even though future consumption may be far away, even though future consumption may occur at a time when the community will be much richer, and even though the current standard of living of many underdeveloped countries is so low that present consumption may be a matter of life or death for some of the population. The extreme represented by the first alternative reflects a view that future consumption is simply unimportant in comparison with present consumption. The other extreme really amounts to growth maximization, since a higher growth rate will eventually produce a larger

total of aggregate consumption if future consumption is not discounted vis-à-vis present consumption. The conflict between these two points of view has sometimes been referred to in literature as that between output maximization and growth maximization.

These traditional debates can also be fully reflected in the methodology in the Guidelines if it is so desired. However, these are extreme cases, and the more usual approach implicitly or explicitly taken by planners amounts to attaching some weight, but a lower one, to future consumption vis-à-vis present consumption. As we have remarked repeatedly throughout the previous chapters, we regard national weights as being initially unknowns in the planning process. What precise values these national weights will take will, it is hoped, emerge from the policy makers' selection of projects. But their logic lies essentially in the policy makers' ethical values, which find expression through the formulation of plans and the choice of projects that go to fill a plan. These considerations will be pursued in detail in Part III.

The discussion so far should make it clear that while the estimation of different types of objectives is a matter for detailed calculation, the over-all assessment of a project is dependent on supplementing these detailed estimations by the use of national weights. Part II of the Guidelines, therefore, should be taken in conjunction with Part III.

Chapter 10

PROJECT EVALUATION UNDER UNCERTAINTY

Throughout the previous chapters we have talked about projects in a way that assumed that future benefits and costs are known. The reader may well wonder what provision we are making in our approach for the uncertainties of the future. Import prices may unexpectedly rise or fall; construction costs may turn out to be more than anticipated; production may not go as planned; and so on. In view of the many ways in which predictions may prove wrong, it is pertinent to ask what values of benefits and costs one should use in the evaluation of projects. One expects that some kind of average of the various possibilities should be used for the estimation of benefits and costs. The question is, what average is really appropriate? In particular, the reader may ask whether the Government should bias its selection against risky projects. In this chapter we go briefly into what the project evaluator should do about uncertainty—briefly, because (1) the subject of decision under uncertainty is still somewhat controversial; that is to say, there appears as yet to be no consensus on the appropriate way of viewing it; and (2) given the approach that we shall be pursuing here, our recommendations are quite simple in principle.

10.1 EXPECTED PRESENT VALUE OF NET BENEFITS

The extent to which an evaluator is confident in the estimates of benefits and costs of a project varies greatly. If various countries have agreed to maintain the price of some exportable commodity, the evaluator may in general have good reason to feel confident of the estimates of the benefits of a project that produces this commodity for export. For other projects, estimates of future prices and quantities may be no more than educated guesses. But even where one is not certain of the future estimates, a distinction is normally drawn between the following two cases: (1) the various possible outcomes can be characterized by numerical probabilities, e.g. the energy output ten years hence of a hydroelectric project on a river for which long, reliable records of stream flow exist can be characterized by a known probability distribution; (2) the probability distribution of the various outcomes is not

known. Economists have for a long time referred to outcomes falling under category (1) as "risky" outcomes and those falling under category (2) as "uncertain" outcomes.

In this chapter we shall be concerned with projects that are risky and, violating the established convention, we shall use the terms "risky" and "uncertain" interchangeably. The reader may object that uncertainties in projects are most frequently of such a nature that it is not known what probability distribution describes them. It might then be thought that we are restricting our discussion in this chapter to very uninteresting cases. But even though the project evaluator may genuinely regard future possibilities as uncertain and may be reluctant to impute probabilities to the various outcomes, one should bear in mind that he is not totally without knowledge. When all the relevant possibilities are thought of and the various arguments bearing on the outcome weighed one against the other, the evaluator will no doubt feel that certain possibilities are highly unlikely and that others may well turn out to be correct. For example, the statement that the export price of bicycles is as likely to go up as down is surely a better description of things than the statement that it is certain to rise by 100 per cent.

In any event, the very fact that individuals make decisions under uncertainty (and not always just "blindly") seems to indicate that they act according to various degrees of belief about the likelihood of different outcomes. Weighing one argument against another, one feels that some outcomes are more likely to occur than others. Naturally, past evidence is often (though not always) of great help. If the evaluator discovers that construction costs have in the past been systematically underestimated in the feasibility reports of industrial projects, he will naturally cast doubt on current estimates of construction costs. He may wish to use past experience to mark up such cost estimates, since his belief is that costs are likely to be higher than stated. Numerical probabilities are a natural expression of such degrees of belief. We shall not go into the question of how one might go about making statistical estimates of the probability of future outcomes, since this would take us far afield. Moreover, there is still a great deal of disagreement among statisticians about how one should use the available information to estimate probabilities. Fortunately, however, there are good reasons for supposing that in general it is sufficient to have only a rough idea of the probability distribution of the benefits and costs of an industrial project. What the evaluator should try to estimate are "expected values" of the benefits and costs, and this is what we discuss below. For the sake of being specific we shall concentrate our discussion entirely on the national objective of maximizing net aggregate-consumption benefits.

For a given year (t) of a project assume that the evaluator judges that the probability that the net benefit of the project will be B_{it} is q_{it}. (The index i represents the "state" of the world and runs over the various possible states.)[17]

---

[17] A "state" is a description of all facts relevant to the project's performance.

We have then, $\sum_{i} q_{it} = 1$. One then says that the expected value of net benefits due to the project in year t is:

$$E(B_{it}) = \sum_{i} q_{it} B_{it} \qquad (10.1)$$

Discounting this expected value at the social rate(s) of discount, one obtains the present value of the expected net benefits yielded in year t. If one now algebraically sums the present values of the expected net benefits for all the years of the project one obtains the expected present value (EPV) of the project. The EPV of a project reflects the average value of its discounted net benefits and is thus a natural index of its desirability. The general rule (exceptions will be discussed in 10.3) is, therefore, to recommend a project having a positive EPV and to reject a project having a negative EPV. If one is evaluating a set of mutually exclusive projects (e.g. if they are project variants) one ought to recommend the project with the highest EPV (provided, of course, that it is positive!).

Now, the expected net benefit in a given year of a project is the algebraic sum of the expected benefits (direct as well as indirect) and the expected costs (direct as well as indirect). If there are good reasons for supposing that the uncertainty in the quantities of the inputs and output(s) of a project is independent of the uncertainty in the shadow prices of these inputs and output(s), the procedure for evaluating the expected costs and benefit(s) is to multiply the expected levels (quantities) of inputs and output(s) by the expected values of the corresponding shadow prices. An example will help to illustrate this. Suppose that the uncertainty in the shadow price (export price perhaps) of ceiling fans is independent of the uncertainty in the output level of a plant producing ceiling fans. Suppose that for a given year it is estimated that the plant will produce 20,000 fans with probability $\frac{1}{2}$ and will produce 25,000 fans with probability $\frac{1}{2}$. It is, moreover, judged that the shadow price of a fan will be Rs360 with probability $\frac{1}{3}$ and that it will be Rs372 with probability $\frac{2}{3}$. Then the expected level of output for that year is $\frac{1}{2} \times 20,000 + \frac{1}{2} \times 25,000 = 22,500$ units. Furthermore, the expected shadow price of fans for that year is $Rs(\frac{1}{3} \times 360 + \frac{2}{3} \times 372) = Rs368$. It follows that the expected value of the benefit from the plant for that year is $Rs22,500 \times 368 = Rs8.28$ million. The procedure for evaluating the expected value of the costs involved in production for that year will be identical (provided, of course, that the uncertainty in the levels of inputs is independent of the uncertainty in the shadow prices of these inputs).

If, however, the uncertainty in the level of output of the project is not independent of the uncertainty in the shadow price of the output (because say, the export price of ceiling fans is sensitive to the volume exported), the foregoing simple procedure for calculating the expected value of the benefit will not suffice. What one has to do in such a case is to consider all the possible values of the benefit, assess their probabilities and use formula 10.1 directly.

That is to say, one has to assess the probability of the export price being Rs372 per fan contingent on a production level of 20,000 units; the probability of the export price being Rs372 per fan contingent on a production level of 25,000 units; and so on. Since there are two possible prices and two possible output levels in our example, there are four possible states of the world relevant to the calculation of the benefit derived from this project (i.e. i runs from 1 to 4). The table provides a description of such a situation.

i	Number of fans	Export price (Rs)	Benefit (Million Rs)	Probability q_i
1	20,000	372	7.44	1/3
2	25,000	372	9.30	1/12
3	20,000	360	7.20	1/3
4	25,000	360	9.00	1/4

Expected value of benefit of project: $= \dfrac{7.44}{3} + \dfrac{9.30}{12} + \dfrac{7.20}{3} + \dfrac{9.00}{4} =$ Rs7.905 million.

10.2 ZERO RISK PREMIUM

The reader may be wondering at this stage whether it is appropriate to assess a project solely through its EPV. Ought one not to penalize an unduly risky project? If the EPV of project A is only just greater than the EPV of project B, but if A is much riskier, is there no case for recommending B? It is indeed true that private firms use a variety of techniques (for example, using a payback period) to take account of uncertainty in calculating commercial profitability. These techniques vary in detail but share the common purpose of biasing project design and selection against uncertain projects. This may or may not be sound practice for private firms.

In any event, there is an important immediate difference between public and private enterprise. The typical private firm specializes in a few products and undertakes a small number of projects. As a result the over-all performance of the firm is highly correlated with the performance of each of its investment projects. Failure of one project may spell bankruptcy. The Government, on the other hand, typically undertakes many projects. The net benefits from each project are (generally speaking) small relative to the aggregate consumption of the economy.[18] Moreover, these net benefits are generally less highly correlated with the level of aggregate consumption than is the contribution of a project's profits to a private firm's total profits. Because of its larger number of projects and the greater diversity of its investment "portfolio", the Government can be much more confident than the private firm that

---

[18] We use "aggregate consumption" and "national income" synonymously here. National income will consist of the country's total consumption and its total investment (revalued at the shadow price of investment to make it comparable to consumption).

unexpected failure of one project will be matched by extraordinary success in another.[19]

By having a large number of projects, the Government, in effect, reduces its risk considerably. That is why a Government may not be overly concerned about the uncertainty in aggregate consumption (national income). Typically, national income will not be very uncertain because of the foregoing argument. Therefore, with a national income that is fairly certain and with projects that are small (i.e. the extent of the uncertainty of any such project is small compared with the level of national income), the Government can be neutral towards risk and ought, therefore, to judge projects only by their EPVs.[20]

10.3 EXCEPTIONAL CASES

In the discussion carried out in the foregoing two sections, we tacitly assumed that (1) the country's aggregate consumption in the absence of the proposed project is fairly accurately predictable; and (2) the proposed project is "small", i.e. the "range" of the net benefits of the project is small compared with the size of aggregate consumption. In this section we consider cases where either of these assumptions may be untrue and discuss what the project evaluator should do in such cases. It might seem plain that the EPV rule will not suffice then. One would like to know what rule should replace it. One would also like to know whether the evaluator would make serious errors if he stuck to the EPV rule in such cases. All this we shall discuss below.

Given the choice of maintaining the same consumption level as previously or taking a chance on a 50—50 probability of increasing or decreasing this income level by a given amount, individuals—especially those with low incomes—will generally opt for the sure thing. That is to say, individuals tend to attach a greater weight to a large decrease in consumption than to an equal increase. It would, therefore, appear appropriate that the Government, as the custodian of society, behave similarly with regard to aggregate consumption. In other words, the Government should prefer a more certain national income, even though it may be at the cost of a higher expected value. The upshot of this is that a tiny contribution of net benefits due to a project should be worth more to a country when its national income is low than when it is

---

[19] A formal example may illustrate the point. Consider N projects, no two of which are correlated, and suppose that each has a return whose expected value is r and whose variance is v. If one invests Rs1 in any one of these projects the expected value of the return is r and the variance of the return is v. But if one invests Rs1/N in each of these projects then the expected return is still r, but now the variance of the return is v/N. If N is "large", v/N is "small". If we associate risk with variance, one reduces the risk in the return to a rupee invested by such a diversification.

[20] It may be argued that this should be true as well for the private sector, since capital markets augment the private sector's capacity to pool risk. In other words, individuals can diversify their portfolios by purchasing shares of various companies. This would be true provided capital markets function in a perfectly competitive manner. But in fact capital markets in developing countries are notoriously imperfect. In any case we argue, in the text, that the Government would be wise in general to be neutral towards risk in the selection of industrial projects.

high. That is to say, a higher weight should be given to the net benefits of a project when aggregate consumption is low than when aggregate consumption is high. The natural way of capturing these considerations is to say that aggregate consumption provides society with "utility" and that the level of utility rises with increasing aggregate consumption, but at a diminishing rate. We now come to two cases where the evaluator, in assessing projects, ought not to rely on the EPV alone.

(1) Suppose that a project is unusually large, that is to say, the extent of the uncertainty in its net benefits in a given year is a substantial fraction of the national income of the economy. It would follow that undertaking the project would render the national income itself uncertain. Such projects are no doubt uncommon for large countries (although projects like the Aswan dam do exist), but they are probably not uncommon for small countries. Undertaking to export a sizable quantity of primary products could render the national income of a small economy uncertain owing to the vicissitudes of export prices. One wants to know what one should do in such a situation. It would be best to see what issues are involved with the help of an example:

Suppose that the national income of an economy in a given year is Rs500 million. A project is proposed which in that year will yield net benefits of Rs100 million with probability $\frac{1}{2}$ and Rs150 million with probability $\frac{1}{2}$. The expected value of its net benefits for that year is, therefore, Rs125 million. Suppose that the central planners judge the utility of aggregate consumption, C, to be $-10,000/C$ units. If the project is undertaken society will enjoy the utility level $-10,000/600$ units with probability $\frac{1}{2}$ and the utility level $-10,000/650$ with probability $\frac{1}{2}$. It follows that the expected value of utility is $\dfrac{-10,000}{2 \times 600} - \dfrac{10,000}{2 \times 650}$, which roughly equals -16.03 units. Now this same level of utility would be attained by a sure project yielding net benefits that year of y, where $\dfrac{-10,000}{500 + y} = -16.03$; that is, y is roughly Rs124 million. In other words, the correction that needs to be made on the expected net benefit of the uncertain project is about Rs1 million, which is less than 1 per cent of the expected net benefit. There seems, therefore, to be fairly good justification for supposing that only small corrections may be required, even for projects as large as the one we have just considered.

(2) In this case we suppose that the national income itself is uncertain. We then suppose that the probability distribution of the net benefits of a project is correlated with the probability distribution of the aggregate consumption of the economy. Such a case is less likely to occur among industrial projects with which we are, in the main, concerned in these Guidelines. But an account should clearly be given of how to handle such a case.

Consider an economy that expects the national income to be Rs500 million if the rainfall is good and Rs300 million if the rainfall is bad. Let the probability of each of these events be $\frac{1}{2}$. The project evaluator is now considering a fertilizer

project that will yield net benefits of Rs10 million if the rainfall is good and zero net benefits if the rainfall is bad. He is also considering an irrigation project that will yield zero net benefits if the rainfall is good and Rs9.8 million of net benefits if the rainfall is bad. In other words, the fertilizer project's benefit is positively correlated with the "goodness" of rainfall and is thus, in turn, positively correlated with aggregate consumption. The irrigation project, on the other hand, is negatively correlated with aggregate consumption. This is quite reasonable for a rather dry region, since moisture and fertilizers are complements, whereas natural precipitation and irrigation are substitutes. The problem that we are interested in is one of ranking the two projects. Now the expected value of the net benefit of the fertilizer project (which is Rs5 million) is higher than the expected value of the net benefit of the irrigation project (which is Rs4.9 million). Does this mean that the fertilizer project will win? Not at all. For if the country embarks on the fertilizer project the expected utility would be $\dfrac{-10{,}000}{2 \times 510} - \dfrac{10{,}000}{2 \times 300} = -26.5$ units.[21] With the irrigation project the expected utility would be $\dfrac{-10{,}000}{2 \times 309.8} - \dfrac{10{,}000}{2 \times 500} = -26.1$ units. Thus, the country would be better off embarking on the irrigation project even though the expected value of its net benefits is lower than that of the fertilizer project. This is simply because the irrigation project provides positive net benefits when the country needs them most. The above argument has an intuitive appeal. Planners often talk of the "insurance value" of irrigation. The foregoing example indicates what this might mean.

So far in this chapter we have been concerned exclusively with the aggregate-consumption objective. In the context of this objective it is probably correct to suppose that the project evaluator would wish to go beyond the EPV rule only under exceptional circumstances. But it is also probably correct to suppose that only under exceptional circumstances is the EPV rule appropriate in the context of a regional-distribution objective. It seems most plausible that the considerations that lead to the first of our two exceptional cases are most often relevant here. That is to say, the success or failure of a project located in a particularly impoverished region may generally have a severe impact on the income of that region. The simple EPV rule will not then suffice in evaluating the net redistribution benefits for precisely the reasons that we have mentioned earlier in this section. Once we recognize what the problem is, we know in principle how to go about tackling it.

Thus, the essential point is to attach a higher weight to a rupee of net redistributional benefits when the project is a failure than when it is a success. This introduces yet another set of national parameters to our system of benefit-cost analysis. It is apparent that these parameters will be especially hard to specify. Indeed, it is our belief that the planning apparatus in most

---

[21] We are assuming that the utility function is of the same form as in the earlier example: i.e. it is $-10{,}000/C$, when C is aggregate consumption.

countries will not be able to generate these national parameters for some time to come. For this reason we do not discuss these specific national parameters in Part III of these Guidelines. We submit that at the present stage what is desirable is an awareness of the kind of considerations that imply the use of such weights. Occasionally, perhaps, these considerations may prove to be decisive in the choice of projects.

10.4 CONCLUDING REMARKS

In the foregoing section we discussed cases where the project evaluator may be well-advised to go beyond the simple EPV rule in evaluating uncertain projects. One may object that it is futile to introduce utilities, since planners rarely think in such terms and the evaluator will not know what function to use. No doubt this is true. But if there are reasons for being averse to taking risks, one must articulate these reasons and the extent to which risky projects are to be penalized. Moreover, it would be desirable to penalize uncertain projects in a consistent way. For such reasons the use of payback periods is an inappropriate method of pruning out uncertain projects. For one thing, different payback periods seem to be used for different sectors of the economy (for reasons that are never explicit); for another, such a technique totally ignores the benefits of a project over the years beyond the period. A stiffer rate of discount is often used to assess an uncertain project. One should bear in mind the consequences of this procedure, which is to attach an even lower weight to the net benefits of later years. The argument for doing this might be that the further away the future the more hazy is the outcome. This may well be true. But there is a good deal of evidence to suggest that the uncertainty in the net benefits of a project in its initial years is particularly high. Construction delays and delays in the delivery of heavy machinery for the installation of a plant are more a rule than an exception. It seems, therefore, that if there are good grounds for going beyond the simple EPV rule, a careful evaluation of the uncertainties involved needs to be made and the EPV of the uncertain project corrected along the lines suggested in the previous section. We do not wish to suggest that this is at all a simple procedure. Indeed, as we have remarked earlier, it is difficult to envisage the use of the national parameters implied by these considerations in the immediate future. One can simply hope for a growing awareness of these issues.

PART III

Application of Methodology at the Active Planning Level

Chapter 11

THE ROLE OF NATIONAL PLANNING
IN PROJECT FORMULATION AND EVALUATION

11.1 THE NEED FOR NATIONAL PARAMETERS

Parts I and II of these Guidelines developed a methodology for project formulation and evaluation that in form resembles calculations of commercial profitability but in substance differs markedly. Formally, calculations of national economic profitability simply replace monetary revenues and monetary costs with social benefits and social costs, and the rate of discount used to aggregate returns and outlays at different times becomes a social rate of discount rather than a private rate of discount. But social benefits and costs differ substantively from monetary revenues and costs. And the social rate of discount appropriate to calculations of national economic profitability will equal the private rate of discount appropriate to calculations of commercial profitability only by accident once we abandon the assumptions of perfect competition that characterize virtually all of welfare economics.

For the project evaluator, the differences between calculations of commercial and national economic profitability are reflected in a variety of ways. The prices used to value the inputs and outputs of these projects differ, and even the definition and classification of inputs and outputs differ. For example, the social cost of employing an additional worker in situations of widespread unemployment is equal to the money wage he receives only by chance, whereas in a commercial calculation of profitability the existence of unemployment does not affect the relevance of the money wage as a measure of cost. (It might affect the level of the money wage but not its relevance.) The use of "shadow wages" in place of money wages is an important difference between national and commercial evaluation of the cost of labour.

The definition and classification of inputs and outputs differ when the focus is changed from commercial to national economic profitability because the nation is properly concerned with many dimensions of projects that do not affect their commercial viability. As examples we may cite the effects of projects on the rate of saving, the distribution of income and the availability of foreign exchange. Thus, the methodology outlined in Parts I and II provides

117

both a set of categories for organizing pertinent data that commercia profitability omits and a set of "prices" for converting these effects into comparable units of measurement.

The project evaluator is obliged to calculate for himself some of the prices appropriate to national economic profitability. Chapter 4 indicated one instance—a project that would add sufficient sugar to domestic supplies to decrease the price to consumers. In this case the evaluator must calculate the price elasticity of demand to measure the willingness to pay for the project's output. But more typically, appropriate measures of social value are not affected by the decisions about any particular project, its size, location, technology, or product mix. Nor are the weights on income-distribution objectives or on other objectives that may enter into national economic profitability typically affected by single projects, unless these are exceptionally large projects like steel mills and high dams. Similarly, the social rate of discount is unlikely to be affected by any single project. Thus, it is natural to assign the calculation of these parameters to the national level rather than to the project level.

11.2 THE CIRCULARITY IN DETERMINING NATIONAL PARAMETERS

These national parameters are the subject matter of this part of these Guidelines. The problem facing the Central Planning Organization (CPO) can be illustrated by means of a simple example.[22] Suppose there are 100 projects under consideration that might contribute to the objective of redistributing consumption towards the poorest region in the country. The total contribution to this region's consumption obviously depends on the extent to which regional consumption is reflected in the formulation of each of the projects as well as on the importance attached to redistribution in their evaluation. But the emphasis appropriate for the regional objective in turn depends upon the extent to which the poorest region will continue to lag behind the rest of the country, which is to say, the decisions taken on all the potential projects that might raise the region's consumption. The circularity is shown schematically in figure 9.

In other words, if the other 99 projects taken together will in fact bring the region's *per capita* income within, say, 10 per cent of the national average, then it might be reasonable to pay little attention to income redistribution in making decisions about project number 100. But formulation and evaluation decisions are taken simultaneously, or virtually so, on all 100; each project is thus in effect number 100, and project formulation and evaluation must

---

[22] We shall designate the national level as the CPO in what follows. Whether the CPO should be thought of as an agency of the Planning Ministry, the Finance Ministry, or as an autonomous organization is an administrative question beyond the scope of these Guidelines. Certainly the answer to this question will vary from country to country and can only be answered in the specific context of each country's governmental apparatus. In the present discussion the CPO serves only the purpose of focusing attention on the national level so we need not be concerned about its precise place in the governmental organization.

Figure 9   Circularity of decision making

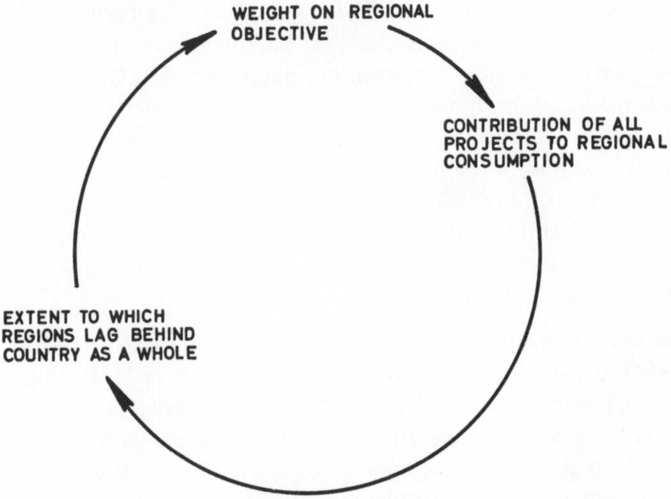

therefore rely explicitly or implicitly on assumptions about what other projects will contribute to development objectives. Thus the dilemma: project formulators and evaluators require the weight on income-redistribution benefits to be specified in advance. But the levels of these parameters can rationally be specified only in the light of the results of all government policies taken together, which determine the progress made towards income parity and the relative importance of further improvement. The dilemma exists for all the national parameters—the social rate of discount, which depends on the distribution of consumption over time; the shadow price of investment, which depends on the extent to which investment is more highly valued at the margin than consumption; the shadow wage, which depends both on the shadow price of investment and the magnitude of productivity differences between "advanced" and "backward" sectors of the economy; the shadow price of foreign exchange, which depends on the availability of foreign exchange relative to domestic resources.

11.3 LEAVING DETERMINATION OF NATIONAL PARAMETERS TO THE PROJECT LEVEL

One way out of the dilemma would be to dispense with the CPO altogether and to have each project formulator and evaluator estimate national parameters for himself on the basis of his best guesses about the results of government policies that affect the distribution of income, the rate of saving, the productivity of labour, the availability of foreign exchange, and a host of other variables that determine the appropriate levels of national parameters. Among other things, this would put each project formulator and evaluator in the position of second-guessing other formulators and evaluators, that is, of predicting their estimates of national parameters. For Jones's estimates

of these parameters would affect Jones's recommendations with respect to the projects under his purview, and Smith would have to take account of Jones's projects, along with everybody else's, in building up the projection of development patterns on which his own estimates depend. Quite apart from the duplication of effort and the virtual certainty of inconsistencies between Smith's estimates of Jones's decisions and Jones's estimates of Smith's decisions, to decentralize estimation of national parameters would put burdens on project evaluators and formulators for which they possess neither adequate information nor adequate training to discharge. Thus, the responsibility for estimating national parameters cannot reasonably fall upon project formulators and evaluators.

But there is a more important reason than inconsistency for not leaving the task of setting national parameters to the project level. Even if by sheer luck, project formulators and evaluators made consistent guesses, this would in itself be no guarantee that the national parameters were correctly specified. In view of the conflict among objectives, hard choices must be made between greater success with respect to one and greater success with respect to another. For example, improving the present distribution of income may conflict with increasing the rate of investment. National parameters, which represent the relative weights on different objectives and the shadow prices of the instruments that contribute to fulfilling these objectives, should reflect conscious political decisions with respect to what are, after all, political questions. To allow project formulators and evaluators to determine national parameters is to turn over political decisions to technicians and to deprive the political leadership of its rightful role in the decision process.

11.4 THE CPO AS THE "VISIBLE HAND"

Hence the CPO is here conceived as a body articulating political choices as it performs the technical function of co-ordination. The role the CPO plays in project evaluation and formulation is analogous to the role the market plays in co-ordinating the decisions of households and firms in idealized models of capitalist economies. A chief difference is that the CPO intervenes consciously and politically. In contrast with this "visible hand", principal virtues claimed for market co-ordination by defenders of *laissez-faire* are (1) that no conscious intervention is required and (2) that the goals realized are those of the co-ordinated rather than those of the co-ordinator.[23]

But the "visible" and political role of the CPO does not logically prevent it from imitating the market mechanism. Indeed, economists like Taylor,

---

[23] Following Adam Smith, generations of economists have devoted their talents to making precise the role played by the "invisible hand" in promoting economic welfare, and we need not duplicate their efforts here. In any event, the important defects of the prices that emerge from market co-ordination of economic activity have been outlined in the discussion in Part I of the limitations of commercial profitability as a guide to public-investment decisions.

Lange, and Lerner,[24] schooled in the orthodox economic myths of perfect competition, have built models of socialist economies in which the activities of separate economic agents are co-ordinated by a central body—the equivalent of our CPO—whose role is precisely to integrate politically determined objectives with technologically determined possibilities in fixing prices that guide decentralized decision-making based on profit-maximization criteria.

If we were to follow the Taylor-Lange-Lerner model, the CPO would mediate between policy makers and project formulators and evaluators by making explicit the value judgements implicit in the pattern of economic development the country is following, and giving these judgements quantitative expression as economic weights. Decisions would thus be taken with respect to projects on the basis of these national parameters. Parameter values would be revised periodically, say, with each new five-year plan, as part of general policy revision based in part on the extent to which the patterns of distribution of consumption among classes and over time, the balance of payments, and other indicators of economic progress conform to the projections on which all economic policies have been based. In addition, changes in economic environment that result from changed domestic or international conditions—changes with respect to war and peace, the weather and harvests, world demand and supply conditions for exports and imports, aid prospects, technology—would affect these periodic revisions in national parameters. Finally, changes in political direction that result from shifts in the domestic balance of political forces will make improvements in the distribution of income, increases in the rate of saving, and other objectives less or more important.

The success of project formulators and evaluators obviously depends on the extent to which the first approximations to national parameters are accurate reflections of national parameters. If they are "prices called out at random" (to use Walras's phrase), project formulation and evaluation become well nigh meaningless. Unless one has reasonable confidence that national parameters reflect national priorities, one cannot put much faith in national economic profitability as measuring anything very important. So if the CPO is to infer national parameters from the prospective pattern of economic development, there must be a reasonable basis for imputing optimality to that pattern of development.

This is where national economic planning comes into the picture and why the link between formulation and evaluation of projects and national planning is crucial. The pattern of economic development from which national parameters are inferred can be considered optimal if national planning is in fact a systematic method for first delineating the set of feasible development patterns, then for choosing one from among the feasible set as the optimal pattern.

---

[24] O. Lange and F. Taylor, *On the Economic Theory of Socialism*, University of Minnesota Press, Minneapolis, 1938; A. Lerner, *The Economics of Control*, Macmillan, London, 1945.

11.5 DETERMINING NATIONAL PARAMETERS FROM AN OPTIMAL NATIONAL PLAN: THE FEASIBILITY FRONTIER

To sharpen our understanding of how national planning might perform each of these functions and how the national parameters implicit in the optimal plan can be made explicit, let us look at the planning process in a model simple enough to be represented in a two-dimensional diagram (figure 10).

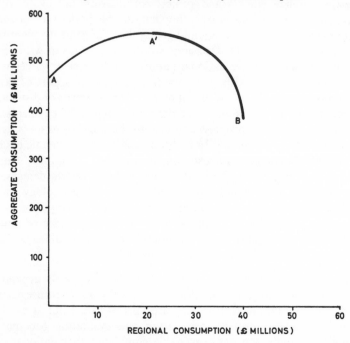

Figure 10   Feasibility frontier of alternative plans

Suppose there are only two objectives, "aggregate consumption" and "regional consumption", the latter a surrogate for the consumption of the poorest region. Assume away all intertemporal problems (problems of constraints on the rate of saving and the optimal intertemporal distribution of consumption), problems of income differences among classes (except as they are reflected in regional differences), problems of unemployment and underemployment, problems of foreign exchange availability and valuation, and finally problems of combining the multitude of different commodities and services in the economy into "aggregate" and "regional" consumption.

Then the first step of planning, the delineation of feasible alternatives, can be represented graphically by the curve labelled AB, called the "feasibility frontier". An enormous amount of analysis must be supposed to underlie the delineation of a feasibility frontier. It is not to be supposed that this analysis is at the same level of detail as that which underlies project formulation and evaluation, else there would be no point to separating project planning from national planning; on the other hand, the feasibility frontier cannot be

defined without analysis of alternative development strategies. The difference between the two types of planning is one of specificity and detail. At the level of national planning, the whole range of government policies, of which project choices are but one element, are variables. At the level of project planning, everything but the decisions with respect to the project in question is taken as given, so there is more room for detailed analysis of the specifics of the particular project.

Each point on AB corresponds to a different national plan. In the present model, with two variables, differences between alternative plans would be primarily differences in the mix of projects, differences in project location and technology, and—for outputs sold in the poorest region—differences in alternative pricing policies.

As the feasibility frontier is drawn in figure 10, the only relevant alternative plans are those represented on the segment A'B, for on AA' there is no conflict between the two objectives of planning; so long as any positive weight is placed on the income of the poorest region, it would serve no purpose to choose the plan corresponding to any point between A and A', for the plan corresponding to A' dominates all such plans.

11.6 USING "EQUAL-WELFARE" CURVES TO CHOOSE THE OPTIMAL PLAN

The next step in this idealized version of the planning process is to designate one of the points on A'B as optimal. This is clearly a political decision, for it ought to reflect judgements with respect to the relative importance of aggregate and regional consumption. To keep the story neat, we can imagine these judgements to be elicited from policy makers in the form of a set of "equal-welfare" curves, as in figure 11, each showing combinations of aggregate and regional consumption judged by policy makers to be equally desirable. Thus, curve 1 indicates that £400 million of aggregate consumption, of which £10 million is consumed in the poorest region, is held by policy makers to be as desirable as an aggregate consumption of £300 million, of which £20 million is consumed in the poorest region. The judgement of policy makers that aggregate and regional consumption are both desirable in and of themselves is reflected in the numbering of the curves: over-all social well-being increases as one moves from lower numbered to higher numbered curves.

The optimal plan can now be identified. It is the one corresponding to the point on A'B that touches the highest attainable equal-welfare curve. If we superimpose figure 11 on figure 10, as in figure 12, we see that this plan is the one corresponding to point C, for there is no other point on the feasibility frontier that touches equal-welfare curve 3 or any higher numbered curve.

The next and final step in linking national planning to project formulation and evaluation is to derive the single national parameter of the model—the weight on regional consumption relative to aggregate consumption—from delineation of the feasibility and the designation of C as the optimal plan. In our idealized version of planning, the CPO's task is easy, almost trivial.

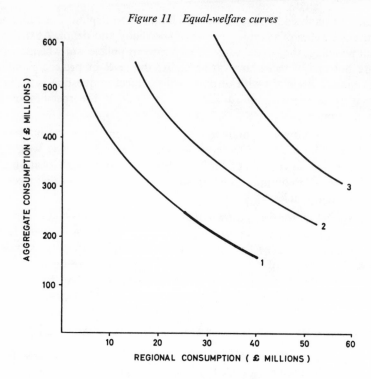

Figure 11   Equal-welfare curves

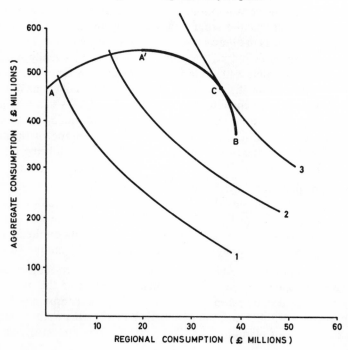

Figure 12   Optimal welfare point

The weight on regional-consumption benefits is by definition the premium the Government places on £1 within the poorest region. Now if one wants to know what premium a policy maker places on regional consumption relative to aggregate consumption, one asks him how much aggregate consumption he would be willing to give up to increase regional consumption by £1. If, for example, he replied £5, he would be saying that £1 of consumption in the poorest region deserves the same weight as £5 of consumption in the country at large, which is to say that regional consumption is weighted 5 times as heavily as aggregate consumption at the margin.[25]

Obviously, the willingness of policy makers to give up aggregate consumption for the sake of increasing consumption in the poorest region is a crucial element in designating C as the optimal national plan. But how does this willingness enter precisely? *In fact, the slope of the equal-welfare curve is exactly the amount of aggregate consumption policy makers showed themselves to be willing to give up to increase regional consumption by £1 when they articulated the equal-welfare curves in figure 11.*

Consider the construction in figure 13. Point D, corresponding to an aggregate consumption of £400 million and a regional consumption of

Figure 13   Welfare trade-off diagram

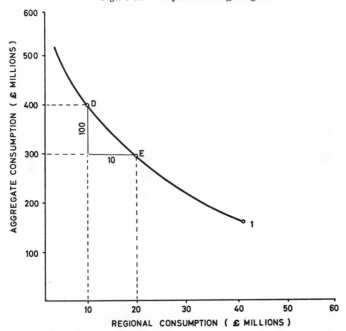

---

[25] The weight on regional consumption is a *premium* because additions to regional consumption that do not reduce consumption elsewhere in the country are properly counted twice, once under the rubric of regional-consumption benefits. Thus, a premium of, say, 0.5 would imply that net increases of consumption in the poorest region are valued 1.5 times as much as net increases outside the region, not half as much, as an overly quick reading might suggest.

£10 million, and point E, corresponding to an aggregate consumption of £300 million and a regional consumption of £20 million, are by assumption equally desirable. Thus, the Government is saying in effect that—assuming aggregate consumption is between £300 million and £400 million and regional consumption is between £10 million and £20 million—it is willing to give up £10 million of aggregate consumption for each £1 million increase in the consumption in the poorest region, which, as we have seen, is tantamount to saying that the Government places a premium of 10 on each £1 of regional consumption. But 10 is the slope of the chord between D and E (10 = 100/10), and if we take D and E closer and closer together, the slope of the chord approaches the slope of the equal-welfare curve itself. This is, of course, what we set out to show.

This construction emphasizes the role of the development pattern in determining the values of national parameters. The equal-welfare curves are bowed in towards the origin rather than being straight lines, which is to say that the relative importance of additional regional consumption decreases as the ratio of regional to aggregate consumption increases. So the weight on regional consumption depends on the pattern of aggregate consumption and

Figure 14   Slope of the optimal welfare point

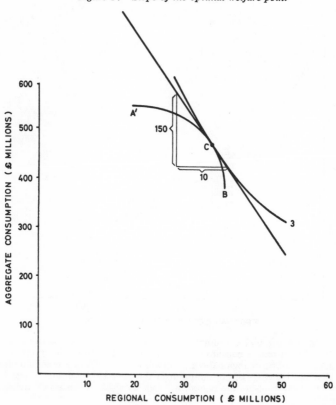

regional consumption (which together constitute the development pattern in this simple model) that emerges from the planning process. In our model it is thus the slope of equal-welfare curve 4 at the point C that is relevant, which, as figure 14 shows, has the numerical value of 15.

So the CPO has no difficulty in this idealized and simplified model of planning. It needs to know only the shape of the equal-welfare curve at the point on the feasibility function corresponding to the optimal plan, from which it calculates the single national parameter of the model and transmits it to project formulators and evaluators. Revision of the weight on regional consumption awaits revision of the national plan, which presumably would take place at stated intervals like five years or before the stated interval has elapsed if drastic changes in the economic environment radically alter the shape of the feasibility frontier.

The analysis we have presented suggests an economy of planning effort that would be desirable even in the context of this simple model. It is needlessly ambitious to oblige policy makers to articulate their value judgements with respect to aggregate and regional consumption over the entire range of possible combinations. It would be enough if policy makers were to articulate these judgements in the neighbourhood of the relevant portion of the feasibility frontier, A'B, the solid portion of the equal-welfare curves in figure 15, for obviously it is here that the choice must be made.

Figure 15   Relevant portions of the equal-welfare curves

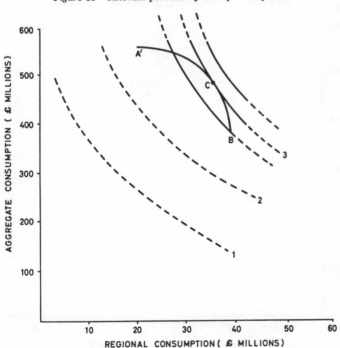

11.7 INFERRING NATIONAL PARAMETERS FROM THE FEASIBILITY FRONTIER

Indeed, the equal-welfare curves need not be explicitly defined at all to determine the weight on regional consumption! The feasibility frontier and the equal-welfare curve are tangent at C, so if it is known that C represents the optimal plan, the slope of the equal-welfare curve can be inferred from the slope of the feasibility frontier. In other words, equality of the two slopes is a condition of optimality. *Thus, knowledge that C is the optimal plan, coupled with knowledge of the shape of the feasibility frontier in the neighbourhood of C, would permit the CPO to calculate the weight on regional consumption without direct knowledge of policy makers' judgements that led them to choose C.*

Why is equality of the slopes of the feasibility frontier and the equal-welfare curve a condition of optimality? The answer is easy to grasp graphically: we saw that the optimal plan was the one corresponding to the point on A'B touching the highest equal-welfare curve. This right away implies tangency, which is to say that the two curves barely touch. For if the feasibility frontier did more than barely touch equal-welfare curve 3 at C, that is, if the two curves crossed one another, C could not represent the optimal plan; another point on A'B would lie on a higher equal-welfare curve.

To see what tangency of the two curves means in terms of the logic of planning, we must understand what the slope of the feasibility frontier means. As we move from A' towards B, locational decisions, pricing policies and

Figure 16   Trade-off along the feasibility frontier

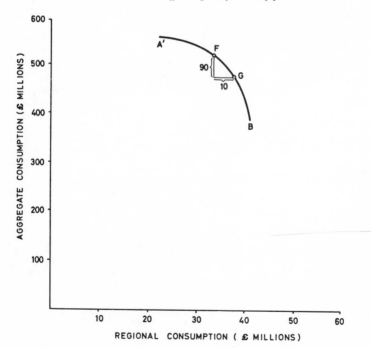

other planning instruments are changed in ways that favour the poorest region at the expense of aggregate consumption. The slope of the feasibility frontier tells the planner how much aggregate consumption must be sacrificed to increase regional consumption £1. Thus, for example, as one moves from F to G in figure 16, one gives up £90 million of aggregate consumption to increase regional consumption by £10 million, or £9 of aggregate consumption per £1 of regional consumption. The slope of the chord connecting F and G approaches the slope of the feasibility frontier as the two parts are brought closer and closer together.

So in the neighbourhood of the optimal plan C, the amount of aggregate consumption that must be sacrificed to increase regional consumption by £1 (the slope of the feasibility frontier) is equal to the amount of aggregate consumption policy makers are prepared to give up to increase regional consumption by £1 (the slope of the equal-welfare curve). Put this way it is perhaps obvious that tangency of the two curves is a condition of optimality and that the slope of one curve can therefore be inferred from the slope of the other at the point corresponding to the optimal point. For if policy makers were prepared to give up more aggregate consumption for £1 of regional consumption than the political and technical constraints underlying A'B obliged them to, C could not be optimal. It would be desirable to change locational, pricing, and other decisions to favour the poorest region. Similarly, if policy makers were prepared to give up less aggregate consumption for an extra £1 of regional consumption than constrained to by the feasibility frontier, it would be desirable to change the plan in the opposite direction.[26]

Thus, to conclude this discussion of the simple, two dimensional model, we may observe that the CPO can calculate its single national parameter from knowledge that C represents the plan that will be implemented coupled with knowledge of the shape of the policy makers' equal-welfare curve at C. Or, lacking explicit knowledge of the policy makers' judgements, the CPO can nevertheless infer the information required to calculate the desired national parameter. To do this it would have to know additionally that C represents an optimal plan, and it must know the shape of the feasibility frontier in the neighbourhood of C.

11.8 FROM THE MODEL TO THE ACTUAL PLANNING ENVIRONMENT: FEASIBILITY AND OPTIMALITY

The possibility that the CPO can, as it were, read the collective mind of policy makers in inferring national parameters from planning decisions is an

---

[26] This discussion presupposes assumptions about the shape of the feasibility frontier and equal-welfare curves that for the most part have been made implicitly rather than explicitly. In addition to the equal-welfare curves being bowed "in" towards the origin, the feasibility curve is assumed to be bowed "out", and all curves are assumed to be smooth. For a more elaborate discussion of the ground covered in sections 11.6, and 11.7, see Stephen A. Marglin, *Public Investment Criteria* (George Allen and Unwin Ltd., London and Massachusetts Institute of Technology, Cambridge, Mass., 1967).

attractive one. It obviously simplifies the job of the CPO if its political role is limited to interpreting policy, to translating the national plan into national parameters. So it becomes essential to examine the extent to which real-world planning corresponds to the idealized scheme of the model. Unfortunately, little of the model survives when translated into real-world conditions.

The most glaring difference between actual situations and the model is the enormous difference in complexity. Even in the simple model we have assumed away significant planning problems in taking the feasibility frontier as a given of the problem. And in actual situations, there is a future as well as a present to be provided for; foreign trade is beset by uncertainties and market imperfections; political constraints inhibit the Government's ability to achieve desirable and technically feasible patterns of development; the representation of technological possibilities is itself a complex task; a multiplicity of goods and services rather than simply "consumption" and "investment" must be reckoned with. When these complications are taken into account, the very delineation of the feasibility frontier, or even a small part of it, becomes a task so formidable that it has eluded planners all over the world. An indication of the difficulties is customarily elaborated in countries that have attempted to use formal planning as an aid to development. Planning commissions are quite satisfied with their efforts if they can produce a single plan that is internally consistent. And if this plan is debated in the Government or in the country at large, the debate revolves primarily around its feasibility rather than its optimality. In terms of our simple model, debate hinges on whether the plan lies inside the feasibility frontier or outside it, not on whether the segment of the feasibility frontier on which it lies is tangent to an equal-welfare curve.

Frequently, the debate hinges on whether planned levels of investment can be attained, that is, on whether the Government will be able to levy sufficient taxes and generate sufficient profits from public-sector enterprises to meet the excess of total investment over private saving. Critics will argue that the plan is too ambitious or not ambitious enough in this respect. In either case the question is more frequently one of what the actual political constraints on taxation and pricing policies are rather than one of whether the balance between consumption and saving is the optimal one among a variety of feasible alternatives. Other questions of feasibility are also raised in such debates: whether foreign trade plans are overly "optimistic" or overly "pessimistic", which is again a question of feasibility rather than of optimality. Or whether technological relationships, for example, in agriculture are "realistic", a question of critical importance, since the availability of agricultural commodities limits the growth of the nonagricultural sector in most developing economies: political constraints put a floor on real wages, and expansion of nonagricultural employment cannot take place without raising the price of agricultural commodities (and therefore increasing the cost of employment in terms of industrial goods) unless domestic agricultural production or imports increase sufficiently. The list of examples could be multiplied. Readers can

undoubtedly find a sufficient number of examples from their own experience to convince themselves that current planning techniques do not produce a set of alternative plans that delineate even in approximation a feasibility frontier. It follows that only the rash would impute optimality to present national plans.

11.9 LIMITATIONS OF MATHEMATICAL PLANNING MODELS

Nor does the state of economic research hold out much hope that the situation will improve much during the 1970s. The mathematical planning models that at an earlier time held out much promise appear now to suffer from defects that will take a long time to remedy. These defects, which can be grouped under six headings, will only be touched on here: (1) All mathematical planning models simplify the objectives of development inordinately. For lack of data on policy makers' judgements as well as for computational simplicity, even the most ambitious do not go beyond a model in which the sole objective is maximization of a discounted present value of aggregate consumption. (2) Again for lack of data, but this time data on consumers' demand functions rather than on policy makers' judgements, no scope for variation in consumption according to relative scarcities is permitted. Instead goods and services are assumed to be necessarily consumed in fixed proportions. (3) Next, the conventional and almost universal approach to technology is to assume that linear input-output systems[27] adequately describe the productive interrelationships of the economy. Again, a combination of ignorance—lack of data—and computational requirements dictate the approach, since it is widely recognized that the assumption of a single linear technique that remains constant over time for each sector of the economy is a drastic oversimplification of the range of choice, a simplification, moreover, that precludes systematic investigation of one of the most important areas of government policy. (4) In addition, computational limitations imposed by even the largest of the present generation of computers force the model-builder to decide between detail in the number of distinct productive sectors he will include or detail in the number of time periods he will cover. Either way, the model suffers as a representation of reality. (5) Moving on to foreign trade, it appears fair to say that no planning model has tried to come to grips with the choices available to the economy in export policies. Again, data are woefully lacking, for industrial exports depend heavily on quality, marketing capabilities and relationships that are difficult to quantify, and raw material exports depend on world conditions that are highly uncertain. The usual convention is to assume that the future will resemble the past. Imports are more tractable, but unless the economy is highly disaggregated (which, as we have just noted, precludes systematic optimization with respect to present and future), it is nearly impossible to represent coherently the policy choices available with respect to import substitution. (6) Finally, and perhaps most importantly,

---

[27] For an introduction to which see William H. Miernyk, *The Elements of Input-Output Analysis*, Random House, New York, 1965.

ignorance of political realities—both lack of data and lack of attention—have led generally to omission of constraints on saving and foreign exchange availabilities imposed by the Government's difficulties in controlling demand for consumer goods. At best these constraints are reflected in a most haphazard fashion that precludes any systematic integration of fiscal and monetary policies as well as technological choice into the model. But such integration is a necessary condition of a planning model that is supposed to generate a feasibility frontier. Nor can it be assumed, as would be necessary to justify the complete omission of distributional considerations in the treatment of development goals, that no political constraints tie the distribution of income to the production decisions that planning models focus on.

11.10 CONSISTENT FORECASTING: A POSITIVE ROLE FOR PLANNING

This description of the shortcomings of the current generation of mathematical planning models is necessarily brief and incomplete, but it is adequate to indicate the gap that exists between the present possibilities of planning and the requirements a plan must fulfil to base national parameters on the assumption that such a plan is optimal. Indeed, it is clear that at present planning serves a much more limited function than it would have to serve in order to be used as the sole basis for determining national parameters. The Soviet Five-Year Plans, the Indian plans, the French "indicative" plans differ according to the political and institutional structures of these countries. But they share the common feature that they serve primarily as an over-all check on the consistency of the development of various aspects of the economy, and secondarily as a basis for estimating the size and composition of the Government's capital budget and the requirements for taxation and borrowing implied by the over-all investment effort. Neither of these tasks is unimportant. It is obviously desirable, for example, that industrial development not be hampered by a lack of electric generating capacity resulting from a failure to anticipate industrial demands. Planning thus serves to reduce the uncertainties in demand that the authorities responsible for individual sectors face.[28] The details of planning methods designed to achieve consistency are outside the scope of the present Guidelines. Material balances[29] or more refined techniques of input-output analysis are commonly used and appear to be satisfactory at least at the level of a first approximation.

The secondary role of providing a basis for the Government's capital budget follows from the primary role of ensuring consistency. The plan serves as a means for assigning over-all magnitudes within which project formulation and evaluation take place. It sets the basic ground rules, so to speak, whereby the group of project formulators and evaluators charged, say, with water

---

[28] Market mechanisms are inadequate because of the long gestation lags in critical sectors like transport and electricity. Simple rules of thumb like extrapolation of the past fail because a developing future will not represent a stagnant past.

[29] See W. Brian Reddaway, *The Development of the Indian Economy* (George Allen and Unwin Ltd., London, 1961) for a description of the use of material balances.

resources development know whether to consider projects whose capital outlay totals £100 million or £1,000 million over the plan period.

Our methodology utilizes the consistent forecasts of the plan in yet another way. Some national parameters reflect characteristics of the pattern of development that have nothing to do with whether that pattern is optimal. The shadow price of investment, for example, depends on capital productivity and the propensity to invest in the economy, as well as on the social rate of discount. The first two—capital productivity and the propensity to invest—are characteristics of the pattern of development that can be inferred from a well-formulated plan. The CPO can utilize these forecasts without assuming that the development pattern is optimal, although to infer a social rate of discount from a national plan, both the optimality of the plan and knowledge of the feasibility frontier in the neighbourhood of the optimal plan are crucial.

In short, a national plan that is a consistent forecast of the future defines a strategy of development, within which project formulation and evaluation are tactical elements. If the strategy is achieved, it is evidently feasible. But the conditions and limitations under which the strategy is elaborated preclude one from imputing optimality to it, unless one is rash enough to impute optimality to whatever actions a Government might take on the specious grounds that if the Government did not consider these actions optimal, it would not take them.

Consequently, the methodology recommended in these Guidelines does not rely on optimality assumptions, and it does not attempt to infer value judgements from comparisons of the plan with "nearby" alternatives. In determining national parameters we counsel utilizing a national plan only as a forecast of what will be, not of what ought to be. In the next chapter we shall outline this part of the methodology. In subsequent chapters we shall fill in the details.

11.11 SUMMARY

The methodology for calculating national economic profitability requires project formulators and evaluators to compute social benefits and social costs utilizing parameters which, though formally resembling market prices, are not to be found in any currently published list of prices. These parameters include the relative weights on the relevant objectives of economic development, the social rate of discount, the shadow price of investment, the shadow wage, and the shadow price of foreign exchange. Because these parameters are in general independent of all decisions taken with respect to individual projects, their calculation is assigned to the national level of the planning process rather than to the project level; they are thus called national parameters.

The key problem in computing national parameters is the circularity that arises from the sensitivity of decisions about each project to the magnitude of national parameters and the sensitivity of the appropriate magnitudes of

national parameters to decisions about all the projects. Ideally, this circularity could be resolved by inferring the appropriate magnitudes of national plan with "nearby" alternative plans rejected as inferior. The CPO would have the role of articulating the value judgements implicit in the national plan, of translating implicit judgements into explicit weights on objectives, weights on consumption over time (the social rate of discount), and the shadow prices of investment, labour, and foreign exchange. The CPO would itself make no value judgements.

Alas, this idealized version of the planning process bears little resemblance to planning as it is actually done. The complexities of the economic and institutional environment make it sufficiently difficult to generate even a single feasible plan that optimality is out of the question, as is the possibility of comparing alternative plans. Nor does the state of current research on mathematical planning models hold out much hope for the next decade.

This is not to say that national planning is irrelevant to project formulation and evaluation. A well-formulated plan can at least provide a consistent forecast of future economic development, even if it is impossible to impute optimality to the forecast. A consistent forecast is of obvious value in determining the size and composition by branch of public investment and determining the framework in which project formulators and evaluators in each branch must work.

Moreover, a well-formulated plan indicates magnitudes whose relevance for estimation of national parameters depends only on the accuracy of the forecasts, not upon their optimality. The shadow price of investment, for example, depends in part on capital productivity and the propensity to invest, regardless of whether capital productivity and the propensity to invest are optimal. So these magnitudes can legitimately be inferred from a national plan whose only virtue is consistency, whereas the remaining determinant of the shadow price of investment—the social rate of discount—cannot be.

National planning thus plays a limited but crucial role in project planning. National planning constrains project planning to fall into line with the over-all development strategy by limiting the outlays in each branch of public invest-ment to mutually consistent amounts. But the tactical decisions that remain to be taken once budget constraints are set cannot be fully resolved by referring to the national plan. Thus, the methodology that we outline in the following chapters turns to other sources for the value judgements that underlie national parameters.

Chapter 12

NATIONAL PARAMETERS:
MEANING, SIGNIFICANCE AND DERIVATION

12.1 DERIVING NATIONAL PARAMETERS FROM EQUAL-WELFARE CURVES: LIMITS TO "TOP-DOWN" PLANNING

The last chapter established that development according to a national plan does not imply optimal development even according to the Government's own lights. However, it does not follow logically from this observation that national parameters cannot be derived from the plan. Recall the simple, two-goal model of the last chapter, which represents a world in which the only considerations are aggregate consumption and regional consumption. One of the ways of deriving the weight on regional-consumption benefits in that model requires the CPO to know only (1) the point C in figure 17 representing the plan that will be followed and (2) the equal-welfare curve through C. If the CPO can elicit directly or indirectly from policy makers their judgements with respect to the relative desirability of increments to the amounts of aggregate consumption and regional consumption represented by C, this organization can quantify these judgements in the form of a weight on regional-consumption benefits, and project formulation and evaluation can proceed accordingly. For the equal-welfare curves in the neighbourhood of C to be relevant, it is necessary to know that the consumption pattern represented by C will be achieved, not that it is optimal to do so.

The rub is that it is far easier to set forth the logic of equal-welfare curves than to set forth a constructive procedure for actually eliciting the relevant value judgements in a way that makes them meaningful for project formulation and evaluation. The key question is whose judgements, whose equal-welfare curves are to count. Unfortunately, yours and mine hardly matter. The relative emphasis to be placed on the consumption of the country as a whole and the consumption of its poorest region is a political question that ought to be resolved by those who are politically responsible and politically accountable for their stewardship of the national interest. It is not the function of administrators and technicians, who supposedly only carry out the will of their political masters and thereby the will of the people.

135

Figure 17   Equal-welfare curve through point C

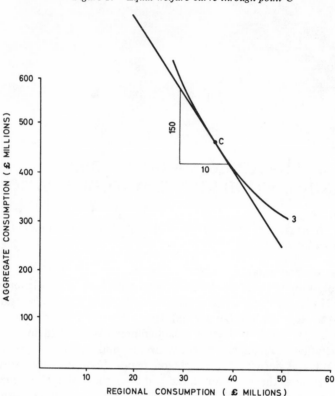

We do not intend here to create the impression that we are so naive as to think that policy makers and civil servants are absolutely distinct groups or will ever be except in extreme idealizations of Government. Civil servants do and must participate in policy formulation: as they prepare and articulate alternatives for their political masters, they necessarily eliminate alternatives, which is to constrain the options available to the political leadership; as they implement their masters' directions, they fill in the gaps in these directions, which in general involves them in policy questions. But making policy and administering policy, though necessarily overlapping, are not identical functions. If the defects of commercial profitability as a measure of project merit are sufficiently important to require its replacement by a substantively different measure of project merit, namely, national profitability, the political leadership should be represented in determining the relative emphasis on different objectives, the relative emphasis on present and future, and other parameters that shape project formulation and evaluation. For civil servants to arrogate these decisions to themselves and treat them as parameters akin to technical standards such as those that determine the safety of a bridge is to deprive the political leadership of its only opportunity to give content to the word "national" in the name of national economic profitability.

On the other hand, the political process appears to discourage rather than encourage the systematic and explicit expression of value judgements by the political leadership that a "top-down" model requires.

The problem is manifold. In the first place, the political leadership serves many functions, the chief of which are to hold the national fabric together and assure its own place in that fabric. Far down the list come the tactical questions with which benefit-cost analysis is concerned.

Second, the qualifications of political leadership are many and varied, but for better or worse a grasp of the tools of economics has never been high on the list. Yet without an understanding of the over-all methodology of benefit-cost analysis elaborated in these Guidelines, it is difficult to imagine that the value judgements necessary for calculation of national parameters could be elicited from the political leadership in the form of equal-welfare curves. For the questioning designed to elicit these curves would be so unfamiliar and appear so "academic" that the exercise would come to nought. And the time of policy makers is all too limited to allow the instruction that would enable them to respond meaningfully to questions about the relative marginal desirability of various national goals. If the world were as simple as the two-objective model utilized in this discussion, the problem might be overcome quickly. But with several objectives and time periods to be considered simultaneously, the problem of eliciting value judgements multiplies rapidly in its complexity. It is unlikely that the thread of the argumentation evolved in eliciting these judgements will be followed by policy makers lacking an appreciation of the whole.

The third and most important reason why the political process discourages rather than encourages explicit quantification of political value judgements with respect to the goals underlying calculations of national economic profitability is that political leaders rely on the support of distinct interest groups that are partially (at least) in conflict with one another. In such circumstances ambiguity has obvious advantages. One can hope to appear all things to all men. The corollary is an understandable if deplorable reluctance to take explicit positions that indicate the precise extent to which the political leader values one objective (with its particular lobby) over another objective (with its particular lobby). Of course, if the balance of interest groups is sufficiently lopsided and a decision serves sufficiently important goals—political, economic, social or emotional—this reluctance can be overcome. Indeed, most readers will be able to think of examples in which the political leadership of their country has come down firmly on one side or the other of controversial questions of concrete policy. But it seems unlikely that the balance of interest groups with respect to the decisions called for on the part of the policy makers in deriving national parameters will appear to policy makers sufficiently lopsided or the decisions themselves sufficiently important to encourage forthright decisions that are bound to offend some groups. A decision to place a premium of £5 per £1 of consumption generated in region X is but a promise of unspecified value to that region, a promise, moreover, that can only add fuel to the fires of political opponents in regions Y and Z.

There is one more point to consider. Civil servants are not without their share of culpability. All too often they discourage the political leadership from intervening in what they wrongfully consider to be their own exclusive sphere of competence. They obfuscate the necessarily political nature of the standards that govern benefit-cost analysis, so much so that any intervention by politically responsible officials into project choice is damned by the mere label "political".[30]

12.2 THE NEED FOR A TRANSITIONAL "BOTTOM-UP" PROCEDURE

All this may be unduly pessimistic if read as a prediction of the future as well as a description of the actual state of affairs in most countries, developed as well as developing. Certainly the political process need not be rigid and can adapt itself to the requirements of project formulation and evaluation once it is recognized that choices with respect to projects may affect the several goals of public policy. Policy makers may attach increasingly more importance to their role in setting the standards that govern calculations of national economic profitability and may devote more time to acquiring the analytic skills necessary to articulate their value judgements in a fashion sufficiently precise and quantitative to be useful in project formulation and evaluation. Likewise, policy makers may become more courageous in taking explicit decisions as they come to understand the desirability of influencing project choices systematically in the articulation of national parameters rather than in the necessarily *ad hoc* fashion to which passivity at the critical stage of setting national parameters consigns them.

However, it is clear that it may take a long time to work the necessary changes in the political process. It is equally clear that change will not come spontaneously. The present need is for a methodology that is not top-down, one that does not require explicit intervention by the political leadership in the setting of national parameters. The methodology ought, however, to draw the political leadership into the decision process in a way that focuses attention on its critical role and prepares the transition to a methodology in which responsible policy makers have the leading role of setting national parameters in advance of project formulation and evaluation. The "bottom-up" procedure outlined in the following paragraphs reflects these considerations.

---

[30] This is not meant to justify the notorious attempts by irresponsible politicians to influence project decisions on an *ad hoc* basis to obtain votes or money. Indeed, one of the advantages of having the political leadership articulate its judgements in the form of national parameters is that the articulation takes place in advance of taking decisions on specific projects. In this way the separation of judgements with respect to personal interest is facilitated. For before specific projects are at issue, the implications that different numerical values of national parameters may have for particular projects cannot be known, and the articulation of value judgements is more likely to be in terms of the policy makers' conception of the national interest than in terms of their personal interest. Special pleading later on would then show up more clearly as an attempt to gain exception to general national policy. (Compare Stephen A. Marglin, *Public Investment Criteria*, George Allen and Unwin Ltd., London and Massachusetts Institute of Technology, Cambridge, Mass., 1967.)

12.3 WEIGHTS AND SHADOW PRICES

First, we distinguish two categories of national parameters, "weights" and "shadow prices". We shall reserve the term weights for those national parameters that directly reflect political value judgements. In this category are the weights reflecting judgements about the distribution of income, and weights on "merit wants" and other objectives that the Government may consider sufficiently important to be reflected in national economic profitability calculations. In addition, this category includes the social rate of discount, which reflects the relative weight on aggregate consumption at different times and is (for reasons alluded to in chapter 3 and discussed more fully in chapter 13) properly a subject of political choice. As chapter 3 pointed out, if we consider aggregate consumption at each time a separate and distinct goal, the present-value method of consolidating consumption at different times is equivalent to computing a weighted sum of consumption year by year, with the rate of discount equal to the rate at which the weight on consumption falls over time.

Shadow prices, of which the principal ones considered here are the prices of investment, labour, and foreign exchange require no new value judgements beyond those that are introduced in the definition of weights and those that implicitly underlie the national plan, "national plan" being understood here as a set of consistent projection of consumption and its distribution, savings, merit wants, and other aspects of the pattern of economic development. The pattern of development, as we shall see, affects shadow prices in two ways. First, indirectly: shadow prices of investment and labour depend on weights and the pattern of development influences the weights. (Weights reflect the marginal importance of various objectives, and the marginal importance depends on the degree of fulfilment of objectives at the point from which marginal departures are measured.) Second, all shadow prices depend directly on the projections embodied in the national plan. Exactly how shadow prices depend on weights and on the plan is the subject matter of subsequent chapters of this part of these Guidelines.

12.4 TREATING WEIGHTS AS UNKNOWN: A SIMPLE MODEL OF "BOTTOM-UP" PLANNING

Consider now the first category of national parameters, the weights. The basic idea of our methodology is for project formulators and evaluators to treat the weights as *unknowns* of the planning problem. Values of weights that make significant differences in the design and operation of projects will be identified, and a set of project variants will be elaborated that are optimal in different ranges of parameter values. The set of variants will then be submitted in its entirety to the responsible policy maker. In this scheme, the CPO has as its principal responsibility the staff function of articulating to the political leadership the implications for the values of national parameters of choosing one variant over the others. In effect, the CPO must say to the political leadership: "If you choose variant X you imply that national para-

meters lie in such and such a range. For choice of variant X is consistent with no other values of the national parameters."

This procedure serves four functions at once: (1) It ensures that all relevant alternatives are brought to the attention of the political leadership. (2) It focuses choice on the relevant variables by relating political decisions to national parameters. (3) It thereby serves to introduce the political leadership to the importance of national parameters. (4) Finally, it forms the basis for deliberate, systematic determination of national parameters when the day finally dawns that these can be specified in advance of project formulation and evaluation.

To fix ideas, let us look first at how this procedure would work in a simple, timeless model. Suppose we are charged with formulating an irrigation project. Imagine that techno-economic studies indicate that the project can provide water for large-scale commercial agriculture or for small-scale peasant farming. If devoted to large-scale commercial agriculture, the available annual water supply of 1 million acre-feet could provide an annual increment of £9 million of aggregate consumption by irrigating 250,000 acres intensively to produce high-valued crops such as citrus fruits, grapes, and vegetables. If devoted to small-scale peasant farming, however, the aggregate consumption produced would be much less. The small peasant farmers of the region are not, let us suppose, completely integrated into the market economy. They regard their own subsistence food needs as a first claim on the land even if they could earn more by producing for the market and buying their own food on the market in the manner of a Kansas wheat farmer or a California citrus grower. Besides, the technologies for growing high-valued crops are complex, and it will be a long time before peasants gain the confidence and sophistication to grow citrus fruits, grapes, and vegetables. To shorten the time appreciably would require agricultural extension services far beyond the country's resources. Suppose, for definiteness, that in primarily subsistence agriculture, the 1 million acre-feet available would cover 500,000 acres (a rate of 2 acre-feet per acre). Let the aggregate consumption attributable to the water be £5 million if applied in this fashion.

To complete the story, let the aggregate consumption costs of constructing and operating the project be £4 million, and assume these costs are borne by the government budget rather than by beneficiaries. Suppose also that the aggregate-consumption benefits of the commercial farming variant (variant A) would be distributed among 250 wealthy landlords, and that the consumption of 40,000 peasants would increase by £2 million, as a result of the employment opportunities created by irrigation. The £5 million of the subsistence farming variant (variant B), on the other hand, would be shared equally by 100,000 peasant families, each family owning 5 acres. Suppose finally that the political leadership has indicated that it is in the national interest to increase the consumption levels of poor peasants even at the expense of aggregate consumption, but for reasons presented at the beginning of this chapter has declined to articulate this judgement more precisely.

Then what is the project formulator supposed to do? He can, of course, reflect his own understanding of the national interest in the formulation of irrigation policy. He may thus be guided to variant B out of sympathy for the small peasant. Or he may judge that distributional objectives may safely be left to the fiscal system, that high charges for the water or high taxes on agricultural incomes can transfer the benefits from the original beneficiaries of variant A, the landlords, to the national treasury, whence they can be passed on to whomsoever the Government judges to be in greatest need. Whatever decision the project formulator and evaluator reach, the political leadership can in principle modify. But intervention at this point to modify a decision taken on "technical" grounds is always suspect, and often with good reason.

12.5 FORMULATING ALTERNATIVE PROJECTS SUITABLE FOR DIFFERENT MAGNITUDES OF THE REDISTRIBUTIONAL WEIGHT

Following our procedure, therefore, the formulator and evaluator prepare alternative projects and attempt to focus the political choice on questions of national interest by confronting the policy maker with the implications of whatever choice he makes for the relative valuation of aggregate consumption and poor peasants' consumption. The table below summarizes the verbal description of the benefits and costs of the two variants.

	Net aggregate consumption (benefits minus costs) (£ Millions)	Peasants' consumption
Variant A	5	2
Variant B	1	5

If we assume that a policy allocating some water for commercial farming and the remainder to peasants is feasible, the range of alternatives is most easily displayed in a graph as in figure 18. This graph is drawn on the assumption that the results of mixed distribution variants are simply weighted averages of the results of the two extreme variants, the weights being the proportions of water allocated to the two types of farming. The points A and B correspond to variants A and B, respectively, and point C corresponds to allocating half the water to commercial farming and half to subsistence farming.

The line AB is a feasibility frontier in some ways analogous to the feasibility frontier encountered in the model of national planning. The important difference between the two is that the present feasibility frontier applies to a single project rather than to the aggregate of all projects. (In fact, one can conceptualize the earlier feasibility frontier as being derived from a set of project frontiers like the present one).

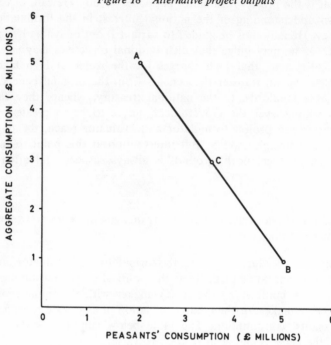

Figure 18   Alternative project outputs

Now if the premium to be placed on peasants' consumption relative to aggregate consumption were known to project formulators and evaluators, planning at the project level would be easily completed with the information we have available. If we denote the aggregate and peasants' consumption by B_1 and B_2, respectively, and the weight on peasants' consumption by w, then the planning goal would be to maximize

$$B_1 + wB_2 \qquad (12.1)$$

subject to the constraint imposed by the basic data, namely,

$$B_1 = 5a + 1(1 - a) \qquad (12.2)$$

$$B_2 = 2a + 5(1 - a) \qquad (12.3)$$

$$0 \le a \le 1 \qquad (12.4)$$

The fraction a represents the allocation of water to commercial agriculture, A, and the fraction $(1 - a)$ represents the fraction allocated to subsistence agriculture, B.

12.6 CALCULATING THE "SWITCHING VALUE" OF THE WEIGHT

Figure 19 shows graphically the solution to this simple problem of choice for a particular value of w, namely, $w = 2$. Superimposed on the feasibility

frontier are equal-NEP lines (NEP for national economic profitability), each of which represents a particular value of the sum

$$B_1 + 2B_2$$

For example, all the points along the equal-NEP line labelled 10 have the equation

$$B_1 + 2B_2 = 10$$

Equal-NEP lines to the "northeast" of this line indicate higher levels of national economic profitability, lines to the "southwest", lower levels. The optimal variant is clearly the one for which national economic profitability is highest, which in this case is variant B, the subsistence-farming variant.

Figure 19   Feasibility frontier and equal national economic profitability (NEP) diagram

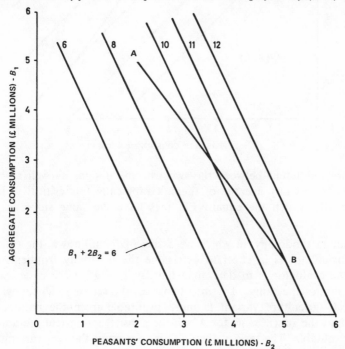

PEASANTS' CONSUMPTION (£ MILLIONS) - B_2

Now, reducing the level of w is tantamount to flattening out the equal-NEP lines, for it should be clear that the steepness of these lines varies directly with w. (That is, the higher the level of w, the greater must be the increase in aggregate consumption to hold national economic profitability at a constant level while reducing peasants' consumption by £1.) Once the equal-NEP lines become flatter than the feasibility frontier—as in figure 20, with, for definiteness, $w = 1$—the commercial-farming variant, A, becomes the optimal choice.

This indicates that there is a critical value of w for which the two alternatives give the same national economic profitability. For this level of w, policy

Figure 20   Feasibility frontier and equal national economic profitability (NEP) diagram

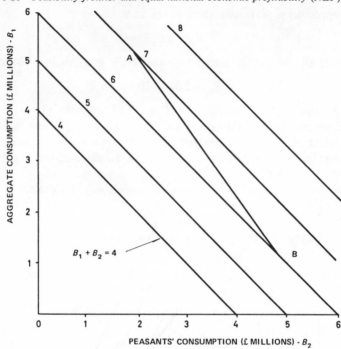

makers are indifferent between the two extreme designs as well as between the extremes and any average of them. Graphically this critical value of w is the one for which the equal-NEP lines have the same slope as AB, as indicated in figure 21.

   In our methodology, in which we assume w is unknown, the task of the project formulator is in effect to determine the feasibility frontier AB. The task of the evaluator is to determine the "switching" value of w, call it $\overline{w}$, which separates the range of w into two sets, the set $(w < \overline{w})$ for which the commercial-agriculture variant is more profitable from the national point of view, and the set $(w > \overline{w})$ for which the subsistence-agriculture alternative is more profitable. The task of the CPO is to present the two variants of the project to the political leadership together with a statement outlining the implications with respect to the two objectives of one choice or the other. That is, the CPO says to the appropriate policy maker: "If you choose variant A, you imply the premium the Government places on peasants' consumption is less than $\overline{w}$. If you endorse variant B, you imply the premium exceeds $\overline{w}$." To facilitate choice, the CPO would also present to the policy maker a summary of the implications of previous decisions on projects that forced choice between poor peasants (or similarly placed groups) and aggregate consumption. Eventually, a consistent pattern of weighting would, it is hoped, emerge from a large number of choices. That is, policy makers would indicate by their choices that they always choose the variant biased towards aggregate

Figure 21   *Switching value of regional-distribution weight*

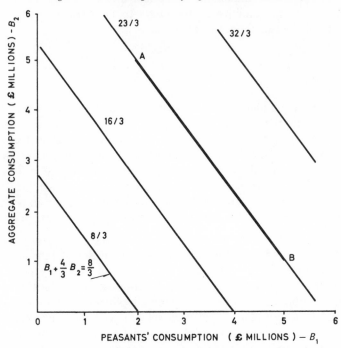

consumption whenever $\bar{w}$ is less than 0.75 and the variant biased towards poor peasants when $\bar{w}$ exceeds 0.75. This would make it possible to specify the weight as 0.75 in advance of project formulation and evaluation.

Of course, project evaluators need not derive $\bar{w}$ graphically. Look again at equations (21.1), (12.2) and (12.3). By substituting from (12.2) and (12.3) into (12.1), we can express national economic profitability as

$$B_1 + wB_2 = 5a + 1\,(1 - a) + w\,[2a + 5\,(1 - a)] \qquad (12.5)$$

When like terms are collected together, the above equation reduces to

$$B_1 + wB_2 = 4a + 1 + w\,(-3a + 5) \qquad (12.6)$$

or to

$$B_1 + wB_2 = (4 - 3w)\,a + 1 + 5w \qquad (12.7)$$

The choice variable of the problem is a, the fraction of water allocated to commercial agriculture. It is clear from (12.7) that national economic profitability is maximized when $a = 0$ for $w > 4/3$. In other words, with the redistributional weight in excess of 4/3, the subsistence-farming alternative is superior. By the same token, (12.7) is maximized when $a = 1$ for $w < 4/3$.[31] Thus $w = 4/3$ is the "switching value" of the present problem; algebraically

---

[31] Note that a is limited to the interval (0, 1) by the logic of the problem. This constraint is reflected in (12.4).

it is the value of w that makes the coefficient of a $(4 - 3w)$ vanish, so that national economic profitability is insensitive to how the available water is divided between the two modes of agriculture.

12.7 EXTENDING THE MODEL TO MORE DIMENSIONS: THE NEED FOR SIMPLIFYING ASSUMPTIONS

The virtue of the algebraic technique over the graphical is that the first is generalizable to the case in which many national parameters are to be estimated. In the general case the coefficient of choice variables like a in the example above will be complicated expressions involving more than one national parameter. But the principle is the same: switching values of national parameters defined by zero values of these coefficients divide the range of national parameters into subranges that indicate the relative importance of various objectives implied by the choice of one project variant over others.

In principle, the number of national parameters can be very large. The weights on income-redistribution objectives and the social rate of discount, as well as the weights on particular merit wants all may vary over time so that the number of national parameters is proportional to the time horizon. In practice, we should expect to see many simplifying assumptions made in order to make the use of national parameters operational. For example, we should probably acquiesce in treating the social rate of discount as constant over time, which implies that the weight on aggregate consumption decreases at a constant rate over time.

Similarly, we should probably agree to express changes in the weight on redistribution objectives relative to aggregate consumption in some equally simple manner. For instance, we might designate a time horizon T over which the relative weight on the consumption of the group or region in question would be constant, with the redistributional weight taken as zero after time T. The determination of a particular value of T would reflect a judgement with respect to the length of time the need for redistribution to the group or region in question is expected to last. In other words, a value of T equal to 20 years would indicate the expectation that after 20 years the consumption level of the group or region will have risen to the point that further redistribution is of insufficient concern to be reflected in calculations of national economic profitability.

Thus, the observation that the relative importance of objectives may change over time is reflected very pragmatically in national economic profitability calculations. In place of a very general formulation allowing for varying weights and rates of discount, the recommended formulation assumes constancy of these parameters, with a sharp discontinuity at the times at which various objectives are expected to be sufficiently well fulfilled that they need not be given prominence. For example, suppose the service life of an irrigation project is 50 years and let the relevant objectives be aggregate consumption and redistribution. Suppose further that the horizon for the redistribution

objective is 20 years. Thus, denoting year t's net aggregate-consumption benefits (benefits minus costs) by B_{1t} and redistributional benefits by B_{2t}, the redistributional weight by w_t and the social rate of discount by i, the project's national economic profitability is represented by

$$\sum_{t=1}^{50} \frac{B_{1t} + w_t B_{2t}}{(1 + i)^t} \qquad \begin{aligned} w_t &= w & t &= 1, \ldots, 20 \\ w_t &= 0 & t &= 21, \ldots, 50 \end{aligned} \qquad (12.8)$$

Equivalently, we could write national economic profitability as

$$\sum_{t=1}^{50} \frac{B_{1t}}{(1 + i)^t} + w \sum_{i=1}^{20} \frac{B_{2t}}{(1 + i)^t} \qquad (12.9)$$

The second formulation expresses national economic profitability as a weighted sum of present values of aggregate-consumption and redistributional benefits, both present values being computed at the social rate of discount. By contrast, the first formulation converts each year's redistributional benefits to their equivalent social value in terms of aggregate consumption before discounting the annual benefits. The two procedures are obviously equivalent, and we take note of the two alternatives only to emphasize that pragmatic necessity has the effect of implying a common rate of discount for all types of benefits, at least over the common part of the time horizon: that is, the same i figures in both terms of expression (12.9). This point will be examined at greater length in the next chapter, which explores the social rate of discount more systematically.

Policy makers can be expected to have the same problems in articulating precise time periods over which various objectives may be of concern as we have suggested they will have in defining the precise numerical magnitudes for the weights on these objectives in any one year. Thus, the horizon for each objective must in our methodology be considered a possible unknown of the problem, like the weights themselves and the social rate of discount.

An extension of our earlier example will illustrate the complexities introduced by bringing time into the picture. Suppose the benefit and cost data from that example are applicable in each of an assumed 50 years of project service life.[32] Then the project's national economic profitability is derived by inserting the data of formula (12.6) into (12.8) or (12.9), with the 20-year horizon replaced by the unknown horizon, T. In the second form we have

$$\sum_{t=1}^{50} \frac{4a + 1}{(1 + i)^t} + w \sum_{t=1}^{T} \frac{-3a + 5}{(1 + i)^t} \qquad (12.10)$$

Making use of the constancy of benefits over time, we can simplify (12.10) using the identity $\sum_{t=1}^{N} \frac{f(x)}{(1 + i)^t} \equiv f(x) \frac{1 - (1 + i)^t}{i}$ so that it becomes

---

[32] To keep matters simple, we shall ignore the "scrap" value of the project 50 years hence.

$$\left[4\frac{1-(1+i)^{-50}}{i}-3w\frac{1-(1+i)^{-T}}{i}\right]a+\frac{1-(1+i)^{-50}}{i}+$$

$$+5w\frac{1-(1+i)^{-T}}{i} \qquad (12.11)$$

All values of the parameters i, w, and T for which the coefficient of a,

$$\left[4\frac{1-(1+i)^{-50}}{i}-3w\frac{1-(1+i)^{-T}}{i}\right] \qquad (12.12)$$

becomes equal to zero are switching values. A few of these are given below, the table entry showing the value of w, which taken together with the indicated values of i and T makes expression (12.12) equal to zero.

		T	
		20	40
i	0.05	1.95	1.42
	0.10	1.60	1.36

The table emphasizes the relative unimportance of the social rate of discount and the redistribution time horizon in choosing between the alternative variants of the project, at least over the range of the two variables represented in the table. Relatively large changes in each of these parameters imply a much less dramatic change in the redistributional weight.

This points up a corollary of our methodology: not every national parameter will be important to every national project. A virtue of our procedure is that it focuses attention on the particular parameters important to each project, and allows policy makers to pay correspondingly less attention to the unimportant.

12.8 THE CPO'S ROLE IN DETERMINING RELEVANT OBJECTIVES

We have thus far been intentionally vague about the list of objectives to be considered in project formulation and evaluation. This is because the objectives will rightly vary from country to country and within each country from one situation to another. The importance of redistribution objectives and the form these take must depend on the specifics of the project and its environment. An irrigation project will offer different scope for redistribution than will a steel mill, and redistribution will be a more important consideration in formulating and evaluating irrigation projects in a country divided into *latifundia* and *minifundia* than in one with an economically homogeneous peasantry. Similarly, the importance of merit wants such as health and education will vary from project to project and place to place. The effects on public health of a dam in tropical Africa may be great, whereas a dam of similar size and scope may have negligible effects on public health in more temperate areas.

Our irrigation example affords a good example of a merit want—the desire to promote peasant proprietorship—that can be expected to vary in importance from country to country. In our analysis we made no distinction between incomes generated to poor peasants as employees of large landowners and incomes gained by the same individuals in exploiting their own holdings. But one Government, preparing for a transition to collective agriculture, may consider peasant ownership a "demerit" want and wish to penalize the subsistence variant accordingly. By contrast a second Government, holding private ownership to be a moral or political virtue, may attach a positive premium to the subsistence variant over and above its redistributional advantage. In either case the premium or penalty is to be treated as an unknown of the problem to be discovered by procedures analogous to those presented for analysing the importance of the redistribution objective.

The relevance of objectives to project formulation and evaluation will depend on the possibilities that choosing one alternative over others affords for contributing to different objectives, as well as on the intrinsic importance of the objectives. Though this point may appear an obvious corollary of our methodology, it is lost sight of often enough to bear repeating. If all conceivable courses of action will lead to the same results with respect to the consumption of the poorest tenth of the population, there is no point emphasizing this objective in project formulation and evaluation however great the policy makers' concern for these people.

Thus, besides summarizing the results of the formulation and evaluation of alternative project designs in a fashion that makes choice intelligible to the policy maker, the CPO must guide each group of formulators and evaluators to a mix of objectives appropriate to the project at hand. After some time—many years most likely—the matching of objectives with projects may become quite routine, for it should become clearer and clearer over time which projects can be effectively harnessed to which objectives. But especially as national economic profitability calculations are undertaken for the first time skilled judgement will be required from the CPO to guide project formulation and evaluation along relevant paths.

12.9 QUANTIFYING SHADOW PRICES

A final task of the CPO is to quantify shadow prices, those national parameters that depend only in part (if at all) on the direct value judgements of policy makers embodied in the weights on objectives we have been considering up to now. Here we shall simply summarize the relationships between shadow prices and weights, since the derivation of these shadow prices is important enough to merit individual chapters.

The *shadow price of investment* has been mentioned repeatedly in earlier parts of these Guidelines. It plays a critical role in project analysis when the market prices of consumption goods and capital goods fail to reflect relative social values. If the rate of saving could be fixed independently of other decisions, no problem could arise: the investment rate would be increased

until relative market prices were equal to relative social values. But two types of constraints must be reckoned with. First, it might be technologically impossible to increase the rate of investment because (1) the full capacity of domestic capital-goods industries is being used in the output of "productive" capital—producers' durables and plant; (2) foreign exchange is being fully utilized to purchase productive capital; and (3) exports cannot be increased to provide more foreign exchange. Second, it might be politically impossible within the existing institutional framework to take measures that would increase the rate of saving. Left to themselves, peasants, workers, and capitalists may be willing to save less than the Government judges optimal, and, more importantly, they may be sufficiently powerful to prevent measures (like taxation) that would put more resources at the disposal of the Government for investment. The Government may not even be able to control the allocation of its own budgets. Internal pressures to distribute the profits of public enterprise to workers and management (in the form of bonuses) and external pressure to reduce prices when public enterprise shows a profit must be reckoned with. Moreover, political pressures to use the public budget for collective consumption goods or for purposes that serve the economic, social, or political interests of important groups (military expenditures are a case in point) may be irresistible.

In general, we judge the political constraints on the rate of investment to be more important than the technological ones. In countries with domestic capital-goods industries, the capacity of these industries is rarely devoted completely—or even approximately so—to producers' goods. Consumers' durables and housing account for a substantial portion of their outputs. And in virtually all countries, a substantial percentage of foreign exchange is devoted to the importation of final consumption goods and intermediates used to produce consumption goods, both durables and nondurables. Moreover, in most countries experts could be increased if the Government were able and willing to resist the pressures that scarcities or higher prices resulting from a reduction in domestic supplies would cause. This is not to condemn either domestic production of durables or the importation of consumption goods. Neither is it to condemn the lack of austerity measures to increase exports. It is rather to recognize the political nature of the restrictions on capital formation. Possibly the Soviet Union in the early years of its development and the People's Republic of China would qualify as examples of countries in which constraints on the rate of investment were at least partially technological in nature, but it would be difficult to find other examples. Thus, our derivation of the shadow price of investment will be based on the assumption that political constraints dominate.

In brief, the shadow price of investment is the present value of the additional consumption that a unit of investment would generate. As we shall see in chapter 14, this shadow price depends on the social rate of discount, but also on the productivity of capital over time as well as on the propensity to reinvest the output that accrues from capital. If these propensities differ

among the various groups of income recipients in the economy, there is not one, but many shadow prices of investment. As chapter 6 showed, the shadow price of investment varies according to who carries out the investment to the extent that the ownership of capital influences the distribution of the income from investment.[33]

In chapter 14, we shall limit the number of groups to three and the number of shadow prices of investment to two by assuming that one of the groups—workers and peasants—saves nothing. The other groups will be the Government and private capitalists. The last group is obviously heterogeneous, including small shopkeepers and large corporations, whose propensities to invest may differ widely. Our tripartite division is not meant to be the last work in classification, but a working model responsive to the likely availability of data in most developing countries.

The social rate of discount belongs to the first category of national parameters that our methodology treats as unknowns of project formulation and evaluation. The productivity of capital and propensities to invest, by contrast, are objective parameters of the economy. Current values can be estimated from national-income statistics and detailed studies of households and firms by econometric techniques. But, since shadow prices of investment depend on the future stream of consumption generated by investment, estimates of current productivity and propensities to invest are insufficient without the assumption that the future will resemble the present. Such an assumption would, however, fly in the face of the structural changes that generally accompany successful economic development. Thus, the estimation of future lack of capital productivity and propensities to invest becomes a real problem for the CPO.

Here is where the national plan comes in. The future course of capital productivity and propensities to invest can be inferred from the national plan, if this document and its supporting studies can be considered a serious projection of productivity, consumption, and distribution figures. Precise formulae for shadow prices of investment are presented in chapter 14.

The *shadow wage of labour* employed to construct or operate a project is not—in terms of aggregate consumption—the money wage unless (1) the money wage is equal to the output forgone elsewhere in the economy by hiring workers for the project and either (2) the creation of jobs on the project in question does not reduce the level of investment elsewhere in the economy or (2′) shadow prices of investment are each equal to one, which is to say that investment and consumption are marginally equally valuable.

The prominence attached to the shadow price of investment in these Guidelines is evidence of our belief that assumption (2′) will be the exception

---

[33] Similarly, the shadow price of investment will vary with the productivity of capital. In so far as capital ownership affects productivity, the shadow price of investment will vary according to ownership even if propensities to invest are identical throughout the economy. In general we shall de-emphasize this problem, not for the usual textbook reason that competition equalizes rates of return throughout the economy, but because quantitative estimates of differences are unlikely to be available.

rather than the rule. Thus, the use of money wages as a measure of the aggregate-consumption cost hinges on assumptions (1) and (2). But violations of these assumptions are to be expected in developing economies. Shifting workers from peasant agriculture or traditional services to public projects may decrease output very little in these sectors, and mobilization of unemployed workers will reduce output not at all. Assumption (1) will therefore not be fulfilled in many situations because the wage received by workers in the public sector (or in capitalistic private employment) may be much higher than the output lost in moving workers from agriculture and services. But valuation of labour services is more than a question of output forgone by putting men to work constructing or operating projects. The increase in public-sector employment may change the composition of total output, increasing consumption at the expense of investment. For if workers are able to maintain real wages in the face of expanding employment and can be neither induced nor obliged to increase their savings, investment must be reduced elsewhere in the economy to meet the increased consumption demands of the new workers. So long as the shadow price of investment exceeds one, the change in the composition of output must be reflected in the shadow wage.

Thus, the shadow wage depends on two factors: (1) the output forgone by moving workers from their previous employment to public-sector jobs and (2) the shift in the composition of output from investment to consumption by the expansion of public-sector employment. The importance of the second factor in turn depends on the shadow price of investment, which in turn makes the shadow wage dependent on the social rate of discount.

Both the productivity of workers in employment alternative to the public sector and the shift in the composition of output attendant to public-sector employment can be estimated from a well-formulated plan. Chapter 15 derives a formula for relating the shadow wage to these factors and the shadow price of investment.

The *shadow price of foreign exchange* is by definition the contribution a unit of foreign exchange makes to aggregate consumption. This obviously depends on how marginal increments of foreign exchange are utilized. For the present and the immediate future, the utilization of marginal increments of foreign exchange can be gleaned from an examination of the allocation of current supplies of foreign exchange. Usually, this will be a matter of government policy, for allocation of foreign exchange is one of the activities over which Governments of developing countries typically exercise the greatest control. Over a longer period, government policy with respect to foreign exchange allocation cannot be determined by current actions, but it can be inferred from a well-formulated national plan. Again, our methodology does not assume that the foreign exchange is or will be optimally utilized; at issue is simply the actual utilization, present and future.

There is one important difference between the shadow price of foreign exchange and the shadow prices of investment and labour. As chapter 16

shows, the shadow price of foreign exchange does not depend directly on any of the weights that are regarded as unknowns in the planning process. Of course, the present and future allocation of foreign exchange is sensitive to the same value judgements that underlie the unknown weights. But the indirect influence of these judgements does not make the shadow price of foreign exchange, unlike the shadow price of investment and the shadow wage, an unknown of the problem of formulating and evaluating projects. It is, as chapter 16 shows, a different story when foreign exchange is valued in order to reduce dependence on foreign sources of capital rather than for its effects on aggregate consumption alone.

12.10 SUMMARY

It is tempting but inappropriate to assume that, by virtue of the existence of a national plan, current and future resource allocations are optimal. This does not in itself make it impossible to derive national parameters from the plan, but to implement planning based on parameters set by those at the top of the planning process would require an ability on the part of policy makers to articulate their value judgements in an explicit, quantitative fashion that is unlikely to be found at present. Thus, initially, we propose a "bottom-up" procedure that inverts the flow of information characteristic of "top-down" planning. We propose to treat those national parameters that are simply quantifications of value judgements—weights on objectives and the social rate of discount—as unknowns of the problem of project formulation and evaluation. National parameters whose magnitudes depend also on observable parameters of economic development—shadow prices of investment and labour—are treated as functions of the unknown weights.

The CPO indicates to formulators and evaluators the objectives relevant to the project at hand. The formulators and evaluators indicate to the CPO the sensitivity of project design to the weights on objectives and the social rate of discount, and the CPO presents variants that are optimal in different ranges of parameter values to policy makers for explicit choice. Policy makers then choose one from among a set of alternatives. The CPO must make policy makers aware of the critical role of national parameters by spelling out the implication for parameter magnitudes of choosing one variant over another.

Gradually, as the awareness, interest and understanding of policy makers grow, it may be possible to move from the bottom-up methodology to a top-down methodology in which policy makers weight and determine shadow prices in advance of project formulation and evaluation. The present methodology has the virtue of preparing the way for such a sophisticated methodology while serving in the interim to bring all the relevant objectives of public policy to bear on project formulation and evaluation.

The next task of these Guidelines is to derive formulae for shadow prices of investment, labour and foreign exchange. An introductory chapter explores the nature and significance of the social rate of discount, a parameter on which both the shadow price of investment and the shadow wage depend.

Chapter 13

INTERTEMPORAL CHOICE:
THE SOCIAL RATE OF DISCOUNT

13.1 THE REASON FOR DISCOUNTING FUTURE BENEFITS AND COSTS

Investment, by definition, yields its fruits only with the passage of time, so that project formulation and evaluation inevitably involve intertemporal choice. The choice between hydroelectric and thermal power, for example, involves a choice between initial capital outlays and operating outlays over the life of the project. So does the choice between canal irrigation from artificial, large-scale, surface-storage reservoirs and tube-well irrigation from natural groundwater reservoirs. But why does this pose problems for project formulation and evaluation? Why can't we simply add up the benefits and costs over the life of the project and use this aggregate as the measure of the project's over-all contribution to each objective?

Were we to do this, we should be assuming, explicitly or implicitly, that benefits and costs are of equal value wherever they occur. Thus, focusing for the moment on the single objective of aggregate consumption, and denoting the net aggregate-consumption benefit (the difference between benefits and costs) in year t by B_t, the over-all aggregate-consumption benefit B^* would be

$$B^* = B_0 + B_1 + \ldots + B_T \qquad (13.1)$$

for a project whose economic life is assumed to be T years. Equal weight on benefits and costs at different times is implicit in formula (13.1), for adding £10 of benefit in year T and subtracting £10 in year 0 would leave the value of the sum B^* unchanged.

But so long as *per capita* aggregate consumption is expected to rise over time, most policy makers would judge an extra £1 to be more valuable today than 20 years hence. Suppose an extra £1 today typically provides milk to milkless diets or blankets to ill-clad workers, whereas an extra £1 in 20 years is expected, by virtue of a higher standard of living, to contribute to the fulfilment of more marginal wants—luxury foods, more attractive clothes, transistor radios. Under such circumstances it is not difficult to accept the assumption that the weight on aggregate-consumption benefits should decline

154

over time. If, following the practice of Parts I and II of the Guidelines, we make present consumption the unit of account and thus fix its weight at 1.0, the over-all aggregate-consumption benefit becomes

$$B^* = B_0 + v_1B_1 + \ldots + v_TB_T \tag{13.2}$$

with the weights $v_1, \ldots, v_T$ declining over time to reflect the diminishing marginal utility of consumption.

Formula (13.2) in effect makes aggregate consumption in each year a separate and distinct category of benefits, just as within any year aggregate-consumption benefits are counted separately and distinctly from redistributional benefits. Only the weighted benefits $B_0, v_1B_1, \ldots, v_TB_T$ are directly comparable; an increase of 1 in the weighted benefit v_tB_t exactly compensates a decrease of £1 in B_0, in the sense that the over-all measure B^* is left unchanged. If the weight v_{20} is equal, for example, to 0.5, it would thus take an increase of £2 in B_{20} to cancel out a decrease of £1 in B_0. So a weight of 0.5 on aggregate consumption 20 years hence implies that an extra £1 of outlay today whose return is deferred 20 years must earn £2 to be worth while.

The weights $v_1, \ldots, v_T$ are sometimes called "discount factors", for they indicate the amount by which future benefits (and costs) must be discounted to make them comparable to present benefits (and costs). The sum (13.2) is called the "discounted present value" of aggregate consumption, "present" reminding us that all benefits and costs, once weighted, are expressed in units exactly comparable to present aggregate consumption.

13.2 THE RELATIONSHIP BETWEEN INTERTEMPORAL WEIGHTS AND THE SOCIAL RATE OF DISCOUNT

The question at issue in this chapter is how to determine the weights $v_1, \ldots, v_T$. This, alas, is a most difficult and thorny subject, and our conclusions are anything but optimistic. But before we explore the problem in detail, we shall make one simplifying assumption. To facilitate the specification of weights both conceptually and operationally, we shall henceforth assume that the weights decline over time at a constant percentage rate. That is,

$$\frac{v_t - v_{t+1}}{v_{t+1}} = \text{const.} \tag{13.3}$$

If we denote this constant rate of decrease by i, we may express the ratio of weights in year t and year $t+1$ as

$$\frac{v_t}{v_{t+1}} = 1 + i \quad \text{or} \quad \frac{v_{t+1}}{v_t} = \frac{1}{1+i} \tag{13.4}$$

Now look again at formula (13.2). It can be written

$$B^* = B_0 + v_1B_1 = \frac{v_2}{v_1} v_1B_2 + \ldots + \left(\frac{v_T}{v_{T-1}} \frac{v_{T-1}}{v_{T-2}} \ldots \frac{v_2}{v_1} v_1 \right) B_T \tag{13.5}$$

For most of the numerators and denominators in expressions of the form

$$\frac{v_{t+1}}{v_t} \frac{v_t}{v_{t-1}} \cdots \frac{v_2}{v_1} v_1 \qquad (13.6)$$

cancel, which reduce these expressions to the simpler form

$$v_{t+1}$$

But substituting from (13.4) into (13.6) transforms (13.6) into

$$\left(\frac{1}{1+i}\right)\left(\frac{1}{1+i}\right) \cdots \left(\frac{1}{1+i}\right)$$

once we take into account that v_1 also is equal to v_{t+1}/v_t, by virtue of the assumption that $v_0 = 1$. Substituting into formula (13.5), we have

$$B^* = B_0 + \frac{B_t}{1+i} + \cdots + \frac{B_T}{(1+i)^T} \qquad (13.7)$$

or, in more compact form,

$$B^* = \sum_{t=0}^{T} \frac{B_t}{(1+i)^t} \qquad (13.8)$$

Formula (13.8) should call to mind the present-value formula first introduced in chapter 2 in the context of commercial profitability.[34] This similarity emphasizes that the differences between analysis of the national profitability of a project and analysis of its commercial profitability are differences in the meaning and significance of benefits and costs and the weights by which different benefits and costs are aggregated into common measures. The mathematical techniques of aggregation of benefits and costs over time are the same for both kinds of analysis.

The metamorphosis of formula (13.2) into formula (13.8), however, does not answer the question of how to determine the weights $v_1, \ldots, v_T$. It merely transforms the question. The question now becomes one of determining i, the rate at which the weight on aggregate consumption falls over time. The parameter i is the *social rate of discount*, the rate at which society's weight on increments to consumption declines over time. The assumption that i is constant over time is one that can be defended only on the grounds that such an approximation to a more complicated path of i is a reasonable one in view of our ignorance about the future.

13.3 DETERMINING THE SOCIAL RATE OF DISCOUNT FROM PREFERENCES REVEALED IN THE MARKET PLACE

It is widely held that the market resolves the problem of choosing the social rate of discount just as it resolves the problem of giving relative values

---

[34] See also section 3.2.

to sugar and cloth, at least for small increments of commodities considered within the framework of the aggregate-consumption objectives. Just as the market price of sugar tells us what consumers are willing to pay for the marginal kilogram of sugar, so, according to one view at least, does the market rate of interest tell us what individuals are willing to pay for future consumption. According to conventional consumption theory, the individual who buys sugar in a free market at 2 shillings per kg must be completely indifferent between having the last 2 shillings he spends and having the last kg of sugar he buys. Were it not so, he would buy more sugar or less sugar, another kg if at the margin he prefers a kg of sugar to 2 shillings, less if he prefers 2 shillings to 1 kg of sugar. Thus, the assumption of marginal indifference between goods and money permits us to infer (marginal) willingness to pay from market price, and to value various components of aggregate consumption by their market prices. Analogously—or so the story goes—an individual who borrows £100 at a 10 per cent rate of interest commits himself to giving up £110 next year in order to have £100 this year. If he can be assumed to be marginally indifferent between £1 today and £1.1 next year—else why would he borrow £100 and not £99 or £101?—he can be assumed to value marginal increments to current consumption 10 per cent more than he values future consumption. In other words, he is willing to pay approximately £0.9 today for £1.0 next year. This is tantamount to saying that, taking present consumption as the unit of account and assigning to it a weight of 1.0, the hypothetical borrower in our story places a weight of 1/1.1 on consumption next year. More generally, if $\check{r}$ is the market rate of interest, individual borrowers can be assumed to weight next year's consumption by

$$\frac{1}{1+\check{r}}$$

Since analogous reasoning applies to more distant years, and to lenders as well as borrowers, conventional consumer theory leads us to identify the time weights $v_1, \ldots, v_T$ with market discount factors

$$\frac{1}{1+\check{r}}, \ldots, \frac{1}{(1+\check{r})^T}$$

or in other words, to equate the social rate of discount i to the market rate of interest $\check{r}$.

Of course, imperfections abound in capital markets, in rich countries as well as poor. It is not unusual for savers (lenders) to earn 5 per cent or less while borrowers pay 20 per cent or more. Nor are capital markets free from rationing. Nevertheless, this approach could be applied in modified form. One could take an average of rates at which different classes of individuals borrow or save, weighted by the shares these individuals bear of project benefits and costs. The principle of "consumer sovereignty" would remain: consumption at different times would be weighted in accordance with relative values inferred from individuals' saving (and dis-saving) behaviour; the social

rate of discount would be taken from market rates of interest in the same way that the social value of sugar is taken from its market price.

In fact, the problem with this approach lies much deeper than the multiplicity of market rates of interest. For this approach assumes a rational, calculating basis for individual decisions on saving and borrowing, a basis that remains, after many years of econometric research, a hypothesis supported more by the preconceptions of its authors than by empirical observations. The reasons for these preconceptions are not hard to find. The whole structure of welfare economics, which traces its intellectual ancestry to Adam Smith, requires the assumption of a rational, calculating "economic man" to justify market outcomes. So intertemporal rationality must be assumed to justify the rate of capital accumulation dictated by market forces in a capitalist economy.[35] Economists steeped in the tradition of Adam Smith generally impute rationality and calculation to individual decisions whenever observed data do not contradict their preconceptions, a methodology enjoined by individuals among the most eminent in the profession. The rub is that in translating hypotheses based on rationality into a form suitable for testing by observable data, little is left of the hypothesis of rationality.[36] Actually, observable data no more support the notion of rationality, calculation and planning in individual decisions as saving and borrowing than they do the contrary hypothesis.

The viewpoint taken here is that the customary treatment of intertemporal choice, which permits one to infer a social rate of discount from rates of interest that individuals earn on what they save or pay for what they borrow, is a misplaced application of the theory of consumer choice. The assumption that an individual who pays 2 shillings per kg for sugar and 1 shilling for wheat values a kg of sugar twice as much at the margin as a kg of wheat is based on a model that finds little applicability in conditions of intertemporal choice. In choosing between wheat and sugar, the individual may be assumed to learn from trial and error. He makes the choice repeatedly, and little time elapses between making the choice and realizing its consequences. So it is not unrealistic to assume that the individual learns from experience and adjusts his shopping basket so that the marginal satisfaction he obtains from the two commodities are in rough proportion to their prices. But the possibility for learning from trial and error is severely limited in the intertemporal context. To impute rationality to a decision on savings, it must be assumed that current consumption is planned in the context of a lifetime consumption plan based on lifetime resources. But one does not have the opportunity to try different combinations of consumption at age 20, or at age 30, or at age 40.

---

[35] To be sure, it is this same line of reasoning that in the Guidelines underlies the use of "willingness to pay" as a measure of benefits and costs with respect to the aggregate-consumption objective. So at least some of our criticism of imputing rationality to observed market behaviour applies more widely than to intertemporal decisions.

[36] See, for example, Milton Friedman, *A Theory of the Consumption Function*, Princeton University Press, Princeton, New Jersey, 1957; Albert Ando and Frances Modigliani, "The 'life-cycle' hypothesis of saving", *American Economic Review*, Volume 53, No. 1, March 1963, pp. 55—84.

For time's arrow, as philosophers and poets—if not economists—are keenly aware, flies in one direction. By the time one may have acquired the experience assumed to underlie rational choice in timeless models, one has no longer the possibility of giving effect to this knowledge in a comparable situation of intertemporal choice.

Moreover, the overwhelming uncertainty that surrounds the estimation of lifetime resources for most people introduces another fundamental difference between the timeless model to which the sugar-wheat choice paradigm belongs and the actual environment of intertemporal decision making. Hence, even if individuals could be assumed to have well-defined preferences with respect to consumption at different moments of their lives, it could not be concluded that their decisions reflect marginal valuations of consumption at these different moments. Unlike the hypothetical consumer in the sugar-wheat paradigm, who by virtue of the money in his pocket controls his consumption of sugar and wheat, the typical peasant or worker does not in fact control his lifetime consumption plan, a circumstance that is largely the result of accidents of nature or of accidents of business cycles that the individual rightly sees himself as helpless to modify. But control over results of decisions, at least in a probabilistic sense, is implicit in any model of rational choice, for decisions are assumed to be taken in anticipation of results.

The observed data on savings behaviour in fact suggest that in an industrialized country like the United States most households save little or nothing of the income that is left after meeting collectively determined obligations such as taxes and union dues, and that a relatively few high-income families save moderate percentages of their disposable incomes. These observations are probably better explained by a few fairly obvious facts than by elaborate models of intertemporal rationality. First, the very act of personal saving should be recognized as an assertion of individual control over the future. It is therefore not to be expected that individuals whose every other act has taught them that control rests with others—the gods, the bosses, the Government, the "system"—are to assert an independent personality in this single economic realm. Much more likely is that income will be spent as fast, or almost, as it is earned. (When incomes are rising, some personal saving will take place as a result of lags in adjusting expenditures to income.) The rich who save do so either because their incomes are rising so fast that they have not yet learned how to spend all that they earn, or because, as members of the local elite, they are in fact in greater control of their lives than the typical individual. In the second case saving is much more an assertion of personality, a form of monument building, than a rationally planned deferral of consumption from which can be inferred intertemporal preferences. The accumulation reflected in the Egyptian pyramids and the enterprises of Calvinist capitalists can hardly be explained in terms of intertemporal consumption rationality.

The intertemporal context is an extreme example of the breakdown of the logic of "consumer sovereignty". But it is not an isolated one. Other

areas of choice, such as education, share enough of the characteristics of decisions on savings, such as the impossibility of learning values by trial and error, to make benefits and costs that accrue in these areas candidates for special treatment (under the rubric of merit wants) in a framework that is otherwise individualist in its emphasis on willingness to pay as the measure of benefits and costs.

There is another defect of the attempt to infer social discount rates from individual savings behaviour that should at least be mentioned. This defect is that markets allow individuals no scope to express their preferences for the rate at which society accumulates capital, as distinct from the rates at which they individually accumulate capital. If it is assumed that individuals plan their savings to achieve optimal individual lifetime consumption plans, it must still be admitted that markets allow individuals no way of expressing a preference for greater social accumulation, unless individual altruism is so strong that one is willing unilaterally to increase one's saving.

The defect of markets at issue is one that is widely recognized, namely, their inability to cope with *externalities*, that is, situations in which my well-being depends on your actions. In the present case, my well-being is increased by the knowledge that society will be better off in the future, and I am willing to increase my rate of saving as part of a collective agreement to achieve this end. My extra saving is, as it were, the price I am willing to pay to induce you and others to do likewise. If there are enough people of a similar bent, we may all be willing to save more on condition that others do so, for even if the altruism of each of us is weak relative to more hedonistic desires, we can all see our own sacrifices multiplied many times over by the twin effects of (1) the sacrifices of others and (2) capital productivity. If such "weak" altruism is sufficiently widespread (and there is no way of gleaning from market behaviour or private philanthropic efforts whether it is), then even an otherwise perfect capital market composed of intertemporally rational individuals could not provide a social rate of discount appropriate for public investment decisions.

13.4 THE SOCIAL RATE OF DISCOUNT AS THE MARGINAL PRODUCTIVITY OF CAPITAL

An alternative view of social discounting is that the appropriate rate of discount for public investment is the marginal productivity of capital in the economy. In its simplest form, the argument is that if £1 invested elsewhere in the economy can earn £1.2 next year, no public-sector project that earns less should be judged acceptable with reference to the aggregate-consumption objective. Conversely, no public-sector project should be required to earn more than can be earned at the margin in the rest of the economy. More generally, if the internal rate of return on the marginal project[37] is equal to q elsewhere in the economy—20 per cent in our simple example—then no public projects that earn less than q are justifiable in terms of the aggregate-

---

[37] See chapter 2 for a discussion of the internal rate of return and related concepts.

consumption objective, and all that earn more are justifiable in terms of this objective. Thus, or so it is argued, the social rate of discount i is equal to q.

In fact, this argument is sound only under a most limited set of assumptions. In the form given, the argument applies only to a two-period model in which the total volume of investment is fixed independently of project choice in the public sector. For in this case marginal productivity provides an adequate measure of an alternative project's contribution to future aggregate consumption; moreover, the assumption that the volume of investment is fixed independently of project choice in the public sector guarantees that this opportunity cost is the appropriate measure of cost, in the same way that current alternative cost is the appropriate measure of current benefits when the supply margin is the relevant one.[38]

A more precise formulation of the argument requires recourse to simple algebra. Recall that the over-all measure of aggregate consumption is the weighted sum of positive and negative contributions to aggregate consumption in each period, which in a two-period model is

$$B^* = B_0 + v_1 B_1$$

If aggregate current investment were simply the sum of project outlays decided independently of one another, it would be correct to measure B_0 for each project by its capital costs. That is, if we denote a typical project's capital requirements by K_0, we would write

$$B_0 = - K_0$$

and

$$B^* = - K_0 + v_1 B_1 \qquad (13.9)$$

But the assumption that the aggregate level of investment is determined independently of project decisions means that the relevant cost of any specific project in terms of aggregate consumption is not today's capital cost. Rather, the cost of project X is the consumption forgone next period because a marginal project must be eliminated to make room in the over-all capital budget, whose size is fixed, for project X. On the assumption that the marginal project earns a net return of £q per £1 of capital invested, the gross consumption forgone on the margin is

$$(1 + q) K_0$$

Of course, this consumption is forgone next period, so it is properly weighted by v_1 before being debited against the account of project X. Thus, in place of (13.9), we have the following expression for the aggregate consumption, net of opportunity costs, traceable to project X:

$$B_X^* = - v_1 (1 + q) K_0 + v_1 B_1 = v_1 [B_1 - (1 + q) K_0] \qquad (13.10)$$

Since (13.10) expresses aggregate-consumption benefits net of opportunity costs, we are interested only in the algebraic sign of this expression: project X

---

[38] See Part II, chapter 4.

is acceptable on the basis of the aggregate-consumption objectives if (13.10) is positive, unacceptable if (13.10) is negative. Now the interesting thing about (13.10) is precisely that its sign is completely independent of v_1 as long as v_1 is any positive number! That is, (13.10) has the same sign as

$$\frac{B_X^*}{v_1} = B_1 - (1 + q) K_0 \qquad (13.11)$$

which, for that matter has the same sign as

$$\frac{B_X^*}{v_1 (1 + q)} = \frac{B_1}{1 + q} - K_0 \qquad (13.12)$$

This brings us to the end of the argument, for the right-hand side of (13.12) is nothing but the present value of benefits less capital costs, with benefits discounted at q!

The algebra notwithstanding, it may appear to be a form of sleight of hand that we have succeeded in banishing v_1 from consideration. Somehow it turns out not to matter what weight we put on next period's consumption relative to this period's consumption; we still end up discounting future benefits by $(1 + q)$ so that q is for all intents and purposes the social rate of discount. But the magic, if any, lies in our assumption of a fixed investment budget. For this assumption means that the costs of project X (or any other project) are not borne today; today's sacrifice is independent of project decisions. Rather, the costs of project X are borne next period, so that in fact no intertemporal weighting is necessary. The only question is how much consumption must be given up next period, a question that is answered by the marginal productivity of capital.

Unfortunately, the logic of this analysis breaks down as soon as we drop either of two critical assumptions: first, that the over-all investment budget is fixed independently of project decisions; and, second, that there are only two time periods to take into account. Consider what happens if we relax just the first assumption. Suppose that only a fraction a of the costs of project X are met by diverting resources from other projects. The remainder, $1 - a$, is assumed to be drawn from current consumption, so that the decision whether to go ahead with project X affects the over-all level of current investment as well as its composition. For the fraction aK_0, the story is as before. This portion of costs is properly debited against the project next period, with the appropriate allowance for the additional consumption forgone as a result of the reduction of marginal investment elsewhere in the economy. Thus, this fraction of costs is debited to the account of project X as

$$- v_1 a (1 + q) K_0 \qquad (13.13)$$

The remainder is debited against the project in the current period, for, by assumption, current consumption is reduced by this amount. Hence, in addition to (13.13),

$$- (1 - a) K_0 \qquad (13.14)$$

is debited against the account of project X. If we take account of (13.13) and (13.14) as well as of the benefits of project X, we have the complete picture:

$$B_X^* = - v_1 a (1 + q) K_0 - (1 - a) K_0 + v_1 B_1 \qquad (13.15)$$

or

$$B_X^* = v_1 B_1 - [a v_1 (1 + q) + (1 - a)] K_0 \qquad (13.16)$$

Now there is no way of eliminating v_1 from consideration, unless $a = 1$, which is the case already dealt with, that is, the case when all the capital resources required for a project come out of marginal investment elsewhere in the economy.

Even if $a = 1$, intertemporal weights cannot be eliminated when there are more than two periods. With more than two periods, we must first determine the time pattern of consumption produced by marginal investments in the economy. This will depend not only on the technical characteristics of marginal investment—its gestation period and economic life—but also on the division of its returns between consumption and further investment. We shall examine these problems in more detail in the next chapter, so now let us take the most simple example imaginable in order to analyse the effects of extending the number of time periods beyond two. Suppose that, as before, the marginal investment of £1 today yields £$(1 + q)$ next period and nothing thereafter. Suppose furthermore that this return is immediately consumed so that problems of reinvestment are obviated. Thus, with $a = 1$, the appropriate measure of the over-all contribution of project X to aggregate consumption is

$$B_X^* = - v_1 (1 + q) K_0 + v_1 B_1 + v_2 B_2 + \ldots + v_T B_T \qquad (13.17)$$

Now, taking account of the relative nature of the weights, we could fix v_1 (rather than v_0, which has been eliminated) arbitrarily at 1.0, so that expression (13.17) becomes

$$B_X^* = - (1 + q) K_0 + B_1 + v_2 B_2 + \ldots + v_T B_T \qquad (13.18)$$

But all we have gained by our labours is the elimination of one weight; we still must specify $v_2, \ldots, v_T$ in order to compute a numerical value for (13.18) or even to compute its sign. Thus, since the two-period model is but a formal abstraction whose only virtue is expository simplicity and in reality there are many more than two periods to consider, the simplifying assumption that public investment displaces marginal private investment ($a = 1$), even if true in approximation, is of little help in determining a social rate of discount.

In the general case, the assumptions required to justify the use of the marginal productivity of capital as the social rate of discount are even more stringent than what is required in the two-period model. Nothing short of the assumption of optimal growth will do. That is, we must assume that the path the economy will follow over time is the best of all feasible paths. To be sure, we may assume that feasibility and optimality are defined with respect to political and institutional constraints on the Government's control over the economy as well as with respect to technological constraints.

Under conditions of optimal growth, the marginal productivity of capital, properly valued, is the social rate of discount, because the logic of optimization dictates that investment be carried to the point where the net (social) return on capital is just sufficient to compensate for the lower value placed on marginal future consumption relative to marginal present consumption, which is to say the point at which the marginal productivity of capital equals the social rate of discount. But the marginal productivity of capital in question is a social marginal productivity that reflects politically and institutionally created scarcities as well as physical scarcities. Thus, for example, suppose political and institutional constraints lead to investment's having a marginal social value (or shadow price) twice that of consumption and that returns from marginal private investment are divided between consumption and reinvestment in the ratio 3:1. Then if marginal investment of £1 this period has a nominal return of £1.2 next period (and nothing thereafter), its social marginal productivity in terms of aggregate consumption is not 20 per cent, but

$$\frac{(0.75 \times 1) + (0.25 \times 2)}{2} \times 0.2 \qquad (13.19)$$

or

$$\frac{1.25}{2} \times 0.2$$

in other words, 12.5 per cent. The logic behind (13.19) is simple. The rate of return on any asset is the ratio of the return to the price of the asset. In this case the nominal net return of 0.2 is assumed to be divided between consumption (75 %) and reinvestment (25 %). The first is valued at the nominal price of 1.0 (since aggregate consumption is the unit of account), the second at the shadow price of 2.0, so the social value per unit of return is 1.25. Thus, the social value of 0.2 units of output is 0.25, but the price of the capital is 2.0, and the ratio of 0.25 to 2.0 is 0.125.

But the fact remains that even with the qualification that the marginal productivity of capital must be its social marginal productivity, the requirement of optimal growth on which the argument rests is not a reasonable assumption. For reasons outlined in chapter 11, only a Candide would impute optimality to the future path of economic development projected for any economy, planned or unplanned. And without this assumption, the social rate of discount cannot be presumed to equal the social marginal productivity once we abandon the simplifying assumptions of a two-period model in which $a = 1$.

13.5 THE SOCIAL RATE OF DISCOUNT AS A VALUE JUDGEMENT

There is thus no escape from the need for the Government to judge the relative weight to be accorded aggregate-consumption benefits and costs at different times. We have indicated that the major reason for placing a lower weight on future benefits and costs is the union of two facts, or, more accurately, two assumptions: first, that *per capita* consumption will rise over time and,

second, that the marginal social significance (or "marginal utility" for short) of consumption diminishes with each rise in consumption. The nature of the value judgement inherent in the social rate of discount may be clarified by examining how the rate of growth of consumption and its marginal utility combine to determine the social rate of discount. Recall formula (13.3)

$$\frac{v_t - v_{t+1}}{v_{t+1}} = \text{const.} = i$$

which expresses the social rate of discount as the rate at which the weight on aggregate consumption falls over time. If we adopt the more compact notation

$$\Delta v_{t+1} = v_{t+1} - v_t \tag{13.20}$$

formula (13.3) becomes

$$i = -\frac{\Delta v_{t+1}}{v_{t+1}} \tag{13.21}$$

Formula (13.21) is equivalent in turn to

$$i = -\left(\frac{\Delta v_{t+1}}{\Delta C_{t+1}} \frac{C_{t+1}}{v_{t+1}}\right)\left(\frac{\Delta C_{t+1}}{C_{t+1}}\right) \tag{13.22}$$

since the new elements C_{t+1} and ΔC_{t+1} $(= C_{t+1} - C_t)$ appear symmetrically in the numerator and the denominator. These new elements represent *per capita* consumption (C_{t+1}) and the (absolute) change in *per capita* consumption (ΔC_{t+1}). Now consider the expressions within parentheses one at a time. The first is equivalent to

$$\frac{\Delta v_{t+1}/v_{t+1}}{\Delta C_{t+1}/C_{t+1}} \tag{13.23}$$

which represents the ratio of the rate of change of the marginal utility of consumption $(\Delta v/v)$ to the rate of change of *per capita* consumption $(\Delta C/C)$, both expressed in percentage terms. Economists have a name for such ratios of percentage changes; they are in general called "elasticities". So expression (13.23) is the elasticity of marginal utility with respect to *per capita* consumption; it shows how much the marginal utility of consumption changes with each 1 per cent increase in the average level of consumption. The second expression

$$\frac{\Delta C_{t+1}}{C_{t+1}} \tag{13.24}$$

is simply the rate of growth of *per capita* consumption in percentage terms. Thus, (13.22) expresses the social rate of discount in terms of the product of the elasticity of marginal utility and the rate of growth of *per capita* consumption:

$$i = - \text{(elasticity of marginal utility)} \times$$
$$\times \text{(rate of growth of } per\ capita \text{ consumption)} =$$
$$= -\frac{\% \text{ change in marginal utility}}{\% \text{ change in consumption}} \times$$
$$\times (\% \text{ change in } per\ capita \text{ consumption}) \tag{13.25}$$

This way of expressing the social rate of discount clearly brings out the relationship between the social rate of discount and the rate of economic growth. With negative elasticities of marginal utility, the social rate of discount varies directly with the rate of growth of *per capita* consumption. Thus, if the elasticity of marginal utility with respect to *per capita* consumption were —2.0 (which would mean that the social significance of extra consumption would decline 2 per cent with each 1 per cent increase in average consumption), a rate of growth of *per capita* consumption of 3 per cent would mean a social rate of discount of 6 per cent, whereas a rate of growth of *per capita* consumption equal to 5 per cent would mean a social rate of discount of 10 per cent. The reality behind these numbers is that if one takes a development plan as a realistic forecast, the richer this plan suggests the future will be relative to the present, the less valuable additional consumption in the future will be. This conclusion reflects itself in a social rate of discount that varies proportionately to the rate of growth of consumption. Thus, the higher the rate of growth of consumption in the absence of the project, the harder it will be for any given project to be acceptable on the basis of its future contributions to aggregate consumption.

A second virtue of formula (13.25) is that it clearly separates its positive or objective determinant from its normative or subjective determinant. At the level of project formulation and evaluation, the future rate of growth of *per capita* consumption is a given datum, notwithstanding that whatever growth rate is achieved is the result of synthesis of economic policies formulated in terms of a variety of political, institutional and technological constraints. In countries with reasonably well-developed planning organizations, the national development plan is the obvious source for estimating the future rate of growth of *per capita* consumption, provided that the plan document is a reliable forecast of future development patterns. Note that the use of the national plan to forecast the rate of growth of consumption in no way implies that planned growth is optimal. The plan is here used as a forecast only of what will be, not what ought to be.

Alas, neither the plan nor any document customarily prepared in national planning organizations provides any guidance as to the normative element of the social rate of discount, the elasticity of the marginal utility of aggregate consumption with respect to *per capita* consumption. To infer an elasticity from the plan, it would be necessary not only to impute realism to the plan (as its use as a base for projecting $\Delta C/C$ requires) but also to impute optimality. Moreover, it would be necessary to know in some detail the intertemporal consumption patterns of alternative plans that have been rejected during the planning process. With such information it would be possible to estimate the social marginal productivity of capital, and, by virtue of the optimality of the plan, to use this marginal productivity as a measure of the social rate of discount.

13.6 THE SOCIAL RATE OF DISCOUNT AS AN UNKNOWN OF PROJECT EVALUATION

However, for reasons outlined in chapter 11, it is in general possible neither to impute optimality to the plan nor to gather any but the most superficial knowledge of discarded alternatives. Thus, the elasticity of marginal utility, if it is to be estimated at all, must be estimated independently of the national economic plan. Unfortunately, the difficulties articulated in chapter 12 make it unlikely that the political process, such as it is presently, is capable of quantitative articulation of such value judgements as the elasticity of marginal utility embodies. For this reason, we counsel treating the social rate of discount, like redistribution weights and merit-want weights, as an unknown of project formulation and evaluation. Sensitivity analysis, along the lines laid out in chapter 12 would indicate for each project the "switching value" of the social rate of discount, the numerical value of the discount rate for which the project's net present value is just zero.

The switching value of the social rate of discount will be recognized by many as the project's internal rate of return, for this concept, like the switching value, is defined as the value of the discount rate that just makes the net present value zero. Algebraically, both are defined as the value of i for which

$$\sum_{t=0}^{T} \frac{B_t}{(1+i)^t} = 0 \qquad (13.26)$$

Thus, our lengthy intertemporal analysis appears to reduce to a calculation of each project's internal rate of return! What then explains the length of the analysis?

First, it has brought out the all-important fact that the switching value or the internal rate of return is not a measure of intrinsic project merit to be compared with the internal rate of return on marginal private investment or with any other "objective" rate of discount. *The calculation of internal rates of return on public investments is proposed not to escape intertemporal value judgements but to facilitate them.* It is meant initially as a means of clarifying to policy makers responsible for decisions with respect to projects what the implications are of various decisions. Ultimately, it may be hoped, the process of confronting the implications of their decisions will permit policy makers to express value judgements before projects are formulated, rather than implicitly in the process of project evaluation. But that, it must be emphasized, is a stage of sophistication in project formulation and evaluation that no country, rich or poor, appears close to achieving.

A second purpose of this discussion has been to prepare the way for the analysis of the shadow price of saving and the shadow wage of labour, which occupy chapters 14 and 15, respectively. Our analysis of the relationship between the public and private sectors suggested that it is only under extremely stringent conditions, unlikely to be met in reality, that the marginal productivity of capital can be considered an appropriate surrogate for the social rate of discount. In general, the productivity of investment alternatives to public

projects is relevant not as a discount rate but as one of the principal determinants of the *opportunity cost* of public investment. In general, the capital cost of a public project will be only partly borne by the economy at the time the investment is made, in that only part of the resources initially required for it will come out of present consumption. The remainder of the resources will typically come out of alternative investments, so that the economy bears the costs when it forgoes the consumption these alternatives would have contributed. The marginal productivity of capital, along with the propensity to reinvest returns, determines the time path of consumption from marginal private investment, and the next chapter shows how this stream of consumption can be expressed as a single number, namely, the present value of the stream. In fact, the present value of the future consumption generated by £1 of marginal investment is by definition the shadow price of saving, for this present value reflects the social value of saving relative to consumption. Of course, to compute this or any present value, the social rate of discount must be specified, so that in project formulation and evaluation the shadow price of saving varies with the shadow rate of discount.

All this will be spelled out in more detail in the next chapter. At present our only aim is to emphasize that our insistence on the value judgement inherent in intertemporal valuation in no way denies the importance of the productivity of capital in the complete intertemporal criterion. But the proper role of the productivity of capital is in determining the value of a unit of resources withdrawn from other investment, not in determining the weight that should be accorded the future relative to the present.

13.7 REDISTRIBUTION AND MERIT-WANT OBJECTIVES

Up to now we have discussed the social rate of discount solely in relationship to the aggregate-consumption objective. This is not because of misplaced emphasis, but because discounting with respect to other objectives is implicitly reflected in the time pattern of weights on these objectives. Since aggregate consumption is the unit of account in each time period, changes in the weights on redistribution or merit-want objectives over time implicitly define rates of discount for these objectives, and the methodology of these Guidelines requires no further specification of discount rates.

Algebraically, the existence of a second objective, redistribution to poor peasants, let us say, requires us to replace B_t by the weighted sum

$$B_{1t} + w_t B_{2t} \tag{13.27}$$

where B_{1t} is the (net) aggregate-consumption benefit and B_{2t} the (net) redistributional benefit. The parameter w is the premium placed on peasants' consumption in year t relative to aggregate consumption in the same year. Thus, the weighted sum (13.2) of the project's lifetime benefits, which we have labelled the present value, becomes

$$B^* = B_{10} + w_0 B_{20} + v_1 (B_{11} + w_1 B_{22}) + v_2 (B_{12} + w_1 B_{22}) +$$
$$+ \ldots + v_T (B_{1T} + w_T B_{2T}) \tag{13.28}$$

Now with the assumption that the v's diminish at a constant rate, i, expression (13.28), like expression (13.2), becomes

$$B^* = \sum_{t=0}^{T} \frac{B_{1t} + w_t B_{2t}}{(1 + i)^t} \tag{13.29}$$

so that no separate discounting of redistributional benefits is required if the methodology proposed in these Guidelines is followed.

But, as chapter 12 indicated, formula (13.29) is equivalent to

$$B^* = \sum_{t=0}^{T} \frac{B_{1t}}{(1 + i)^t} + w \sum_{t=0}^{T'} \frac{B_{2t}}{(1 + i)^t} \tag{13.30}$$

provided that the weight on redistributional benefits relative to contemporaneous aggregate consumption remains constant over a period of T' $(\leq T)$ years and then falls to zero. Algebraically, the assumption involved in rewriting (13.29) in the form of (13.30) is

$$w_t = w \qquad t = 0, \ldots, T'$$
$$w_t = 0 \qquad t = T' + 1, \ldots, T$$

In the form of expression (13.30), over-all project benefits are expressed as the weighted sum of discounted present values of aggregate consumption and redistributional benefits, both discounted at a common social rate of discount, i. The assumption of a constant weight, w, permits us to express over-all project benefits in this form because it allows us to rewrite (13.28) as

$$B^* = B_{10} + v_1 B_{11} + \ldots + v_T B_{1T} +$$
$$+ w (B_{20} + v_1 B_{21} + \ldots + v_{T'} B_{2T'}) \tag{13.31}$$

From (13.31) it is an easy step to (13.30) once we assume that the v's decline at a constant rate.

The complication introduced into project formulation and evaluation by the existence of multiple objectives is thus not one of increasing the number of discount rates. But the sensitivity analysis proposed to determine the switching value of the social rate of discount for each project is complicated by the existence of multiple objectives. For projects producing substantial redistributional or merit-want benefits, the internal rate of return will increase with the weight accorded to these benefits, as well as with the length of time over which these objectives are taken into account; switching values of parameters must be presented in tabular form, as described in chapter 12, rather than as single numbers. Only in the event that the aggregate-consumption objective is the sole objective does the internal rate of return give the only switching value relevant to the exercise of judgements in the evaluation process.

13.8 SUMMARY

Benefits and costs that occur in the future are less valuable than current benefits and costs if *per capita* consumption is expected to rise and if it is assumed that the marginal social significance of consumption is inversely related to the level of *per capita* consumption. Thus, the appropriate measure of the aggregate consumption attributable to an investment is a weighted sum of the present and future benefits and costs of the project. If the weights on increments to aggregate consumption diminish at a constant rate, i, the stream of consumption $B_0, \ldots, B_T$ is equivalent to

$$\sum_{t=0}^{T} \frac{B_t}{(1 + i)^t}$$

which is commonly called the project's net present value. The parameter i is the social rate of discount.

Were we naively to apply the logic of willingness to pay to the choice of a social rate of discount, we should be committed to identifying the social rate of discount with an average of the rates of interest individuals pay on borrowings or earn on savings. For such interest rates "reveal" what individuals are "willing to pay" to advance consumption or what they must be paid to defer consumption. However, we find the logic of consumer choice that justifies inferring social values from market actions wanting when applied to intertemporal choices. Thus, even within the context of the aggregate-consumption objective we depart from the basic premise of this objective —valuation based on consumer sovereignty—when it comes to intertemporal comparisons of benefits and costs.[39] Even if all borrowers paid 10 per cent and all savers earned 10 per cent we are not ready to accept that the social rate of discount would necessarily be 10 per cent.

Equally unsatisfactory as a basis for the social rate of discount are observed rates of capital productivity in the private sector. The proposition that the social rate of discount is the marginal (social) productivity of private investment requires stringent assumptions to justify it. Even within the framework of a two-period model, the marginal productivity of capital can be used as a surrogate for the social rate of discount only if it is assumed that the resources required for the project under investigation are drawn entirely from marginal investment in the private sector.

Once we shift the locus of analysis from a two-period to a multi-period model, nothing short of the assumption of optimal growth will justify discounting future benefits and costs at a rate equal to the marginal productivity of capital. Under conditions of optimal growth, the use of a marginal productivity of capital of, say, 20 per cent as an indication of the social rate of discount amounts to little more than the assertion that policy makers insist, at the margin, on exactly £1.2 worth of consumption next year for each £1.0 of

---

[39] An alternative basis for rejecting market actions as the basis for intertemporal evaluation is the presence of externalities in intertemporal choices.

consumption sacrificed this year. In other words, £1.2 next year has exactly the same value in the eyes of policy makers as £1.0 this year, which is to say that policy makers discount future consumption at a rate of 20 per cent. Were this not the case, or so the logic of optimization goes, more investment or less would be desirable, and investment would be increased or decreased until its marginal productivity became exactly equal to the social rate of discount.

The logic by which the social rate of discount may be inferred from the marginal productivity of capital under conditions of optimal growth is thus a special application of the logic spelled out in chapter 11 for inferring national parameters from optimal development plans. And it is subject to all the limitations outlined in chapter 11. Specifically, the story breaks down as soon as it is admitted that to impute optimality to development plans is in general to argue that whatever decisions a Government takes must be optimal, at least relative to the politics, institutions and technologies that constrain these decisions. If not, or so such Candide-like optimism goes, the Government would take different decisions.

We rather believe that the fractionization of power in the process of government decision making, the existence of important special interests that influence and sometimes even control government decisions, and the complexity of planning problems all combine to make a mockery of "optimality" of policies that determine the over-all allocation of resources between present and future. We therefore counsel against the resolution of intertemporal valuation problems by appeal to the "objective" criterion of capital productivity in the private sector.

This is not to say that the productivity of capital in the private sector is irrelevant to the evaluation of public investment. On the contrary. But it is the present value of the consumption stream forgone when such investment is displaced that is relevant, and this present value is relevant as a cost, not as a discount rate. The next chapter describes in detail a procedure for calculating this cost and illustrates the differences for project choice that result from reflecting private-sector capital productivity as an opportunity cost rather than as a rate of discount.

Since neither individuals' market-revealed "preferences" nor observed rates of capital productivity determine the social rate of discount, policy makers must determine this parameter by making an implicit or explicit value judgement with respect to the intertemporal distribution of increments to consumption. Notwithstanding the virtues of an explicit judgement made prior to the formulation of investment proposals, it appears to us at the very least premature to propose such a procedure. Intertemporal value judgements are very likely among the most difficult to conceptualize, and chapter 12 presents several reasons why responsible policy makers are at present unable to quantify their values in any meaningful way, even without the complications resulting from comparisons of present with future.

We therefore treat the social rate of discount as an unknown of the planning problem, in line with the general procedure described in chapter 12. Where aggregate consumption is the only objective, the suggested procedure of calculating values of the unknown parameter that change the project design in significant ways—the so-called "switching values" of national parameters—reduces in general to a calculation of the project's internal rate of return.

But it is important to distinguish the purposes that the internal rate of return serves in our methodology from the role it plays in other treatments of project formulation and evaluation. Here the internal rate of return is meant solely to confront policy makers with the consequences of their choices. The internal rate of return is directly comparable neither with market rates of interest nor with observed rates of capital productivity. Unlike more conventional use of the internal rate of return, there is no objectively determined bench mark with which each project can be compared. The only relevant bench mark is the intention of responsible policy makers, which, after sufficient exercise, may be quantifiable into a consistent cut-off rate of return that would fulfil the condition required of a social rate of discount.

The problem of intertemporal choice becomes even more complicated when additional objectives like redistribution and merit wants enter the picture. This is not because these objectives require separate rates of discount; for each objective this rate of discount is implicit in the weights placed on benefits with respect to that objective relative to aggregate consumption benefits. Rather, the problem is that with more than one unknown parameter in the planning problem, switching values can no longer be represented by simple numbers. So the switching value of the social rate of discount—the internal rate of return—can be interpreted only with reference to given values of other parameters, and, conversely, the switching values of other parameters can be interpreted only with reference to a given value of the social rate of discount. This obviously makes it more difficult to infer clear-cut value judgements with respect to any single parameter when more than one objective is present and makes it all the more difficult to infer a single, consistent pattern of values from policy makers' decisions.

Thus, one should not look to benefit-cost analysis as a means of substituting "objective", "quantitative", and "hard" analysis for "subjective", "qualitative", and "soft" judgements, at least not for some time to come. Benefit-cost analysis can sharpen the focus of policy makers' intervention in project evaluation, but it cannot as yet reduce this process to a routine that, once set in motion by appropriate value judgements on the part of those politically responsible and accountable, would—like the universe of the deists—run its course without further interference from the top.

Chapter 14

INTERTEMPORAL CHOICE:
THE SOCIAL VALUE OF INVESTMENT

14.1 THE SHADOW PRICE OF INVESTMENT IN THE SIMPLEST CASE

The last chapter emphasized the distinction between the marginal productivity of capital as a determinant of the social rate of discount and as a determinant of the opportunity costs of the projects whose formulation and evaluation are at issue. With respect to the social rate of discount, the influence of the marginal productivity of capital is at best indirect. With respect to opportunity costs (and by the same token, benefits), the marginal productivity of capital plays a direct role. The purpose of this chapter is to examine that role in some detail.

The conventional procedure in project evaluation is to debit a project's account for capital costs at the time capital outlays are made. But from the point of view of national economic profitability, this is appropriate only if the economy's sacrifice of consumption for the sake of the project is exactly equal in magnitude and timing to this capital outlay. For the project's net present value

$$B^* = B_0 + v_1 B_1 + \ldots + v_T B_T = \sum_{t=0}^{T} \frac{B_t}{(1+i)^t} \qquad (14.1)$$

is supposed to represent a weighted sum of aggregate consumption, B_t representing the *incremental aggregate consumption*, or its equivalent, attributable to the project in year t. If, for simplicity, we assume the capital cost to be concentrated in year 0, and we denote its magnitude by K_0, the conventional formula

$$B^* = -K_0 + v_1 B_1 + \ldots + v_T B_T = \sum_{t=1}^{T} \frac{B_t}{(1+i)^t} - K_0 \qquad (14.2)$$

is an appropriate surrogate for (14.1) only if the economy sacrifices consumption whose value is K_0 in year 0.

More typically, a portion of the resources required for a public project come out of alternative investment, and for this portion of costs the sacrifice

173

of consumption is deferred until the time the displaced investments would themselves have yielded consumption. In a two-period model in which the entire impact of a public project is borne by alternative investment, the computation of costs at the time consumption is actually sacrificed is equivalent, as the last chapter showed, to discounting the returns of public investment at a rate equal to the marginal productivity of capital, designated as q. But once we extend the time horizon beyond two periods, this equivalence disappears. Suppose, for example, that the marginal £1 invested in the economy yields a projected stream of returns of £q per year. Since the life of capital is assumed to be infinite in this example, q represents the marginal productivity of capital. Now suppose that this return of £q per year is immediately consumed as it becomes available. Then the weighted sum of incremental aggregate consumption due to a public project is represented not by (14.2) but by the expression

$$B^* = 0 + v_1 (B_1 - qK_0) + \ldots + v_T (B_T - qK_0) - \ldots - v_t qK_0 - \ldots =$$
$$= \sum_{t=1}^{T} \frac{B_t}{(1+i)^t} - \sum_{t=1}^{\infty} \frac{qK_0}{(1+i)^t} \qquad (14.3)$$

Expression (14.3) can be simplified because of the assumption that the *return on marginal investment*, q, is constant over time. This permits us to write

$$\sum_{t=1}^{\infty} \frac{qK_0}{(1+i)^t} = qK_0 \sum_{t=1}^{\infty} \frac{1}{(1+i)^t} \qquad (14.4)$$

which in turn simplifies to

$$qK_0 \sum_{t=1}^{\infty} \frac{1}{(1+i)^t} = \frac{q}{i} K_0 \qquad (14.5)$$

by virtue of the identity

$$\sum_{t=1}^{\infty} \frac{1}{(1+i)^t} = \frac{1}{i} \qquad (14.6)$$

an identity that holds for any positive i. Substituting into (14.3), we have

$$B^* = \sum_{t=1}^{\infty} \frac{B_t}{(1+i)^t} - \frac{q}{i} K_0 \qquad (14.7)$$

If expression (14.7) is compared with (14.2), we can clearly see the difference between debiting capital outlays to the public project's account at the time consumption is actually sacrificed, as in (14.7), and debiting the project's account at the time capital outlays are made. The present value of the consumption stream forgone by displacing marginal investment is q/i times the magnitude of the investment itself, for the cost of K_0 in (14.2) becomes $(q/i)K_0$ in (14.7). If q exceeds i, the opportunity cost $(q/i)K_0$ will exceed the nominal cost K_0; that is to say, the present value of the return from displaced investment exceeds the nominal cost of the investment whenever the marginal productivity of

capital, q, exceeds the social rate of discount, i. Thus, the opportunity cost is not only a function of the productivity of capital alone, but a function of the social rate of discount as well.

In general, we have termed the opportunity cost of a single unit of resources the "shadow price" of the resource. Thus, the shadow price of investment, P^{inv}, is by definition the present value of the aggregate-consumption stream generated by £1 of marginal investment. To the extent the present example is representative of real-world conditions, the shadow price of investment would be given by the formula

$$P^{\text{inv}} = \frac{q}{i} \qquad (14.8)$$

and (14.7) would be written

$$B^* = \sum_{t=1}^{T} \frac{B_t}{(1+i)^t} - P^{\text{inv}} K_0 \qquad (14.9)$$

14.2 A MORE REALISTIC MODEL: REINVESTMENT

Formula (14.8), however, must be viewed as the result of a preliminary exercise designed to illustrate the principles behind the calculation of the shadow price of investment rather than as an acceptable approximation to reality. Even as a first approximation it is unrealistic to assume that all returns from investment are immediately consumed, as the story behind formula (14.8) does. Rather, a fraction, s, will in general be reinvested, and only the remainder, $(1-s)$, will be consumed. This does not mean, however, that all we need do is to replace q by $(1-s)q$ in the numerator of (14.8). For we must take into account the indirect consumption produced by reinvestment along with the direct consumption, $(1-s)q$. A convenient way of accounting for the indirect consumption attributable to displaced investment is to analyse the consumption stream in terms of the returns from the capital accumulated by adding the proceeds of reinvestment to the original stake. If reinvestment from the returns of an initial £1 investment leads to an accumulated investment of a_t in year t, the over-all—direct and indirect—return from this investment will be

$$qA_t$$

Assuming the fraction $(1-s)$ of this return is consumed, the contribution to aggregate consumption in year t is

$$(1-s)\, qA_t$$

The shadow price of investment, the present value of the entire stream of consumption, is thus

$$P^{\text{inv}} = \sum_{t=1}^{\infty} \frac{(1-s)\, qA_t}{(1+i)^t} \qquad (14.10)$$

To evaluate (14.10), we must have a way of expressing A_t in computable terms. This is readily at hand, since A_t depends only on the propensity to

invest, s, and the marginal productivity of capital, q. In year 1 the accumulated capital is still the original stake of £1:

$$A_1 = 1$$

By year 2, however, the original stake is augmented by the reinvestment of £sq, the fraction of the first year's return (q) assumed to be plowed back into capital formation. Thus, in year 2

$$A_2 = A_1 + sqA_1 = (1 + sq)\, A_1 = 1 + sq \tag{14.11}$$

In year 3, the accumulated capital includes the reinvestment of a fraction of year 2's return as well as the earlier reinvestment. Year 2's return is

$$qA_2$$

and so the reinvested portion is

$$sqA_2$$

Thus, the capital accumulated by year 3 is

$$A_3 = A_2 + sqA_2 = (1 + sq)\, A_2 = (1 + sq)^2 \tag{14.12}$$

The general pattern that emerges should be clear: the capital accumulated in year t is the sum of the capital on hand during the previous year, A_{t-1}, and the reinvestment from the returns of the previous year, sqA_{t-1}:

$$A_t = A_{t-1} + sqA_{t-1} = (1 + sq)\, A_{t-1}$$

Since the same logic holds for year $t-1$, we have

$$A_{t-1} = A_{t-2} + sqA_{t-2} = (1 + sq)\, A_{t-2}$$

so that

$$A_t = (1 + sq)^2 A_{t-2}$$

Working backwards to year 1, we have the general formula

$$A_t = (1 + sq)^{t-1} \tag{14.13}$$

of which (14.11) and (14.12) are special cases.

Now we can substitute from (14.12) into (14.10). We then have

$$P^{\text{inv}} = \sum_{t=1}^{\infty} \frac{(1 - s)\, q\, (1 + sq)^{t-1}}{(1 + i)^t}$$

or, equivalently,

$$P^{\text{inv}} = \frac{(1 - s)q}{1 + sq} \sum_{t=1}^{\infty} \left(\frac{1 + sq}{1 + i} \right)^t \tag{14.14}$$

The series of terms summed in (14.14)

$$\sum_{t=1}^{\infty} \left(\frac{1 + sq}{1 + i} \right)^t = \frac{1 + sq}{1 + i} + \left(\frac{1 + sq}{1 + i} \right)^2 + \dots + \left(\frac{1 + sq}{1 + i} \right)^t + \dots$$

is, like the sum

$$\sum_{t=1}^{\infty} \frac{1}{(1+i)^t} = \frac{1}{1+i} + \frac{1}{(1+i)^2} + \cdots + \frac{1}{(1+i)^t} + \cdots$$

a "geometric sum", which can be written in a compact form even though it includes an infinite number of terms. In strict analogy with the identity

$$\sum_{t=1}^{\infty} \frac{1}{(1+i)^t} = \frac{1}{i}$$

the identity

$$\sum_{t=1}^{\infty} \left(\frac{1+sq}{1+i}\right)^t = \frac{1+sq}{i-sq} \tag{14.15}$$

holds whenever i exceeds sq. Thus, substituting from (14.15) into (14.14), we have

$$P^{\text{inv}} = \frac{(1-s)q}{i-sq} \tag{14.16}$$

Formula (14.16) expresses the shadow price of investment as the product of the share of consumption in the marginal return from investment, $(1-s)$, and the marginal rate of return, q, divided by the difference between the social rate of discount, i, and the rate at which capital accumulates, sq. As the ratio of $(1-s)q$ to $(i-sq)$, P^{inv} can also be thought of as the present value of the stream of consumption directly attributable to marginal investment, $(1-s)q$, discounted at an artificial rate of discount, $i-sq$, representing the social rate of discount corrected for reinvestment by substituting the rate of accumulation sq from i. Either way we view P^{inv}, $s+q$ are, therefore, the two values that must be estimated for the economy as a whole.

14.3 A DIFFERENT DERIVATION OF P^{inv}

Formula (14.14) can be reached by a different argument, which has the virtue of clarifying the relationship between the marginal productivity of capital, the social rate of discount and the shadow price of investment. Instead of computing the present value of the consumption stream attributable directly and indirectly to marginal investment, we can compute the present value of the sum of (1) direct contributions to consumption, $(1-s)q$, and (2) direct contributions to investment, sq, valuing the contribution to investment at the shadow price, P^{inv}. Viewed in this way the annual return from a £1 investment is

$$(1-s)q + P^{\text{inv}} sq \tag{14.17}$$

The present value of these returns is equal to the shadow price of investment, which is to say

$$P^{\text{inv}} = \sum_{t=1}^{\infty} \frac{(1-s)q + P^{\text{inv}} sq}{(1+i)^t}$$

Making use of the fact that this, too, is a geometric sum, we can rewrite it in the more compact form

$$P^{\text{inv}} = \frac{(1-s)\,q + P^{\text{inv}}\,sq}{i} \tag{14.18}$$

Now solve (14.18) for P^{inv} to obtain

$$P^{\text{inv}} = \frac{(1-s)\,q}{i - sq} \tag{14.16}$$

which is exactly the formula obtained by calculating the present value of the stream of direct and indirect consumption.

14.4 The social marginal productivity of capital and the social rate of return

Now we can examine the relationship of the marginal productivity of capital, the social rate of discount and the shadow price of reinvestment. In our first example, all returns from marginal investment were assumed to be immediately consumed, and q was unambiguously the social marginal productivity of capital. In symbols:

$$\text{SMP} = q$$

In the absence of reinvestment, therefore, the shadow price of investment is simply the ratio of the social marginal productivity of capital to the social rate of discount, q/i. In the second example the same rule holds, although the social marginal productivity of capital becomes more difficult to identify. Given that a portion of the returns from marginal investment is reinvested, a proper social accounting requires us to value this portion at the shadow price of investment. Thus, the social marginal productivity of capital (SMP) becomes

$$\text{SMP} = (1-s)\,q + P^{\text{inv}}\,sq$$

as in (14.17) rather than simply q. Thus, as examination of (14.18) shows, the same rule governs the shadow price in both examples, namely, the formula

$$P^{\text{inv}} = \frac{\text{SMP}}{i} \tag{14.19}$$

In both cases, the shadow price of investment is the ratio of the social marginal productivity of capital to the social rate of discount. In the second case it is necessary to eliminate P^{inv} from the right-hand side in order to express this parameter in terms of s, q, and i, but that does not affect the fundamental symmetry between the two examples.

There is one more concept that should be introduced to complete this aspect of the discussion of the social value of investment, namely, the concept of the social rate of return. Barring changes in asset values over time, the rate of return on any asset is the ratio of the gross return to the value of the asset. For example, if a machine worth £100 returns £10 per year, the rate of return

on the machine is 0.10, so long as the machine does not depreciate (or appreciate) in value over the course of the year. Thus, provided the price of capital goods remains constant, the rate of return on a unit of capital of infinite durability is the ratio of the marginal productivity of capital to the price of a unit of capital. Symbolically, the rate of return is given by the ratio

$$\frac{\text{MP}}{P_K} \qquad (14.20)$$

where MP represents marginal productivity and P_K the price of a unit of capital. To value capital in money terms is to attach a price of £1 to a unit of capital, so that the *nominal* rate of return becomes equal to the marginal productivity of capital.

The *social* rate of return on capital, which we shall denote r, is defined analogously, as the ratio of the social marginal productivity of capital to the shadow price of capital. Symbolically,

$$r = \frac{\text{SMP}}{P^{\text{inv}}} \qquad (14.21)$$

But the conclusion that the rate of return is identical to the marginal productivity of capital no longer holds, for the shadow price of capital is not £1, but P^{inv}, which will exceed £1 as long as q exceeds i. Thus, the social rate of return will in general be less than the social marginal productivity of capital. Indeed, substituting from (14.30) into (14.32), we have

$$r = \frac{\text{SMP}}{\frac{\text{SMP}}{i}}$$

which is to say

$$r = i \qquad (14.22)$$

Now (14.22) says that the social rate of discount is always equal to the social rate of return! However, the equality of r and i is a logical consequence of the definitions of (1) the shadow price of investment and (2) the social rate of return. The parameter r is, therefore, not an independently observable datum by which one can estimate i. For this reason there is no inconsistency between (14.22) and the arguments of the previous chapter that led us to reject observable measures of capital productivity as a basis for determining the social rate of discount. Since r cannot be determined without first specifying P^{inv}, and P^{inv} cannot be determined without first specifying i, estimates of r cannot possibly serve as the basis for estimates of i.

There is only one circumstance under which r might be estimated before i and could therefore be used as a basis for estimating i. That is when, in addition to the shadow price P^{inv}, which by definition measures the social *value* of investment, (1) there exists an independent estimate of the social *cost* of investment, and (2) these two independent estimates are equal. For under these circumstances, the social cost of investment can be used in place

of the social value of private investment in equation (14.21); thus, r can be estimated from the formula

$$r = \frac{\text{SMP}}{P^{\text{inv}}}$$

and i, in turn, can be estimated from the formula

$$i = r$$

The key assumption is that the social cost of investment does not depend directly on the social rate of discount.

By the social cost of investment we mean the amount of aggregate consumption that the economy must give up in order to increase investment by £1. Do not fall into the trap of thinking that by virtue of the common monetary unit of measure of consumption and investment this cost is necessarily £1. Institutional and political constraints, an example of which will be given in the next chapter, may make it necessary to sacrifice more than £1 to increase investment by £1. But the social cost of investment may not be readily approximated, and even if it can be, one cannot expect that the second precondition of independent estimation of r—equality between the social value and the social cost of investment—will be met. For equality between the value and cost of investment is nothing less than the marginal condition of an optimal rate of investment, which is to say an optimal rate of growth! All the reasons given in chapter 11 for rejecting the temptation to impute optimality to planned rates of growth, as well as the very real issue of whether planned rates of growth will be realized, need not be resurrected here. Suffice it to recall them, and to emphasize that without the assumption that the rate of investment is optimal, the social value of investment cannot be estimated from its social cost, and hence formulae (14.21) and (14.22) cannot be used to infer i from objective data.

14.5 CHANGES OVER TIME IN P^{inv}

Up to this point, our discussion has assumed that all the parameters that determine the social value of investment—the rate of saving, the marginal productivity of capital and the social rate of discount—remain constant over time. If any of these parameters change over time, the simple formulae for P^{inv} derived earlier in this chapter no longer suffice, and, moreover, P^{inv} will not itself remain constant over time. That is, the social value of next year's investment in terms of next year's consumption will differ from the social value of present investment in terms of present consumption.

To calculate P^{inv} without the simplifying assumption of constant s and q is not, however, impossible. The reader who is interested in the details of this calculation should turn to appendix A of this chapter. Here we note only that if the time horizon over which i exceeds sq is large, formula (14.16) will remain a reasonable approximation to P^{inv}.

14.6 OPPORTUNITY COSTS WHEN RESOURCES ARE DRAWN FROM BOTH CONSUMP-
TION AND INVESTMENT

We have been concerned up to now with evaluating the opportunity
costs of public investment that displaces marginal investment. If the resources
required for public investment come out of consumption rather than alternative
investment, adjustments of the type we have discussed here are not appropriate.
Since consumption is the unit of account, £1 of consumption currently forgone
should be debited to the project's account as £1. In general, if the fraction a^{inv}
of a project's capital costs is drawn from investment and the fraction a^{con}
is taken out of consumption, the appropriate present-value formula is not

$$B^* = \sum_{t=1}^{T} \frac{B_t}{(1+i)^t} - P^{inv} K_0 \qquad (14.9)$$

but

$$B^* = \sum_{t=1}^{T} \frac{B_t}{(1+i)^t} - (a^{inv} P^{inv} + a^{con}) K_0 \qquad (14.23)$$

If the proportion of capital costs that come out of investment is the same as
the marginal propensity to invest, that is, if

$$a^{inv} = s,$$

and if the total economic activity forgone is equal to £1 per £1 of capital
outlay, so that

$$a^{con} = 1 - a^{inv}$$

then

$$a^{inv} P^{inv} + a^{con} = sP^{inv} + (1 - s)$$

and by substituting from (14.16) we have

$$sP^{inv} + (1 - s) = \frac{(1 - s) i}{i - sq}$$

which represents the corrected opportunity cost per £1 of nominal cost.

14.7 PUBLIC AND PRIVATE INVESTMENT

But even with this correction, the story remains incomplete in several
respects. First, in focusing our attention on marginal investment and consumption, we have completely neglected the sectoral distribution of displaced
investment. If marginal public investment is displaced by a particular project,
the productivity of public-sector capital and the propensity to invest the profit
of public enterprise are relevant rather than private-sector q and s. If we
denote the shadow price of a unit of government capital by P^{gov}, then an
argument analogous to the one that led to (14.16) gives the result

$$P^{gov} = \frac{(1 - s^{gov}) q^{gov}}{i - s^{gov} q^{gov}} \qquad (14.24)$$

Several remarks are in order. First, formula (14.24) assumes that the Government recaptures the productivity of its marginal investment in the form of revenues. Second, formula (14.24) assumes constant q and s. Since the results of extending the analysis to comprehend the case of non-constant q and s would be completely symmetrical with our analysis in an undifferentiated economy (see appendix A), conciseness dictates forbearance with respect to such repetition. Third, it should be noted that the social rate of discount is not specifically labelled "gov". The assumption implicit throughout this analysis is that the Government is indifferent as to whether consumption originates in the public or the private sector. Any preference for one over the other properly comes under the heading of merit wants. Fourth, formula (14.24) assumes that the shadow price of public consumption is one, which is to say that—at the margin—a £1 public outlay towards filling current needs produces aggregate-consumption benefits of exactly £1. All these assumptions could be relaxed, but at a higher expositional cost than value.

The existence of two pools of investment from which resources may be drawn not only leads to a second shadow price but also complicates the calculation of the shadow price of resources drawn from the other pool. For the benefits of private investment cannot be assumed to remain completely in the private sector unless the marginal effective tax rate is zero. To the extent that the level of public investment depends on revenues derived from taxation of private profits (and other forms of income), the social value of private investment depends on the rate of taxation and the difference between public and private capital productivities and investment propensities.[40] In other words, the consumption stream attributable directly and indirectly to a unit of private investment must allow for the marginal public investment and public consumption made possible by tax revenues generated by private investment.

Assuming constant values of the relevant parameters, the easiest way of calculating the value of P^{pri} is to use equation (14.19), which has the form

$$P^{\mathrm{pri}} = \frac{\mathrm{SMP}}{i} \tag{14.25}$$

Of course, in a two-sector model, the social marginal productivity of private investment is no longer

$$\mathrm{SMP} = (1 - s)\, q + P^{\mathrm{inv}}\, sq$$

but rather

$$\mathrm{SMP}^{\mathrm{pri}} = [(1 - s^{\mathrm{pri}})\, q^{\mathrm{pri}} + P^{\mathrm{pri}}\, s^{\mathrm{pri}}\, q^{\mathrm{pri}}]\,[1 - m] +$$
$$+ [(1 - s^{\mathrm{gov}})\, q^{\mathrm{pri}} + P^{\mathrm{gov}}\, s^{\mathrm{gov}}\, q^{\mathrm{pri}}]\, m \tag{14.26}$$

when m is the effective marginal tax rate on the product q^{pri}. Formula (14.26) expresses the social marginal productivity of private capital as the value of

---

[40] The productivity of private investment may also depend upon the level of public investment, but we shall assume that the marginal productivity of private capital is independent of marginal public investment.

THE SOCIAL VALUE OF INVESTMENT

the annual product of £1 of private capital: namely, the sum of (1) private consumption and investment

$$[(1 - s^{\mathrm{pri}})\, q^{\mathrm{pri}} + P^{\mathrm{pri}}\, s^{\mathrm{pri}}\, q^{\mathrm{pri}}]\,[1 - m]$$

valued at appropriate shadow prices and (2) the public consumption and investment

$$[(1 - s^{\mathrm{gov}})\, q^{\mathrm{pri}} + P^{\mathrm{gov}}\, s^{\mathrm{gov}}\, q^{\mathrm{pri}}]\, m$$

also valued at appropriate shadow prices. Substituting from (14.26) into (14.25) we have

$$P^{\mathrm{pri}} = \frac{[(1 - s^{\mathrm{pri}})\, q^{\mathrm{pri}} + P^{\mathrm{pri}}\, s^{\mathrm{pri}}\, q^{\mathrm{pri}}]\,[1 - m] + [(1 - s^{\mathrm{gov}})\, q^{\mathrm{pri}} + P^{\mathrm{gov}}\, s^{\mathrm{gov}}\, q^{\mathrm{pri}}]\, m}{i} \tag{14.27}$$

Now if we substitute the value of P^{gov} from formula (14.24) and solve (14.27) for P^{pri}, we obtain the complicated expression

$$P^{\mathrm{pri}} = \frac{(1 - s^{\mathrm{pri}})\, q^{\mathrm{pri}}\, (1 - m)}{i - s^{\mathrm{pri}}\, q^{\mathrm{pri}}\, (1 - m)} + \frac{(1 - s^{\mathrm{gov}})\, q^{\mathrm{pri}}\, m}{i - s^{\mathrm{pri}}\, q^{\mathrm{pri}}\, (1 - m)} +$$

$$+ \frac{s^{\mathrm{gov}}\, q^{\mathrm{pri}}\, (1 - s^{\mathrm{gov}})\, q^{\mathrm{gov}}\, m}{[i - s^{\mathrm{pri}}\, q^{\mathrm{pri}}\, (1 - m)]\,[i - s^{\mathrm{gov}}\, q^{\mathrm{gov}}]} \tag{14.28}$$

Formula (14.28) is more comprehensible if considered term by term. The first term

$$\frac{(1 - s^{\mathrm{pri}})\, q^{\mathrm{pri}}\, (1 - m)}{i - s^{\mathrm{pri}}\, q^{\mathrm{pri}}\, (1 - m)}$$

is the discounted present value of the private consumption generated directly and indirectly by £1 of private investment. The second term

$$\frac{(1 - s^{\mathrm{gov}})\, q^{\mathrm{pri}}\, m}{i - s^{\mathrm{pri}}\, q^{\mathrm{pri}}\, (1 - m)}$$

is the present value of the public consumption generated directly by the tax payments of the private sector on the income q^{pri}. The third term

$$\frac{s^{\mathrm{gov}}\, q^{\mathrm{pri}}\, (1 - s^{\mathrm{gov}})\, q^{\mathrm{gov}}\, m}{[i - s^{\mathrm{pri}}\, q^{\mathrm{pri}}\, (1 - m)]\,[i - s^{\mathrm{gov}}\, q^{\mathrm{gov}}]}$$

is the present value of the consumption generated by the public investment resulting from the stream of tax revenues mq^{pri}.

The appropriate present-value formula for project formulation and evaluation is now

$$B^* = \sum_{t=1}^{T} \frac{B_t}{(1 + i)^t}\, [a^{\mathrm{pri}}\, P^{\mathrm{pri}} + a^{\mathrm{gov}}\, P^{\mathrm{gov}} + a^{\mathrm{con}}]\, K_0 \tag{14.29}$$

where a^{pri} and a^{gov} are the shares of capital costs that come out of private and public investment, respectively, with a^{con} representing the sum of public and private consumption displaced at the margin.

The extent to which (14.29) represents an improvement over (14.23) obviously depends upon the extent to which P^{pri} and P^{gov} differ, which in turn depends on the extent of differences between public and private propensities to save—s^{gov} and s^{pri}—and the extent of differences between public and private capital productivities—q^{gov} and q^{pri}. In some situations, these differences will be small enough to be ignored; in others the differences may be large, but the estimates of the propensity to save and the productivity of capital so crude and so highly aggregated that it is impossible to distinguish between public and private s and q. In recognition of these hard realities of project formulation and evaluation, the case studies that form Part IV of these Guidelines assume common values of s^{pri} and s^{gov} as well as common values of q^{pri} and q^{gov}. This makes P^{pri} and P^{gov} equal and permits the use of a single shadow price, P^{inv}, the derivation of which has already been discussed.

14.8 Reinvestment of benefits

Up to now we have concerned ourselves solely with costs and have said nothing about the evaluation of benefits. But when a portion of project benefits is reinvested, the principles for evaluation of these benefits are symmetrical with the evaluation of outlays that displace investment. Thus, the appropriate present-value criterion becomes

$$B^* = \sum_{t=1}^{T} \frac{(a_t^{\mathrm{pri}} \, P^{\mathrm{pri}} + a_t^{\mathrm{gov}} \, P^{\mathrm{gov}} + a_t^{\mathrm{con}}) \, B_t}{(1+i)^t} -$$
$$- (a_0^{\mathrm{pri}} \, P^{\mathrm{pri}} + a_0^{\mathrm{gov}} \, P^{\mathrm{gov}} + a_0^{\mathrm{con}}) \, K_0 \qquad (14.30)$$

with a_t^{pri}, a_t^{gov}, and a_t^{con} representing the year-by-year distribution of benefits among private investment, public investment and consumption respectively. Formula (14.30) collapses to

$$B^* = \sum_{t=1}^{T} \frac{(a_t^{\mathrm{inv}} \, P^{\mathrm{inv}} + a_t^{\mathrm{con}}) \, B_t}{(1+i)^t} - (a_0^{\mathrm{inv}} \, P^{\mathrm{inv}} + a_0^{\mathrm{con}}) \, K_0 \qquad (14.31)$$

in the event P^{pri} and P^{gov} are estimated by the common parameter P^{inv} either because the two parameters are estimated to be sufficiently close together or because a paucity of information precludes separate estimation.

Examination of formulae (14.30) and (14.31) shows that segregating benefits and costs into investment and consumption portions and evaluating the investment portion at the shadow price(s) of investment does not affect the ranking of projects whenever (1) the shadow price(s) of investment are constant over time and (2) the distributive shares a^{pri}, a^{gov}, and a^{con} (or a^{inv} and a^{con}) remain constant over time. For in this case we could factor out the expression

$$a^{\mathrm{pri}} \, P^{\mathrm{pri}} + a^{\mathrm{gov}} \, P^{\mathrm{gov}} + a^{\mathrm{con}}$$

and (14.30) would become

$$B^* = (a^{\mathrm{pri}}\, P^{\mathrm{pri}} + a^{\mathrm{gov}}\, P^{\mathrm{gov}} + a^{\mathrm{con}}) \left(\sum_{t=1}^{T} \frac{B_t}{(1+i)^t} - K_0 \right) \qquad (14.32)$$

with the result that the algebraic sign of B^* and even its relative value among different projects would be unaffected by the re-evaluation of costs and benefits elaborated in this chapter. In effect, the reinvestment of benefits would just cancel out the loss of consumption from investment displaced at the time the project is undertaken.

But the stringency of the assumptions required to eliminate an essential role for the shadow price(s) of investment is sufficient to vitiate the significance of what must at first blush appear to be a most striking result. Even if we must be satisfied with the assumption of constant shadow price(s) of investment, we can rarely be satisfied with the assumption that the parameter values a_0^{pri}, a_0^{gov}, and a_0^{con} are identical with a_t^{pri}, a_t^{gov}, and a_t^{con} for future periods. In general, the immediate outlay of resources for construction of projects will lead to a relatively greater impact on investment than will the realization of the project's benefits. Indeed, since tax policies and government expenditures on current account are generally quite rigid in the short run, the major impact of the outlays required to construct an additional public project will usually fall on other public investment. A secondary impact will be felt by private investment if deficit spending and monetary policy are used marginally to raise resources from the private sector. Very little of the marginal investment burden will be borne by decreasing consumption. On the other hand, consumption will tend to share much more generously in the fruits of public investment. To some extent, the benefits of public investment will flow directly to the private sector, and the Government's ability to direct the flow of these benefits into investment will be limited by the political and institutional constraints that circumscribe its power to tax; as far as the income of private beneficiaries is concerned, the relevant determinant of the disposition of benefits is as much the private sector's as the Government's propensity to invest. This will tend to reduce the future level of a^{pri} relative to its present level.

But even if the Government recaptures benefits—whether directly in the form of project revenues or indirectly in the form of taxes—it cannot be assumed that the Government will come close to completely reinvesting these benefits. Rather, the greater the Government's income because of its previous investments, the less are the pressures on the finance minister to increase taxes or slow down the expansion of programmes providing current consumption, both of which have the effect of reducing the future level of a^{gov} relative to its present level. For these reasons we should expect future levels of a^{con} to be higher than the present negligible level, even at the level of a first approximation.

The distribution of project income within the private sector plays an important role in determining the future level of a^{pri}. Organizations such as corporations in general save a much higher percentage of their net income than do individuals. And there is evidence that the rich save more than the

poor. By the same token, the distribution of project income between the private sector and the Government will affect the future value of a^{pri} and a^{gov}, all of which makes it quite clear that the Government cannot be neutral with respect to the distribution of projects even within confines so narrow as the aggregate-consumption objective. It must, however, be remembered that the distribution of income favourable to a project's performance with respect to the present value of its aggregate-consumption benefits—income to savers—may be undesirable in terms of over-all government policy, which may emphasize income to the poor, who are generally not savers. Thus, the conflict between the aggregate-consumption objective and income-redistribution objectives may be even more acute viewed in the intertemporal context than it is in the static context.

14.9 CONSTRAINTS ON SAVING VERSUS CONSTRAINTS ON INVESTMENT: THE DISTRIBUTION OF PROJECT INCOME VERSUS THE FORM OF PROJECT OUTPUT

Our emphasis on the distribution of project income as the determinant of the values of a^{pri}, a^{gov}, and a^{con} may appear to be misplaced. It might seem more appropriate to emphasize the form of the project's output. If the Government builds a steel mill, the argument runs, it necessarily adds to future investment, for steel—consumer durables aside—can be used only to build more capital goods. A cloth mill, on the other hand, must add to future consumption, since cloth is principally used in the manufacture of consumer goods.

The argument that the form a project's output takes may affect the rate of saving is correct up to a certain point. It is very likely true, for example, that construction of an automobile assembly plant makes it more difficult for the Government to restrict the allocation of resources to satisfying upper and middle class demands for automobiles, and construction of fertilizer plants may ultimately reduce the price of food and fibre. Each of these investments affects the distribution of real income and thereby—in so far as propensities to save differ among income classes—the rate of saving. But this link between the form of project outputs and the rate of saving is an indirect one, through the distribution of income.

The direct relationship between the form of project output and the rate of saving is more difficult to assess. To argue that constructing a steel mill increases future saving more than constructing a textile mill because of the nature of the output is to put undue emphasis on the technical constraints that limit the supply of capital goods, as opposed to the political constraints that limit the demand for capital goods. In our view the supply of capital goods is not the critical limitation on the rate of saving in most poor countries. Even where the present domestic output of capital goods is far below what current investment plans require, there are generally no technical bars to the increase of exports, which would provide foreign exchange for the importation of capital goods; nor are there technical bars to curtailing the importation

of consumer goods or intermediates used in the production of consumer goods. As for the future, the decision to construct a steel mill today is no guarantee of a net increase in the future supply of steel. Instead, the decision to build a particular steel mill today may be the reason for rejecting another steel project tomorrow, or for cutting imports. Either of these results would in effect mean that the output of the steel project presently in question would merely substitute for other sources of supply rather than adding to the total supplies available to the economy. Indeed, in extreme cases, an attempt to expand the rate of saving by increasing the output of steel and allied products might even lead to export of these goods if the effective demand for saving is not adequate to absorb the domestic production of capital goods.

Similar arguments apply in reverse to the output of "light" industries such as textiles. The decision to construct a particular textile mill does not necessarily increase the domestic supply of textiles; even if it does change the total supply of textiles, only the proportions of the various goods consumers buy may be changed, not total consumption.

In short, the seductive appeal of the idea that choosing "heavy" industrial projects over "light" industrial projects is a means to increasing the rate of saving is by and large a misreading of recent efforts to industrialize, especially the successful effort of the Government of the Union of Soviet Socialist Republics. Heavy industry and a high rate of saving did indeed go hand in hand in the Soviet Union, but cause and effect ran in the opposite direction from that supposed by the champions of heavy industry as a means to the goal of accumulation. Once it had consolidated political power, the Soviet Government applied this power to increasing the rate of saving, from which followed the choice of heavy industrial projects.

We thus view the principal constraints on the rate of saving as political in nature, the critical determinant being the distribution of disposable income among organizations—such as the Government, private pension funds, private corporations (and possibly some rich people)—with high propensities to save and the middle and lower income groups who save virtually nothing. Once income reaches individuals, governmental control over consumption rests on its ability to manipulate the price level of consumer goods, either through sales and excise taxes or more generalized fiscal and monetary measures. However, powerful groups of workers, civil servants and capitalists are able either to insulate their consumption against the effects of inflation or to resist successfully government efforts to mobilize resources by taxation, deficit spending, or monetary measures, so most Governments are rather limited in their ability purposefully to manipulate the consumer price level with a view to augmenting the rate of saving. Again the problem is one of political will rather than technical means; few Governments are prepared to challenge the basic interests of the groups they rely on for support and even survival.

For these reasons we lay more stress on the distribution of project income than on the form of project output in calculating effects on the rate of saving. At the level of project formulation and evaluation, we think it appropriate

to employ shadow price(s) of investment based on the propensities to save and capital productivities of the principal classes of beneficiaries and cost bearers, so that project-level planners have only to determine the distribution of direct benefits and costs between investment and consumption.

14.10 COMPARISONS WITH OTHER INTERTEMPORAL CRITERIA

It may be appropriate, by way of conclusion, to illustrate the operational differences between the procedures proposed here and more conventional ways of taking capital productivity and time preference into account in intertemporal criteria. For the sake of simplicity we shall employ a single shadow price of investment, P^{inv}, based on the assumption of a uniform marginal propensity to save $s = 0.25$ and a uniform marginal productivity of capital $q = 0.20$. Assuming these parameters remain constant over time we have

$$P^{\text{inv}} = \frac{(1-s)\,q}{i - sq} = \frac{(0.75)\,(0.20)}{i - 0.05} = \frac{0.15}{i - 0.05} \qquad (14.33)$$

Now consider a hypothetical project that costs £1 in initial capital outlays and yields an annual return $b = 0.18$ every year in perpetuity, which is to say that the project has an "internal rate of return" of 18 per cent. If we make no corrections for the social value of investment, we would calculate the project's net present value as

$$B^* = \sum_{t=1}^{\infty} \frac{b}{(1+i)^t} - 1 = \frac{0.18}{i} - 1 \qquad (14.34)$$

Two preliminary observations can be quickly made. First, were we to use the nominal marginal productivity of capital directly as a social discount rate, that is, were we to adopt the convention

$$q = i$$

we should unambiguously reject the project. Formula (14.34) would in this case be

$$B^* = \frac{0.18}{0.20} - 1 = 0.9 - 1 = -0.1$$

which is to say that the project's net present value is negative. But for reasons elaborated in the last chapter, we reject the use of the productivity of capital as a discount rate. As an alternative we proposed a sensitivity analysis with respect to the discount rate, treating this parameter in effect as an unknown of project formulation and evaluation.

This brings us to our second preliminary observation: were we to apply the sensitivity analysis urged in the last chapter without correcting for the social value of investment, we would immediately find that the "switching value" of the social rate of discount is $i = 0.18$. For (14.34) is positive for all values of i less than 0.18 and negative for all values of i greater than 0.18.

In other words, the decision with respect to this project would depend simply on whether policy makers placed a premium of more than 18 per cent on additions to this year's consumption over additions to next year's, on additions to next year's over the following year's, and so forth.

But if we correct the analysis to take account of the social value of investment, the results change dramatically. Suppose, again for the sake of simplicity, that all the project's costs are financed by measures that displace alternative investments, so that

$$a_0^{inv} = 1; \, a_0^{con} = 0$$

Suppose furthermore that all benefits immediately augment consumption, with no portion of these benefits being reinvested. Thus,

$$a_t^{inv} = 0; \, a_t^{con} = 1$$

for all future t. With these assumptions, the net present value becomes

$$B^* = \frac{0.18}{i} - P^{inv} = \frac{0.18}{i} - \frac{0.15}{i - 0.05} \tag{14.35}$$

The first effect of this correction is to limit the potential range of social discount rates to rates above 0.05. As the derivation of the formula

$$P^{inv} = \frac{(1 - s) \, q}{i - sq}$$

emphasized, this equation holds only when

$$i > sq$$

Otherwise, the social value of investment, P^{inv}, is infinite, for the consumption arising out of reinvestment grows faster than the rate at which this incremental consumption is discounted.

But the imposition of a lower bound on i is not tremendously helpful, for the domain of possible social rates of discount is still open-ended on the upward side. Thus, it remains necessary to treat i as an unknown of project planning, and algebraic manipulation reveals that $i = 0.3$ is the switching value for (14.35) in the sense that

$$B^* < 0 \text{ for } 0.05 < i < 0.3$$
$$B^* > 0 \text{ for } i > 0.3$$

Several aspects of this calculation should be noted. First, the switching value is greater in (14.35) than it is in (14.34)—0.3 versus 0.18. Second, and more surprising, the direction of change at the switching value is reversed. In (14.34), a social discount rate below 0.18 is necessary to make the project acceptable, but in (14.35) a social discount rate above 0.30 is required. A high social discount rate is required to reduce the present value of the future consumption generated by alternative investments to the point that the present value of

the project's benefits outweighs its consumption costs. Third, the assumption that the annual return, b, was less than q leads to the result that the switching value of i exceeds q. The social rate of discount must exceed the nominal productivity of capital for a project whose nominal rate of return is less than q to be justified.

A fourth observation is in order, too. If the annual return of this hypothetical project had been less than £0.15, no rate of discount would make its present value positive. For in this case (14.35) would become

$$B^* = \frac{b}{i} - \frac{0.15}{i - 0.05} < \frac{0.15}{i} - \frac{0.15}{i - 0.05} \qquad (14.36)$$

and it is easy to verify that there is no (positive) value of i for which the right hand side of (14.36) is positive!

These observations, separately and together, should at least give pause to those who believe that the social rate of discount is nothing but a device to make the benefit-cost analysis of projects "look" better in order to justify wasteful public expenditures. The procedures proposed in these Guidelines do not allow planners to reach any conclusions they might like by manipulating the rate of discount.

Confined as it is to a single perpetuity, this example does not, however, bring out important differences between the procedures proposed in these Guidelines and more conventional procedures. Consider two mutually exclusive projects—say, a tube-well irrigation scheme and a surface-storage irrigation scheme. Let the two entail equal initial outlays, on the assumption that the less capital-intensive tube-well scheme will cover a larger area than the surface-storage scheme. Normalizing capital costs at £1 for each project suppose the net annual benefits of the tube-well scheme are

$$b_{\text{TW}} = 0.28$$

but that, after 10 years, the installations must be totally replaced or abandoned. Suppose that the project is replaced every 10 years; benefits are consumed as they become available; and capital costs are financed by displacing alternative investment. The tube-well scheme's net present value is then

$$B^*_{\text{TW}} = \frac{b_{\text{TW}}}{i} - P^{\text{inv}}\left[1 + \frac{1}{(1+i)^{10}} + \frac{1}{(1+i)^{20}} + \cdots\right] =$$

$$= \frac{b_{\text{TW}}}{i} - P^{\text{inv}}\left[\frac{1}{1 - \frac{1}{(1+i)^{10}}}\right] =$$

$$= \frac{0.28}{i} - \frac{0.15}{i - 0.05}\left[\frac{1}{1 - \frac{1}{(1+i)^{10}}}\right] \qquad (14.37)$$

(The compact notation in the second and third lines of the formula reflects the fact that reinstallation costs represent a geometric sum.)

The surface-storage project will be assumed to be infinitely durable, so that once in place it will last for ever. Its net annual return will be assumed to be

$$b_{SS} = 0.24$$

and the impact of costs and benefits on investment and consumption will be assumed to be symmetric with the tube-well project. The net present value of the surface-storage scheme is thus

$$B_{SS}^* = \frac{b_{SS}}{i} - P^{inv} = \frac{0.24}{i} - \frac{0.15}{i - 0.05} \qquad (14.38)$$

Now calculation of the values of B_{TW}^* and B_{SS}^* at various discount rates shows that the switching values for the two schemes are $i = 0.16$ and $i = 0.133$ respectively; the acceptance of the tube-well scheme would imply a social rate of discount of at least 16 per cent, and acceptance of the surface-storage alternative a social rate of discount of at least 13.3 per cent. If the projects were not mutually exclusive, nothing more could be gleaned from the analysis. But the "either-or" nature of the choice allows us to draw further implications from the choice of one of the two schemes. Further calculation with (14.37) and (14.38) shows that the surface-storage scheme has the higher present value of the two at all discount rates below 0.195, whereas the tube-well scheme has the higher present value at discount rates above 0.195. That is, $i = 0.195$ is the switching value between the two projects.

The calculations can now be summarized in diagram 1:

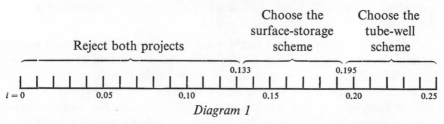

Diagram 1

As chapter 13 emphasized, the relationship between choice and discount rates is symmetric. One can specify the value of the discount rate and read from the table the appropriate decision. Or, if one trusts that the choices of planners are representative of the Government's preferences—one can read from the table the interval of discount rates consistent with particular choices with respect to the two alternatives.

Now compare the results summarized in table 14.1 with more conventional modes of analysis. If we use the nominal productivity of capital as a discount rate, we would choose the tube-well scheme and reject the surface-storage scheme. For with $i = q$, the shadow price of investment is one, and equations (14.37) and (14.38) become

$$B_{TW}^* = \frac{0.28}{0.20} - \frac{1}{1 - \frac{1}{(1.20)^{10}}} \qquad (14.39)$$

and

$$B_{SS}^* = \frac{0.24}{0.20} - 1 \qquad\qquad (14.40)$$

It is easy to verify that (14.39) exceeds (14.40).

Similarly, if we were to calculate the nominal internal rates of return of the two alternatives and rank them accordingly, we would choose the tube-well scheme over the surface-storage scheme. For the nominal internal rate of return of the tube-well scheme, the value of i for which

$$\frac{0.28}{i} - \frac{1}{1 - \frac{1}{(1+i)^{10}}}$$

is equal to zero is 0.25. And the internal rate of return of the surface-storage scheme, the value of i for which

$$\frac{0.24}{i} - 1$$

is equal to zero is 0.24.

Thus, use of conventional criteria leads to a bias in favour of less durable, less capital-intensive alternatives whenever the Government's marginal time preference is less than the nominal productivity of capital. In the present example, both ignoring the opportunity costs of displaced investment altogether (as in the nominal rate of return calculation) and reflecting these opportunity costs incorrectly in the discount rate (as in the present-value calculation with $i = q$) result in a decision that is inappropriate over a wide range of potentially relevant discount rates—even when appropriate allowance is made for the productivity of capital.

This is not to suggest that simple examples capture all the relevant aspects of investment decisions. Even leaving aside the distribution of benefits and costs, an example like the present one immediately introduces the question of uncertainty and many related issues. It might well be that the flexibility of the tube-well scheme would make it preferable to the surface-storage scheme at any rate of discount. Or the lack of a suitable acquifer might make the assumption of renewal of the tube well every 10 years a dubious one, and might render the above analysis irrelevant. If, for example, the acquifer would support the tube-well scheme only 10 years, the net present value of this alternative would be

$$B_{TW}^* = \sum_{t=1}^{10} \frac{0.28}{(1+i)^{10}} - \frac{0.15}{i-0.05} = \frac{0.28}{i}\left[1 - \frac{1}{(1+i)^{10}}\right] - \frac{0.15}{i-0.05}$$

Comparison of this equation with (14.38)

$$B_{SS}^* = \frac{0.24}{i} - \frac{0.15}{i-0.05}$$

makes it clear that under the present assumption, the opportunity costs of the two alternatives, being indentical, are irrelevant to the analysis, except

to provide a floor to the discount rate at which the two alternatives become desirable. Repetition of the analysis summarized in diagram 1 would now lead to the results below:

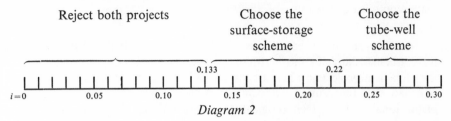

Diagram 2

The switching value of i between the two schemes now takes place at 0.22 rather than at 0.195.

Important as these issues are, the place to introduce them is not in the choice of an intertemporal criterion, where their importance is submerged in a host of other issues; rather, it is imperative that these issues be introduced specifically in a manner that allows them to be systematically integrated into the analysis.

14.11 SUMMARY

The social value, or shadow price, of investment is the net present value of the aggregate-consumption stream resulting directly and indirectly from a unit of marginal investment. In the simplest model, with no reinvestment of benefits, there are only direct benefits to take into consideration, and the shadow price of investment depends only on capital productivity and the social rate of discount at which returns are converted into present equivalents.

In more realistic models, the shadow price of investment must also reflect the consumption produced indirectly by the reinvestment of a portion of the immediate output of investment. Thus, the marginal propensity to save enters as an additional determinant of the shadow price of investment.

The shadow price of investment may vary over time, since it depends on present and future rates of capital productivity and saving, and these may vary over the planning horizon. But if the time at which the nominal capital productivity and the social rate of discount are expected to become equal is sufficiently far in the future, little distortion will be introduced by assuming a constant value for P^{inv}. In any event, a lack of data may compel such an assumption. (See appendix A to this chapter.)

The shadow price of investment is the appropriate measure of value for resources a project draws from alternative investment or for project-generated incomes ploughed back into further investment. Resources drawn from consumption and income consumed are properly valued at unity, since consumption is the unit of account. Typically, the share of capital costs borne by alternative investment will be greater than the share of project incomes devoted to investment.

When the data permit a sectoral disaggregation of investment, it may be important to distinguish between the shadow price of public investment and the shadow price of private investment. The algebra, however, becomes much more complicated because of the interdependence of the resources in the two sectors.

Our approach to benefit-cost analysis emphasizes the distribution of project benefits and costs rather than the form of project output in determining the impact of projects on investment and consumption. This emphasis reflects our view that the primary constraints on capital formation are political and institutional and not technological. In mixed economies, public and private policy can fairly easily thwart efforts to force a higher rate of saving by concentrating on "heavy" industry. The lesson to be learned from socialist development on the Soviet model is not that heavy industry creates a higher rate of saving, but that a higher rate of saving—brought about by political and institutional changes—creates the economic demand for heavy industry.

This chapter concluded with a comparison between our intertemporal criterion, which joins the social rate of discount with the shadow price of investment, and more conventional criteria. Contrary to the objections raised in some quarters, the criterion proposed here does not create any motivation to employ unreasonably low discount rates. For any increases in the present value of benefits gained thereby are more than offset by increases in the present value of costs, as reflected in the shadow price of investment. Indeed, the real purpose of the somewhat elaborate criterion proposed here emerges clearly from the examples analysed in the concluding section. This purpose is to prevent bias in favour of short-lived, non-durable investment introduced by conventional criteria in situations where the Government's marginal time preference in consumption is less than the nominal productivity of capital. The intertemporal criterion proposed here may be somewhat more difficult to apply than conventional criteria, but this difficulty is inescapable if value judgements and opportunity costs are to play their appropriate roles.

APPENDIX A

FORMULA FOR P^{inv} WHEN NATIONAL PARAMETERS CHANGE OVER TIME

To calculate P^{inv} without the simplifying assumption of constant s and q is not an impossible task. It is merely more cumbersome. The key difference is that in place of the simple formula

$$A_t = (1 + sq) A_{t-1} = (1 + sq)^{t-1}$$

we have the more complicated formula

$$A_t = (1 + s_{t-1} q_{t-1}) A_{t-1} = (1 + s_{t-1} q_{t-1}) (1 + s_{t-2} q_{t-2}) \ldots (1 + s_1 q_1) \quad (14.41)$$

the subscripts denoting rates of saving and productivity specific to each year. In place of the formula for the (constant) shadow price of investment

$$P^{inv} = \sum_{t=1}^{\infty} \frac{(1-s)\,qA_t}{(1+i)^t} \tag{14.10}$$

we have the formula

$$P_0^{inv} = \sum_{t=1}^{\infty} \frac{(1-s_t)\,q_t A_t}{(1+i)^t} \tag{14.42}$$

the subscript zero on P_0^{inv} emphasizing that the calculation is valid only for the present shadow price of investment. Substituting from (14.23) into (14.24) gives the formula

$$P_0^{inv} = \sum_{t=1}^{\infty} \frac{(1-s_t)\,q_t\,[(1+s_{t-1}\,q_{t-1})\,(1+s_{t-2}\,q_{t-2})\ldots(1+s_1\,q_1)]}{(1+i)^t} \tag{14.43}$$

Analogously, the shadow price of investment in year u, P_u^{inv}, is defined as the present value, discounted to year u, of the consumption stream directly or indirectly attributable to an investment of £1 made in year u. If we denote the capital in year t from investment in year u by $A_{t,u}$ we shall arrive at the formula

$$P_u^{inv} = \sum_{t=u+1}^{\infty} \frac{(1-s_t)\,q_t A_{t,u}}{(1+i)^{t-u}} \tag{14.44}$$

Since by extending (14.41) we have

$$A_{t,u} = (1+s_{t-1}\,q_{t-1})\,A_{t-1,u} = (1+s_{t-1}\,q_{t-1})\ldots(1+s_{u+1}\,q_{u+1}) \tag{14.45}$$

we may write (14.44) in the form

$$P_u^{inv} = \sum_{t=u+1}^{\infty} \frac{(1-s_t)\,[(1+s_{t-1}\,q_{t-1})\ldots(1+s_{u+1}\,q_{u+1})]}{(1+i)^{t-u}} \tag{14.46}$$

which subsumes (14.43) as the special case $u = 0$.

Expression (14.46) can be simplified by taking advantage of its recursive feature. If we decompose (14.46) into two sums by separating the consumption stream before and after t_0, we have

$$P_u^{inv} = \sum_{t=u+1}^{t_0} \frac{(1-s_t)\,q_t\,[(1+s_{t-1}\,q_{t-1})\ldots(1+s_{u+1}\,q_{u+1})]}{(1+i)^{t-u}} +$$

$$+ \sum_{t=t_0+1}^{\infty} \frac{(1-s_t)\,q_t\,[(1+s_{t-1}\,q_{t-1})\ldots(1+s_{u+1}\,q_{u+1})]}{(1+i)^{t-u}}$$

If we now factor

$$\frac{(1+s_{t_0}\,q_{t_0})\ldots(1+s_{u+1}\,q_{u+1})}{(1+i)^{t_0-u}}$$

out of each term in the second sum, we have

$$P_u^{inv} = \sum_{t=u+1}^{t_0} \frac{(1-s_t)\, q_t\, [(1+s_{t+1}\, q_{t+1}) \cdots (1+s_{u+1}\, q_{u+1})]}{(1+i)^{t-u}} +$$

$$+ \frac{(1+s_{t_0}\, q_{t_0}) \cdots (1+s_{u+1} q_{u+1})}{(1+i)^{t_0-u}} \sum_{t=t_0+1}^{\infty} \frac{(1-s_t)\, q_t\, [(1+s_{t-1}\, q_{t-1}) \cdots (1+s_{t_0}\, q_{t_0+1})]}{(1+i)^{t-t_0}}$$

Now look closely at everything to the right of the second summation sign; by directly applying (14.28) we have

$$P_{t_0}^{inv} = \sum_{t=t_0+1}^{\infty} \frac{(1-s_t)\, q_t\, [(1+s_{t-1}\, q_{t-1}) \cdots (1+s_{t_0+1}\, q_{t_0+1})]}{(1+i)^{t-t_0}} \qquad (14.47)$$

from which it follows that

$$P_u^{inv} = \sum_{t=u+1}^{\infty} \frac{(1-s_t)\, q_t\, [(1+s_{t-1}\, q_{t-1}) \cdots (1+s_{u+1}\, q_{u+1})]}{(1+i)^{t-u}} +$$

$$+ \frac{(1+s_{t_0}\, q_{t_0}) \cdots (1+s_{u+1}\, q_{u+1})}{(1+i)^{t_0-u}} P_{t_0}^{inv} \qquad (14.48)$$

Formula (14.48) says that the shadow price of investment in year u is equal to the sum of "joint products:" (1) the present value in year u of the consumption stream generated between year u and year t_0 and (2) the present value in year u of the capital accumulated at year t_0. The interpretation of term (1) is straightforward:

$$\sum_{t=u+1}^{T} \frac{(1-s_t)\, q_t\, [(1+s_{t-1}\, q_{t-1}) \cdots (1+s_{u+1}\, q_{u+1})]}{(1+i)^{t-t_0}}$$

is the sum of the present value of consumption generated directly and indirectly between year u and year t from the investment of £1 in year u. Term (2) perhaps needs more explanation. So consider the three factors one by one:

$$(1+s_{t_0}\, q_{t_0}) \cdots (1+s_{u+1}\, q_{u+1})$$

represents the accumulation of capital in year t_0 from a £1 investment in year u; $P_{t_0}^{inv}$ is the social value in year t_0 of each £1;

$$\frac{1}{(1+i)^{t_0-u}}$$

is the present value in year u of each £1 worth of capital in year t_0. Hence, the product of the three factors is, as asserted, the present value in year u of the capital accumulated in year t from the original investment of £1.

Formula (14.48) is particularly useful if national planning is sufficiently organized to provide estimates of the period of time it will take the economy to close the gap between the nominal marginal productivity of capital and the social rate of discount. For once q and i become equal, the shadow price of investment becomes equal to its nominal price. Symbolically, if there exists a time t_0 such that

$$q_t = i \qquad t = t_0 + 1, \, t_0 + 2, \ldots,$$

then

$$P_{t_0}^{\mathrm{inv}} = \sum_{t=t_0+1}^{\infty} \frac{(1 - s_t) \, q_t \, [(1 + s_{t-1} \, q_{t-1}) \ldots (1 + s_{t_0+1} \, q_{t_0+1})]}{(1 + i)^{t-t_0}} = 1$$

independently of the marginal propensity to save s_t. In this case formula (14.30) becomes

$$P_u^{\mathrm{inv}} = \sum_{t=u+1}^{t_0} \frac{(1 - s_t) \, q_t \, [(1 + s_{t-1} \, q_{t-1}) \ldots (1 + s_{u+1} \, q_{u+1})]}{(1 + i)^{t-u}} +$$

$$+ \frac{(1 + s_{t_0} \, q_{t_0}) \ldots (1 + s_{u+1} \, q_{u+1})}{(1 + i)^{t_0-u}} \tag{14.49}$$

Now (14.49) is easier to compute than (14.37) or (14.48) because it requires estimates of the parameters s and q over a period of t_0 years rather than over an infinite future. Equipped with the knowledge that the shadow price of investment will become equal to the nominal price of £1 after t_0 years, calculation of the current shadow price requires estimates only of (1) the year-by-year contribution to consumption between now and t_0 and (2) the capital accumulated by year t_0.

But estimates of changes in q and s even over a limited period of time may be beyond the capacity of planning organizations, including those capable of estimating the period t_0 that it will take to close the gap between q_t and i. Therefore, it may be necessary to assume that q and s retain their current values until t_0, which reduces formula (14.49) to

$$P_u^{\mathrm{inv}} = \sum_{t=u+1}^{t_0} \frac{(1 - s) \, q \, (1 + sq)^{t-u-1}}{(1 + i)^{t-u}} + \left(\frac{1 + sq}{1 + i} \right)^{t_0-u} \tag{14.50}$$

Formula (14.50) can be simplified even further by making use of the identity

$$\sum_{t=u+1}^{t_0} \frac{(1 - s) \, q \, (1 + sq)^{t-u-1}}{(1 + i)^{t-u}} = \frac{(1 - s) \, q}{i - sq} \left[1 - \left(\frac{1 + sq}{1 + i} \right)^{t_0-u} \right] \tag{14.51}$$

Substituting from (14.51) changes (14.50) to

$$P_u^{\mathrm{inv}} = \frac{(1 - s) \, q}{i - sq} \left[1 - \left(\frac{1 + sq}{1 + i} \right)^{t_0-u} \right] + \left(\frac{1 + sq}{1 + i} \right)^{t_0-u} \tag{14.52}$$

If (14.52) is used to approximate P_u^{inv}, only three parameters—in addition to i—must be estimated: s, q, and t_0.

One further point should be noted. If t_0 is large relative to u and i exceeds q, then all terms of (14.52) that are raised to the power t_0-u become negligible, and (14.52) reduces to

$$P_u^{\mathrm{inv}} \cong \frac{(1 - s) \, q}{i - sq} \tag{14.53}$$

for all u, which is to say

$$P_0^{\text{inv}} = P_1^{\text{inv}} = \ldots = P_u^{\text{inv}} = \ldots$$

This is the formula derived on the assumption of perpetual inequality between q and i, namely, formula (14.16). Thus, if the time of closing the gap between q and i is sufficiently far in the future, little distortion can be introduced by assuming that the present gap between q and i will continue in perpetuity. This is the assumption that underlies the use of (14.16) in the case studies in Part IV of these Guidelines.

APPENDIX B

THE RELATIONSHIP OF THE SOCIAL RATE OF DISCOUNT AND THE SOCIAL VALUE OF INVESTMENT TO THE RATE OF GROWTH AND THE VOLUME OF INVESTMENT

The purpose of this appendix is to pull together remarks scattered through the previous two chapters relating i and P^{inv} to the rate of growth and the volume of investment. It is equally intended to supplement those remarks with precautions designed to prevent the most obvious kinds of misinterpretation.

In chapter 13, a direct relationship between the social rate of discount and the rate of growth of *per capita* consumption was elaborated. The basic formula

$$i = -\frac{\Delta v_{t+1}}{v_{t+1}} \tag{13.21}$$

was expanded by simultaneously multiplying and dividing (13.21) by the growth rate

$$\frac{\Delta C_{t+1}}{C_{t+1}}$$

to read

$$i = -\frac{\Delta v_{t+1}/v_{t+1}}{\Delta C_{t+1}/C_{t+1}} \frac{\Delta C_{t+1}}{C_{t+1}}$$

which can be interpreted as

$i =$ (Elasticity of marginal utility) $\times$ (Rate of growth of *per capita* consumption)

or, using the symbols E and G for the elasticity and the rate of growth,

$$i = -EG$$

The elasticity of marginal utility was shown to reflect normative judgements with respect to the rate at which the marginal utility of consumption declines as the level of consumption increases. Given the elasticity of the marginal utility of consumption, the social rate of discount varies directly with the rate of growth of *per capita* consumption.

The social value of investment is more difficult to relate to the rate of growth and the level of investment. The formula

$$P^{\text{inv}} = \frac{(1 - s)\, q}{i - sq}$$

(14.16)

reminds us that the shadow price of investment depends on marginal rates of saving and capital productivity as well as on the social rate of discount. Thus, quantitative specification of the relationship of all three parameters to the rates of growth and investment is required. Rather than following this tack, we shall analyse the social cost of investment, which, as chapter 14 pointed out, is equal to the social value of investment when the level of investment is optimal. This relationship is more straightforward. If additional investment becomes harder and harder to mobilize as the level of investment increases—whether for political, institutional, or technological reasons—the social marginal cost of investment rises with the level of investment. This we believe to be the typical case, so long as the political, institutional, and technological environments remain unchanged.

So we can state two rules that will be generally valid so long as policy makers' value judgements remain unchanged, and so long as the political, institutional and technological conditions under which the economy operates remain constant. *First, the social rate of discount will vary directly with the rate of growth of per capita consumption. Second, if the rate of investment is optimal, the shadow price of investment will vary directly with the level of investment.*

As for the interpretation of these rules, the most obvious question to ask is whether an increase in the level of investment brought about by policy changes designed to increase the rate of growth will lead to increases in i and P^{inv}. Naive application of our rules might lead one to believe so. But the reality is that changes in the level of investment or the rate of growth almost always result from a combination of changes in the political judgements governing growth and development and changes in the political, institutional or technological environments. Thus, the assumptions required for one to be able to infer changes in i and P^{inv} from changes in the level of investment and the rate of growth are virtually always violated. If, for example, a new Government comes to power and decides to emphasize growth and development more than its predecessor, it does not follow that the social rate of discount and the shadow price of investment should be increased. For the shift of political power will first of all lead to changes in the value judgements underlying the elasticity of the marginal utility of consumption; with E changing at the same time as G, it no longer follows from the formula

$$i = - EG$$

that an increase in G implies an increase in i. And if the shift in political power is sufficiently radical, the political and institutional environment may change to such a great extent that the marginal cost of investment is changed

substantially at every level of investment. Thus, it is conceivable that the old lower level of investment and the new higher level might both be "optimal", but "optimal" with respect to different value judgements and different constraints. In such a case nothing can be inferred about the direction of change in P^{inv} accompanying an increase in the level of investment.

Chapter 15

THE SHADOW WAGE
IN A SURPLUS-LABOUR ECONOMY

15.1 INTRODUCTION

In textbook models of perfect competition, the market wage rate is the appropriate shadow price for labour, just as any market price is the appropriate shadow price for a good or service. In the dreamworld of neoclassical theory, there is no involuntary unemployment, and the wage is equal to the productivity of the marginal worker. So the market wages measure the opportunity cost of labour to the public sector, the social value of the goods lost by adding another worker to the public-sector payroll.

But Part I of these Guidelines suggested several reasons why the market wage is an inappropriate price for social evaluation of employment in the presence of widespread underemployment and unemployment. First, the wage rate obviously does not reflect the opportunity cost of an unemployed man; to a first approximation, the economy loses nothing apart from the disutility of work, from the creation of new jobs. Second, redistribution accompanies new jobs. This redistribution has two aspects. To the extent that (1) the immediate gainers (the formerly unemployed) save less than the immediate losers (capitalists, employed workers, civil servants), and (2) the shadow price of investment exceeds one, the redistribution reduces the present value of aggregate consumption, and employment thus represents a positive cost in terms of aggregate consumption. In other words, though the direct opportunity cost of employment in terms of aggregate consumption—the first approximation—may be zero, there is in general an indirect opportunity cost whose magnitude depends on the propensities to save of the newly employed and others in the economy, as well as on the shadow price of investment. On the other hand, higher weights may be attached to the income of the newly employed than to the income of more prosperous members of the community, either on the basis of a redistribution objective or on the basis of an employment objective.[41]

---

[41] The difference between the two was explored in chapter 8 of Part II. In brief, the redistribution objective values employment because it puts income in the hands of the poor, while the employment objective values it because unemployment is socially undesirable even apart from the poverty that usually accompanies it.

This chapter is in the main devoted to translating these general considerations into quantitative measures of the shadow price of labour. As background to this, however, a few remarks on the meaning of surplus labour are undoubtedly in order.

15.2 THE MEANING OF "SURPLUS LABOUR"

In some models of economic development, surplus labour has been identified only with visible unemployment, or with underemployment so pronounced that the marginal productivity of labour is zero. In particular, it has been argued that in peasant agriculture, population pressure is often so great that agricultural employment could be substantially reduced without reducing agricultural output. This has led other economists to charge that the concept of surplus labour is an empty one, in the sense that few if any actual economies fulfil this definition. The ensuing debate over whether the marginal productivity of labour in agriculture or in traditional services (of which the shoeshine boy, the pedicab driver and the lottery-ticket vendor are archetypes) is literally zero is very likely a monument of irrelevance. For the definition of surplus labour in terms of unemployment or zero marginal productivity is rightly to be understood as a simplification of the kind that is made in all theorizing, and not as a literal description of the economies that the theory attempts to describe.

The essence of surplus labour lies in the gap between the market wage in the organized, capitalistic sectors of the economy and the social value of the marginal product of labour in the rest of the economy, and not in the value of the marginal product *per se*. Of course, if perfect competition prevailed in the rest of the economy—in peasant agriculture, services and similar activities—as well as in the capitalist sector, and if the rate of saving were socially optimal, the market mechanism could be relied upon to equate the marginal product to the wage.

But in the traditional "rest of the economy", incomes are not in general determined by the rules of perfect competition. The incomes of self-employed members of a peasant family, for example, are not determined by wages equal to the marginal productivity of a man-hour multiplied by the number of hours each works, plus "dividends" equal to their respective shares of the product imputed to family land and capital. Rather, the allocation of income and work is determined by traditional rules of behaviour that are in all probability modified only slightly by the personalities and productivities of the various members of the particular family in question.

Economic relationships outside the family are probably equally complicated within traditional societies. In any event it is certain that employment bargains are not the impersonal exchanges of labour-power against goods that they are in a capitalist economy. Therefore, there is no reason to expect that wage rates and marginal productivities will be equal within traditional societies even where there is a "market" for labour that nominally resembles the market

for labour in the capitalistic sector. The owner of a small plot may prefer to work his own land intensively even if this implies a marginal productivity of labour much below the going agricultural wage, if the alternative of wage labour on a large landlord's holding implies political and social obligations that put him in a dependent status and reduce his prestige below that of one who works only his own land. But the same peasant may insist on a wage from industry at least equal to the average productivity of labour on his small holding, if this is what he would forgo by abandoning his traditional occupation, residence and claim on the family enterprise.

In short, the coexistence of traditional and capitalist sectors can be expected to produce the essential feature of surplus labour—the existence of underemployment in the traditional sectors. One has to be careful with the term "underemployment". Underemployment does not mean that people have nothing useful to do. Still less does it mean that there are not enough workers in these sectors. (Quite the opposite!) Rather, people are underemployed in traditional sectors if the social value of their marginal product is less than the wage rate the Government must pay them for public-sector employment, which will generally be determined by the wage rate in the advanced, capitalistic sector of the economy. In addition—but this is not a necessary condition of surplus labour—there may be significant numbers of workers without any employment whatsoever. These potential workers will in general be concentrated in the shanties and slums of large cities, living off the largesse of their more fortunate brothers, cousins, and friends who have managed to find work.

Surplus labour thus refers primarily to a pool of unskilled labour. This does not, however, limit the applicability of the concept to employment in which only the most primitive abilities are required, like pick-and-shovel work on a road gang. Many jobs in the public sector or in private industry require skills that can be learned in a matter of weeks or months, and the concepts developed here for the evaluation of surplus labour are relevant to the evaluation of the costs of such semi-skilled employment as well as to the evaluation of labour costs for "totally" unskilled work. Indeed, higher rates of unemployment among the educated classes are not unknown in developing economies. The growth of jobs suitable for high school and college graduates often does not keep pace with the spread of education, especially since suitability is as much culturally as economically determined.

15.3 DIRECT OPPORTUNITY COST

We shall take up, in order, each of the three considerations that determine the shadow price of labour: the direct opportunity cost, the indirect cost and the redistribution of income.[42] The first, the direct opportunity cost, is perhaps the most tractable from a conceptual point of view and the least tractable from the point of view of empirical measurement. In a word, the direct

---

[42] See chapters 6 and 7 for a preliminary discussion of this.

opportunity cost of public-sector employment is the social value of the marginal product forgone by adding a worker to the public payroll. If the creation of a new job in the public sector actually increases total employment, so that directly or indirectly the effect of hiring an additional worker in the public sector is to reduce unemployment, the identification of the direct opportunity cost is conceptually and empirically easy: no product is forgone, so the direct opportunity cost is zero. However, when the primary problem is one of underemployment rather than visible unemployment, the identification remains conceptually easy but becomes empirically difficult. The social value of the marginal products forgone remains the measure of the direct opportunity cost, but it becomes exceedingly difficult to measure this parameter. If it is assumed that the forgone output would have been entirely consumed, it becomes possible to ignore the ramifications involved in the differential (social) values of investment and consumption and to identify the social value of the marginal product with the market value of marginal product.

But this simplification helps only a little; the estimation of the private marginal productivity of labour, in capitalistic or traditional sectors, is itself a formidable task. Probably nothing less than a detailed study of the consequences for production of withdrawing labour from traditional sectors will provide a suitable framework for estimating direct opportunity costs. (The design of such a study is beyond the scope of these Guidelines.) Suffice it to say that project formulation and evaluation cannot wait until one is satisfied that the requisite study has been properly designed and carried out. In the meantime, crude approximations must suffice. One approximation is the incomes of individuals in traditional sectors who possess only their own labour power, lacking capital and land; for example, the wages paid landless labourers in agriculture, or the net incomes of pedi-cab drivers who divide the gross with the cab owner. The wage income of landless labour is, for reasons suggested earlier, likely to overestimate the marginal productivity of the smallholder. But so long as the direction of bias is clear, the use of traditional-sector wages that overestimate the marginal productivity may be a suitable first approximation to the direct opportunity cost, particularly if these wage rates are sufficiently below the capitalistic- or public-sector wage that there is no danger of obscuring the gap between wage payments by public authorities and the direct opportunity cost of the labour employed on public projects.

In many countries, it should be emphasized, these problems of estimation are irrelevant. As has been indicated, when overt unemployment or under-employment is so widespread that one can be reasonably confident that nothing is being forgone as a result of new public-sector employment, the opportunity cost can be taken to be zero.

We shall designate the direct opportunity cost of labour by the parameter z. In what follows, we shall assume that z is less than the capitalistic-sector wage, w, which we shall suppose is the relevant wage for industrial projects in the public sector.

15.4 INDIRECT COSTS: EFFECTS ON THE RATE OF SAVING

We turn our attention now to the indirect cost incurred by public-sector employment, as a result of the reallocation of resources in favour of consumption that typically accompanies expansion of employment. Central to the analysis of this reallocation is the concept of the shadow price of investment, a concept analysed in the previous chapter. The shadow price of investment takes on a special form in the labour-surplus economy, which is derived in the following manner:

If a unit of investment creates ℓ jobs,[43] then the annual increment to the income of capitalists[44] is equal to the nominal profit rate

$$y - w\ell,$$

where y measures the annual increment to output provided by one unit of capital[45] and $w\ell$ measures the wage bill associated with the marginal unit of capital. If capitalists save a fraction s^{cap} of their incomes and consume the remainder, the aggregate-consumption value of their annual income from a marginal unit of investment is

$$P^{\text{inv}} s^{\text{cap}} (y - w\ell) + (1 - s^{\text{cap}}) (y - w\ell) \tag{15.1}$$

In addition, if workers save nothing, the consumption they derive from a marginal unit of investment is measured by

$$(w - z)\ell \tag{15.2}$$

If we add the two together, the aggregate-consumption value of the income generated by a unit investment is

$$P^{\text{inv}} s^{\text{cap}} (y - w\ell) + (1 - s^{\text{cap}}) (y - w\ell) + (w - z)\ell \tag{15.3}$$

The shadow price of investment can be defined as the present value, at the social rate of discount, of the entire stream of aggregate-consumption increments represented by (15.3).

If the labour surplus is sufficiently large that the parameters of (15.3) can be treated as constant over-all future time (a special case), we can derive the shadow price of investment from the formula for the present value of a perpetuity, as in equation (14.19). That is, P^{inv} is the ratio of (15.3) to the social rate of discount, i:

$$P^{\text{inv}} = \frac{P^{\text{inv}} s^{\text{cap}} (y - w\ell) + (1 - s^{\text{cap}}) (y - w\ell) + (w - z)\ell}{i} \tag{15.4}$$

If we now solve (15.4) for P^{inv}, we obtain the result

$$P^{\text{inv}} = \frac{(1 - s^{\text{cap}}) (y - w\ell) + (w - z)\ell}{i - s^{\text{cap}} (y - w\ell)} \tag{15.5}$$

---

[43] ℓ in other words is the marginal labour: capital ratio.
[44] In this text "capitalist" is used as a short notation for "owners of capital".
[45] y is thus the incremental output: capital ratio.

One word of caution is in comparing (15.5) with the corresponding results of chapter 14. The propensity to save utilized here, s^{cap}, is the propensity to save out of capitalists' income. This is to be contrasted with the over-all propensity to save, denoted s, employed in chapter 14. The parameter s is, of course, smaller than s^{cap}, since it is an average of propensities to save throughout the economy, including the propensity to save out of wages, which is assumed to be zero in the present model. Moreover, the parameter y here measures the incremental output: capital ratio, which is equal to the direct social yield of capital, denoted q in chapter 14, only if $z = 0$. More generally, the relationships between the variables appropriate to the surplus-labour situation and the variables utilized in the more abstract discussion of chapter 14 are given in the following formulae:

$$y - z\ell = q,$$

and

$$s^{\text{cap}} (y - w\ell) = sq$$

so that

$$(1 - s) q = (1 - s^{\text{cap}}) (y - w\ell) + (w - z) \ell$$

Now that we have, in formula (15.5), an appropriate expression for the shadow price of investment in the surplus-labour economy, we can measure the indirect costs of employment. Suppose that the cost of additional public-sector employment is financed in increased taxation of capitalists, which reduces their consumption and investment in the ratio $(1 - s^{\text{cap}}) : s^{\text{cap}}$. Under these circumstances public-sector employment implies a transfer of income from capitalists to workers equal to the wage bill. For each worker who receives a wage of w, capitalists suffer a loss in after-tax income of w.

The effect on current aggregate consumption of this transfer is positive: capitalists' consumption declines by $(1 - s^{\text{cap}}) w$ and workers' consumption rises by w. If our attention were riveted blindly on the present, we should count this transfer as a benefit, even without considering that workers' consumption ought to receive a greater weight than capitalists' because of their lower standard of living. But the aggregate-consumption objective places a weight on current investment equal to the discounted present value of future contributions to consumption attributable to the marginal unit of investment. And for reasons explored at length in the previous chapter, this weight, the shadow price P^{inv}, is likely to exceed one. When the loss of current investment entailed by reducing capitalists' income by w is taken into account, the aggregate-consumption value of the income reduction becomes

$$[(1 - s^{\text{cap}}) + P^{\text{inv}} s^{\text{cap}}] w \tag{15.6}$$

instead of $(1 - s^{\text{cap}}) w$. The expression $(1 - s^{\text{cap}}) w$ continues to measure the current reduction in aggregate consumption and $P^{\text{inv}} s^{\text{cap}} w$ measures the aggregate-consumption value of the reduction in investment. Against the loss measured by (15.6) must be counted the increased consumption of the additional worker, namely, w. If we subtract w from (15.6), the indirect cost of employment due to the transfer of income from capitalists to workers becomes

$$[(1 - s^{\text{cap}}) + P^{\text{inv}} s^{\text{cap}}] w - w = s^{\text{cap}} (P^{\text{inv}} - 1) w \qquad (15.7)$$

The shadow wage, including direct and indirect effects, is thus

$$w^* = z + s^{\text{cap}} (P^{\text{inv}} - 1) w \qquad (15.8)$$

Expression (15.8) requires further explanation. It defines a shadow wage with respect to a single objective, aggregate consumption. Surprisingly, perhaps, this shadow wage may exceed the nominal wage even in the presence of unemployment so widespread that the direct opportunity cost is zero. If, for example, $s^{\text{cap}} = 0.5$ and $P^{\text{inv}} = 3.0$, w^* will be at least $1.5w$ (more if z is positive). The reason for this seemingly paradoxical result is that the market wage does not reflect the effects on investment of the transfer of income from capitalists to workers. When these effects are taken into account, the aggregate-consumption cost of employment easily may exceed the nominal wage.

This does not mean that employment is socially less desirable than the market indicates. For one thing, the costs of all goods and services, not just labour, must be consistently evaluated. In choosing among alternative ways of constructing or operating a project, the relevant question is not the absolute cost of labour, but its cost relative to the cost of capital; measured in terms of aggregate consumption, this relative cost will in general be less than the relative cost indicated by uncorrected market values.[46] Equally important, aggregate consumption is but one objective, and the effects of a redistribution of income from capitalists to workers should not be ignored in a calculation of national economic profitability.

---

[46] Consider, for example, a choice between alternative construction techniques governed by cost-minimization considerations. With respect to commercial profitability, the relative costs of utilizing a unit of capital and utilizing one worker is the ratio of the profit rate to the wage rate:

$$\frac{y - w\ell}{w}$$

With respect to national profitability, the analogous (aggregate-consumption) costs are the social marginal productivity of capital,

$$\text{SMP} = s^{\text{cap}} P^{\text{inv}} (y - w\ell) + (1 - s^{\text{cap}}) (y - w\ell) + (w - z) \ell \qquad (15.3)$$

and the shadow wage rate,

$$w^* = z + s^{\text{cap}} (P^{\text{inv}} - 1)w$$

whose ratio is

$$\frac{\text{SMP}}{w^*} = \frac{[s^{\text{cap}} P^{\text{inv}} + (1 - s^{\text{cap}})] [y - w\ell] + (w - z) \ell}{z + s^{\text{cap}} (P^{\text{inv}} - 1) w}$$

Now subtracting $(w - z\ell)$ from the numerator and adding $w - z$ to the denominator, we obtain the inequality

$$\frac{\text{SMP}}{w^*} > \frac{[s^{\text{cap}} P^{\text{inv}} + (1 - s^{\text{cap}})] [y - w\ell]}{[s^{\text{cap}} P^{\text{inv}} + (1 - s^{\text{cap}})] w} = \frac{y - w\ell}{w},$$

which shows that the ratio of capital to labour costs is higher when costs are measured with respect to the aggregate-consumption objective than when costs are measured with respect to commercial profitability. Thus, under conditions of surplus labour, cost-minimization will in general dictate substituting labour for capital when the national criterion of aggregate consumption is substituted for the private criterion of commercial profits.

15.5 REDISTRIBUTIONAL BENEFITS AND COSTS

If income-redistribution objectives are pursued in project choice, unemployed and underemployed workers will generally be one of the groups whose consumption is accorded a greater social weight than consumption in the aggregate. If we incorporate this consideration into the computation of the shadow wage, the logic that led to (15.8) must be modified; the aggregate-consumption cost continues to be measured by

$$z + s^{\text{cap}} (P^{\text{inv}} - 1) \, w \tag{15.9}$$

but we must add appropriate redistributional weights to the gains and losses of workers and capitalists. If we suppose, for the moment, that capitalists are accorded a neutral redistributional weight of 0.0, capitalists are fully taken account of in (15.9). This leaves workers' consumption to be added in a second time, with a redistributional premium of v. The newly employed workers' immediate gain is

$$w - z \tag{15.10}$$

But against this gain must be counted the loss of future wages due to the reduction in private investment. As the rate of capital formation decreases, so do future employment and future wages. For each unit of investment forgone, ℓ jobs are forgone in perpetuity, each of which would produce a net annual consumption increment of $w - z$. The present value of workers' forgone consumption, assuming the weight on workers' consumption relative to aggregate consumption remains constant over the entire future, is P^{wkr}, defined by

$$P^{\text{wkr}} = \frac{(w - z) \, \ell}{i - s^{\text{cap}} (y - w\ell)} \tag{15.11}$$

The loss for each present job created in the public sector is the product of the loss per unit of investment displaced, P^{wkr}, and the loss of investment per job created, $s^{\text{cap}} \, w$. Thus, the present value of future workers' consumption forgone for each job created today in the public sector is

$$P^{\text{wkr}} \, s^{\text{cap}} \, w \tag{15.12}$$

The aggregate-consumption value of this loss is

$$v \, P^{\text{wkr}} \, s^{\text{cap}} \, w \tag{15.13}$$

The net gain to workers is the difference between (15.10) and (15.13)

$$v \, (w - z) - v \, P^{\text{wkr}} \, s^{\text{cap}} \, w \tag{15.14}$$

The net social cost of employment is the difference between (15.9) and (15.14)

$$w^* = z + s^{\text{cap}} (P^{\text{inv}} - 1) \, w + v \, [z + (s^{\text{cap}} \, P^{\text{wkr}} - 1) \, w] \tag{15.15}$$

If (15.15) is compared with (15.8) it is clear that even the direction of the impact on the shadow wage of introducing redistribution objectives explicitly

into the calculation cannot be predicted *a priori*, without explicit knowledge of the parameters i, s^{cap}, y, w, ℓ, and z. Only when s^{cap} is unity, so that capitalists' consumption disappears from the calculus, is the effect on w^* of including redistribution unambiguous. In this case, the shadow wage is increased proportionately to the redistributional weight, v.

Separating redistributional costs from the aggregate-consumption costs may be conceptually desirable in that it shows clearly the role of each of the elements that determine the social cost of employment. However, this separation relies on what must be admitted to be a gratuitous assumption, namely, that capitalists' consumption counts in the same manner as other groups not singled out for special attention, for example, skilled workers and middle-class peasants. It can be argued even on orthodox precedent that capitalists should receive a special redistributional weight—a negative one in view of their high initial level of consumption, with respect to which increments are computed.

If capitalists are accorded a non-zero redistributional weight, the shadow wage represented by (15.16) ceases to be relevant because the shadow price of investment computed according to (15.4) and (15.5) is no longer relevant. P^{inv} measures the present value of consumption generated by a unit of investment without regard to recipient. But the relevant parametrization is now in terms of capitalists' consumption and workers' consumption, with the shadow price of consumption workers forgo in the future defined by (15.11) and the shadow price of capitalists' future forgone consumption by

$$P^{cap} = \frac{(1 - s^{cap})\,(y - w\ell)}{i - s^{cap}\,(y - w\ell)}$$

The formulae for P^{wkr} and P^{cap} both assume a constant weight on capitalists' consumption relative to aggregate consumption.

The present value of the effects of employment on capitalists' and workers' consumption must take into account present as well as future changes in consumption. For workers, the present change is positive, $w - z$. For capitalists, there is a loss, equal to $(1 - s^{cap})$. Formulae comprehending both present and future effects are presented in table 15.1.

TABLE 15.1   THE EFFECTS OF EMPLOYMENT ON CONSUMPTION OF DIFFERENT CLASSES

Capitalists' consumption	Workers' consumption
$-\,[(1 - s^{cap}) + s^{cap}\,P^{cap}]\,w$	$-\,[z + (s^{cap}\,P^{wkr} - 1)\,w]$

If redistribution premiums of v^{cap} and v^{wkr} are assigned to the two categories of consumption, the shadow wage becomes

$$w^* = [1 + v^{cap}]\,[(1 - s^{cap}) + s^{cap}\,P^{cap}]\,w +$$
$$+ [1 + v^{wkr}]\,[z + (s^{cap}\,P^{wkr} - 1)\,w] \qquad (15.16)$$

210 GUIDELINES FOR PROJECT EVALUATION

Presumably policy makers will judge capitalists' consumption to be marginally no more valuable than aggregate consumption, so that $v^{cap} \leq 0$, and workers' consumption to be no less valuable than aggregate consumption, so that $v^{wkr} \geq 0$. At one extreme, the Government might be indifferent to distribution, with

$$v^{cap} = v^{wkr} = 0$$

In this case expression (15.16) reduces to (15.8), since

$$P^{inv} = P^{wkr} + P^{cap}$$

At the other extreme, a strongly egalitarian Government may judge capitalists' consumption to be socially valueless, at least at the margin, which is to say

$$v^{wkr} \geq 0; \; v^{cap} = -1$$

In this case (15.16) reduces to

$$w^* = (1 + v^{wkr}) [z + (s^{cap} P^{wkr} - 1) w] \tag{15.17}$$

Equation (15.17), it has been noted, cannot even be given a definite algebraic sign *a priori*. With redistribution included, the cost of employment can be positive or negative, depending on the values of s^{cap} and P^{wkr}.

15.6 EXTENSIONS OF THE ANALYSIS

The analysis elaborated thus far is limited by the various simplifying assumptions made along the way, particularly the assumption that all parameters remain constant over time and the assumption that all saving, at least at the margin, is done by capitalists' organizations and individuals. We could relax these assumptions in the manner described in appendix A to chapter 14 and produce formulae for nonconstant parameters. We could also apply the arguments of chapter 14 to the case where both the capitalist class and the Government save, and the two are linked by the fact that one source of government saving is taxes on the private sector. The first exercise is sufficiently mechanical that little understanding, and hence little improvement of these Guidelines, is to be gained by it.

The second is perhaps less mechanical, but it may be even more devoid of content in the sense that the formulae that emerge involve parameters that are not likely to be measurable for years to come—if ever. Thus, the assumption that saving is done by capitalists must be understood to limit the relevance of the shadow wage as calculated here to transfers of resources from the private sector to the public sector. In other words, the shadow wage as measured by (15.15) or (15.16) measures the social cost of labour for a public project when the impact of the accompanying redistribution is borne by the capitalist sector.

So long as capitalists are assigned a neutral distribution weight of zero, the analysis can, however, be applied without significant modification to the case where both public and private investment are affected by a marginal public-sector project. It is only necessary to assume that the marginal rate

of saving and the nominal rate of profit are the same for the Government as for private capitalists. With this assumption, the shadow wage measures the social cost of labour independently of whether the public project in question competes with other public projects or with capitalists for the resources it utilizes. In place of (15.15), in which capitalists are assigned a neutral redistributional weight equal to zero, we have

$$w^* = z + \bar{s}\,(P^{\mathrm{inv}} - 1)\,w + v\,[z + (\bar{s}\,P^{\mathrm{wkr}} - 1)\,w] \qquad (15.18)$$

where

$$P^{\mathrm{inv}} = \frac{(1 - \bar{s})\,(\bar{y} - w\bar{\ell}) + (w - z)\,\bar{\ell}}{i - \bar{s}\,(\bar{y} - w\bar{\ell})} \qquad (15.19)$$

and

$$P^{\mathrm{wkr}} = \frac{(w - z)\,\bar{\ell}}{i - \bar{s}\,(\bar{y} - w\bar{\ell})} \qquad (15.20)$$

In these expressions, the parameter $\bar{s}$ represents the (common) marginal rate of saving of the Government and the capitalist class, which are assumed between them to do all the saving. The parameters $\bar{y}$ and $\bar{\ell}$ are assumed to measure common marginal output : capital and labour : capital ratios.

The distributional neutrality towards resources drawn from profits that characterizes (15.18) is more reasonable if these resources are drawn from the public sector rather than from the private sector. In any event, formula (15.18) is probably the best that we can do. To modify (15.16), in which the neutrality assumption is abandoned, to fit the present case would require us to apply the same redistributional weight assigned to resources withdrawn from other public projects as is applied to resources taken from private capitalists.

15.7 SUMMARY

The market wage may fail to measure the social cost of labour for three reasons. First, in traditional sectors of the economy, labour is not allocated or rewarded according to textbook principles of competitive markets. So even in the absence of visible unemployment, there may be a gap between the direct opportunity cost, the marginal productivity of labour outside the capitalist sector, and the wage that private capitalists and the Government are obliged to pay. The presence of visible unemployment makes the argument all the more imposing without changing its form: the marginal productivity of an unemployed person is zero, so a gap exists *ipso facto* between the wage and the direct opportunity cost.

Second, expansion of public-sector employment generally involves a transfer of income from capitalists to workers, a transfer that reduces investment and expands consumption. So long as the shadow price of investment exceeds one, this transfer creates an indirect cost that must be added to the direct opportunity cost in calculating the shadow wage.

Third, the same transfer changes the time distribution of workers' consumption. Present consumption is increased, but future consumption

reduced as a result of the reduction in the rate of investment. If a special redistributional weight is attached to workers' consumption, the present value of the changes in workers' consumption must be included, with an appropriate weight, in the calculation of the social cost of labour.

If the burden of employment expansion entailed by a given project is entirely borne by capitalists, a strong case can be made for reducing the shadow wage by placing a negative redistributional weight on the present and future consumption losses of capitalists. This complicates the algebra; the shadow price of investment is defined as the present value of consumption generated by a unit of investment—without regard to its distribution—and consequently must be replaced by separate shadow prices of capitalists' and workers' consumption. But no new parameters are involved. So operationally, if not conceptually, reflection in the shadow wage of a negative redistributional weight on capitalists' consumption poses no difficulties beyond the formidable ones posed by the calculation of direct and indirect aggregate-consumption costs, and the determination of redistributional weights.

Strictly speaking, the formulae presented here are limited in applicability to the analysis of expansion of public-sector employment at the expense of private capital formation and capitalists' consumption. To apply these formulae to projects that draw resources from elsewhere in the public sector, it is necessary to assume that the Government's marginal rate of saving is the same as the marginal rate of saving of private capitalists, and that common marginal output : capital and labour : capital ratios obtain in the public sector and the private (capitalistic) sector. Such assumptions must strike the reader as heroic, but it is unlikely that the data likely to become available over the next decade will allow much improvement over this assumption. At such time as it becomes possible to differentiate between public and private saving rates, output : capital ratios and labour : capital ratios, it will be easy enough to recast the formulae developed here to take the differences into account.

Finally, a word about the magnitude of the shadow wage relative to the market wage is in order. The fact is that we can say very little *a priori*. Only the direct opportunity cost can generally be assumed to be smaller than the market wage. Once indirect costs and redistributional weights are taken into account, it is entirely possible that the shadow wage will exceed the market wage. This does not, however, mean that public projects should be more sparing of labour than a calculation of private profitability would indicate. Shadow prices must be used consistently throughout the formulation and evaluation of public projects for the calculation of national economic profitability to be meaningful. Specifically, in choosing between alternative techniques for constructing a public project, the calculation of the social cost of capital goods must also reflect the indirect effects on investment and the distribution of consumption as well as the direct effects on output. In general, the relative social costs of labour and capital will favour employment of people over machines more than their relative costs as measured by market prices.

Chapter 16

THE VALUE OF FOREIGN EXCHANGE

16.1 WHY DO OFFICIAL EXCHANGE RATES UNDERVALUE FOREIGN CURRENCIES?

It is difficult to think of a developing country that is content with its balance of payments. Most place considerable emphasis on improving the foreign exchange situation both in the formulation of general economic policies and in the choice of specific projects. Yet the emphasis on increasing exports and decreasing imports is matched by confusion and uncertainty on how to integrate a due concern for the balance of payments into calculations of national economic profitability.

One approach would be to consider contributions to the balance of payments a distinct objective (a merit want) on a par with aggregate consumption and income distribution. Alternatively, and we shall consider this alternative first, amelioration of a country's foreign-exchange position can be viewed solely as instrumental to the aggregate-consumption objective.[47] In this case, foreign exchange earnings are amenable to evaluation solely on terms of the aggregate consumption that foreign exchange makes available, which obviates the need to introduce new value judgements to compare contributions to the balance of payments with contributions to domestic income. To the extent that foreign exchange is viewed at the margin simply as instrumental to aggregate consumption, the numerical value of a unit of foreign exchange is a shadow price, not a weight like the social rate of discount or the weight on redistribution to disadvantaged groups.

But why, in this case, is there any need for a shadow price? Why doesn't the official exchange rate perform adequately in translating foreign currency (let us say "francs") into domestic currency ("rupees")? One might point to the "free" market discounts that exist for the currencies of many developing countries as good reason for rejecting official rates as indicators of the domestic value of foreign exchange. And it is tempting to do so. For if the value of foreign exchange is determined by the ratio of its price in free markets to the official price, the problem of determining the shadow price of foreign exchange can be solved by periodic perusal of the financial pages of the more internationally minded of the world's daily newspapers.

---

[47] See the preliminary discussion in section 9.3.

Alas, such a view of the shadow price of foreign exchange is naive in the extreme. The reasons for rejecting the official exchange rate are more basic than the discounts that exist in many markets, as witness the fact that countries whose currencies trade at par in free markets are in general as concerned with the balance of payments as countries whose currencies sell at substantial discounts.

In part, the reasons for the almost universal existence of a balance-of-payments problem in developing countries is the result of development itself. The process of development increases the demand for imported capital goods that are beyond the productive capacities of most developing countries. In part, however, the disproportionate increase in demand for foreign exchange is the result of the inequalities that characterize the distribution of income in many developing countries rather than the result of development pure and simple. As incomes rise, the demand for consumer goods rises. The more skewed the income distribution, the greater the proportion of increases in demand that are channelled towards imported goods. And the more skewed the income distribution, the less is the likelihood that the Government will be able to take effective measures to curb the demand of the more affluent sections of the society, for Governments tend to rely most heavily on the support of the affluent when the income distribution is highly skewed. Indeed, the most that many Governments are able to do is to channel the demand for imports towards the domestic market, and even this method of conserving scarce foreign exchange frequently turns out to be illusory. Projects of "import substitution" nominally designed to produce consumer goods domestically often turn out on close examination to require significant amounts of imported raw materials or intermediates and to make no significant impact on the balance-of-payments problem. Automobile "production" that hardly goes beyond assembly of parts manufactured abroad is an example that has been repeated throughout the developing world. Such projects in fact often do more harm than good, since they conceal the drain of resources and allow affluent consumers to utilize quantities of scarce foreign exchange that would be politically intolerable if they were visible.

Whereas the demand for imports of capital goods is thus endogenous to growth and the demand for imports of consumer goods (or components) is endogenous to free market growth, there is no built-in mechanism for expanding exports to balance the pressures to increase imports. As "hewers of wood and drawers of water" for the industrially advanced countries, the poorer countries are faced with markets that in the aggregate expand slowly over time, so that major efforts are required of a country even to maintain the value of its exports of primary products. Prodigious efforts are necessary to initiate non-traditional exports at any substantial level.

The balance-of-payments problem reveals itself in a variety of ways apart from a discount on a country's currency. Most developing countries have found it necessary to devalue their currencies periodically, to erect substantial tariff barriers and provide export subsidies, or to place quotas

or outright prohibitions on some categories of imports; and many countries have found it necessary to rely on all these instruments, one at a time or jointly.[48] The need to resort to any of these policies is symptomatic of an undervaluation of foreign currencies in relation to the domestic currency: a rupee's worth of francs provides goods worth more than a rupee in terms of aggregate consumption. In consequence, the shadow price of foreign exchange appropriate to project formulation and evaluation exceeds its nominal price.

16.2 CALCULATING THE SHADOW PRICE OF FOREIGN EXCHANGE

A simple example will both illustrate this point and indicate a general procedure for determining the shadow price of foreign exchange. Suppose that as foreign exchange becomes available at the margin it is used to import French cognac at a c.i.f. price of FF15 per bottle. Suppose further that at the official rate of exchange, one franc is worth two rupees, so the official c.i.f. cost of a bottle of cognac is Rs30. Finally, suppose that there are no taxes of import duties on cognac, but that it is sufficiently scarce that its domestic market-clearing price is Rs45. In this case an additional FF15 of foreign exchange—Rs30 at the official exchange rate—permits the importation of a good whose domestic value in terms of aggregate consumption is Rs45. In other words, each rupee's worth of foreign exchange—"worth" measured at the official rate of exchange—provides goods worth Rs1.5—"worth" measured in terms of domestic willingness to pay. The shadow price of foreign exchange is thus Rs1.5 per rupee.

The principle can be generalized to any number of commodities. Let f_i be the fraction of foreign exchange allocated to the ith of n commodities at the margin. And let P_i^D represent the domestic market-clearing price, that is, the price reflecting the marginal willingness to pay for the ith import. Finally let P_i^{cif} represent the c.i.f. price in rupees calculated at the official rate of exchange. Then f_i/P_i^{cif} represents the quantity of the ith import that will be purchased if an extra rupee of foreign exchange (FF0.5) becomes available. For example, if three tenths of marginal foreign exchange earnings are allocated to cognac, then each rupee's worth of foreign exchange will provide

$$0.30 \times \frac{1}{30} = 0.01$$

bottles of cognac. In other words, it takes Rs100 worth of foreign exchange to provide a bottle of cognac if only 30 per cent of foreign exchange is allocated to cognac.

---

[48] Moreover, many developing countries have relied on foreign private investment or on foreign aid to balance their international accounts and are either unwilling—because of the "strings" inevitably attaching to foreign ownership or aid—or unable—because of a lack of suitors—to continue this dependence in the future. To the extent that unwillingness rather than inability is the issue, the premium of foreign exchange reflects a merit want and is therefore as much a political judgement as the weights discussed in earlier chapters. For the present we shall confine ourselves here to the value of foreign exchange in terms of aggregate consumption.

Now the quantities of good $1, \ldots, n$,

$$\frac{f_1}{P_1^{\text{cif}}}, \ldots, \frac{f_i}{P_i^{\text{cif}}}, \ldots, \frac{f_n}{P_n^{\text{cif}}}$$

have the respective unit values

$$P_1^D, \ldots, P_i^D, \ldots, P_n^D$$

in terms of aggregate consumption. The total aggregate-consumption value of the imported goods is therefore

$$P_1^D \frac{f_1}{P_1^{\text{cif}}} + \ldots + P_i^D \frac{f_i}{P_i^{\text{cif}}} + \ldots + P_n^D \frac{f_n}{P_n^{\text{cif}}}$$

with

$$f_1 + \ldots + f_i + \ldots + f_n = 1$$

This expression defines the shadow price of foreign exchange, which we shall denote P^F from here on. Equivalently, P^F can be written

$$P^F = \sum_{i=1}^{n} f_i \frac{P_i^D}{P_i^{\text{cif}}}, \tag{16.1}$$

which is to say that the shadow price of foreign exchange is a weighted average of the ratios of market-clearing to official c.i.f. prices, the weights reflecting the content of the marginal import bill.

Conceivably, enhanced earnings of foreign exchange might relieve the pressure to export rather than being totally utilized to expand imports. This can be accommodated within our general procedure by treating reductions in exports as increases in imports. Let

$$x_{n+1}, \ldots, x_i, \ldots, x_{n+h}$$

represent the rupee amount by which each of h exports falls in response to earnings of foreign exchange; let P_i^D represent the market-clearing price of export i; and let P_i^{fob} represent the f.o.b. price at the official rate of exchange. Then, in place of formula (16.1), we have

$$P^F = \sum_{i=1}^{n} f_i \frac{P_i^D}{P_i^{\text{cif}}} + \sum_{i=n+1}^{n+h} x_i \frac{P_i^D}{P_i^{\text{fob}}} \tag{16.2}$$

with

$$\sum_{i=1}^{n} f_i + \sum_{i=n+1}^{n} x_i = 1$$

Just as P_i^D and P_i^{cif} will differ only in the presence of tariffs or import controls, so will P_i^D and P_i^{fob} differ only in the presence of export subsidies or export quotas. In general, we would judge that the x's are likely to be small relative to the f's. It is usually imports that respond to changes in the availability of foreign exchange, not exports. But Governments that are successfully

promoting exports to the extent that home industries or consumers are seriously deprived by shortages of domestically produced goods may respond to a marginal increment of foreign exchange by relieving these shortages, and formula (16.2) comprehends this possibility.

16.3 ACTUAL VERSUS OPTIMAL TRADE POLICY

Straightforward as formulae (16.1) and (16.2) may appear at first glance, many important assumptions implicitly underlie them. First, consistent with the general approach of these Guidelines, these formulae for the shadow price of foreign exchange are based on actual and projected trade policies, not on optimal policies. A simple example will illustrate this point. Suppose that, at the margin, foreign exchange is divided between two imports, cognac and transistor radios. That is, in our general formula, let $n = 2$. (For this exercise, assume that exports are at the margin unresponsive to foreign exchange availabilities: all the x's are equal to zero.) Let transistor radios sell for Rs70 c.i.f. at the official exchange rate and Rs140 in the domestic market. Let foreign exchange be divided at the margin between cognac and transistor radios in the ratio $3 : 7$, so that $f_1 = 0.3$ and $f_2 = 0.7$. In this case, formula (16.1) gives the shadow price of foreign exchange as

$$P^F = f_1 \frac{P_1^D}{P_1^{\text{cif}}} + f_2 \frac{P_2^D}{P_2^{\text{cif}}} = 0.3 \frac{45}{30} + 0.7 \frac{140}{70}$$

or

$$P^F = 1.85$$

Now it can be argued that if the Government is following a trade policy that is optimal with respect to aggregate consumption, it is mistaken in allocating foreign exchange to cognac. It should allocate all foreign exchange, at the margin at least, to transistor radios and none to cognac. For with $f_1 = 0$ and $f_2 = 1.0$, the value of foreign exchange becomes

$$P^F = 1.0 \frac{140}{70} = 2.0$$

It might appear, therefore, that project formulation should be based on the higher shadow price, and the shortcomings of trade policy called to the attention of the trade authorities.

We take a different view in these Guidelines. First of all, while our primary focus in this chapter is on the relationship between foreign exchange and aggregate consumption, trade policy is formulated in terms of a wider range of goals and in response to the pressures of various interest groups. The notion of an "optimal" trade policy cannot be interpreted so narrowly as optimal with respect to aggregate consumption.

In reality, however, it is doubtful that the notion of an optimal trade policy is a useful one in the contexts for which these Guidelines are designed. It seems more useful to consider the trade policies that developing countries

follow as the outcome of a bargaining process between various interest groups, foreign and domestic, inside the Government and outside. In our view, only a Candide would label the outcome of this bargaining process as optimal. Marginal allocations of foreign exchange are likely to reflect these same conflicts rather than a deliberate and conscious policy aimed at maximizing the contribution to a well-defined objective function subject to well-articulated constraints. Project analysis should, in our view, reflect what will (or, more realistically, what is likely to) happen, not what ought to happen. The shadow price of foreign exchange thus depends on how increments of foreign exchange will be divided among alternative uses, not on the wishful thinking of the project analyst who perceives (or misperceives) the irrationality of the over-all policy framework in which he operates. Only when "what is" is approaching "what ought to be" with sufficient speed that transition problems can be ignored is it appropriate to base the shadow price of foreign exchange (or any other shadow price) on a perception of what ought to be. To us it seems more appropriate to regard the allocation of foreign exchange at the margin as a given parameter of project decisions than to regard the allocation vector as a choice variable. This assumption reflects the general viewpoint of these Guidelines: that the appropriate realm for project formulation and evaluation is the tactical, not the strategic.

16.4 THE EFFECTS OF "REVERSE IMPORT SUBSTITUTION"

A second assumption implicit in the formulae we propose for calculating the shadow price of foreign exchange is that the increments to supplies measured by the ratios

$$\frac{f_1}{P_1^{\text{cif}}}, \ldots, \frac{f_n}{P_n^{\text{cif}}}, \frac{x_{n+1}}{P_{n+1}^{\text{fob}}}, \ldots, \frac{x_{n+h}}{P_{n+h}^{\text{fob}}}$$

are net additions. It could be otherwise: increases of imports could lead to a reallocation of domestic factors of production, so that the ultimate impact of a marginal rupee's worth of foreign exchange could be very different from that indicated by formulae (16.1) and (16.2). Take our one-commodity example. The implicit assumption in this example is that marginal imports of cognac add to the economy's consumption of liquor. But if the domestic production of brandy were to fall by one bottle every time an additional bottle of imported cognac became available, and the resources were to be used for production of table grapes, the ultimate effect of increasing the availability of foreign exchange would—assuming away differences in quality and price between the domestic and imported liquor—be the aggregate-consumption value of the table grapes that additional imports of cognac indirectly made available, not the value of the cognac itself.[49]

---

[49] Under certain circumstances, specifically when the marginal costs of the goods involved in the substitution chain are equal to their respective prices, the calculations are unaffected by these substitutions. Formulae (16.1) and (16.2) would therefore continue to hold irrespective of whether imports are substituted for domestic production.

We shall assume, with one important exception, that no such "reverse import substitution" takes place, in other words, that marginal imports in general represent net additions to the economy-wide supplies of the commodities in question. The exception is for capital goods.

To assume that the net availability of capital goods is affected at the margin by the availability of foreign exchange would be to assume that the rate of capital formation, the rate of investment, is constrained by the balance of international payments. This is a popular view and a frequently heard justification for foreign aid. But in our view it generally results from a misunderstanding. To be sure, the content of imports and the volume of exports are related to the rate of investment. The direction of causality, however, generally runs opposite to the line of the argument to the effect that investment depends on the availability of foreign exchange. It is our view that throughout most of the developing world, political and institutional constraints determine the rate of investment. (Foreign aid may be important in certain situations, but its importance is more because it puts resources in the hands of Governments whose class basis or timidity prevents them from raising resources domestically than because the resources that external aid makes available are foreign.) These political and institutional constraints prevent Governments from taking actions that would substantially reallocate resources from consumption to investment, and these constraints act for the most part independently of whether the resources at issue are foreign or domestic.

In other words, we are arguing that the appearance of capital goods in the marginal import bill is, for purposes of analysing the value of foreign exchange, illusory. In countries with reasonably well-developed capital goods industries, the import of capital goods substitutes for domestic production. And in most countries, whether or not in possession of capital goods industries, the statistical relationship between imports and capital formation is the result of the simultaneous dependence of both on income. As countries get richer, they both save and import more, and some of the increased savings is reflected in increased imports. It is not increases in foreign exchange that of themselves make greater capital formation possible, but the increases in domestic income, which are normally highly correlated with increases in exports as well as imports. Foreign exchange is often more valuable in terms of aggregate consumption than the official rate of exchange indicates, but not, at least not very often, because the rate of investment is inhibited by a lack of foreign exchange.

Indications of the degree to which our view of the relationship between foreign exchange and the rate of investment is or is not appropriate to any particular country may be obtained by studying the country's sources and uses of foreign exchange. To the extent that a country imports consumer goods or intermediates utilized in the domestic manufacture of consumer goods, foreign exchange could be made available for the importation of capital goods. To this extent it is the political power of the consumers and manufacturing interests that depend on imports that constrain the rate of

capital formation, not a lack of foreign exchange itself. To the extent that a country refrains from taking actions (like subsidies) to promote exports out of a fear of the inflationary consequences of restricting domestic supplies of the exported goods, it is once again political constraints that determine the proportion of national income allocated to investment, not independent constraints on the availability of foreign exchange.

If our view of the general relationship of the availability of foreign exchange to the rate of investment accords with the facts of a country's experience, the impact of a project on the rate of saving is determined by the size and distribution of the income it generates, not by its impact on the balance of payments. Hence, it is appropriate to exclude imports of capital goods from the calculations of the marginal import bill in formulae (16.1) and (16.2). The allocation vector $(f_1, \ldots, f_n)$ should be limited to consumer goods and intermediates used for the production of consumer goods so that, with this restriction, either

$$\sum_{i=1}^{n} f_i = 1$$

or

$$\sum_{i=1}^{n} f_i + \sum_{i=n+1}^{n+h} x_i = 1$$

depending on whether or not exports are thought to be sensitive to the availability of foreign exchange from other sources.

16.5 EFFECTS OF FOREIGN EXCHANGE ON THE GOVERNMENT'S CONTROL OF RESOURCES

There is one way in which earnings of foreign exchange may augment the rate of investment that the argument we have presented does not take fairly into account. If the foreign exchange a project earns affects the distribution of income between the public and private sectors differently than other earnings, and if the rate of investment is sensitive to the distribution of income, it is appropriate to reflect this feature of foreign exchange earnings in project formulation and evaluation.

That political and institutional constraints inhibit the Governments of most developing countries from extracting resources from its citizens through taxation is well known. Many poor countries would tax more and spend more on collective consumption activities as well as on capital formation if it were felt to be politically feasible. But those who have the most capacity to pay also have the most capacity to resist taxation or to evade it. And institutions such as the family farm or business make it difficult to establish an effective taxation system, offering as they do all kinds of possibilities for evading taxes that are unavailable to salaried personnel. In this context, indirect taxes, especially taxes on imports and exports, are important instruments of public finance and are an important means by which Governments win control of resources from the private sector. Thus, the transfer of income

that results from tariffs, export duties and the monopoly profits of government enterprises engaged in international trade may play a significant role in project formulation and evaluation.

It is important to emphasize that this role is logically distinct from the role of the shadow price of foreign exchange. First of all, the transfer of resources from the private to the public sector does not affect the direct value of foreign exchange, which formulae (16.1) and (16.2) are designed to reflect. These formulae hold independently of whether the Government or the private sector reaps the gains from differences between the c.i.f. prices of imports calculated at official exchange rates and their market-clearing prices. Second, the arguments made here apply equally to goods produced wholly for domestic markets on which the Government, by virtue of an excise tax or a monopoly, effectuates transfers from the private to the public sector. But since the relative administrative and political ease of taxing imports and exports makes these goods bear a heavy burden of taxation in developing countries, the present chapter is an appropriate place to analyse the effect of such transfers on project formulation and evaluation.

At issue is the point made in chapter 14 that resources in the hands of the Government may have a different value from resources in the hands of the private sector. To deal with this possibility, separate formulae were developed for the shadow prices of public investment[50]

$$P^{\text{gov}} = \frac{(1 - s^{\text{gov}}) \, q^{\text{gov}}}{i - s^{\text{gov}} \, q^{\text{gov}}}$$

and private investment[51]

$$P^{\text{pri}} = \frac{(1 - s^{\text{pri}}) \, q^{\text{pri}} \, (1 - m)}{i - s^{\text{pri}} \, q^{\text{pri}} \, (1 - m)} + \frac{(1 - s^{\text{gov}}) \, q^{\text{pri}} \, m}{i - s^{\text{pri}} \, q^{\text{pri}} \, (1 - m)} +$$

$$+ \frac{s^{\text{gov}} \, q^{\text{pri}} \, (1 - s^{\text{gov}}) \, q^{\text{gov}} \, m}{[i - s^{\text{pri}} \, q^{\text{pri}} \, (1 - m)] \, [i - s^{\text{gov}} \, q^{\text{gov}}]}$$

In these formulae P^{gov} and P^{pri} are the respective shadow prices of Government and private investment; s^{gov} and s^{pri} are respective propensities to save out of government and private income; q^{gov} and q^{pri} are respective productivities of government and private capital, each assumed to be recaptured (except for taxes) by the sector making the investment; i is the social rate of discount; and m is the marginal effective tax rate on private income.

Now let u_i measure the sum of indirect taxes (import duties, excises and the like) and monopoly profits of public importing concerns, per unit of the ith import. Then u_i / P_i^{cif} measures the transfer of income from the private sector to the Government for each rupee's worth of foreign exchange allocated to the ith import. And

---

[50] See equation (14.24).
[51] See equation (14.28).

$$T = \sum_{i=1}^{n} f_i \frac{u_i}{P_i^{\text{cif}}}$$

represents the total transfer of income from the private to the public sector per rupee's worth of foreign exchange, on the assumption that all increments of foreign exchange are allocated to imports, that is, on the assumption

$$\sum_{i=1}^{n} f_i = 1$$

(The treatment of imports is symmetric. If increased availability of foreign exchange reduces exports, and if r represents the per unit subsidy for the ith export, then

$$T = \sum_{i=1}^{n} f_i \frac{u_i}{P_i^{\text{cif}}} + \sum_{i=n+1}^{n+h} x_i \frac{r_i}{P_i^{\text{fob}}}$$

with

$$\sum_{i=1}^{n} f_i + \sum_{i=n+1}^{n+h} x_i = 1)$$

In a project's aggregate-consumption account, foreign exchange earnings of Rs100 would then show up in two places. First, these earnings would show up in terms of their direct value, $P^F \times 100$. Second, these earnings would lead to intersectoral flows whose net contribution to aggregate consumption would be

$$(s^{\text{gov}} P^{\text{gov}} - s^{\text{pri}} P^{\text{pri}}) T \times 100$$

That is, assuming publicly generated consumption has the same value as the private consumption it displaces, the net value of the transfer depends on the difference between the value of public and private investment, weighted by the respective marginal propensities to invest.

One important technical qualification should be mentioned here. To the extent that the transfer takes the form of the profits of a government trade monopoly rather than the form of taxes, the calculation of marginal profits must take account of the elasticity of domestic demand. If an additional bottle of cognac can be sold by a government cognac monopoly only by reducing the price slightly, the loss of profit on every bottle of cognac must be taken into account. Ignoring the variable costs of operating the government cognac monopoly, the correct formula for measuring the marginal profit of importing cognac is

$$u_1 = MR_1 - P_1^{\text{cif}}$$

where MR_1 is the marginal revenue from cognac; MR_1 is in turn given by the formula

$$MR_1 = \left(1 + \frac{1}{e_1}\right) P_1^D,$$

in which e_1 represents the (negative) elasticity of domestic demand for cognac. In the limiting case of an infinitely elastic demand (that is, when the demand

schedule is horizontal), the marginal revenue reduces to the market-clearing price; with $e_1 = -\infty$, we have

$$u_1 = P_1^D - P_1^{cif}$$

We emphasize the role of the elasticity of demand in this context because it is one of the few places where, apart from large changes in supplies, the slope of demand curves affects the analysis of national economic profitability. The reason elasticities matter here and not elsewhere is that, in the calculation of aggregate-consumption benefits and costs, losses of producers' surplus generally cancel gains in consumers' surplus, leaving only the (usually) inconsequential surplus on the increments to total supplies. But here it is precisely the difference in the value of resources in the hands of the Government (the "producer" of cognac) and resources in the hands of the private sector (the consumer) that engages our attention.

In the analysis of transfers, intermediate goods pose a special question: If the final product (say, automobiles) is subject to a significant excise in addition to or instead of the duty on imported intermediates (components in automobile manufacture), are the taxes on the final product properly reflected in the calculation of the transfer? The answer is a qualified "yes". If domestic production of a good depends at the margin on imported components, it is appropriate to credit the excises levied by the Government on the finished product to marginal imports of components. If, for example, expansion of domestic production of automobiles depends on imported engines, the excise tax levied on the cars produced with engines financed out of marginal supplies of foreign exchange is properly included in the transfer-of-resources calculation.

One final word on taxes and government profits from international trade is appropriate. The operational significance of transfers is limited by the ability to distinguish between the value of resources in public and private hands. Transfers cannot be reflected in project formulation and evaluation until meaningful data on sectoral propensities to save and capital productivities have been gathered and analysed. For most countries this is well in the future.

16.6 RATIONING

Up to now it has been implicitly assumed that imported goods are distributed through the market mechanism, even though decisions as to which goods to import may not be left to the market. The weight of this assumption is reflected in the fact that the prices $P_1^D, \ldots, P_n^D$ are market-clearing prices reflecting domestic willingness to pay. If an import is rationed domestically, its market price underestimates the willingness to pay for the good. In the presence of rationing, it is necessary to simulate demand curves in order to estimate willingness to pay.

This is easier said than done. One might hope to impute the demand for rationed intermediates (for example, components of automobiles or radios)

from the market prices of the non-rationed final goods into whose production they enter. Unfortunately, the stringent conditions that must be met for such an importation procedure to be valid are unlikely to be realized in practice. If a competitive producer utilizes rationed imports, and if all other inputs are purchased in competitive markets, the residual surplus that remains after deducting the costs of production (including normal competitive profits) can be attributed to the rationed imports. An imputed willingness to pay for these imports can be calculated as the sum of the actual payments under rationing and the residual surplus.[52]

Alas, this method of imputing willingness to pay breaks down if producers are not perfect competitors, and they generally are not. With production dominated by oligopolies and monopolies, it is impossible to separate the surplus earned on privileged access to a rationed import from other sources of profit, a separation that is possible under competitive conditions because of the possibility of estimating normal profits and treating this category of surplus like a cost of production. By contrast, a "normal" oligopoly or monopoly profit does not even exist in principle.

The best operational procedure is probably to eliminate rationed goods from the calculation of formulae (16.1) and (16.2) entirely. The weights $(f_1, \ldots, f_n, x_{n+1}, \ldots, x)$ on the remaining goods must then be adjusted so that they add up to unity.

16.7 FOREIGN EXCHANGE AS A MERIT WANT

Up to now we have looked upon foreign exchange solely as an instrument, as a means to the goal of aggregate consumption. From this standpoint, the shadow price of foreign exchange reflects the marginal value of foreign resources independently of how debits and credits on international account are brought into balance. In other words, the shadow price of foreign exchange, P^F, answers the question, "Given the level and composition of imports and exports, either actual or prospective, what is (will be) the value in domestic terms of the goods that a marginal unit of foreign exchange would make available?" Nowhere does this analysis put the question "What is the appropriate level of imports, in the light of export possibilities and the prospects of covering trade deficits by foreign aid or private capital inflows?" In effect, to treat foreign exchange as instrumental to aggregate consumption is to assume that an optimal balance has been struck between the aggregate-consumption objective, redistribution objectives, and the objective, to which most countries pay at least formal allegiance, of independence from the strings that inevitably attach to foreign aid or foreign private investment.[53]

---

[52] See section 5.4.

[53] The only gesture towards realism in this formulation is the assumption that the marginal import bill is determined by considerations other than aggregate consumption, so that the allocation of foreign exchange between commodities is not necessarily the allocation that would maximize the value of foreign exchange in terms of aggregate consumption.

If we revert for the sake of simplicity to our assumptions that exports are fixed exogenously and that a single import receives all foreign exchange available at the margin, the relationship between the instrumental nature of foreign exchange and the optimality of the balance between objectives can be shown very simply. Figure 22 shows a hypothetical feasibility frontier, FF, analogous to the feasibility frontier introduced in chapter 11, but relating the total availability of foreign exchange for imports (rather than regional consumption, which was the second objective considered in chapter 11) to the level of aggregate consumption. Our procedure for calculating the shadow price of foreign exchange amounts in this simple model to calculating the slope of the feasibility frontier at a given point, such as A. For the slope of FF, equal to 1.5 in the present example, represents the amount by which aggregate consumption increases when foreign exchange is increased by an amount equal to Rs1 at the official rate of exchange.

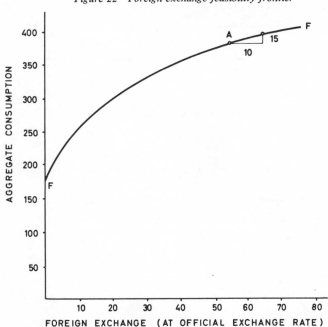

Figure 22   Foreign exchange feasibility frontier

The important point for present purposes is that to infer a shadow price from the slope of a feasibility frontier at a specific point like A is, barring exceptional circumstances,[54] to assume that the point A represents an optimal mix of objectives. The superimposition of equal-welfare curves, as in figures 23 and 24, makes this clear. In figures 23 and 24 over-all social well-being increases as we move to the north or northwest, in the direction of the arrow. Figure 23's

---

[54] Such as a straight-line feasibility frontier or an adjustment of domestic production to changes in imports of the kind ruled out in section 16.4.

Figure 23   Equal-welfare curves and feasibility frontier

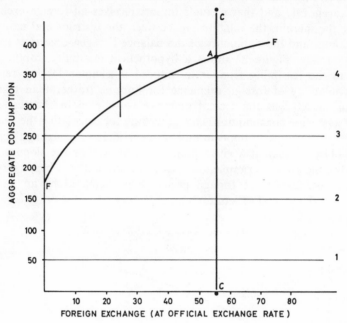

Figure 24   Equal-welfare curves and feasibility frontier

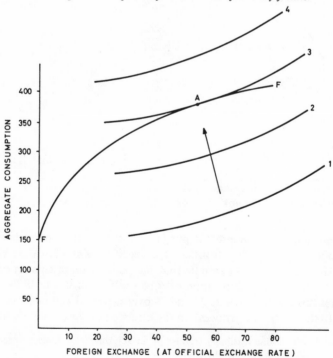

equal-welfare curves say that the more aggregate consumption, the greater is over-all well-being. Figure 24 says additionally that well-being increases inversely with the amount of foreign exchange that the economy utilizes—not, we should emphasize, because foreign trade is judged to be a social evil, but rather because the economy is assumed to depend at the margin on foreign aid and foreign private investment to finance imports. In figure 23 constraints on foreign aid and private investment, reflected in the vertical line marked CC, are assumed to put the economy at the point A. In figure 24 the equal-welfare curve labelled "3" is tangent to FF at A. In both cases point A represents the highest level of well-being attainable, and—what matters for project formulation and evaluation—the marginal value of foreign exchange can be inferred from the slope of FF, or more generally by formulae (16.1) and (16.2) without the need for additional judgements by policy makers.

Now, contrast figure 25 with figures 23 and 24. Here the equal-welfare curve at A has a slope of 2.5, indicating a willingness to sacrifice 2.5 rupees' worth of aggregate consumption to reduce foreign exchange utilization (and, more specifically, the accompanying strings) by one rupee. Thus, earnings of foreign exchange produced by projects or foreign exchange costs incurred by projects should be evaluated at Rs2.5 per rupee rather than the Rs1.5 that represents the equivalent in terms of aggregate consumption. In the situation described in figure 25 foreign exchange earnings or savings have

Figure 25   Equal-welfare curves and feasibility frontier

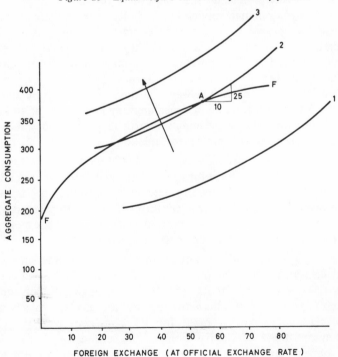

value as a merit want over and above their value in providing aggregate consumption.

In principle, it may be possible to elicit from policy makers in advance of project formulation and evaluation the weight W^F to be placed on foreign exchange, considered a merit want. But for reasons spelled out in chapters 11 and 12, we think it an unrealistic demand to place on policy makers, at least for the time being. Instead, we propose to reverse the direction of information flow. Just as with the redistributional weight and the social rate of discount, we propose that, where foreign exchange is considered a merit want, alternative designs be formulated whenever significant differences in the impact on the balance of payments appear to be realizable by varying one feature or another of a project's design. Benefits and costs in terms of foreign resources should be counted separately from benefits and costs in terms of domestic resources, and no attempt should be made at the formulation stage to aggregate the impacts on the two kinds of resources.

The implications for the weight on foreign exchange appear during the evaluation and choice stage of project planning. Just as choice between alternative water-distribution schemes would reveal a range of weights on the benefits to poor peasants relative to aggregate-consumption benefits in the example of chapter 12, and choice between alternative techniques of irrigation would reveal a range of social discount rates in the example of chapter 14 so would the choice among alternatives that differ with respect to their impact on foreign and domestic resources reveal the range in which the weight on foreign exchange implicit in the choice between these alternatives lies. Conceivably, repeated choices among competing designs, coupled with systematic dialogue between technicians and policy makers to reveal the sources of apparent inconsistencies between the choices, may narrow the range of the weight to an interval that for operational purposes can be reduced to a single number. From that point in time onwards, a point in time, to be sure, that lies well in the future, information can meaningfully flow from the top downwards; that is, weights can be meaningfully articulated by policy makers to guide technicians charged with project formulation.

So far in this discussion we have assumed that at the very least it is known whether foreign exchange is valued for its own sake as a merit want in addition to its instrumental value in increasing aggregate consumption. It must be admitted, however, that sometimes project formulation has to proceed without even this knowledge. The rhetoric of pronouncements on public policy may well obscure rather than enlighten this basic distinction.

Fortunately, a variant of the bottom-up procedure of inferring weights from actual decisions can be employed to test whether foreign exchange is valued as a merit want and for its contribution to aggregate consumption. The first step is to formulate alternative designs for several projects and to determine a reasonably narrow range for W^F consistent with the choices made from among these alternative designs. The second step is to calculate the shadow price P^F according to the procedures elaborated in the preceding

sections. The final step is to compare the results of the two exercises. If the range determined in step one for W^F includes the value calculated for P^F, it is reasonable to conclude that foreign exchange is important for its own sake as well as for its contribution to aggregate consumption.[55]

16.8 SUMMARY

There are two ways of viewing foreign exchange in the calculation of national economic profitability. First, foreign exchange can be viewed simply as instrumental to aggregate consumption; the value of foreign exchange is then the amount of aggregate consumption that would be obtainable with a unit of foreign exchange. Second, foreign exchange earnings or savings can be regarded as a goal in themselves prized over and above their contribution to aggregate consumption. Presumably elevation of foreign exchange to the status of a merit-want objective reflects a desire to reduce the influence of foreign Governments or capitalists implicit in reliance on foreign aid or foreign private investment to finance trade deficits.

In the event that foreign exchange is regarded only as instrumental to aggregate consumption, its value can be reflected in a shadow price that requires no judgement additional to the basic one that foreign exchange is purely an instrument. This shadow price can be calculated by the weighted average of the ratios of domestic market-clearing prices to c.i.f. prices calculated at the official rate of exchange. The appropriate weights are the fractions of foreign exchange allocated at the margin to the various imports.

To the extent that the effects of foreign exchange earnings at the margin include a reduction of the pressure to export, the increased availability of domestic supplies of exportable goods must find expression in the calculation of the shadow price of foreign exchange. The aggregate-consumption value of the supplies of exportable goods released to the domestic market is measured by the ratio of domestic market-clearing prices to f.o.b. prices (at the official exchange rate), and the weight attached to each export is the monetary value, measured in domestic currency at the official exchange rate, of the increases in domestic supplies of the good that takes place in response to a unit increase in the availability of foreign exchange.

It is important to emphasize as well as to list the assumptions that lie behind this formulation of the shadow price of foreign exchange, for these assumptions indicate both the limitations of the present formulations and its strengths. In first place is the assumption that it is the actual and projected allocations that matter in determining the shadow price, not a hypothetical optimum that differs from what is and what is likely to be. The rationale of this assumption is that project formulation and evaluation must be conceived

---

[55] A value of P^F lying above the range of merit-want values of foreign exchange suggests that policy makers in fact judge foreign exchange to be less valuable than its instrumental usefulness in terms of producing aggregate consumption. Since, in principle, P^F is a lower bound for the value of foreign exchange, such a finding would indicate a fundamental error in one of the sets of calculations.

of as tactical rather than strategic decisions, and in general it can be expected that these decisions take place in an over-all environment that is more likely to reflect the conflicts, resolved and unresolved, of various classes and interest groups rather than a consciously articulated strategy of maximization subject to well-defined constraints. Project formulation and evaluation, in short, are tactical decisions, but it is less than certain, to put it mildly, that a coherent strategy, much less an optimal one, underlies the tactics.

The effect of this assumption is to render meaningless—from the point of view of project decisions—calculations of the value of foreign exchange based on hypothetical allocations demonstrably superior to the actual or projected allocation in terms of their impact on aggregate consumption. This is not to say that such calculations have no point whatsoever; they may be useful in analysing and rationalizing trade policy, for example. But the appropriate basis for calculating the shadow price of foreign exchange with respect to project formulation and evaluation is the manner in which foreign exchange will in fact be allocated at the margin, not how it ought to be.

Other assumptions underlying our procedure for calculating the shadow price of foreign exchange are more technical in nature. For one thing, it is assumed that at the margin foreign exchange is allocated directly or indirectly to consumption goods and that marginal imports represent net additions to the supplies of goods available domestically. The idea behind the assumption that foreign exchange is allocated to consumption goods is that the rate of investment is determined in the first instance politically and institutionally, and that subject to these political and institutional constraints the chief determinant at the margin of savings is income and its distribution. Thus, the impact of project earnings on investment is through its impact on income, not through its impact on foreign exchange. The consumption goods and intermediates imported at the margin are assumed to represent net additions to domestic supplies in order to obviate the need for analysing the chain reaction of effects that would follow from "reverse import substitution" (substitution, at the margin, of imports for domestic production).

Additionally, it is important to note that the shadow price of foreign exchange measures only the direct impact on aggregate consumption of improvements in the balance of payments. Indirect effects will be significant for Governments that rely heavily on imports as sources of revenue for financing public investment, assuming that it is possible to differentiate the propensity and value of public investment from the propensity and value of private investment. In principle, at least, there is no difficulty in measuring the value of the transfer of resources from the private to the public sector that accompanies an increment of foreign-exchange earnings.

Finally, the calculation of the shadow price of foreign exchange in terms of a weighted average of domestic to international prices presupposes that domestic prices reflect marginal willingness to pay. This in turn has the effect of assuming away rationing or other non-market techniques of distributing imports. For although it is theoretically possible to simulate demand curves

and thereby to simulate willingness to pay, operationally it does not seem feasible to do so. The more practicable procedure appears to be to exclude rationed goods from the calculation altogether, and to adjust the weights on imports (and exports) so that they continue to add up to one.

A quite different approach to the whole question of evaluating foreign exchange begins from the judgement that weakening the strings attaching to foreign-capital inflows, whether those inflows take the form of government loans or grants or the form of private investment, is an achievement worth a sacrifice of aggregate consumption. To make this assumption operative at the level of project formulation and evaluation, it is sufficient to assume that, at the margin, foreign-exchange earnings replace foreign-capital inflows, and that the amount of aggregate consumption policy makers are willing to sacrifice to reduce foreign-capital inflows by one unit exceeds the aggregate-consumption value (that is, the shadow price) of foreign exchange.

This is tantamount to assigning merit-want status to earnings of foreign exchange. The value of foreign exchange thus becomes a weight reflecting a direct judgement, rather than a shadow price whose value can be calculated on the basis of prior judgements. As with other weights, we do not believe it operationally feasible to expect policy makers to initiate the design process by specifying the value of the weight on foreign exchange. Instead of such a "top-down" process, we propose a "bottom-up" process in which the flow of information is reversed: technicians should prepare alternative designs wherever significant scope exists for varying foreign exchange earnings or savings by altering one of the features of a project's design. Choice by policy makers of one alternative over others implies a range of weights, namely, the range in which the chosen variant is more "profitable" than the rejected alternatives. Besides sharpening the differences between alternatives, this process serves to focus policy makers' attention on the significance of their decisions in terms of conflicts between the objectives that projects are designed to further. Hopefully, repeated application of this bottom-up version of the design process will also narrow the range of the foreign exchange weight sufficiently that a top-down process of designing projects in terms of pre-assigned weights becomes feasible.

Chapter 17

CO-ORDINATION OF INVESTMENT DECISIONS

17.1 CO-ORDINATION THROUGH MARKET PRICES AND NATIONAL PARAMETERS

The methodology of social benefit-cost analysis proposed in these Guidelines for calculating national economic profitability is an example, *par excellence*, of what economists call partial-equilibrium analysis. Central to this approach is the assumption that projects can be meaningfully analysed one at a time, without tracing the entire chain of effects step by step. In the language of engineering, our approach amounts to analysing each project as a "free body".

Obviously, "projects" that are intimately linked in physical terms cannot be analysed as "free bodies". Steelmaking and steelworking projects cannot be meaningfully judged independently because the profitability (both commercial and national) of one may depend critically on the existence of the other. Such investments can be analysed only as a unit, as a single "free body".

But including investments with important physical linkages together as single projects does not solve the problem of co-ordination. Projects so defined still compete with each other for the same resources and provide outputs that are at least partially substitutable for one another. Social benefit-cost analysis does not ignore these interactions. Rather, it seeks to summarize the interactions between a particular project and the rest of the economy in a set of parameters: market prices (corrected as need be by the methods outlined in Part II) and national parameters. Thus, the effects of a proposed textile mill on the economy are taken into account not by a minute examination of the project's impact on the production, foreign trade, distribution and consumption of every good in the economy, but by an analysis of the net income generated to the Government, private capitalists and workers, now and in the future.

In the main it is assumed that market prices, corrected for the most flagrant deviations from willingness to pay, reflect relative values with sufficient accuracy to be useful in project formulation and evaluation. National parameters supplement market prices by providing a means of evaluating the differential impact of income that is saved from income that is consumed; the differential social impact of income that accrues to the rich from income

232

that accrues to the poor; the differential impact of income generated in the form of foreign exchange from income in the form of domestic currency; and, finally, the differential impact of "income" that takes the form of merit wants from income in general. These national parameters reflect value judgements, as required, on the distribution of consumption over time and among classes and regions, as well as the importance of paying for imports with exports rather than foreign debt, whether economic or political, and the importance of specific merit wants that may be relevant. National parameters provide information about the rest of the economy that is essential for formulating and evaluating any single project, but that the project-level planner is in no position to gather for himself.

17.2 An example of the derivation of a national parameter from a national plan: the shadow price of investment

Because national parameters combine in varying degrees factual information about the economy and judgements about the relative importance of various objectives, we have distinguished *weights*, which are the direct expression of values, from *shadow prices*, which depend on weights but require no new judgements for their estimation. Thus, the social rate of discount is a weight; it expresses a judgement on the relative importance of present and future consumption. The social value of investment, by contrast, is a shadow price; it depends on factual information about the productivity of capital and the propensity to save as well as on the social rate of discount, but requires no value judgement additional to the one embodied in the social rate of discount.

In one sense, however, the distinction between the two classes of national parameters may be misleading. All national parameters, whether weights or shadow prices, are expressions of the impact of projects on the economy as a whole that are valid only at the margin, only for small changes in the quantities with which they deal. The value judgement on income distribution reflected in a premium on peasants' or workers' incomes depends on the extent to which peasants and workers lag behind the middle and upper classes. If in spite of, or as a result of, over-all government policy the relative position of peasants and workers deteriorates, it is reasonable to place a higher premium on their incomes than would be justified under more egalitarian conditions.

This means that national parameters cannot be meaningfully articulated in a vacuum. Whether a top-down or a bottom-up version of project formulation and evaluation is envisioned, national parameters can be articulated only in the light of over-all development tendencies and trends. National parameters, in short, depend on an overview of the economy, which, because of the durability implicit in the very notion of an investment project, must include a forecast of the future.

This is one of the main links between project planning and national planning in the present methodology. As chapters 11 and 12 suggested, a national plan can provide the reference point for the marginal evaluations

and judgements on the future that national parameters embody. Let us examine how this might work in a simplified but concrete example, now that weights and shadow prices have been described in sufficient detail to make the connexion between project and national planning reasonably clear.

Take, for instance, the shadow price of investment, as formulated at the end of our discussion of the labour-surplus economy:

$$P^{\text{inv}} = \frac{(1 - \bar{s})\,(\bar{y} - w\bar{\ell}) + (w - z)\,\bar{\ell}}{i - \bar{s}\,(\bar{y} - w\bar{\ell})} \qquad (17.1)$$

where $\bar{s}$ is the common marginal propensity to save out of private profit and public-sector income; $\bar{y}$ is the common marginal output: capital ratio of the advanced sectors of the economy; w is the wage rate; z is the direct opportunity cost of labour, reflecting the loss of output in the economy's traditional sectors; and $\bar{\ell}$ is the marginal output: capital ratio of the advanced sectors. Finally, i is the social rate of discount. In this simple formulation, all these parameters are assumed to be constant over time, and all but the social rate of discount reflect the factual state of the economy rather than a direct value judgement.

Any national plan worthy of the name contains important information about the factual parameters $\bar{y}$, $\bar{\ell}$, and $\bar{s}$. Indeed, $\bar{y}$ and $\bar{\ell}$ can be estimated directly from output, investment, and employment plans for the sectors from which public projects divert capital formation at the margin. Assume, for example, that in "Sarania" mining, factory manufacturing and transport industries utilize all the resources that become available for investment at the margin, so that P^{inv} can be calculated in terms of the economic characteristics of these sectors. Now suppose that a study of the current five-year plan (1971—1975) reveals the information summarized in tables 17.1, 17.2 and 17.3. Then rough and ready approximations to $\bar{y}$ and $\bar{\ell}$ can be obtained from the crude ratios of the changes in income and employment to the total investment over the plan period. That is, we can use the formulae

$$\bar{y} = \frac{\Delta Q}{I}$$

$$\bar{\ell} = \frac{\Delta L}{I}$$

where ΔQ represents the change in output (value added) in the three sectors over the plan period, I represents investment over the period, and ΔL represents the change in employment. From table 17.1 we have $\Delta Q = £480$ million. From table 17.2, we have $\Delta L = 1.2$ million. From table 17.3, we have $I = £1,200$ million. Thus,

$$\bar{y} = \frac{480}{1200} = 0.40$$

$$\bar{\ell} = \frac{1.2}{1200} = 0.001$$

TABLE 17.1 GOVERNMENT OF SARANIA, FIVE-YEAR PLAN
NATIONAL INCOME BY INDUSTRIAL ORIGIN
(£ millions)

	1971 (actual)	1975 (planned)
Mining	50	125
Manufacturing (factory)	420	665
Transport	100	260
Total: mining, manufacturing and transport	570	1,050

TABLE 17.2 GOVERNMENT OF SARANIA, FIVE-YEAR PLAN
SECTORAL DISTRIBUTION OF EMPLOYMENT
(Thousand workers)

	1971 (actual)	1975 (planned)
Mining	100	200
Manufacturing (factory)	1,200	1,855
Transport	500	945
Total: mining, manufacturing and transport	1,800	3,000

TABLE 17.3 GOVERNMENT OF SARANIA, FIVE-YEAR PLAN
ESTIMATED NET INVESTMENT BY SECTOR, 1971—1975
(£ millions)

Mining	150
Manufacturing (factory)	650
Transport	400
Total: mining, manufacturing and transport	1,200

It is important that the limitations of these estimates be understood. Not only do we assume in formula 17.1 that all the parameters have constant values over time, in the post-plan period and in the years 1971—1975. Additionally, our estimates of $\bar{y}$ and $\bar{l}$ implicitly assume that *marginal* investment is allocated among the sectors in the same proportions that table 17.3 reflects for total investment.[56] Moreover, the relationships between output, investment, and employment projected for the plan period as a whole are assumed to apply at the margin as well, during and after the plan. Despite these objections, the procedure outlined here appears acceptable when more reliable and detailed forecasts of the structure of output, investment and employment are lacking. What matters above all is that the national economic

[56] Denoting the marginal values of sectoral output: capital and labour: capital ratios by y_i and l_i we have in general
$$\bar{y} = \Sigma a_i y_i$$
$$\bar{l} = \Sigma a_i l_i$$
where a_i is the fraction of marginal investment allocated to the ith sector.

plan be a reliable forecast of the future, as distinct from a hortatory propaganda document. If this condition is met, the plan can provide at least crude estimates of the relevant parameters.

The next parameter is the marginal propensity to save, $\bar{s}$. In the labour-surplus model, the operative assumption is that all after-tax wage income is consumed, and the relevant propensity is the propensity to save out of non-wage income. The obvious temptation is to infer this propensity from marginal saving rates implicit in the plan in the same way that output : capital and labour : capital ratios are inferred from projections of output, investment and employment. Let us see how this would work. First, assume that in Sarania the only saving that takes place out of income generated in the three sectors in which marginal investment takes place—mining, manufacturing, and transport—is private saving out of corporate profits and public saving out of the profits of government enterprises and tax revenues, so that the assumption underlying expression 17.1 is fulfilled. Now look at tables 17.4 and 17.5.

TABLE 17.4   GOVERNMENT OF SARANIA, FIVE-YEAR PLAN
CONSOLIDATED CORPORATE ACCOUNTS: MINING, MANUFACTURING, AND TRANSPORT
(£ millions)

	1971 (actual)	1975 (planned)
Corporate profits before taxes	300	450
Taxes	100	150
After-tax profits	200	300
Retained earnings	110	165
Dividends	90	135

TABLE 17.5   GOVERNMENT OF SARANIA, FIVE-YEAR PLAN
CONSOLIDATED GOVERNMENT ACCOUNTS
(£ millions)

	1971 (actual)	1975 (planned)
Purchases of goods and services	630	830
Current consumption	280	370
Net capital formation	350	460

In the private sector, the ratio of incremental retained earnings to incremental after-tax profits is 55,000 : 100,000, or 0.55. In the public sector, the ratio of incremental investment to incremental expenditure is 90,000 : 200,000, or 0.45. This suggests that the working hypothesis of a common marginal propensity to save in the two sectors is defensible, at least so long as incremental saving propensities are inferred from incremental saving. An average value of $\bar{s} = 0.50$ would appear a reasonable approximation on this basis.

The problem with this procedure is that when incremental saving propensities are inferred from incremental saving rates, a key assumption

of linearity is implicit, just as it is in inferring incremental output: capital and labour: capital ratios from aggregate projections of output, employment and investment. But the assumption of linearity is even less defensible here. It may be that the actual structure of allocation of resources between consumption and saving is quite non-linear in both the corporate and government sectors. In the corporate sector, for example, the accustomed level of dividends may have the first claim on earnings, and the *marginal* retention propensity may be much higher than the indicated rate of 0.55. In the public sector, salaries and operating expenditures may conceivably grow independently of revenues and have first claim on revenues, with investment taking most of the residual; this would imply a marginal saving propensity nearer 1.00 than 0.45. Once again, the data could hide the true propensity because of a reasonably smooth growth path. Thus, the data revealed by plan documents with respect to savings rates must be interpreted in terms of the institutional structure of resource allocation. The plain fact is that no figure "speaks for itself".

For computing P^{inv} we need estimates of w and z as well as estimates of $\bar{y}$, $\bar{l}$ and $\bar{s}$. And these parameters are in general more tenuously related to anything that appears in plan documents than are $\bar{y}$, $\bar{l}$ and $\bar{s}$. However, under the visible tip of the planning iceberg that appears in published documents one can expect to find studies of wages and labour productivities needed to estimate w and z. The wage rate, w, is in general the easiest of the parameters to estimate, since most Governments have reasonably accurate time series of wage statistics in the advanced sectors of the economy. It is important to bear in mind that the surplus-labour model that we are here using to illustrate a general procedure presupposes that at the margin, at least, workers are drawn from the pool of unemployed and underemployed workers coming from the traditional, subsistence sectors of the economy. This in turn presupposes the absence of highly specialized jobs requiring qualifications beyond what can be acquired in the normal course of on-the-job training. To the extent that this assumption is not realized in practice, it becomes necessary to modify the calculations. The easiest procedure is probably to deduct the cost of scarce highly skilled labour from net output in the numerator of $\bar{y}$, treating such labour in effect as a material input. For this example, however, let us ignore this complication and assume that the appropriate (annual) wage is $w = £250$.

The direct opportunity cost of labour drawn from traditional sectors, z, is extremely difficult to estimate, as has already been pointed out in chapter 15. Suffice it to say here that in most countries, for some time to come, crude numbers that are more realistically called guesses than estimates will have to be used. In some cases the average annual wage of landless labourers will serve adequately to estimate z, even though this figure will, if anything, probably overestimate the direct opportunity cost. We shall assume $z = £100$.

If, despite all the difficulties we have indicated, the figures gleaned from the plan and other statistical sources are judged consistent with what is known of the structure of the economy through microeconomic studies and the

accumulated wisdom of planners, sufficient data now exist to attempt crude estimates of P^{inv}. Using the parameters

$$\bar{y} = 0.40 \qquad\qquad w = 250$$
$$\bar{\ell} = 0.001 \qquad\qquad z = 100$$
$$\bar{s} = 0.5$$

we have

$$P^{\text{inv}} = \frac{(0.5)(0.40 - 0.25) + (0.25 - 0.10)}{i - (0.5)(0.40 - 0.25)} = \frac{0.225}{i - 0.075}$$

Thus, for representative values of the social rate of discount between 0.10 and 0.20, we have the values for the shadow price of investment presented in table 17.6. It is in any event meant to be only illustrative. But it does suggest

TABLE 17.6   VALUES OF THE SHADOW PRICE OF INVESTMENT FOR VARIOUS VALUES OF THE SOCIAL RATE OF DISCOUNT

i	P^{inv}
0.10	9.0
0.125	4.5
0.15	3.0
0.175	2.25
0.20	1.80

This discussion has been necessarily brief and schematic.

both the uses of data gleaned from national economic plans and the pitfalls inherent in such data. The two main lessons are: first, plan data are useful only so far as they are a reliable forecast of the future; second, plan data must be supplemented by a reasonable knowledge of the technological and institutional structure of the economy.

17.3 LIMITATIONS OF THE PRICE MECHANISM

It is, in principle at least, a conceivable goal to place the entire burden of co-ordination on (corrected) market prices and national parameters. One can imagine a day when all necessary value judgements have been articulated by policy makers, all shadow prices computed, whether by procedures akin to those laid out in the preceding pages or by more sophisticated procedures. In this glorious future, the appropriate rule for project formulation and evaluation will be to adopt all projects for which the benefits, weighted according to objective and discounted to the present, exceed the costs, similarly weighted and discounted. Where projects are mutually exclusive, such as a thermal electric and a hydroelectric project, the rule becomes one of choosing the project for which benefits are most in excess of costs.

For many years to come, however, nothing remotely resembling this state of affairs can reasonably be anticipated. Indeed, a Government that

tried too precipitously to depend completely on market prices and national parameters for co-ordination of projects might find itself with a set of "desirable" projects in one branch alone—projects for which the benefits exceed the costs—whose capital costs were far greater than the resources available for public investment in the aggregate. A theorist might take comfort in the fact that such an event would "merely" signal that the market prices had been inadequately corrected and national parameters were inappropriate. Repeated revision of both prices and parameters coupled with reformulation and re-evaluation of projects on the basis of revised prices and parameters would (barring certain theoretical complications) eventually lead to a set of projects whose costs were consistent with over-all resources availabilities. But this is small comfort. Repeated revision of prices, together with reformulation and re-evaluation of projects, is a time-consuming process, and public invest- ment cannot simply be suspended until prices and parameters converge to values that bring project designs into line with resource availabilities. Nor would introducing the iterative process of revising prices, parameters and project designs with a long lead time overcome the difficulty. For apart from the theoretical considerations on which convergence depends, the stable environment that such an iterative procedure presupposes may be altogether absent. The longer the lead time the greater the likelihood that dramatic changes will take place in the environment with respect to questions of war and peace, international trade, aid and investment flows, famine and agricultural plenty, etc. Such developments may be wholly unanticipated; they are hardly capable of being reflected in an iterative process that seeks to establish appropriate market prices and national parameters for tactical decisions of project design. And yet such fundamental changes in the economic climate (and much less dramatic changes, too) would likely render the whole iterative exercise irrelevant. It is fair to say, by way of summary, that iterative adjustment can realistically bear little of the burden of establishing appropriate prices and parameters. Not until the formidable problems that inhibit meaningful national planning are overcome,[57] so that the prices and parameters emerge from the national plan itself, can primary reliance be placed on these prices and parameters for guiding project-level decisions.

17.4 BUDGETARY CONTROL AS AN INSTRUMENT OF CO-ORDINATION

In short, for the immediate future, other instruments will have to be used to co-ordinate public projects with each other and with the private economy. Undoubtedly the chief instrument of co-ordination in the public sector will be the government budget, which allocates funds by branches of investment, and may even earmark funds for specific projects.

In the actual setting of project decisions, budgetary control serves several goals. First, to the extent that the allocation among branches derives from an over-all plan, the budgetary process can ensure a rough over-all consistency

---

[57] A cursory discussion of these problems is contained in chapter 11.

of proportions among various branches of investment. Thus, transportation can be allocated a proportion of new capital formation that guarantees that the economy's ability to move goods will increase roughly apace with its ability to produce goods, regardless of errors in market prices or national parameters or in the computation of benefits and costs at the project level that might suggest that no transportation projects are worth undertaking. Second, the level of the budget for each branch or ministry indicates to those responsible at the branch or ministry level the range in which the total investment outlay for projects under their jurisdiction must fall. Thus, if the energy ministry receives an over-all investment allocation of 50 million, it knows that it must choose two out of a dozen large-scale hydroelectric projects, and not five.

Viewed this way, budgetary control is the cutting edge of the national-planning sword. It will for some time to come be the principal instrument for achieving over-all consistency and focusing attention on the relevant tactical choices. But an important difficulty arises from the bureaucratic conflicts that characterize many Governments. Usually the finance ministry is an old, established organization with extensive power, often inherited from a colonial regime for whom financial accounts were the paramount consideration. The planning ministry is by contrast invariably a new body, lacking both the authority that goes with effective lines of communication to the sources of political power and an established bureaucracy. In such circumstances the finance ministry's inevitable reluctance to subordinate itself to the newer body is likely to be successful. In the power struggles between the planning ministry and the finance ministry, it is usually the finance ministry, with its emphasis on short-run exigencies, that emerges victorious.

Thus, the budget usually has only tenuous connexion with the national economic plan. Moreover, operating ministries and agencies are encouraged to deal with the finance ministry and to bypass or even ignore the planning ministry. Questions of short-run finance easily come to dominate questions of social benefits and costs, whatever lip service may be paid to benefit-cost analysis. Thus, for example, even the recurrent costs to which projects commit the Government often receive inadequate attention, for "sufficient unto the day are the evils thereof" is all too often the unofficial motto of operating agencies and finance ministries alike.

The solution to this problem obviously lies in integrating planning and finance. But this solution may be as difficult to achieve as it is obvious. It may be thought highly dangerous to centralize so much power in one ministry. The operating ministries as well as the chief executive may prefer the diffusion of power that accompanies the division of these two functions. And the finance ministry, too, may find its hands quite full without assuming the additional responsibility for over-all planning. Finally, the traditional orientation of the finance ministry may render planning ineffective even if the obstacles to formal integration can be overcome. Nevertheless, integration of planning and finance appears to be among the most important administrative steps required for the successful introduction of benefit-cost analysis.

17.5 THE SCOPE OF BENEFIT-COST ANALYSIS

Whether or not integrated with planning, budgetary control is likely to remain a principal instrument of co-ordination for a long time to come. This has important implications for the role of benefit-cost analysis. First of all, benefit-cost analysis will not be used in the immediate future to allocate resources among branches or ministries. Rather, calculations of national economic profitability will be restricted to comparisons of projects that fall within a single ministry or agency's budget and to comparisons of alternative designs of a single project. The surface-storage versus tube-well example of chapter 14 is one such application of benefit-cost analysis. The example of commercial versus subsistence utilization of irrigation in chapter 12 is another. In the first case we were concerned with alternative sources supplying the same good, in the second with alternative uses of the same physical resources. Both these choices were tactical ones; both would be left open by any over-all decision with respect to the amount of investment funds to be allocated to the irrigation ministry.

It seems eminently reasonable to restrict the scope of benefit-cost analysis when considerations of national economic profitability are introduced into government decision making. For one thing, limiting its scope allows benefit-cost analysis to fit more or less neatly into existing procedures. For another, benefit-cost analysis is thus introduced at the point where it can be used with most confidence, for the alternatives being analysed are sufficiently similar that meaningful comparisons can be made between them. And, finally, the very similarity of the alternatives will make it easier to develop and refine the general techniques according to the specific requirements of each country.

After the methodology has been developed to the point that it can adequately deal with comparisons of physically similar alternatives, the scope of benefit-cost analysis can be gradually extended. One can imagine textile mills being compared with steel mills, or even industrial projects with agricultural projects. The principal purpose of such comparisons would be to check on the budgetary allocations dictated by the over-all plan. If, for example, the marginal agricultural project were found to be overwhelmingly superior to the marginal industrial project in terms of calculations of national economic profitability, grounds would exist for re-examining the plan with a view to shifting emphasis from industry to agriculture.

As for other areas of public expenditure—health, education, warfare—it appears likely that the role of benefit-cost analysis will always be a minimal one. The non-quantifiable elements of decisions of these areas overshadow the quantifiable ones and thereby limit the scope of benefit-cost analysis considerably. Certainly it would be naive in the extreme to think that the day will soon come when a steel mill will be meaningfully compared with a malaria-eradication project, or indeed a project for expanding university education with a project for expanding primary-school education. And, "naive" is hardly strong enough to describe the idea that the techniques

developed in these Guidelines have any real applicability to the calculus of death and destruction that masquerades under the economics of "defence".

We dwell on the limitations of benefit-cost analysis because of a firm conviction that nothing will condemn the methodology developed here to oblivion more quickly and effectively than its indiscriminate application. For benefit-cost analysis to achieve anything like its potential value as a policy instrument, both the technique must be carefully developed and the technicians trained with full awareness of the possibilities and problems specific to each country. The approach developed in these Guidelines is widely applicable, or so we believe. But the present work is deliberately general, and we necessarily emphasize the spirit of the approach rather than the letter. A set of guidelines designed to be useful in countries with widely different incomes, populations, class structures, international trade prospects, and widely differing social, political and economic institutions can realistically do no more than paint in broad strokes. But for the picture to be appreciated, it must be understood not as an end in itself, but as the starting point, and an operational manual must develop as much out of the experience and practice of project analysis as out of theoretical principles. It is to help define reasonable goals and expectations that we emphasize limitations as well as advantages.

17.6 SUMMARY

Market prices are supposed in theory to provide a set of signals to each economic agent that co-ordinates his activities with the activities of others in a manner that achieves an optimal allocation of resources. Social benefit-cost analysis aims at utilizing the price mechanism for co-ordinating separate activities, while providing both for corrections to market prices and for supplementary parameters, called national parameters, where market prices are totally lacking or irrelevant. Part II of these Guidelines describes the specific corrections that must be made where actual prices fail conspicuously to reflect willingness to pay. This part of these Guidelines describes the national parameters that must be introduced where willingness to pay is judged an inadequate basis for valuation, as in the case of merit wants, or where institutional constraints impede the optimal allocation of resources and make it desirable to take account of a project's effects on the personal distribution of income or the rate of saving or the balance of payments. The common denominator of the two classes of national parameters is that both are general to all projects, rather than, as with the market-price corrections analysed in Parts I and II, specific to particular projects.

Although it is useful to distinguish between the positive and the normative dimensions of national parameters, the distinction between shadow prices that reflect factual characteristics of the economy and weights that reflect value judgements conceals an important common element: namely, both shadow prices and weights are definable only with reference to a given economic structure and a specific allocation of resources, and any particular estimate

of a national parameter is valid only at the margin. In a labour-surplus economy, for example, the shadow price of investment can be defined in terms of the output : capital ratio, the wage rate, the labour : capital ratio, the marginal propensity to save and the social rate of discount. All these are variables whose magnitudes vary with the ratio of investment to income, the allocation of investment, tax rates, corporate dividend policy and myriad other dimensions of the economy.

A national plan, together with the economic and statistical studies that normally underlie it, is—or at least ought to be—precisely a description of the economic structure and allocation of resources that will prevail in the future. The plan thus provides the point of reference with respect to which national parameters can be estimated in concrete numerical terms. For this purpose, the issue is the accuracy of the plan as a forecast, not its optimality.

It must be recognized that even with the corrections to market prices described in the earlier parts of these Guidelines and the addition of national parameters, the price mechanism will not adequately co-ordinate investment decisions. For the immediate future, the chief burden of co-ordination in the public sector will undoubtedly fall on the annual budget, and it is therefore obviously important that budgeting be integrated with planning. This is, alas, easier said than done, since the typical finance ministry will neither willingly subordinate itself to the planning ministry nor enthusiastically discharge the responsibilities of planning itself.

Benefit-cost analysis will thus for some time to come play the modest role of facilitating comparison and choice between similar kinds of projects within a single branch of the public sector, rather than the more ambitious role of determining the allocation of public-sector resources among branches or the even more ambitious role of determining the allocation of resources between the public sector and the private sector. Interbranch and intersectoral allocation discussions may one day be amenable to benefit-cost analysis, but nothing would more inhibit the realization of the potentialities of this technique than its premature extension to areas of analysis in which a lack of meaningful data prevents meaningful quantification and comparison.

Chapter 18

CONFLICT AND CHOICE: A SUMMING UP

18.1 FROM COMMERCIAL TO NATIONAL PROFITABILITY

The basic problem of these Guidelines is the analysis of the economic consequences of a proposed public investment. More precisely, we have taken as our task the *valuation* of a project's consequences, assuming that these consequences can be quantified in the form of "outputs" and "inputs". To put matters more simply, we are concerned with translating inputs and outputs expressed in terms of tons of steel or yards of cloth into dollars, pounds, francs or rupees. But money is supposed to account for *national* economic profitability, not private profitability.

Early in these Guidelines commercial profitability was found wanting as an index of social welfare, however useful an index of private well-being it may be. This observation will hardly surprise many readers of these Guidelines, who would never suppose that commercial profitability would be of concern to anybody but the private business man. Indeed, a fair number may accuse us of having set up a straw man and elaborately contrived its destruction! After all, interest in calculations of national economic profitability implies a recognition of the inadequacy of commercial profitability as a criterion of public-investment decisions.

What necessitates the detailed discussion of the limitations of commercial profitability is the widespread acceptance among economists of a theory that justifies, even deifies, commercial profits as an index of social as well as private welfare. The theory in question—neoclassical theory—might be dismissed as mere ideology were it not for the plain fact that, having rejected the theory, we go on in these Guidelines to construct our own methodology of social benefit-cost analysis using the principal tool of neoclassical theory, namely, marginal analysis.

There is no logical difficulty here. In one sense, tools are neutral,[58] and the applicability of marginal analysis depends logically only on the assumption

---

[58] The neutrality of the tools is completely compatible with the view that neoclassical theory itself has grown out of the political interests of the dominant classes in the leading capitalistic countries.

that each project under consideration is so small relative to the economy as a whole that the parameters that measure the values of project outputs and inputs are insensitive to decisions made with respect to the project.[59] The neutrality of the tools, however, says nothing about the social usefulness of making better decisions at the margin. The utility of improving things at the margin obviously depends on value judgements on the particular allocation of resources that serves as the starting point for the marginal analysis. In addition to the judgemental problem, computational problems arise from the attempt to adapt a tool that admirably serves neoclassical theory, given its assumptions, to a context in which the basic assumptions of that theory are found inapplicable.

In the neoclassical world, a specific set of assumptions about human nature, technology, the absence of market power and the functioning of the Government permit one to impute optimality to the allocation of resources that results from the self-seeking activities in the private sector. It follows that *at the margin* the benefits of any project, public or private, are reflected in the market value of the project's output, and costs are reflected in the market value of the project's inputs. Commercial profit—the difference between the market value of outputs and inputs—is an index of social as well as of private gain, and marginal analysis reduces to a simple computation of market values. Thus, both the judgemental and the computational problems are resolved by a single theoretical blow.

Central to our approach, however, is the explicit recognition of the obstacles, chiefly institutional, to achieving an optimal allocation of resources. This recognition does not imply that marginal analysis is inapplicable to project formulation and evaluation, but it does greatly increase the complexity of applying marginal analysis; values that in the neoclassical model are determined in the market place must be directly estimated by the project or national level planner.

Some of these values can at least be based on market prices, and Part II of these Guidelines describes procedures for correcting market prices to reflect social values. An example is the estimation of the value of cement used in the construction of a concrete dam. If the cement is diverted from other uses, its market value, adjusted for consumers' surplus, can be taken as an indication of its social value, at least with respect to aggregate consumption. But if the increase in demand represented by the dam leads to an increase in the supply of cement, the relevant measure of value is the marginal cost of production. Once the assumptions of the neoclassical model are abandoned, there is no reason to expect that market price equals marginal cost, and the presence of excise taxes or monopoly in cement production would be *prima facie* evidence of a difference between these two measures of value. In this case, the project-level analyst must determine the source of the raw material and correct the market price accordingly.

---

[59] Indeed, the procedure described in chapter 4 allows one to come to grips with a project that makes a large change in the supply of a single good.

If this were all there were to the story, calculations of national economic profitability would be difficult, but straightforward. More serious problems arise from the restrictions that market measures of gains and losses, no matter how accurately they may reflect willingness to pay, impart to the concepts of benefits and costs. In brief, willingness to pay reflects benefits and costs in one dimension of welfare only, aggregate consumption. This is suitable in the neoclassical model in which the distribution of income among classes and over time and all merit wants are irrelevant to project decisions. The consequences of projects for the personal distribution of income is ignored on the grounds that the existing distribution—reflecting more governmental intervention or less—is assumed to be optimal. The intertemporal distribution of income is ignored on the grounds that individual decisions on consumption versus savings produce an optimal allocation of resources over time, with the result that the market rate of interest can be utilized, like any other market price, as a measure of the social premium on present as against future consumption exactly analogous to the measures of social values attaching to market prices of apples and pears at the same moment of time. Merit wants are ignored on the grounds that they violate the axiom of consumer sovereignty.

The actual environment of investment decisions, as distinct from the neoclassical model, requires that explicit and serious consideration be given to distributional and merit-want questions in project formulation and evaluation. In our view actual income distributions reflect power rather than any optimal balancing of the claims of various segments of the population; the intertemporal distribution of consumption reflects the institutional organization of societies and economies; and consumer sovereignty reflects more an ideology than an understanding of the relationship between individual and social needs and wants.

Thus, benefits and costs must be separated according to their impact on the institutional and personal distribution of income, according to the time at which they accrue and according to specific categories whenever particular goods are designated as especially meritorious. But—and here is the difficulty at the heart of social benefit-cost analysis—benefits and costs once separated must be put back together again in order to arrive at a single number reflecting a project's national economic profitability. In principle this is easy to do. Weights are assigned to the income generated to certain disadvantaged groups and regions and the weighted income is added to the net aggregate-consumption benefit.[60] Moreover, a social rate of discount establishes a pattern of weights for aggregating future benefits and costs with present benefits and costs. And, finally, merit-want weights, such as the weights on foreign exchange earnings, come into play whenever they exceed shadow

---

[60] Indeed, conceptually one need not limit oneself to positive premiums for disadvantaged groups; capitalists and landlords can be assigned negative penalities reflecting the lack of social value attaching to making the rich richer. In the limit, a penalty of —1 would indicate that additional income to the group had no social value whatsoever, for redistributional "dis-benefits" would then just cancel out aggregate-consumption benefits.

prices defined in terms of aggregate-consumption. With these weights, shadow prices, however difficult to calculate, can be defined that share with market prices a certain objectivity: no value judgements are required for calculation of shadow prices apart from those embodied in weights.

18.2 ELICITING WEIGHTS FROM CHOICES

The difficulty of implementing benefit-cost analysis is not one of defining weights in principle, but of defining them operationally. We are roughly in the position of the mice of Aesop's fable who found their ingenious plan of putting a bell on the cat to warn them of his presence foiled by the lack of a suitable means of implementing the plan. Who is to "bell the cat?" It ought to be the political leadership that defines the weights, for the value judgements at issue are inherently political in nature, reflecting as they do conflicts and strains between various classes and sections of the population. But it is unlikely that the political leadership will of its own volition undertake the responsibilities envisioned for it, and we see no way of bypassing the political leadership that retains meaning for benefit-cost analysis.

Hence, as an alternative to the "top-down" procedure of formulating weights and shadow prices prior to projects, which would logically transform commercial profitability into national profitability, we have proposed a "bottom-up" procedure that at least in the beginning puts the initiative in the hands of project formulators and evaluators. Wherever alternatives exist that have significantly different implications for the personal distribution of income, for the distribution of income over time, or for foreign exchange earnings or other merit-wants judged important on a case-by-case basis, project-level planners are enjoined to formulate alternative designs, each oriented towards a different developmental objective. These alternatives are then presented to the political leadership for a decision. This decision in turn places bounds on the weights in question and corresponding bounds on the shadow prices that are functions of the weights.

The short-run goal is to focus policy makers' attention on the relevant political choices inherent in project design and to extract political decisions with respect to these choices. In this context, the bounds on weights and shadow prices serve to illuminate the value judgements implicit in one decision or another. The long-run goal is to narrow the bounds on weights and shadow prices to a sufficiently small range that the top-down version of planning becomes feasible.

Our bottom-up version of planning amounts to a reversal of the flow of information implicit in neoclassical theory. Rather than acting as signals that guide project-level planners in the manner of market prices, weights emerge from the planning process. In fact, weights are best understood as the focus of a dialogue deliberately instituted to force policy makers to face political decisions. The dialogue, between the project-level planner and the Minister of Industries, would ideally take place somewhat as follows:

Project-level planner: Sir, before you is the report on the pulp and paper mill project assigned to me and my colleagues for formulation. Since two objectives appeared relevant to this choice—aggregate consumption and redistribution—we have prepared two alternative designs. They differ chiefly with respect to location. Alternative A, responsive only to the aggregate-consumption objective, would be located in the district of Guptania, where a well-developed infrastructure would keep investment costs down to a minimum. Alternative B is responsive to the redistribution objective; it would be located in Sendesh, which is both poor and un-developed, though equally well-endowed with forest resources as Guptania.

The chief differences between the alternatives are: (1) the capital costs of B are significantly higher because of the investment in roads and other infrastructure; and (2) B would bring income and employment to the poorest region of the country, whereas A would cost less initially but would contribute to the economic polarization of the country. The real costs in terms of aggregate consumption, of operating the two projects are about equal. On the one hand, the direct opportunity cost of unskilled labour is practically zero in Sendesh, but approximately equal to the market wage in Guptania. On the other hand, transport costs for inputs and outputs will be higher for B even after the infrastructure has been completed. Distances to markets and sources of supply are greater. Moreover, supervisory personnel would have in any case to come from Guptania for some time to come, and they would require a wage supple-ment to balance the higher cost of transporting goods to Sendesh. These two tendencies work in opposite directions and just about cancel each other out.

The aggregate-consumption benefits of the two projects are equal. The two alternatives produce essentially identical outputs.

The question, Sir, is, which alternative will you implement?

Minister of Industries (who prides himself on the knowledge of business economics he has acquired): How can I answer that question without more facts? Compute present values and I shall recommend the alternative with the higher present value.

Project planner: Yes, Sir, I already have, at least on a parametric basis for various values of the social rate of discount and the weight on income generated to Sendesh. You see, Sir, present values are sensitive to the premium attached to Sendesh and the discount rate used to calculate the shadow price of investment. Here is a summary of our data.

SUMMARY OF DATA ON ALTERNATIVE PROJECTS
(£ thousands)

	Aggregate consumption			Annual consumption
	Annual benefit	*Annual operating cost*	*Capital cost*	*Generated to Sendesh*
Alternative A	200	100	500	0
Alternative B	200	100	600	50

Assuming the project will last indefinitely, and that the gap between Sendesh and the rest of the country will remain at its present level indefinitely, the two present values are given by the formulae:

$$\text{NPV}_A = [sP^{\text{inv}} + (1-s)]\frac{200-100}{i} - P^{\text{inv}} \times 500$$

$$\text{NPV}_B = [sP^{\text{inv}} + (1-s)]\frac{200-100}{i} - P^{\text{inv}} \times 600 + W\frac{50}{i}$$

s = marginal propensity to save, assumed equal to the reinvestment propensity for both alternatives;

i = social rate of discount;

P^{inv} = shadow price of investment;

W = premium on income generated to Sendesh.

Thus, we have

$$\text{NPV}_A \begin{Bmatrix}\geq\\=\\\leq\end{Bmatrix} \text{NPV}_B \text{ as } - P^{\text{inv}} \times 500 \begin{Bmatrix}\geq\\=\\\leq\end{Bmatrix} - P^{\text{inv}} \times 600 + W\frac{50}{i}$$

Using a formula for the shadow price of investment derived from the national plan,[61]

$$P^{\text{inv}} = \frac{0.225}{i-0.075},$$

the comparison of present values reduces to

$$\text{NPV}_A \begin{Bmatrix}\geq\\=\\\leq\end{Bmatrix} \text{NPV}_B \text{ as } - \frac{0.225}{i-0.075} \times 500 \begin{Bmatrix}\geq\\=\\\leq\end{Bmatrix} - \frac{0.225}{i-0.075} \times 600 + \frac{W}{i}50$$

So, you see, Sir, we need to know both the social rate of discount and the premium on Sendesh income in order to compute the present values of the two projects in a manner that is meaningful for social choice.

Minister: But I don't know what they are. How am I supposed to determine these parameters? Am I supposed to pull them out of the air? It seems to me that it's a technical job to compute these parameters, and I'm no technician.

Project planner: No, Sir, it is most emphatically not a technical matter. The value judgement inherent in this choice is essentially political, for it pits the interests of Sendesh against the interests of the rest of the economy. The most my colleagues and I can do to facilitate choice is to spell out the implications of choosing one alternative over another.

Minister: Well, I'm certainly inclined to the Sendesh alternative. Offhand, an extra capital outlay of £100,000 seems a small price to pay to generate £50,000 per year to Sendesh.

---

[61] See chapter 17.

Project planner: Well, in that case, you can see from our drawing (figure 26) that your choice implies a combination of i and W somewhere to the northeast of LL, which is to say that for social rates of discount ranging from 0.20 down to 0.10, the implied value of W is at least in the range of 0.72 to 1.8. That is, if we can reasonably put the social rate of

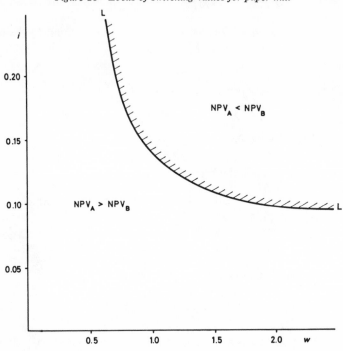

Figure 26   Locus of switching values for paper mill

discount in the range 0.10—0.20, then choosing alternative B implies that £1 of income generated to Sendesh has a social value equal at the very least to £1.72—2.80 to income generated in richer regions of the country.

Minister: How do you figure that?

Project planner: The locus LL is the locus of "switching values" of i and W; it represents the combinations of i and W such that the present values of the two alternatives are equal. As the drawing indicates, B is more profitable (in national terms) than A for combinations of i and W above LL, and A is more profitable for combinations of i and W below LL. If we suppose that an intuitive judgement in favour of B is to be rationalized in terms of national profitability, then the implied values of i and W must lie above LL. That is why we can infer that with i in the range 0.20—0.10, W must lie above the range 0.72—1.8.

Minister: Well, it certainly seems reasonable to value income to Sendesh roughly two to three times as much as income elsewhere. This

region has hardly shared in the country's economic growth and shows every prospect of continuing to lag behind. Your graph only confirms my feeling.

But tell me, why do the switching values of W and i vary inversely with each other? I would have thought the relationship would be a direct one, for in effect we are investing an extra £100,000 to redistribute £50,000 annually to Sendesh. On the assumption of a constant weight for Sendesh relative to current aggregate consumption, the present value of the redistribution is directly proportional to W/i. So the higher the value of i, the higher the value of W required to justify the redistribution. Thus, the switching-value locus should have an upward slope as in figure 27.

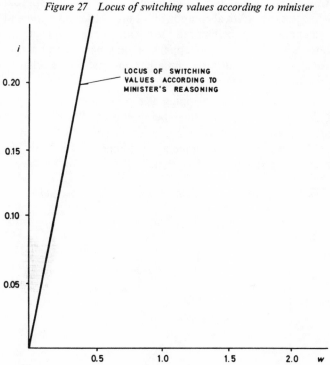

Figure 27   Locus of switching values according to minister

In fact, the ratio of W/i required to justify the redistribution is precisely 2.0, for the equation

$$100 = \frac{W}{i}\, 50$$

defines the set of switching values, at least according to my way of looking at the problem.

Project planner: Your approach would be correct if the nominal price of capital did not understate its value in terms of aggregate

consumption. It is perfectly true that alternative B ties up £100,000 more capital than A. But each unit of that capital could produce a stream of aggregate consumption whose present value is

$$P^{\mathrm{inv}} = \frac{0.225}{i - 0.075}$$

And this present value, like the present value of the redistribution to Sendesh, varies inversely with the social rate of discount. Thus, an increase in *i reduces* the aggregate-consumption *cost* of the redistribution as well as the redistributional *benefit*. Hence, the relationship of LL depicted in figure 26. An increase in the social rate of discount reduces the weight on Sendesh required to rationalize the redistribution.

At this point all that can be claimed for the present approach is that it clearly delineates the political component of project formulation and evaluation, and facilitates choice by spelling out the consequences of one choice or another. But repeated application of this apparatus may narrow the range of *W* and *i* so that for operational purposes these parameters can be regarded as known rather than unknown parameters.

Let us resume our eavesdropping at a point some weeks or months later, when the location of a steel mill is being chosen. Sendesh, let us assume, is once more a possibility, but to avoid duplication, let us assume that the minister's decision has already gone against Sendesh this time. The locus L′L′ in figure 28 is supposed to reflect switching values for the steel mill: choice

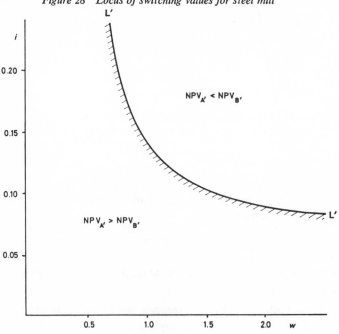

Figure 28   Locus of switching values for steel mill

of alternative A' (the non-Sendesh alternative) over alternative B' (in Sendesh) implies values of W and i below and to the left of L'L'.

Project planner: If we compare your decision against Sendesh in the case of the steel mill and your earlier decision with respect to this paper mill, we can narrow the range of W and i to the shaded area between LL and L'L', which are superimposed on figure 29.

Figure 29   Loci of switching values for paper mill and steel mill

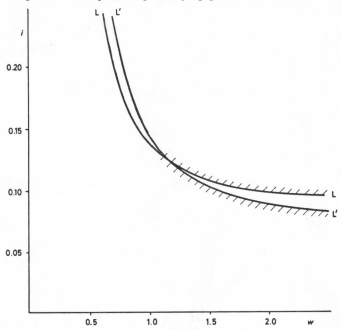

Minister: Explain.

Project planner: Well, the shaded area of the graph represents the only values of W and i consistent with both your decisions, that is, with the decision to choose B over A and A' over B'. Any other values would lead to a higher present value for at least one of the rejected alternatives.

A third project, let us say a textile mill, for which the switching-value locus is L"L" in figure 30, completes the story. If the non-Sendesh alternative, A", is chosen, then the range of values of W and i compatible with all three choices is reduced, as in figure 31, to an area small enough that it can be taken to a single point. Values of W and i equal to 0.95 and 0.15, respectively, can be reasonably taken as representing the minister's implicit value judgements with respect to distribution across regions and over time.

Needless to say, this presentation of dialogue between project planners and policy makers has been highly stylized and considerably idealized. It is not so much the level of sophistication of the hypothetical discussion that is

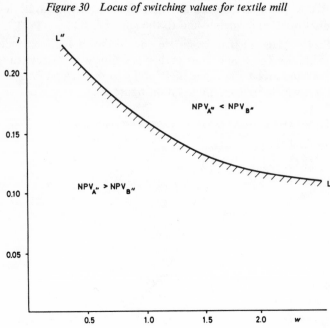

Figure 30   Locus of switching values for textile mill

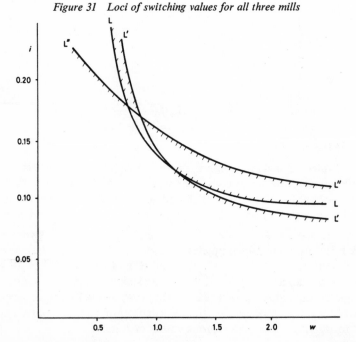

Figure 31   Loci of switching values for all three mills

misleading as the rapid and orderly progress in generating information about parameters as we move from one project to another. Little or no new information is likely to be generated by many projects, as would be the case if a decision

in favour of Sendesh had been taken with respect to the steel and textile mills as well as the paper mill. For in this case, the shaded area of values compatible with choosing B, B', and B'' is hardly different from the area compatible with any one of these choices, as figure 32 shows.

Figure 32   Loci of switching values

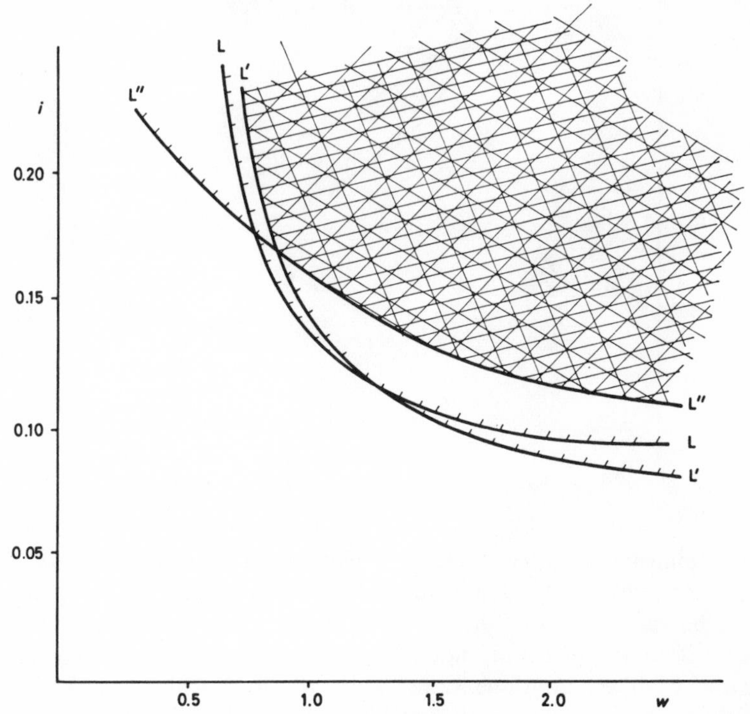

Worse still, inconsistencies may emerge from the process of choosing. Suppose that rather than B, A' and A'', the minister's choices had been A, B' and—initially at least—B''. Now, as figure 33 shows, any two of these choices are compatible, but all three are not. A and B' together define the shaded area in the southeast portion of the diagram as the range of W and i, and B'' implies that the area below and to the right of L''L'' is the appropriate range for the two parameters. At this point the role of the project planner is to call the inconsistency to the attention of the policy maker.

Project planner: Sir, your decisions with respect to the paper mill and the steel mill delimited a range for W and i that is incompatible with your present intention to locate the textile mill in Sendesh. For example, with W in the range 1.25—2.0, the value of i compatible with your earlier decisions is from 0.10 down to 0.085. Yet with W in the range 1.25—2.0, the decision to locate the textile mill in Sendesh can be rationalized only by a discount rate above 0.15.

Figure 33   Loci of switching values

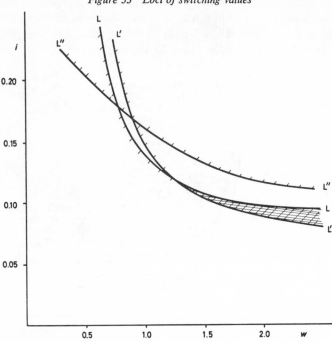

The minister now has three reasonable lines of response open to him. First, he can reverse his tentative decision with respect to the textile mill. Second, he can regret one of his earlier decisions (and maybe even actually reverse it if commitments are not yet too deep and too public). Third, he can point out that there are dimensions to one or more of the three projects that the technicians have failed to consider adequately, dimensions that make comparisons in terms of the regional and intertemporal distribution of consumption incomplete.[62]

Project formulation and evaluation will be sharpened whichever of the three lines of response is followed. But to realize the hope of narrowing the range of parameters to an area small enough to be reduced to a point, it is obviously necessary that technicians exercise some skill in focusing the discussion on projects that are in fact comparable in terms of the dimensions of welfare they impinge upon. Equally obviously, the smaller the number of these dimensions, the faster the dialogue can proceed.

18.3 CONFLICT

It may be argued that the methodology advanced in these Guidelines is likely to exacerbate conflict in situations where the national interest requires

---

[62] Indeed, the third line of response is tautologically implicit in a rejection of the first two!

unity and consensus. It is the view of these Guidelines, however, that conflict is the product of the institutions that channel economic development along particular paths. The desirability of suppressing the specific manifestations of conflict that appear in project formulation and evaluation is more a function of class and even narrower bonds of interest than of general national interest. Exacerbating conflict, or more accurately, making conflict explicit, is undesirable only to the extent that power and position depend on the sublimation, suppression or muting of conflict.

Established interests—those that possess economic, political, and social power and privilege—will undoubtedly find it easier to sway project decisions in their favour if comparisons between alternative courses of action can be suppressed and the pretence maintained that project formulation and evaluation are apolitical and technocratic in nature. By the same token, the less powerful, with official rhetoric and ideology on their side, will find explicit recognition of the conflict between their interests and the interests of others to their advantage. Indeed, in the world view underlying these Guidelines, a precondition for resolving conflicts constructively is an understanding and consciousness of the nature of these conflicts. Project formulation and evaluation can, if carried out along the lines proposed here, facilitate and focus the growth of such consciousness. Otherwise, benefit-cost analysis will contribute only to the obfuscation of basic political choices.

No methodology of project formulation and evaluation is a panacea, a solution to all or even a significant portion of the conflicts generated by development. The scope of benefit-cost analysis is inherently limited by its basic marginalism. At best, benefit-cost analysis will raise questions about developmental objectives and institutional constraints, whose implications extend far beyond the projects at issue. But the answers to these questions are to be found more in the distribution of economic, social and political power than in any analytical technique.

Let us give one example. Our preoccupation with the shadow price of investment stems from a view of development that places chief emphasis on the institutions that constrain saving. The rate of saving in our view is determined by the distribution of income, in the first instance the distribution between savings-oriented organizations and consumption-oriented individuals. Once income passes to the control of a group or individual, the Government will have little further influence over it. Thus, a project that places income in the hands of organizations like corporations with high propensities to save contributes more to the (discounted present value of) aggregate consumption than a project that places a like amount of income in the hands of wage earners whose propensity to save is virtually zero. This obviously biases project decisions in favour of projects that generate income to corporations rather than to workers. If corporations could be counted on to reinvest almost all of their profits, in the manner of the nineteenth century entrepreneurial class for whom accumulation was supposedly just about a commandment, one might accept these distributional implications with complacency. But with

a significant portion of profit supporting a managerial and owning class in affluence, the distributional implications can be suffered less gladly. To be sure, the adverse distributional impact that logically follows from aggregate-consumption maximization can be offset by explicit introduction of a redistribution objective, but the conflict between savings and growth on the one hand and a more equal distribution of consumption on the other is heightened by an institutional structure that makes the consumption by elites a necessary cost of growth. Obviously, project decisions, as decisions at the margin, can directly do little more than reflect this basic conflict. But indirectly the need to choose between alternatives that contribute to saving and growth at the price of skewing the distribution of consumption further towards the rich and alternatives that equalize consumption at the price of inhibiting growth may serve to focus attention on the institutions that limit alternatives so drastically.

Recognition of the limitations imposed by the institutional structure is but a first step. Recognition at best will indicate necessary changes in the distribution of economic, social and political power, but will not of itself bring about these changes.

18.4 SUMMARY

Our approach to benefit-cost analysis is in a way paradoxical. Rejecting the basic premises of a theory of economics designed to demonstrate the virtues of *laissez-faire*, we go on to adopt the principal tool of that theory, marginal analysis. The chief virtue of marginal analysis in a neoclassical world, however, is lost in the process: once the neoclassical assumptions are abandoned, social well-being is no longer reflected in commercial profits, and market prices are no longer indices of social values. Not only must market prices be substantially corrected and revised, but additional parameters must be introduced to reflect the performance of projects in dimensions that are irrelevant in the neoclassical framework, at the margin in any event.

The articulation of the parameters that directly reflect political judgements is precisely the most serious obstacle to the implementation of the methodology advanced here. Indeed, in the beginning, weights must be considered unknowns. It is in effect necessary for technicians to take the initiative and to force political leaders to reveal their value judgements. By refusing to play the traditional game of preparing a single project plan that represents a compromise between contending interests, technicians will put political choice in the hands of those who bear the responsibility for these choices—the political leaders who are accountable to the people for the manner in which conflict is resolved. By confronting the political leadership with alternatives that emphasize the various dimensions of social welfare in differing degrees, technicians will make it impossible to maintain the pretence that project analysis is technical and apolitical.

Not only will conflicts be faced squarely: a series of decisions between alternative designs responsive in differing degrees to the same set of dimensions

of welfare may narrow the range of parameter values sufficiently that for operational purposes each parameter can be expressed as a single number. At this point, a top-down planning procedure will become feasible, and calculations of national economic profitability will come to resemble calculations of commercial profitability, superficially at least. The results of these calculations will be capable of being expressed in a single number, and the ranking of projects by their profitability will become a valid index of their relative desirability.

The present methodology thus provides for the systematic accumulation of the information required to define weights and shadow prices numerically. At the same time it provides a transitional procedure for project formulation and evaluation that makes it possible to introduce the essential features of the present approach without waiting for the day when national economic profitability becomes quantifiable.

The obstacles to the adoption of the procedures outlined here can presumably be best left to others to deal with. But one objection can be anticipated, namely, that our approach runs counter to the obvious wisdom of letting sleeping dogs lie. Do we not go out of our way to create conflicts in project choice where none has existed up to now? Do we not at least emphasize conflict where the goal of Government ought to be to emphasize consensus? Our position is that the substance of conflict is determined by the paths along which a country's economic, social and political institutions channel development, and that muting conflict is by no means an absolute good. Letting sleeping dogs lie appeals naturally to the more powerful segments of the population, who can expect customary forms of compromise to be compatible with their interests. It is less appealing to the groups who have traditionally received the worse end of the bargain. One must finally, as Albert Camus once wrote, choose between the executioners and the martyrs. If choosing for the martyrs eventually calls into question institutions that assign some segments of society the role of executioners and consign others to the role of involuntary martyrs, so much the worse for these institutions.

PART IV

Case Studies

Chapter 19

SOCIAL BENEFIT-COST ANALYSIS OF A PULP
AND PAPER MILL IN SARANIA

19.1 BACKGROUND

The northern province of Sarakand in the country of Sarania is characterized chiefly by a minimum of industrial development. The western part of the province is marked by an extreme dependence on primitive agriculture and a very dense population. Even casual observation suggests that there is fairly large-scale unemployment in this region. The eastern part of the province consists of dense forests covering some 1 million hectares of land, which, until recently, were largely untapped. A common characteristic of all the natural forests in eastern Sarakand is the heterogeneity of their composition. Some 35 per cent of the growing stock consists of hornbeam and about 25 per cent of beech. The remaining 40 per cent consists of maple, alder, oak, elm and linden. To exploit these rich forest resources and to provide a better life for the people of Sarakand, the Sarakand Forest Authority (SFA), a public corporation formed in 1965, embarked on a broad programme of forestry development using the abundant labour force available in the west. To enable timber to be transported from the forest land to the main highways, some 200 kilometres of feeder roads have already been constructed.

Initially, the SFA encouraged the existing small-scale industries, which produce furniture and a variety of wood works. More recently, as a result of the Government's overt concern to promote industrial development in Sarania, the SFA has begun to explore the possibility of introducing large-scale manufacturing units so as to utilize more fully the forest resources. One such proposal is the pulp and paper mill whose feasibility study is now available and whose economic evaluation is the purpose of this chapter.

19.2 OUTPUT OF THE PROJECT

The proposed pulp and paper mill, to be located in central Sarakand, is to produce annually 40,000 tons of rayon-grade pulp and 20,000 tons of corrugating medium, when operating at 100 per cent capacity. The rayon-grade pulp will be used by a private rayon manufacturing factory installed recently

just south of the province's border. At present, rayon-grade pulp is imported into Sarania for the rayon factory. The annual output of rayon-grade pulp of the proposed mill will, therefore, substitute for that much of import. Corrugating medium is currently imported into Sarania by several domestic paper-conversion manufacturing firms. The annual output of corrugating medium by the proposed mill will, therefore, substitute for much of the import. The feasibility report states that on completion of the pulp and paper mill Sarania will become self-sufficient in both rayon-grade pulp and corrugating medium.

19.3 TECHNICAL ASPECTS

For the production of rayon-grade pulp, the feasibility study recommends what is known as the discontinuous prehydrolysis sulphate process. A brief account of this process will make it easier to understand the financial aspects of the project. Wood logs are first barked and chipped and then carried by conveyors to the "digestors", where water is added to the chips. The temperature of the digestor is then raised to about 175° C for approximately two hours. Cooking liquor (containing mainly caustic soda) is then added to the digestor, and the wood is cooked for about two hours at a pressure of 7—8 atmospheres. At the end of the cooking, the pulp and the black liquor, containing the spent cooking chemicals, are blown into blow tanks. The pulp is then washed, screened and sent to the bleach plant. A portion of the black liquor is used as a diluent for the cooking liquor. The remainder is sent to the recovery unit of the pulp mill, where the cooking chemicals are reclaimed.

For the production of corrugating medium, the feasibility report recommends a technique known as the continuous neutral sulphite semi-chemical process. In this process the mixed broad-leaved wood is chipped and then cooked with sodium sulphite and an admixture of alkali (caustic soda, sodium carbonate, bicarbonate of soda). This impregnation is carried out in continuous digestors. After impregnation the chips are mechanically disintegrated and dehydrated, and the semi-chemical pulp produced is then further manipulated in the mill.

The feasibility report goes on to state that the proposed plant is small compared with the competing export pulp mills in other countries. The smallness of the plant, it is claimed, is necessitated by the limited domestic demand for both the products. It is, moreover, thought that the export prospects in the near future are limited.

It would appear from the foregoing description of the production process that the prerequisites for the operation of the mill, other than the mixed broad-leaved wood, are the availability of water, chemicals, power and skilled labour. The mill will get its water from deep wells to be drilled near the plant site. The chemicals will be mainly of foreign origin. Generators will be purchased for the production of power. And finally, it will be seen that much of the skilled labour will be imported from abroad.

19.4 FINANCIAL ASPECTS

The pulp and paper mill will be constructed, administered and operated by the SFA. The construction will cover a period of three years, starting in 1973 (which we shall denote as year 0), at a total cost of 320 million creons.[63] This cost will be phased over the three-year period so that 60 million creons will be spent in each of years 0 and 1 and 200 million creons in year 2. The mill is expected to start operating in year 3, and its expected operating lifetime is 12 years, at the end of which the project will be terminated, i.e. a new decision will then be taken as to whether new machinery will be installed to continue the project. Table 19.1 gives a time series of the output of the mill. It will be

TABLE 19.1   OUTPUT OF PULP AND PAPER MILL
(Tons)

Product	Year				
	0—2	*3*	*4*	*5—10*	*11—14*
(1) Rayon-grade pulp	0	20,000	30,000	40,000	44,000
(2) Corrugating medium	0	20,000	20,000	20,000	22,000
Total	0	40,000	50,000	60,000	66,000

observed that the mill will operate at 100 per cent capacity between years 5 through 10 and will operate at 110 per cent capacity during its last four years.

Of the investment cost (320 million creons) in fixed capital, 210 million creons will be in foreign exchange (dollars, for simplicity) and the remaining 110 million creons in domestic currency. Tables 19.2 and 19.3 give a detailed

TABLE 19.2   FOREIGN EXCHANGE COMPONENT OF CONSTRUCTION COSTS
(Thousand creons)

Item	Year			Total
	0	*1*	*2*	
(1) Buildings, structure and civil works	8,270	—	—	8,270
(2) Processing facilities	—	—	125,300	125,300
(3) Power, water and auxiliary facilities	22,200	25,650	2,630	50,480
(4) Chemical generation equipment	—	6,100	3,000	9,100
(5) Welfare and housing	610	—	—	610
(6) Engineering costs and consultants' fees	5,620	2,200	1,400	9,220
(7) Preliminary expenses	—	—	800	800
(8) Contingencies	—	—	6,220	6,220
Total	36,700	33,950	139,350	210,000

breakdown of the construction costs in terms of the requirements of foreign exchange and domestic resources, respectively.

---

[63] The Saranian currency is 1 creon. The official exchange rate is: 10 creons = 1 dollar.

TABLE 19.3   DOMESTIC COMPONENT OF CONSTRUCTION COSTS
(Thousand creons)

Item	Year			Total
	0	1	2	
(1) Land and site preparation	9,500	—	—	9,500
(2) Buildings, structures and civil works	9,520	17,200	13,340	40,060
(3) Processing facilities	—	—	29,700	29,700
(4) Power, water and auxiliary facilities	3,650	6,250	150	10,050
(5) Chemical generation equipment	—	600	600	1,200
(6) Welfare and housing	—	1,000	2,440	3,440
(7) Engineering costs and consultants' fees	630	1,000	1,000	2,630
(8) Preliminary charges	—	—	5,600	5,600
(9) Contingencies	—	—	7,820	7,820
Total	23,300	26,050	60,650	10,000

It is proposed that the foreign exchange component of construction costs be financed by a World Bank loan and the remaining 110 million creons be covered by funds borrowed from the Central Treasury. The World Bank loan is to be amortized over a 10-year period following completion of the project with an effective rate of interest of 7 per cent on the due balance. The Treasury will also allow a 10-year term for amortization, with an interest rate of 5 per cent on the due balance. It is expected that both the World Bank and the Treasury will grant a period of grace during the construction of the project and charge no interest until production is under way. Assuming that equal annual instalments are to be paid over the full term of amortization of each loan, the annual value of the repayment of these loans can be calculated from the annuity tables as follows:

World Bank loan — 210 million creons at 7% over 10 years (years 3—12)
= 210 million × 0.1424 creons annually
= 29,904,000 creons annually.

Treasury loan   — 110 million creons at 5% over 10 years (years 3—12)
= 110 million × 0.1295 creons annually
= 14,245,000 creons annually.

The operating costs of the project are to be incurred by the SFA at an annual rate of 63.485 million creons when the mill is operated at 100 per cent capacity. It is proposed that the SFA will build up a working capital worth 20 million creons during the years 3, 4 and 5. This working capital will be composed of raw materials, such as pulpwood and chemicals, and the whole of it will be recovered by the SFA at the termination of the project (year 15). As tables 19.2 and 19.3 show, of the total construction costs, 4.05 million creons will be spent on welfare and housing programmes for the employees of the project. It has been decided that housing will be provided free of charge to all employees.

The feasibility report assumes that all fixed capital other than buildings and structures will have a perfect productive life for 12 years after its installation,

but that at the end of this period (i.e. year 15) it will collapse with no residual value. The report further assumes a linear depreciation allotment of 4 per cent per annum on the buildings and structures. This implies that the scrap value of the plant will be about 24.16 million creons (i.e. about half the original investment of 48.33 million creons on buildings and structures).

19.5 PRICING POLICY

It was mentioned in section 19.2 that both rayon-grade pulp and corrugating medium are currently imported into Sarania. The c.i.f. prices of these two commodities are 1,770 creons per ton and 1,400 creons per ton, respectively.[64] The Government of Sarania charges tariffs amounting to 354 creons per ton on the rayon-grade pulp and 560 creons per ton on the corrugating medium. That is, domestic purchasers currently pay about 2,124 creons per ton on the rayon-grade pulp and 1,960 creons per ton on the corrugating medium. The feasibility report states that when the mill is completed the SFA will charge 2,124 creons per ton on the rayon-grade pulp and 1,960 creons per ton on the corrugating medium. In other words, domestic purchasers will be paying exactly what they are currently paying for the two products. Table 19.4 summarizes the annual revenues that the SFA will capture when the project is in operation.

TABLE 19.4   GROSS REVENUE FOR SFA

(Thousand creons)

Product	Year			
	3	4	5—10	11—14
(1) Rayon-grade pulp (2,124 creons per ton)	42,480	63,720	84,960	93,460
(2) Corrugating medium (1,960 creons per ton) .	39,200	39,200	39,200	43,120
Total	81,680	102,920	124,160	136,580

We bring together all the financial aspects discussed so far in table 19.5, which gives the gross cash payments and receipts of the SFA for each year of the project. It includes the operating costs (5) that have been quoted from the feasibility report and that will be discussed later in this chapter. In the first three years the outlay on the construction of the works is matched exactly by the loans from the World Bank and the Central Treasury. In year 3, the loan-repayment instalments, working capital and operating costs exceed the receipts from the sales of the two products, so that there is a net cash outflow from the SFA of 18.793 million creons. In year 4, output (and hence revenue) has increased sufficiently to yield a net cash inflow of 1.866 million creons. In year 5, when the mill begins to work at 100 per cent capacity, net cash inflow

---

[64] We assume, for want of better information, that Sarania faces constant world prices for these two commodities, i.e. the c.i.f. prices remain constant irrespective of the volume of the Saranian imports of these two items. Had they not been constant one would have to assess the marginal import costs of the rayon-grade pulp and the corrugating medium. In such a case the marginal import costs would, presumably, exceed the c.i.f. prices. Here we assume that marginal import cost = constant = c.i.f. price.

TABLE 19.5 SFA ACCOUNT
(Thousand creons)

Item	Year									
	0	1	2	3	4	5	6—10	11—12	13—14	15
Payments										
(1) Construction costs	60,000	60,000	200,000	—	—	—	—	—	—	—
(2) Working capital	—	—	—	14,000	4,000	2,000	—	—	—	—
(3) World Bank loan	—	—	—	29,904	29,904	29,904	29,904	29,904	—	—
(4) Treasury loan	—	—	—	14,245	14,245	14,245	14,245	14,245	—	—
(5) Operating costs	—	—	—	42,324	52,905	63,485	63,485	69,830	69,830	—
Total.............	60,000	60,000	200,000	100,473	101,054	109,634	107,634	113,979	69,830	—
Receipts										
(6) World Bank loan	36,700	33,950	139,350	—	—	—	—	—	—	—
(7) Treasury loan	23,300	26,050	60,650	—	—	—	—	—	—	—
(8) Revenue	—	—	—	81,680	102,920	124,160	124,160	136,580	136,580	—
(9) Scrap value and working capital	—	—	—	—	—	—	—	—	—	44,160
Total.............	60,000	60,000	200,000	81,680	102,920	124,160	124,160	136,580	136,580	44,160
Net cash inflow	0	0	0	−18,793	1,866	14,524	16,526	22,601	66,750	44,160

increases to 14.524 million creons, and so on, until a maximum net cash inflow of 66.750 million creons is reached during years 13 and 14 when the mill is operating at 110 per cent capacity and there is no further loan repayment to be made.

Even a glance at the net cash inflow item of table 19.5 suggests that the project appears extremely desirable from the point of view of the SFA. The rate of return to the SFA in undertaking the project is spectacularly high—about 80 per cent. In view of this high rate of return, the feasibility report, which was sponsored by the SFA, recommends strongly the construction of the pulp and paper mill.

19.6 NATIONAL ECONOMIC PROFITABILITY OF PULP AND PAPER MILL INVESTMENT AND THE VALUE OF OUTPUT

A central objective mentioned in the Draft of the Second Five-Year Plan of Sarania is to increase aggregate-consumption benefits for Sarania. A second objective is to redistribute consumption benefits to the backward province of Sarakand. We shall, therefore, evaluate the pulp and paper mill in the light of these two objectives.

As we recall from the discussions in chapters 4 and 5, in the evaluation of benefits and costs of this project it will be necessary to distinguish between imported and domestically supplied material inputs and between different types of labour. Therefore, the resource categories used for grouping the resource flows will be as follows: domestic inputs (outputs), foreign exchange inputs (outputs), unskilled labour and skilled labour. Machinery and parts (other than some simple machine tools), iron and steel, fuel and various kinds of chemicals are all currently imported into Sarania, as the feasibility report indicates. It will be assumed, for want of better information, that they will continue to be imported throughout the life of the project. All other material inputs are produced domestically.

It was mentioned earlier (section 19.2) that the direct benefits from this project (i.e. rayon-grade pulp and corrugating medium) will replace the imports of these two commodities. It follows that these benefits are to be measured in terms of the foreign exchange resources saved as a result of not importing (see chapter 4). In table 19.6 we present a year-by-year breakdown of the foreign exchange saved because of the project.

TABLE 19.6   SOCIAL VALUE OF OUTPUT OF MILL
(Thousand creons)

Product	Year			
	3	*4*	*5—10*	*11—14*
(1) Rayon-grade pulp (1,770 creons per ton) c.i.f. price	35,400	53,100	70,800	77,880
(2) Corrugating medium (1,440 creons per ton) c.i.f. price	28,000	28,000	28,000	30,800
Total foreign exchange saved	63,400	81,100	98,800	108,680

As already noted, table 19.3, which was supplied in the feasibility report, gives a detailed breakdown by year of the domestic resource requirements in the construction of the project. The total figure over the three years' construction period of 110 million creons exactly matches the loan provided to the SFA by the Central Treasury. It is, however, necessary to categorize this domestic component of the construction costs into (a) unskilled labour; (b) skilled labour; and (c) domestic materials.

Table 19.7 provides the unskilled labour component of the domestic construction costs on a year-by-year basis. From a study of the feasibility

TABLE 19.7　UNSKILLED LABOUR COMPONENT OF CONSTRUCTION COSTS
(Thousand creons)

Item	Year		
	0	1	2
(1) Land and site preparation (item 1 of table 19.3)	5,500	—	—
(2) Buildings, structures and civil works (20% of (2), table 19.3)	1,904	3,440	2,668
(3) Processing facilities (10% of (4), table 19.3)	365	625	15
(4) Welfare and housing (50% of (6), table 19.3)	—	500	1,220
Total	7,769	4,565	3,903

report it was deduced that of the 9.5 million creons involved in land and site preparation, item (1) of table 19.3, about 5.5 million creons is formed of wages to unskilled labour. Furthermore, in table 19.3, about 20 per cent of (2), 10 per cent of (4), and 50 per cent of (6) consist of such wages. All these figures have been incorporated in table 19.7.

Skilled labour being scarce in Sarania, many of the technicians involved in the project will, in fact, be recruited from abroad. There will, nevertheless, be some who will be recruited locally. For the purposes of this study we have classified engineers, draftsmen and surveyors as skilled workers. Foremen and truck drivers etc. we shall regard as semi-skilled workers. Their wages appear to be a rather small component of the construction costs of the project. Consequently, we have not separated out this wage bill from the construction costs. But salaries to domestic skilled employees during construction are not

TABLE 19.8　SALARIES TO SKILLED DOMESTIC EMPLOYEES DURING CONSTRUCTION
(Thousand creons)

Item	Year		
	0	1	2
(1) Land and site preparation ((1), table 19.3)	200	—	—
(2) Buildings, structures etc. (5% of (2), table 19.3)	476	860	667
(3) Welfare and housing (5% of (6), table 19.3)	—	50	122
(4) Engineering costs etc. (100% of (7), table 19.3)	630	1,000	1,000
Total	1,306	1,910	1,789

negligible. We have, therefore, presented in table 19.8 a year-by-year breakdown of the skilled labour component of domestic construction costs.

For a given year in the construction of the project the domestic investment cost minus wage payments to unskilled and skilled labour represents the domestic materials involved in construction. For completeness, table 19.9 provides a year-by-year breakdown of the costs of these materials in construction.

TABLE 19.9   COST OF DOMESTIC MATERIALS IN CONSTRUCTION
(Thousand creons)

	Year		
	0	*1*	*2*
Domestic materials	14,225	19,575	54,958

The foreign exchange cost involved in the construction of the project totals 210 million creons and is spread over the first three years. Table 19.2, provided by the feasibility report, gives a detailed breakdown of the foreign exchange component of construction costs by item. It will be observed that item (6) consists wholly of salaries paid to foreign personnel. All other items consist of payment for foreign materials.

Using tables 19.2, 19.3, 19.7, 19.8 and 19.9 we have compiled the various resources used in the construction of the project and presented them in table 19.10.

TABLE 19.10   RESOURCES USED IN CONSTRUCTION
(Thousand creons)

Resource	Year			Total
	0	*1*	*2*	
(1) Domestic materials	14,225	19,575	54,958	88,758
(2) Unskilled labour	7,769	4,565	3,903	16,237
(3) Skilled labour	1,306	1,910	1,789	5,005
(4) Foreign exchange	36,700	33,950	139,350	210,000
(a) Materials	(31,080)	(31,750)	(137,950)	—
(b) Personnel	(5,620)	(2,200)	(1,400)	—
Total	60,000	60,000	200,000	320,000

TABLE 19.11   WORKING CAPITAL
(Thousand creons)

Resource	Year			Total
	3	*4*	*5*	
(1) Foreign exchange	10,000	—	—	10,000
(2) Domestic materials	4,000	4,000	2,000	10,000
Total	14,000	4,000	2,000	20,000

The SFA will also build up a working capital worth 20 million creons over years 3 through 5. Table 19.11 gives a breakdown of this working capital on a year-by-year basis, showing the resources used as well.

19.7 OPERATING COSTS

The feasibility study states that when operated at 100 per cent capacity the mill's annual requirement of pulpwood is 260,000 solid cubic metres (m^3) of hardwood. Since the forest resources of eastern Sarakand have not, so far, been exploited much, pulpwood at the present moment is not sold as such in Sarania. The pulpwood requirement of the mill will be met by the following arrangement. The logging operation will be conducted by the SFA using machinery (such as tractors, trailers and timber loaders) borrowed from the Ministry of Forestry of the Government of Sarania. Because of the importance of forestry operations, no rentals will be charged for the use of such machines. Transportation of the pulpwood from the forest to the mill is an important cost item, and the SFA will use a private transportation firm that will charge 26.8 creons per m^3 of pulpwood delivered to the mill. The feasibility report states that the cost to the SFA of logging 1 m^3 of pulpwood will be about 67.9 creons. In other words, for logging and transporting to the mill 1 m^3 of pulpwood, the SFA will incur a cost of 94.7 creons.

Since the pulpwood is the most important raw material in the production of pulp and paper, a careful analysis of its cost is required. As the use of pulpwood by the mill will not reduce its supply in the rest of the economy,

TABLE 19.12   CAPITAL COST IN LOGGING 28,000 m^3 OF PULPWOOD
(Thousand creons)

Item of equipment	No.	Resource Foreign exchange	Resource Domestic materials
(1) Tractors	4	680	—
(2) Timber loader	1	150	—
(3) Trailer	8	220	—
(4) Pickup truck	1	40	—
(5) Jeep	1	40	—
(6) Motorcycle	2	10	—
(7) Mules	10	—	20
(8) Cable winches	3	—	60
(9) Diesel generator	1	—	80
(10) Mechanical equipment (welding, cutting, drilling, etc.)	—	—	30
(11) Water-supply equipment	—	—	10
(12) Fuel tanks	—	—	10
(13) Tools (for felling, extraction etc.)	—	—	10
(14) Camp	—	—	260
(15) Equipment for telecommunications etc. .	—	—	40
Total		1,140	520

Total capital cost = 1,660.

we shall have to determine the value of the resources used in producing the pulpwood to assess its cost (see chapter 5). For this purpose we studied a separate document provided by the SFA giving a detailed account of the logging operations that are required in the forest regions of eastern Sarakand.

Table 19.12 presents the capital cost estimates for logging. The estimates refer to one logging unit of approximately 10,000 hectares, producing annually 28,000 m^3 of mixed broad-leaved wood from roughly 165 hectares net felling area. On the assumption that only simple machine tools are produced domestically, we have split up the capital cost for the logging operation according to the resources used, namely, foreign exchange and domestic materials. Depreciation figures for these capital goods were provided by the SFA report on the logging operation. In table 19.13 we have compiled these figures. The figures are high, but not too high, in view of the nature of the operations involved.

TABLE 19.13   ANNUAL DEPRECIATION OF FIXED CAPITAL IN LOGGING 28,000 m^3 OF PULPWOOD

Item of equipment	Depreciation (per cent)	Foreign exchange	Domestic materials	Total
		Resource		
		(thousand creons)		
(1) Tractors	25	170	—	170
(2) Timber loader	25	37	—	37
(3) Trailer	20	44	—	44
(4) Pickup truck	20	8	—	8
(5) Jeep	20	8	—	8
(6) Motorcycle	30	3	—	3
(7) Mules	50	—	10	10
(8) Cable winches	75	—	45	45
(9) Diesel generator	50	—	40	40
(10) Mechanical equipment	66	—	20	20
(11) Water-supply tank	50	—	5	5
(12) Fuel tanks	50	—	5	5
(13) Tools	100	—	10	10
(14) Camp	75	—	193	193
(15) Equipment for telecommunications etc.	50	—	20	20
Total		270	348	618

In table 19.14 we present the annual operating cost of logging 28,000 m^3 of pulpwood according to the resources used. The absence of skilled workers as a separate category in this table requires some explanation. Skilled workers (e.g. forest engineers and surveyors) are required mainly when the forests are surveyed and the logging is contemplated. Since the SFA has already surveyed the forest resources of Sarakand, we clearly cannot now impute the survey costs to the pulp and paper mill under contemplation. For the actual operation of logging, only semi-skilled workers and unskilled workers are required. Assuming that semi-skilled workers are paid wages that reflect their opportunity

TABLE 19.14   OPERATING COST OF LOGGING 28,000 m³ OF PULPWOOD
(Thousand creons)

Item	Foreign exchange	Domestic resources	Unskilled labour	Total
Materials				
(1) Fuels and lubricants	130	—	—	130
(2) Tires	—	90	—	90
(3) Maintenance and repair	—	185	—	185
(4) Insurance	—	17	—	17
Wages				
(5) Semi-skilled	—	1,025	—	1,025
(6) Unskilled	—	—	55	55
Total	130	1,317	55	1,502

costs, we have in table 19.14 placed the 1.025 million creons of such wages in the category of domestic resources.

Using tables 19.12—19.14 we can now calculate the cost of logging and transporting 28,000 m³ of pulpwood. For this we use the formula:

$$\text{Cost} = \text{interest on capital} + \text{depreciation} +$$
$$+ \text{ operating cost (materials and personnel)} + \text{transport cost}[65]$$

The interest rate we use in the above formula is, naturally, the social rate of discount (see chapter 13). The figure that we use is 10 per cent per annum, assumed constant over the lifetime of the project.[66]

In table 19.15 we have compiled the cost of logging and delivering 28,000 m³ of pulpwood according to the various resources used on the basis of the foregoing formula. The total cost comes to 3.036 million creons. From this it

TABLE 19.15   COST OF LOGGING AND DELIVERING 28,000 m³ OF PULPWOOD
(Thousand creons)

Resource	Interest on capital	Depreciation	Operating cost	Transport cost	Total
(1) Foreign exchange ..	$0.1 \times 1{,}140$	270	130	—	514.0
(2) Domestic materials (including semi-skilled labour)	$0.1 \times\ \ 520$	348	1,317	26.8×28	2,467.4
(3) Unskilled labour ...	—	—	55	—	55.0
Total	166	618	1,502	750.4	3,036.4

Cost of 1 m³ of pulpwood $= \dfrac{3{,}036{,}400}{28{,}000} = 108.4$ creons.

---

[65] In the SFA report on logging operations, prices of machines have been assumed to remain constant over time. There are, therefore, no capital gains (losses) in the imputation of the rentals on the machines in the above formula.

[66] Clearly the cost of logging and transportation will vary according to the selection of the social rate of discount in the sensitivity analysis. We stick to a figure of 10 per cent, since not much error will be committed in using a single value such as this.

follows immediately that the logging and delivery of 1 m³ of pulpwood consumes resources worth about 108.4 creons. This is somewhat higher than the 94.7 creons quoted in the feasibility study. The difference arises because the feasibility report assessed the financial aspects of the project from the point of view of the SFA, and the SFA is not required to pay any rental charges to the Ministry of Forestry for the machinery the ministry loans. But the use of such machinery involves a cost to the Saranian economy as a whole and so must be included in the costing of the pulpwood.[67]

When operating at 100 per cent capacity, the mill requires 260,000 m³ of pulpwood annually. For completeness we have compiled in table 19.16 the cost of providing 260,000 m³ of pulpwood to the mill according to the resources used.

TABLE 19.16   COST OF LOGGING AND DELIVERING 260,000 m³ OF PULPWOOD
(Thousand creons)

Resource	Cost	
(1) Foreign exchange	$\dfrac{514 \times 260}{28} =$	4,772.1
(2) Domestic materials	$\dfrac{2,467.4 \times 260}{28} =$	22,911.1
(3) Unskilled labour	$\dfrac{55 \times 260}{28} =$	510.7
Total		28,193.9

Having costed the pulpwood we can now calculate the annual operating costs of the mill when it is operating at 100 per cent capacity (see table 19.17). The figures of table 19.17, except for the pulpwood, have been taken from the feasibility report without any serious modifications. For sulphuric acid (3), sodium sulphate (4) and sulphur (5) we have used world prices, since, although these three items are supplied domestically, they are judged to be potentially exportable. This modification does not really affect the operating costs (these three items add up to very little as compared with the other items). We have, nevertheless, made the correction for the sake of consistency. At 100 per cent capacity the annual operating costs amount to about 66.962 million creons. This is somewhat larger than the 63.485 million creons quoted in the feasibility report and incorporated in table 19.5 as the operating costs met by the SFA. At the risk of restating the obvious, this difference arises largely because the SFA uses the machinery involved in logging operations free of charge.

The pulp and paper mill will operate at 100 per cent capacity during years 5 through 10. In table 19.1 it was seen that the output *configuration* of the project will change over years 3, 4 and 5. Now the two outputs of the mill will require inputs in somewhat different proportions. For example, a ton of corrugating medium requires for its manufacture much less pulpwood than a ton of rayon-grade pulp does, although the two require roughly the same

---

[67] We are, of course, assuming that these pieces of machinery are not currently lying idle.

TABLE 19.17   ANNUAL OPERATING COSTS OF MILL (AT 100% CAPACITY)
(Thousand creons)

Item	Foreign exchange	Domestic materials	Unskilled labour
(1) Pulpwood	4,745.0	22,912.5	520.0
(2) Sodium chloride (imported)	660.0	—	—
(3) Sulphuric acid (exportable)	81.0	—	—
(4) Sodium sulphate (exportable)	966.7	—	—
(5) Sulphur (exportable)	386.8	—	—
(6) Limestone	—	80.0	—
(7) Salt	—	1,600.0	—
(8) Fuel oil (imported)	5,958.4	—	—
(9) Water (purification chemicals, filters etc.) ..	640.0	200.0	—
(10) Other materials (repairs and supplies)	3,880.0	1,600.0	—
(11) Plant office and purchasing	370.0	590.0	—
(12) Payroll expenses	150.0	2,650.0	—
(13) Local freight	—	1,030.0	—
(14) Plant overhead	200.0	1,500.0	—
(15) Insurance	—	1,100.0	—
(16) Distribution and selling	—	1,000.0	—
(17) General expenses	350.0	550.0	—
Personnel			
(18) Operating labour	3,460.0	2,854.0	1,192.0
(19) Plant supervision	500.0	500.0	—
(20) Maintenance labour	2,620.0	1,476.0	640.0
Total	24,967.9	39,642.5	2,352.0

Total annual operating cost = 66,962.45.

amounts of some of the chemicals. But even though the total output of the mill in year 3 will be four sixths of its total output in year 5, some of the items (e.g. (19) and (20) in table 19.17) of the operating costs will be much the same in these two years. As a result the feasibility report suggests that the operating costs in years 3 and 4 are roughly four sixths and five sixths, respectively, of the operating costs in year 5. We shall assume this as well, since the feasibility report does not give a detailed breakdown of the production costs involved in each of the two outputs of the mill. On this basis we have compiled in table 19.18 the year-by-year operating costs of the mill according to the resources used.

TABLE 19.18   OPERATING COSTS OF MILL
(Thousand creons)

Resource	Year			
	3	4	5—10	11—14
(1) Foreign exchange	16,660	20,800	24,968	27,470
(2) Domestic materials	26,420	33,050	39,643	43,600
(3) Unskilled labour	1,560	1,950	2,352	2,590
Total	44,640	55,800	66,963	73,660

19.8 INDIRECT BENEFITS

Of the total investment outlay of the project, expenditure on welfare and housing amounts to 4.05 million creons (see tables 19.2 and 19.3). This expenditure yields an indirect benefit by the project that should now be assessed. It was stated earlier that the SFA will provide the housing and welfare facilities free of charge to the project employees. We have assumed that roughly two thirds of the total expenditure of 4.05 million creons on welfare and housing will be for foreign personnel and the remaining 1.35 million creons (wholly domestic expenditure) will be for Saranian employees. For the purpose of aggregate-consumption benefits to Sarania, the indirect benefits must be evaluated from the housing provided to Saranian employees only. Assuming an annual rate of return of 15 per cent[68] on the 1.35 million creons, we assess the annual indirect benefits due to housing to be about 203 thousand creons.

19.9 RESOURCE FLOWS DUE TO THE PROJECT

We now turn to table 19.19, which has been compiled from tables 19.6, 19.10, 19.11, 19.17 and 19.18. It provides a comprehensive summary of all the resource flows brought about by the pulp and paper mill. Item (1) gives the annual social value of the output of the mill and has been compiled from table 19.6. Item (2) gives the annual indirect benefits provided by the project in the form of the housing and welfare facilities discussed in the previous paragraph. Item (3) consists of the construction costs in terms of the resources used and has been incorporated from table 19.10. Item (4) giving the buildup of working capital has been obtained from table 19.11. Item (5), which gives the annual operating costs, has been compiled from tables 19.17 and 19.18. But in the process we have made an extension in the classification that should be explained. We have in table 19.19 split up the foreign exchange component of operating costs into materials (5-a) and foreign personnel (5-b). We have computed (5-b) from the foreign exchange components of items (18), (19) and (20) in table 19.17. It follows that the foreign exchange component of items (1—17) in table 19.17 yields item (5-a) in table 19.19. Turning to the domestic resource component of operating costs, we have, in table 19.19, split it up into domestic materials (5-c) and semi-skilled labour (5-d). Now wages paid to semi-skilled labour appear in table 19.17 as items (18), (19) and (20) as well as a part of (1). These items, therefore, yield item (5-d) in table 19.19.[69] The remainder of the domestic resource component of operating costs (table 19.17) appears as item (5-c) in table 19.19. Finally, we come to item (6) in table 19.19. It consists of the working capital recovered by the SFA and

---

[68] Discussed in the appendix after chapter 20.

[69] It should be pointed out that the 1.025 million creons of wages to semi-skilled labour in item (5) of table 19.14 is for logging 28,000 m³ of pulpwood. For a normal year of the mill (i.e. 100% capacity) the wage to semi-skilled labour in logging is: $\dfrac{1.025 \times 260}{28} \times 9.730$ million creons. It follows that 9.730 million creons is the portion of item (1) of table 17 that has to be added to items (18), (19) and (20) in table 17 to arrive at the total wages paid to semi-skilled labour in operating costs.

TABLE 19.19   RESOURCE FLOWS FOR THE PULP AND PAPER MILL
(Thousand creons)

									Year							
	0	1	2	3	4	5	6	7	8	9	10	11	12	13	14	15
(1) Output (foreign exchange) …	—	—	—	63,400	81,100	98,800	98,800	98,800	98,800	98,800	98,800	108,680	108,680	108,680	108,680	108,680
(2) Housing (domestic) …	—	203	203	203	203	203	203	203	203	203	203	203	203	203	203	203
(3) Construction costs																
Foreign exchange (3-a) …	31,080	31,750	137,950	—	—	—	—	—	—	—	—	—	—	—	—	—
(3-b) …	5,620	2,200	1,400	—	—	—	—	—	—	—	—	—	—	—	—	—
Subtotal ……	36,700	33,950	139,350	—	—	—	—	—	—	—	—	—	—	—	—	—
Unskilled labour (3-c) …	7,769	4,565	3,903	—	—	—	—	—	—	—	—	—	—	—	—	—
Domestic materials (3-d) …	14,225	19,575	54,958	—	—	—	—	—	—	—	—	—	—	—	—	—
Skilled labour (3-e) …	1,306	1,910	1,789	—	—	—	—	—	—	—	—	—	—	—	—	—
Total (3) ……	60,000	60,000	200,000	—	—	—	—	—	—	—	—	—	—	—	—	—
(a) Working capital ……	—	—	—	14,000	4,000	2,000	—	—	—	—	—	—	—	—	—	—
Foreign exchange (4-a) …	—	—	—	10,000	—	—	—	—	—	—	—	—	—	—	—	—
Domestic materials (4-b) …	—	—	—	4,000	4,000	2,000	—	—	—	—	—	—	—	—	—	—

		C1	C2	C3	C4	C5	C6	C7	C8	C9	C10	C11	C12	C13	C14
(5) Operating costs															
Foreign exchange	(5-a)	12,280	15,350	18,388	18,388	18,388	18,388	18,388	18,388	20,230	20,230	20,230	20,230	—	—
	(5-b)	4,380	5,450	6,580	6,580	6,580	6,580	6,580	6,580	7,240	7,240	7,240	7,240	—	—
Subtotal		16,660	20,800	24,968	24,968	24,968	24,968	24,968	24,968	27,470	27,470	27,470	27,470	—	
Domestic materials	(5-c)	17,720	20,900	25,083	25,083	25,083	25,083	25,083	25,083	27,590	27,590	27,590	27,590	—	
Semi-skilled labour	(5-d)	9,700	12,150	14,560	14,560	14,560	14,560	14,560	14,560	16,010	16,010	16,010	16,010	—	
Unskilled labour	(5-e)	1,560	1,950	2,352	2,352	2,352	2,352	2,352	2,352	2,590	2,590	2,590	2,590	—	
Total	(5)	45,640	55,800	66,963	66,963	66,963	66,963	66,963	66,963	73,660	73,660	73,660	73,660	—	
(6) Working capital and scrap value															
Foreign exchange	(6-a)	—	—	—	—	—	—	—	—	—	—	—	—	—	10,000
Domestic materials	(6-b)	—	—	—	—	—	—	—	—	—	—	—	—	—	34,160
Total	(6)	—	—	—	—	—	—	—	—	—	—	—	—	—	44,160

the scrap value of the project. It was mentioned at the end of section 19.4 that the scrap value of the plant is estimated to be about 24.16 million creons. We assume that it will be wholly in terms of domestic materials.[70] Of the 20 million creons working capital, 10 million is in foreign exchange. This explains (6-a) and (6-b) in table 19.19.

19.10 EVALUATION OF AGGREGATE-CONSUMPTION BENEFITS

The evaluation of the net aggregate-consumption benefits of the pulp and paper mill is carried out best in successive stages of approximation. The first—and the most straightforward—step is to assess the benefits and costs under the assumption that market prices adequately reflect social opportunity costs and, therefore, the ultimate consumption benefits and costs involved. On this basis the aggregate-consumption benefits of the project consist of items (1), (2) and (6) in table 19.19 and the consumption costs include items (3), (4) and (5).[71] Items (1), (2) and (6) correspond to real gains for the Saranian economy as a whole and would not have come about in the absence of the project. Analogously, items (3), (4) and (5) correspond to payments for resources that could have been used elsewhere—were it not for this project—and which, therefore, measure the sacrifice of consumption possibilities that the Saranian economy sustains because of the project.

The market value of net aggregate-consumption benefits in any given year of the project is, therefore, given by

$$MC = (1) + (2) - (3) - (4) - (5) + (6) \qquad (19.1)$$

MC represents the first approximation to the net aggregate-consumption benefits of the project. The second approximation involves the adjustment of the market prices of specific resources wherever these prices do not reflect the real contribution of the resources to the aggregate-consumption objective—i.e. their "social opportunity cost". Throughout these Guidelines we have noted that such discrepancies can occur for a variety of reasons and in a variety of ways. In the evaluation of this project three resources are singled out for price adjustment: foreign exchange, skilled labour and unskilled labour. It is tacitly assumed that all the remaining resources of the project are correctly priced by the competitive market mechanism.

In the case of foreign exchange, it is noted that the heavy pressure on the Saranian balance of payments (brought about by the implementation of their recent Five-Year Plan) has resulted in strict quantitative import controls and export subsidies to maintain the dollar value of the creon. It is clear to the Government that one dollar of foreign exchange is worth substantially more than 10 creons, the official rate of exchange. In what follows the opportunity

---

[70] This is reasonable, since we have assumed that only buildings and structures will remain as scrap and much of the cost in constructing buildings and structures involved the use of domestic materials (see tables 19.2 and 19.3).

[71] From now on all references are to table 19.19 unless otherwise stated.

cost of foreign exchange relative to its official market price will be denoted by $(1 + \Phi)$. That is to say, Φ represents the foreign exchange premium, which is currently positive in Sarania and which is expected to remain constant over the lifetime of the project.

It was noted earlier that considerable surplus unskilled labour exists in western Sarania. The case of unskilled labour, therefore, is opposite to that of foreign exchange. The opportunity cost of unskilled labour, relative to the market wage rate, will be denoted by $(1 + \lambda)$. That is to say, λ represents the unskilled labour premium (negative in our case).

Although skilled labour in Sarania is assumed to be fully employed, it is generally acknowledged that skilled workers are underpaid in the country. That is, it is assumed that the marginal skilled worker contributes more to aggregate-consumption benefits than the wage he commands. In parallel with Φ and λ, $\varkappa$ is defined as the social premium on the market wage of skilled labour. We have assumed that semi-skilled labour commands its opportunity cost, and thus no correction is required for this category of labour.

We now express the net aggregate-consumption benefits in a given year of the pulp and paper mill, after incorporating the opportunity cost premiums, as:

$$SC^* = MC + \Phi F' + \lambda L + \varkappa W$$
$$\text{where } F' = (1) - (3\text{-a}) - (3\text{-b}) - (4\text{-a}) - (5\text{-a}) - (5\text{-b}) + (6\text{-a})$$
$$L = -(3\text{-c}) - (5\text{-e})$$
$$W = -(3\text{-e}) \tag{19.2}$$

SC^* is obtained by adding three terms to the first approximation, MC. The first term corrects MC for the opportunity cost of foreign exchange by multiplying the net foreign exchange component of benefits and costs, F', by the (positive) foreign exchange premium, Φ. The second term corrects MC for the opportunity cost of unskilled labour by multiplying the net unskilled labour component, L, by the (negative) labour premium, λ. The third term does the same for skilled labour with its (positive) premium, $\varkappa$.

But actually we have overcorrected. We have included the foreign exchange premium on the total salary paid to foreign personnel (items (3-b) and (5-b)). But in fact a portion of this salary will be spent in Sarakand. For this portion the foreign exchange correction is not necessary, since the dollar value of this part is converted into creons at the official exchange rate and thus Sarania does not lose the extra value of the foreign exchange. Denoting by δ, $(0 < \delta < 1)$ the fraction of the foreign personnel salary that is not removed from Sarania, the correct formula for the second approximation reads now as:

$$SC = MC + \Phi F + \lambda L + \varkappa W \tag{19.3}$$
$$\text{where } F = (1) - (3\text{-a}) - (3\text{-b}) + (3\text{-b}) - (4\text{-a}) - (5\text{-a}) - (5\text{-b}) +$$
$$+ \delta(5\text{-b}) + (6\text{-a}) \tag{19.3a}$$
$$L = -(3\text{-c}) - (5\text{-e}) \tag{19.3b}$$
$$W = -(3\text{-e}) \tag{19.3c}$$

We now turn to the third and final approximation to the net aggregate-consumption benefits of the project. This consists in taking into account that the social value of funds devoted to investment exceeds the social value of the same funds devoted to consumption. This feature has arisen in Sarania owing to the inability of the central Government to use its fiscal and monetary powers to bring about the rate of investment it deems optimal for the country as a whole. This was discussed at length in chapters 6 and 14. To evaluate the indirect future benefits (and costs) of the project, we shall have to assess the net effect on the mix of consumption and investment in the economy due to the project. To the extent that the project results in a net increase of investment relative to consumption in any given year, the corresponding aggregate-consumption benefits, evaluated at the relevant social rate of discount, are increased above the level measured by the second approximation, SC. To evaluate the net effect to the project on the rate of investment, it is necessary to distinguish all the benefits and cost flows that make up SC, as well as any accompanying cash transfers, according to the group that gains or loses, and to estimate the respective marginal savings propensities of each group.

For this purpose, three broad groups of gainers and losers have been distinguished with respect to the pulp and paper mill: semi-skilled and unskilled workers, L; the Government, G; and the private sector, P. G includes all branches of the Saranian Government—the SFA, the Ministry of Forestry etc.—for they all operate under a common budget. Each of the benefit and cost flows that enter into SC, as defined in equation (19.3), can be identified with one of these three groups. We proceed to do this now with more detailed comments.

To begin with, at the present time both rayon-grade pulp and corrugating medium are imported into Sarania at 1,770 creons per ton and 1,400 creons per ton, respectively, and payment is made for these at the official rate of exchange. Since the Government of Sarania controls the foreign exchange market in Sarania, it effectively bears the cost of the foreign exchange premium associated with the imported products. The Government, on the other hand, charges a duty of 354 creons per ton and 560 creons per ton, respectively, on the two products. The purchasers, therefore, pay 2,124 creons per ton and 1,960 creons per ton on these products. Once the project is in operation the purchasers will be required to pay exactly what they were paying before (but now, of course, the whole 2,124 creons per ton on rayon-grade pulp and 1,960 creons per ton on corrugating medium will be paid to the Government). So, from the point of view of the domestic purchasers it does not make any difference whether the output is produced at home or imported. But with the project in operation the Government earns an extra 1,770 creons per ton on the rayon-grade pulp and 1,440 creons per ton on the corrugating medium. Moreover, it now no longer loses the foreign exchange premium it used to lose. Thus, both item (1) and $\Phi(1)$ [i.e. Φ multiplied by (1)] are direct benefits the Government captures as a result of the project. Next, the housing and welfare benefits, item (2), are gained by L.

The identification of the group that pays for construction costs, item (3), depends on the manner in which these costs are financed—in particular, from whom the corresponding resources are ultimately diverted. If the construction costs of the project are paid out of government revenues without any corresponding receipts (i.e. there is no additional taxation or borrowing by the Government), then G is the loser. Part of the cost of the present project is financed by a World Bank loan and the rest by the Saranian Government. It is assumed that the World Bank loan would have been available to the Government on the same terms in the absence of this project (i.e. the loan is not tied). Hence, it is G that pays for the foreign exchange component (3-a) and (3-b), which it could have used on an alternative project.[72]. In addition to the market value of this foreign exchange component, G also loses the extra opportunity cost, represented by Φ(3-a) and $(1-\delta)\Phi$(3-b). In the case of the funds provided in domestic currency by the Central Treasury loan, it is assumed that these funds are met from Government revenues without any corresponding additional taxation or borrowing. It follows that G loses (3-c), (3-d) and (3-e).

The costs of operating the project and the working capital are financed by the SFA. That is, G loses (4) and (5). Moreover, the additional opportunity costs Φ(4-a)Φ(5-a) and $(1-\delta)\Phi$(5-b) are also borne by G. Finally, at the termination of the project G captures (6) as well as Φ(6-a).[73]

It is assumed that the skilled domestic labour required during the construction of the project is drawn away from the private sector, P, which therefore loses the extra opportunity cost of skilled labour, i.e. P loses $\varkappa$(3-e).

It now remains to consider the (negative) costs included in SC, which are represented by the unskilled labour premium, λL (defined in equation (19.3b)). This premium corresponds to the margin by which the total project wage bill for unskilled labour exceeds the amount necessary to attract unskilled workers to the project, i.e. earnings in alternative employment plus the costs of transfer. This margin corresponds exactly to the net extra income received by the unskilled labour on account of the project. That is, the (negative) costs $\lambda[(3\text{-c}) + (5\text{-e})]$ accrue to L.

The distribution by group of the second approximation to net consumption benefits, SC, can now be summarized as follows:

$$SC = SC^G + SC^P + SC^L \tag{19.4}$$

where

$$SC^G = MC - (2) + \Phi(1) - \Phi(3\text{-a}) - (1 - \delta)\,\Phi(3\text{-b}) - \Phi(4\text{-a}) -$$
$$- \Phi(5\text{-a}) - (1 - \delta)\,\Phi(5\text{-b}) + \Phi(6\text{-a}) \tag{19.4a}$$
$$SC^P = -\varkappa(3\text{-a}) \tag{19.4b}$$
$$SC^L = -\lambda[(3\text{-c}) + (5\text{-e})] + (2) \tag{19.4c}$$

---

[72] Notice that since the loan is untied, it is regarded as a cost due to the project when the loan is given and not when it is repaid. Had the loan been tied to the project we would not regard it as a cost due to the project until the repayments are actually made. See chapter 5, section 5.4.

[73] See section 16.5 for a discussion of this.

where SC^G, SC^P and SC^L represent the value of net consumption benefits flowing to G, P and L, respectively. To arrive at the final social value of net aggregate-consumption benefits, C, it is necessary to correct SC^G, SC^P and SC^L according to the proportions in which each is divided between consumption and investment. Thus, if the average unskilled (and semi-skilled) worker saves a proportion s_L of his marginal gains, the "social value" of the net consumption benefits flowing to unskilled labour is:

$$C^L = [(1 - s_L) + s_L \, P^{\text{inv}}] \, SC^L$$

where P^{inv} is the shadow price of investment.[74] Similarly, if G and P save proportions s_G and s_P of their marginal gains, respectively, then the social value of net consumption benefits flowing to G and to P is:

$$C^G = [(1 - s_G) + s_G \, P^{\text{inv}}] \, SC^G$$
$$C^P = [(1 - s_P) + s_P \, P^{\text{inv}}] \, SC^P$$

We may now write the third and final approximation to the value of net aggregate-consumption benefits, C, to Sarania as a whole in any given year as the sum of the social value of net benefits flowing to each distinct group (see equation 6.7 in chapter 6):

$$C = C^G + C^L + C^P \tag{19.5}$$

19.11 REDISTRIBUTION TO SARAKAND

The second national objective that we consider in the evaluation of the pulp and paper mill is the objective of redistributing benefits to the under-developed province of Sarakand. Some of the benefits and cost flows shown in table 19.19 are relevant to the welfare of Sarakand and some are not. Moreover, the relevant items may affect the redistribution objective differently from the way in which they affect the aggregate-consumption objective.

Neither the value of the outputs (1) nor the extra value of the foreign exchange $\Phi(1)$ can be regarded as direct benefits to Sarakand, since both are captured by the Saranian Central Government. However, the indirect housing and welfare benefits (2) are captured by Sarakand residents and thus must be regarded as a benefit to Sarakand. Among the cost flows, both construction and operating costs are met by the Central Government, so that neither item can be regarded as a loss to Sarakand.

Wage payments require careful handling. Unskilled labour is surplus in Sarakand and is likely to remain so over the lifetime of the project. The wage bill of unskilled labour in both construction and operating costs, i.e. (3-c) and (5-e), therefore, represents benefits to Sarakand. The case of domestic skilled and semi-skilled workers is somewhat different, of course. But we can assume that the employment of domestic skilled and semi-skilled workers in this project causes no corresponding reduction in the Sarakand labour force,

---

[74] See equation A6.12 in the appendix to chapter 6.

since there will be a corresponding immigration of labour into the province. Accordingly, we regard such wage bills (3-e) and (5-d) as benefits to Sarakand. Of the total salary paid to foreign personnel, i.e. (3-b) and (5-b), a fraction δ is assumed to be spent in Sarakand, and the rest $(1 - \delta)$ is removed from Sarania. It follows that δ(3-b) and δ(5-b) also represent benefits to Sarakand.

Finally, neither the working capital nor the scrap value can be regarded as either a cost or benefit to Sarakand, since the payments are made by and to the Central Government.

It follows that the total value of net aggregate-consumption benefits redistributed to Sarakand in any given year can be expressed as:

$$(DR)_s = (2) + (3\text{-c}) + (3\text{-e}) + (5\text{-e}) + (5\text{-d}) + (3\text{-b}) + (5\text{-b}) \quad (19.6)$$

Unlike the first approximation to net aggregate-consumption benefits, MC, $(DR)_s$ does not have to be corrected for the social opportunity costs of foreign exchange, unskilled labour and investment vis-à-vis consumption. What is an opportunity cost with respect to the aggregate-consumption benefits of a country is not necessarily an opportunity cost for a particular region. Thus, although Sarania as a whole enjoys benefits equal to the opportunity cost of foreign exchange when foreign personnel spend a fraction (δ) of their salary in Sarania, the gain due to the extra social value of the foreign exchange is spread over the whole country, and its effect on Sarakand can be assumed to be negligible. Similarly, the benefits to Sarakand of employing unskilled labour are not limited to the excess of the market wage over the amount actually necessary to attract the labour; the latter represents a cost to Sarania as a whole, and very little to Sarakand. Finally, if investment is valued higher than the equivalent current consumption in calculating aggregate-consumption benefits, this is because the increased consumption flow provided by investment is a gain to the country as a whole. The fraction of the gain reaching Sarakand may be ignored for practical purposes.

One important adjustment of $(DR)_s$ remains to be made to assess the total net consumption benefits distributed to Sarakand by the project. Whether the direct benefits measured by $(DR)_s$ are consumed or invested, a part of them will be respent within Sarakand; and to the extent that they result in a net transfer of wage and profit earnings from elsewhere in Sarania to Sarakand or activate otherwise idle resources in Sarakand they will result in a new round of benefits to the region. This was discussed in detail in chapter 7. There it was shown that if γ represents the proportion of marginal benefits to Sarakand which, when respent, results in additional benefits to the region, then the total value of net regional consumption benefits in any one year is given by:

$$R_s = (DR)_s \times \left(\frac{1}{1 - \gamma}\right) \quad (19.7)$$

19.12 EVALUATION OF THE PROJECT

In the course of the two previous sections of this case study dealing with the two principal objectives of the Saranian Government vis-à-vis the proposed

project, various parameters were introduced for which values are required to evaluate the project. In principle, each of these parameters is a function of time, and the appropriate values may therefore change according to the year in which the benefits and costs are being measured. To simplify the computations, however, it will be assumed for the purpose of this case study that the value of each parameter remains constant over the entire lifetime of the project. In table 19.20 each parameter is listed with the corresponding numerical value that is tentatively assumed to be appropriate to the Saranian economy.

TABLE 19.20   VALUES OF NATIONAL PARAMETERS

(1) Foreign exchange premium	Φ = 0.5
(2) Unskilled labour premium	λ = —1.0
(3) Domestic skilled labour premium	χ = +1.0
(4) Marginal rate of return on investment	q = 0.20
(5) Marginal rate of savings	s = 0.3
(6) Social rate of discount	i = 0.08, 0.1, 0.12
(7) Shadow price of investment[a]	P^{inv} = 7, 3.5, 2.33
(8) Marginal propensities to save:	
(a) Government	s_G = 1.0
(b) Private sector	s_P = 0.6
(c) Unskilled and semi-skilled labour	s_L = 0.0
(9) Marginal propensity to respend in Sarakand	γ = 0.2
(10) Proportion of foreign personnel salary spent in Sarakand..	δ = 0.2
(11) Weights on objectives:	
(a) Aggregate consumption	Θ^c = 1.0
(b) Redistribution to Sarakand	Θ^{RS} = (unknown)

[a] The shadow price of investment, P^{inv}, is calculated according to formula 14.16 (see chapter 14). We verify that

$$P^{inv} = \frac{(i-s)\,q}{i-sq} = 3.5 \text{ for } i = 0.1$$

Foreign exchange is assumed to be worth one-and-a-half times its value at the official exchange rate (i.e. $\Phi = +0.5$). In view of the overpopulation and backwardness of the Sarakand region, it may not be unreasonable to regard the opportunity cost of unskilled labour as equal to zero (i.e. $\lambda = -1.0$). In contrast, the opportunity cost of domestic skilled workers is assumed to be twice the market wage (i.e. $\chi = +1.0$).

In line with the general principles advocated throughout these Guidelines, we do not assume that the Saranian Government has stipulated a certain social rate of discount. Instead, the project is evaluated on the basis of a set of values for this national parameter. Specifically, we consider the values of 8 per cent, 10 per cent and 12 per cent (i.e. $i = 0.08$, 0.1 and 0.12). Given a marginal rate of return of 20 per cent on investment ($q = 0.20$) and a marginal rate of savings of 30 per cent ($s = 0.30$), the social value of investment relative to consumption can be derived from equation (14.16).[75] It turns out that the shadow price of investment, P^{inv}, for the three selected values of i are 7, 3.5 and 2.33, respectively. As for propensities to save (resulting in investment),

---

[75] See chapter 14.

the private sector is assumed to consume 40 per cent of its profits (i.e., $s_p = 0.6$), while unskilled (and semi-skilled) workers consume all their wages ($s_L = 0.0$). The Saranian Government—in view of the high value of investment—is ready to devote all available funds to that purpose (i.e. $s_G = 1.0$). Next, the marginal propensity to respend within Sarakand is assumed to be 20 per cent ($\gamma = 0.2$), and, finally, foreign personnel are assumed to spend 20 per cent of their salary in Sarakand (i.e., $\delta = 0.2$).[76]

Given the values of the parameters (1) to (10) in table 19.20, and given all the relevant flows over time in table 19.19, it is now possible to calculate the pulp and paper mill's contributions to each of the two objectives in each year of the project by substituting into the appropriate equations derived in this chapter. To calculate the total contribution to each objective, all that is needed in addition is a set of weights to put the contributions in different years on a comparable basis.

Since all the relevant parameters are assumed to be constant, it is not necessary to make separate calculations for each year of the project. Instead, all the time flows in table 19.19 can be converted into their equivalent present values by discounting back to year 0 at the common rate of discount, and the present values of each flow item can then be substituted into the equations

TABLE 19.21   PRESENT VALUES IN YEAR 0 OF ITEMS IN TABLE 19.19
(Thousand creons)

Item	Social rate of discount		
	8%	*10%*	*12%*
(1) Output (foreign exchange)	612,287	529,810	461,174
(2) Housing and welfare	1,675	1,800	1,346
(3) Construction costs	286,960	279,830	272,980
(3-a) Foreign exchange (materials) ...	178,704	173,940	169,379
(3-b) Foreign exchange (personnel)...	8,857	8,780	8,700
(3-c) Unskilled labour	15,341	15,150	14,956
(3-d) Domestic materials	79,450	17,440	75,507
(3-e) Skilled labour	4,608	4,520	4,438
(4) Working capital	15,418	14,490	13,646
(4-a) Foreign exchange	7,940	7,510	7,120
(4-b) Domestic materials	7,478	6,980	6,526
(5) Operating costs	417,719	360,900	314,998
(5-a) Foreign exchange (materials) ...	114,529	99,150	86,339
(5-b) Foreign exchange (personnel)...	40,942	35,440	30,859
(5-c) Domestic materials	156,961	135,180	118,434
(5-d) Semi-skilled labour	90,652	78,470	68,336
(5-e) Unskilled labour	14,635	12,660	11,030
(6) Working capital and Scrap value	13,910	10,570	8,081
(6-a) Foreign exchange	3,150	2,390	1,830
(6-b) Domestic materials	10,760	8,180	6,251

[76] This last figure may appear too low; but it is plausible, since housing will be provided free of charge and many of the consumer durables will be imported from abroad by the personnel.

given earlier to compute the project's total contribution to the different objectives. Table 19.21 lists the present value in year 0 of each of the flows (items) of table 19.19, discounted at the rates of 8 per cent, 10 per cent and 12 per cent. These results are brought together in table 19.22.

TABLE 19.22   PRESENT VALUE OF NET BENEFITS OF PULP AND PAPER MILL IN YEAR 0
(Thousand creons)

Item	Equation number	Social rate of discount		
		8%	*10%*	*12%*
Aggregate consumption				
MC	(19.1)	— 92,227	—113,040	—131,023
F	(19.3a)	+271,174	+216,230	+169,113
L	(19.3b)	— 29,976	— 27,810	— 25,986
W	(19.3c)	— 4,608	— 4,520	— 4,438
SC	(19.3)	+ 68,728	+ 18,370	— 24,918
SC^G	(19.4a)	+ 43,360	— 6,730	— 47,812
SC^P	(19.4b)	— 4,608	— 4,520	— 4,438
SC^L	(19.4c)	+ 31,627	+ 29,610	+ 27,332
C	(19.5)	+313,950	— 6,245	— 92,040
Redistribution to Sarakand				
R$_S$	(19.7)	+220,175	+ 196,025	+ 174,581

To explain this table, we consider only the case where the social rate of discount is chosen at 10 per cent per annum. The present value of net aggregate-consumption benefits is shown in successive stages of approximation. Using market prices, the present value, MC, turns out to be negative at a level of 113 million creons.

The second approximation, SC, turns out to be positive, but comparatively low, at about 18.3 million creons. This increase has come about because: (*a*) the net foreign exchange contribution of the project (all the output is measured in terms of foreign exchange but only a part of the costs involve the use of foreign exchange); and (*b*) the 27.8 million creons of wage bill to unskilled labour has been replaced by the corresponding social opportunity cost of zero.

The final approximation, C, however, indicates that the pulp and paper mill actually makes a decidedly negative contribution to the aggregate-consumption objective. This is due to the fairly high social value of investment relative to consumption ($P^{inv} = 3.5$) in conjunction with the unfavourable over-all effect of the project on the rate of investment elsewhere in the Saranian economy. The two groups with the highest propensity to invest, the Saranian Government and the private sector, suffer net losses on account of the project. Funds raised to finance the construction of the project carry a high opportunity cost, for they would have been wholly invested on alternative projects. On the other hand, the beneficiaries of the project, unskilled workers, consume all their benefits and add nothing to investment in the country. The result is that,

using the given set of values for the Saranian national parameter, the net aggregate-consumption benefits of the project amount to about minus 6 million creons.

As against this negative contribution to aggregate consumption, the project does make substantially positive contributions to the redistribution objective. The province of Sarakand pays a negligible part of the high price of drawing funds away from investment elsewhere in Sarania, but it does reap many of the benefits of the investment itself. According to table 19.22, the present value of net benefits—direct and indirect—to Sarakand is equal to 196 million creons. It is clear that on aggregate-consumption grounds alone the pulp and paper mill is not justified at a social rate of discount of 10 per cent. It is acceptable only if the Saranian Government places a non-negligible extra weight on consumption in the Sarakand region.

19.13 SENSITIVITY ANALYSIS

Both the social rate of discount and the redistributional weight for Sarakand are regarded as unknowns of the project analysis. Given the two national objectives that were mentioned earlier, the net present value, V, of the Sarakand project can be expressed as

$$V = \Theta^c C + \Theta^{RS} R_S \qquad (19.8)$$

Regarding present aggregate consumption as our unit of account, we can clearly set $\Theta^c = 1$. It remains for us to see how the value of V varies with varying values for the social rate of discount, i, and the redistributional weight, Θ^{RS}.

Using the values of C and R_S presented in table 19.22, it is simple to check that at a value of 10 per cent for the social rate of discount, V is positive if and only if Θ^{RS} exceeds approximately 0.03. That is to say, for $i = 0.1$, the switching value of Θ^{RS} is roughly 0.03. Similarly, it is simple to verify that for $i = 0.08$ and 0.12 the switching values for Θ^{RS} are -1.42 and 0.53, respectively. In figure 34 we have plotted these switching values and have drawn a tentative curve through these points. For points on this curve, $V = 0$. For combinations of i and Θ^{RS} that lie to the right of this curve, V is negative, implying that the project is not acceptable. For combinations to the left of the curve, V is positive, implying that the Sarakand project is desirable.

But, in fact, our zone of ignorance about Saranian national weights is not that large. We know in advance that negative values for Θ^{RS} are not to be contemplated, since the Saranian Development Plan specifically expresses the desire for extra consideration for income generated in Sarakand. It would follow that one's interest is concentrated exclusively on the positive quadrant of figure 34. If, then, the policy makers of Sarania ultimately reject the Sarakand project, an inspection of the $V = 0$ curve would suggest that values of the social rate of discount less than roughly 10 per cent should not be considered for Sarania. On the other hand, if they accept the project, we do not learn

much about the values for the two national weights. It is only after repeated application of this procedure for a large set of projects and project variants that one will, it is hoped, be able to converge to the values of these national weights that reflect the policy makers' judgement.

Figure 34   Switching curve for project acceptance or rejection

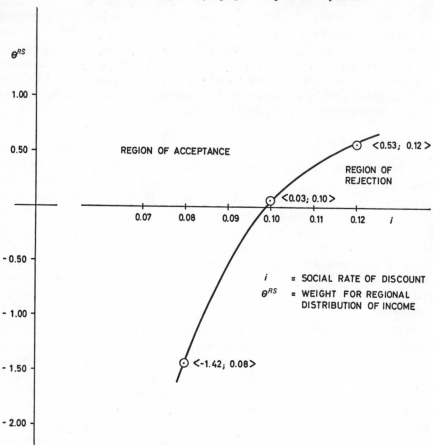

Chapter 20

SOCIAL BENEFIT-COST ANALYSIS
OF A CHEMICAL PLANT IN PALAVIA

20.1 INTRODUCTION

The following study is based on a feasibility report produced jointly by Reynold's Corporation of the United States and Kaja Inc. of Palavia. The report is concerned with the establishment of an inorganic chemical plant some 10 miles outside Sindhor, the capital of Palavia.

Palavia, which only recently proclaimed itself a republic, is a large and overpopulated country with a small industrial base. In its First Five-Year Plan Draft the Government of Palavia emphasized the importance of attracting foreign capital into the country in order to "lay the foundations of a modern industrial state". The project to be evaluated in this chapter is presumably in direct response to this encouragement. It is a joint venture on the part of Reynold's Corporation and Kaja Inc.

20.2 DESCRIPTION OF PROJECT

The proposed project, to be initiated in 1975 (to be referred to as year 0), has an expected lifetime of 24 years. The construction of the project will take 4 years (starting in year 0) and on completion will produce primarily supersulphate, sulphuric acid and alumina sulphate. Normal production is expected to commence in year 5 and will continue till year 23. In year 4 it is expected that output will be about 60 per cent of output in a normal year. Table 20.1 gives a time profile of the outputs of the plant.

TABLE 20.1   NET OUTPUTS
(Tons)

Output	Year	
	4	5—23
(1) Supersulphate	39,000	65,000
(2) Sulphuric acid	12,000	20,000
(3) Alumina sulphate	9,600	16,000
(4) Other inorganic chemicals (e.g. nitric acid, sodium sulphide, hydrochloric acid etc.)	3,000	5,000

All inorganic chemicals are currently imported into Palavia. The outputs of the plant, it is stated in the feasibility report, will substitute for equivalent amounts of the imports. Table 20.2 presents the c.i.f. prices of these outputs in domestic currency[77] and the foreign exchange saved by Palavia as a result of the project. The Government of Palavia currently charges a uniform 20 per cent tariff on the nominal total value of imported inorganic chemicals. Table 20.3 provides a time series of the total tariffs associated with the outputs of the proposed project, i.e. the tariffs that the Government charges for the

TABLE 20.2   VALUE OF OUTPUTS

Output	C.i.f. price (per ton)	Value of output in year 4 (thousand guildas)	Value of output in years 5—23 (thousand guildas)
(1) Supersulphate	182	7,098	11,830
(2) Sulphuric acid	149	1,788	2,980
(3) Alumina sulphate	381	3,658	6,096
(4) Other inorganic chemicals	419 (weighted average)	1,257	2,095
Total		13,801	23,001
Total (rounded)		13,800	23,000

TABLE 20.3   TARIFF ON DISPLACED IMPORTS
(Thousand guildas)

Import	Year	
	4	5—23
(1) Supersulphate	1,419	2,366
(2) Sulphuric acid	358	596
(3) Alumina sulphate	732	1,219
(4) Other inorganic chemicals	251	419
Total	2,760	4,600

TABLE 20.4   GROSS REVENUE FROM PROJECT
(Thousand guildas)

Product	Year	
	4	5—23
(1) Supersulphate	8,517	14,196
(2) Sulphuric acid	2,146	3,576
(3) Alumina sulphate	4,390	7,315
(4) Other inorganic chemicals	1,508	2,514
Total	16,561	27,601
Total (rounded off)	16,560	27,600

---

[77] The Palavian currency is 1 guilda; the official exchange rate: 4 guildas = 1 dollar.

imports that the project will replace. The feasibility report states that the products of the plant will be sold to domestic purchasers at the price they are currently paying (i.e. import cost plus tariffs). Table 20.4, which has been compiled with the help of tables 20.2 and 20.3, provides a time series of the gross revenue accruing to the owners of the project.

20.3 FINANCIAL ASPECTS

The project will be constructed, operated and administered by Kaja Inc. of Palavia in conjunction with Reynold's Corporation of the United States. The total investment requirement of the project is estimated at 18.4 million guildas and will be met entirely through equity capital. It is proposed that 50 per cent of the equity will be supplied by Kaja Inc. and 50 per cent by Reynold's Corporation.[78] Investment in fixed capital amounts to 14.4 million guildas and is spread over years 0 through 3. Table 20.5 provides a time

TABLE 20.5 INVESTMENT IN FIXED CAPITAL
(Thousand guildas)

Item	Year				Total
	0	1	2	3	
(1) Land	250	—	—	—	250
(2) Construction works	150	50	—	—	200
(3) Buildings and structures	220	220	110	—	550
(4) Machinery and equipment	—	3,500	4,000	2,500	10,000
(5) Vehicles	—	55	75	20	150
(6) Salaries to skilled labour	300	350	360	490	1,500
(7) Wages to unskilled labour	400	350	210	40	1,000
(8) Office furniture etc.	25	125	150	50	350
(9) Contingencies	400	—	—	—	400
Total	1,745	4,650	4,905	3,100	14,400

series of this investment according to various items. The plant will be constructed on 150 hectares of unused land owned by the Government of Palavia. The Government has agreed to charge a nominal sum of 250,000 guildas (to be paid in year 0) for the use of the land. It will be observed in table 20.5 that no provision appears in the investment outlay for housing of personnel. The feasibility report states that housing estates already exist fairly near the location of the plant, and thus separate housing establishments were not deemed necessary. Moreover, the total number of unskilled workers required by the project is rather small, and these workers are to be recruited from neighbouring villages. No housing facilities are required for them either.

---

[78] The feasibility report actually states that Kaja Inc. is to provide 51 per cent of the equity and Reynold's Corporation to provide 49 per cent. We have altered the proportions for ease of calculation. Little damage will be caused in the evaluation of the project owing to this change.

Working capital required by the project, worth 4 million guildas (of which 2 million are in foreign exchange and 2 million in domestic materials) will be built up over years 4, 5 and 6. Table 20.6 provides a breakdown of this working capital.

Table 20.7 provides an account of the operating costs of the plant over the lifetime of the project. It has been assumed in the feasibility report that

TABLE 20.6   WORKING CAPITAL
(Thousand guildas)

Resource	Year			Total
	4	5	6	
(1) Foreign exchange	650	650	700	2,000
(2) Domestic materials	300	450	1,250	2,000
Total	950	1,100	1,950	4,000

TABLE 20.7   OPERATING COSTS
(Thousand guildas)

	Year	
	4	5—23
Energy and water		
(1) Water	40	47
(2) Electricity and coal	185	218
(3) Petroleum	40	54
(4) Fuel oils	335	358
Direct production materials		
(5) Gypsum	15	21
(6) Rock phosphate	3,000	4,570
(7) Sulphur	2,725	4,017
(8) Soda ash	3	3
(9) Bauxite	215	400
(10) Sodium nitrate	100	185
(11) Alumina	125	220
(12) Other materials	315	600
(13) Duty on imported material inputs	882	1,470
Packaging materials		
(14) Polythene bags, glass materials etc.	530	1,050
(15) Metal containers, gunny bags	655	1,290
(16) Duty on imported packaging materials	78	155
Maintenance and repair		
(17) Parts and materials	387	400
(18) Miscellaneous	585	600
Salaries, wages and depreciation		
(19) Salaries to skilled labour	2,780	3,000
(20) Wages to unskilled labour	76	80
(21) Depreciation	720	720
Total	13,785	19,458

the plant, buildings and equipment will have a perfect productive life for 20 years after their installation, but that at the end of this period (i.e. year 24) they will all collapse with no residual value. The report then goes on to assume a linear depreciation allotment of 5 per cent per annum on fixed capital. This implies an annual depreciation allowance of 0.720 million guildas, as item (21) in table 20.7 shows. The total operating costs in year 4 come to 13.785 million guildas. In subsequent years they total 19.458 million guildas annually.

TABLE 20.8   CASH FLOW ACCOUNT FOR FIRM
(Thousand guildas)

Item	Year							
	0	1	2	3	4	5	6	7—23
(1) Gross revenue	—	—	—	—	14,560	27,600	27,600	27,600
(2) Investment in fixed capital	1,745	4,650	4,905	3,100	—	—	—	—
(3) Working capital	—	—	—	—	950	1,100	1,950	—
(4) Operating costs	—	—	—	—	13,785	19,458	19,458	19,458
(5) Gross profits	—	—	—	—	1,825	7,042	6,192	8,142
(6) Corporate tax	—	—	—	—	—	—	—	2,443
(7) After-tax profits	—	—	—	—	1,825	7,042	6,192	5,699
(8) Dividends	—	—	—	—	1,825	7,042	6,192	5,699
(9) Return on investment ..	—	—	—	—	—	—	—	31%

We now come to table 20.8, which was provided in the feasibility report and which gives a time series of the cash flow for the joint enterprise. The Government of Palavia imposes a 30 per cent corporate tax on gross profits, but has agreed on a three-year period of grace after production commences. That is, corporate tax will be charged only from year 7 onwards. Item (7) in the table provides the time series of profits after tax. The feasibility report states that all after-tax profits will be returned to shareholders in the form of dividends. The time series of dividends paid out is shown in item (8). It is observed that the return on equity to the shareholders is about 31 per cent from year 7 onwards. Moreover, it is suggested in the feasibility report that a year after the termination of the project (i.e. year 24) the total equity capital will be returned to the shareholders. The project, therefore, appears extremely attractive from the point of view of the enterprise undertaking it.

20.4 NATIONAL ECONOMIC PROFITABILITY

The two most important national objectives mentioned in the First Five-Year Plan Draft of Palavia are the increase in net aggregate-consumption benefits and the redistribution of consumption in favour of several depressed regions of the country. The region surrounding Sindhor is not mentioned as requiring special consideration with regard to the redistribution of consumption. This is not surprising, for this region is among the most prosperous in Palavia. We shall, therefore, evaluate the proposed project only in the light of the national objective of increasing net aggregate-consumption benefits.

As we recall from the discussion in chapter 5, in the evaluation of the costs of this project it is necessary to distinguish between imported and domestically supplied inputs and between different types of labour. For the purposes of this case study we categorize the various resources in the following way: domestic inputs (outputs), foreign exchange inputs (outputs), unskilled labour and skilled labour. All machinery and parts (other than simple machine tools), iron and steel, fuel oils and inorganic chemicals are imported into Palavia. It is assumed that they will continue to be imported throughout the lifetime of the project. All other material inputs, it is assumed, are produced domestically.

We now proceed to lay the framework for evaluating the project in two broad stages. We first reconstruct each of tables 20.1 to 20.7 according to the various resources required (or provided). We then isolate the *actual resource flows* for Palavia. These two stages are distinct for this project, since one need only recall that only 50 per cent of the total investment outlay comes from Palavian resources. Moreover, when 50 per cent of the dividends are paid to foreign shareholders, this part consists of resources lost to Palavia.

It was mentioned that the net outputs of the plant will substitute for equivalent quantities of imports. It follows that the gross benefits of the project are to be measured by the foreign exchange saved as a result of not importing (see chapter 4). Table 20.9 is simply a restatement of table 20.2 and gives the time series of the gross benefits of the project in terms of the resource it saves (i.e. foreign exchange). Table 20.10, which provides the time

TABLE 20.9   SOCIAL VALUE OF OUTPUTS
(Thousand guildas)

Output	Year	
	4	*5—23*
(1) Supersulphate	7,098	11,830
(2) Sulphuric acid	1,788	2,980
(3) Alumina sulphate	3,658	6,096
(4) Other inorganic chemicals	1,257	2,095
Total (rounded) foreign exchange saved	13,800	23,000

TABLE 20.10   INVESTMENT IN FIXED CAPITAL
(Thousand guildas)

Resource	Year				Total
	0	*1*	*2*	*3*	
(1) Foreign exchange	—	3,555	4,075	2,520	10,150
(2) Foreign personnel	150	175	180	245	750
(3) Skilled domestic labour	150	175	180	245	750
(4) Unskilled labour	400	350	210	40	1,000
(5) Domestic materials	1,045	395	260	50	1,750
Total	1,745	4,650	4,905	3,100	14,400

flow of investment in fixed capital in terms of the various resources required, has been compiled from table 20.5. The feasibility report states that items (4) and (5) of table 20.5 require the direct use of foreign exchange. Moreover, it states that about 50 per cent of the salaries to skilled labour (item (6) of table 20.5) consists of salaries to foreign personnel. This now explains items (1—3) of table 20.10. Item (4) in table 20.10 is the same as item (7) in table 20.5. It is tacitly assumed that the rest of the items in table 20.5 reflect the use of domestic materials. This enables one to construct item (5) in table 20.10.

As for working capital, table 20.6 already provides a breakdown in terms of the resource requirements, so that no further comment is required.

We now come to table 20.11, which provides a breakdown in terms of the resources used in the operating costs of the project. Table 20.11 has been constructed from table 20.7. The feasibility report states that in table 20.7, items (3), (4), (6), (7), (10), (14) and (17) require the direct use of foreign exchange. They provide item (1) of table 20.11. It is mentioned in the report that about 50 per cent of the salaries to skilled labour (item (19) in table 20.7) consists of payments to foreign personnel. This explains items (2) and (3) of table 20.11. Item (4) in table 20.11 is the same as item (20) in table 20.7. Now, items (13) and (16) of table 20.7 consist of taxes paid to the Government for the import of production and packaging materials. They form item (5) in table 20.11. Item (21), depreciation, in table 20.7 is reproduced as item (6) in table 20.11. It is assumed that all other items in table 20.7 involve the use of domestic materials. This allows one to construct item (7) in table 20.11.

TABLE 20.11   OPERATING COSTS
(Thousand guildas)

Resource	Year	
	4	*5—23*
(1) Foreign exchange	7,242	10,854
(2) Foreign personnel	1,390	1,500
(3) Domestic skilled labour	1,390	1,500
(4) Unskilled labour	70	80
(5) Duty on imported materials	960	1,625
(6) Depreciation	720	720
(7) Domestic materials	2,013	3,179
Total	13,785	19,458

We now come to the second stage in establishing the framework for evaluating the project. To begin with, recall that of the total equity capital of 18.4 million guildas, 9.2 million is provided by foreign shareholders. Now, it is clearly sensible to assume that this foreign capital would not have been supplied in the absence of the project. It follows that for Palavia this foreign capital has zero opportunity cost. We assume that this 9.2 million guildas of foreign capital helps to finance the cost of machinery, equipment and vehicles required during the construction of the project. We assume that all foreign

personnel are paid in guildas but that they are allowed to take whatever part
of their salary they wish out of Palavia. With this understanding we come
to table 20.12, which gives an account of the actual use to which the domestic
equity is put. Table 20.12 has been constructed with the help of table 20.10.
It was seen in table 20.10 that the cost of machinery, equipment and vehicles
totalled 10.150 million guildas. Foreign equity amounts to 9.2 million guildas.
It has, therefore, been arranged that the deficit of 0.950 million guildas in
foreign exchange will be met in year 3 from domestic equity. This explains
table 20.12. It shows that a total of 5.2 million guildas in construction costs
is to be met by domestic equity. Finally, the whole of the working capital
(4 million guildas) is to be built up with domestic equity.

TABLE 20.12   ACTUAL PALAVIAN FUNDS USED IN INVESTMENT IN FIXED CAPITAL
(*Thousand guildas*)

Resource	Year				Total
	0	1	2	3	
(1) Foreign exchange (materials)	—	—	—	950	950
(2) Foreign personnel	150	175	180	245	750
(3) Domestic skilled labour	150	175	180	245	750
(4) Unskilled labour	400	350	210	40	1,000
(5) Domestic materials	1,045	395	260	50	1,750
Total	1,745	1,095	830	1,530	5,200

Next comes the all-important table 20.13, which provides a comprehensive
summary of all Palavian resource flows and resulting cash transfers brought
about by the project.

Item (1) of table 20.13 has been obtained from table 20.9 and gives the
flow of gross benefits the project provides to Palavia. Item (2) gives the actual
resources of Palavia consumed in the process of constructing the plant. It is
identical to table 20.12 except in one point. In year 0, the firm is to pay
0.250 million guildas to the Government for the use of the land on which the
plant is to be built. It was stated that this piece of land is not currently in use.
We assume, for want of better information, that it would have continued to be
unused. It follows that the opportunity cost of this land is zero. Therefore,
the payment of 0.250 million guildas simply reflects a cash transfer from the
private firm to the Government and does not reflect any use of Palavian
resources. Consequently, in item (2-b) of table 20.13, the Palavian resources
used up in year 0 are not 1.045 million guildas (as in item (5), table 20.12),
but only 0.795 million guildas.

Item (3) in table 20.13 has been obtained from table 20.6 and requires
very little comment. All the working capital is to be met from domestic equity
and hence must be regarded as a cost to Palavia. Item (4) of table 20.13
comprises all items in table 20.11 except item (5), duty on imported materials,
and item (6), depreciation. This is as it should be. The payment of duty on

TABLE 20.13 BENEFITS, COSTS AND CASH TRANSFERS BY YEAR
(Thousand guildas)

Item	0	1	2	3	4	5	6	7—23	24
					Year				
(1) Output (foreign exchange) ...	—	—	—	—	13,800	23,000	23,000	23,000	—
(2) Construction costs ...	1,495	1,095	830	1,530	—	—	—	—	—
(2-a) Foreign exchange (materials)	—	—	—	950	—	—	—	—	—
(2-b) Domestic materials	795	395	260	50	—	—	—	—	—
(2-c) Foreign personnel	150	175	180	245	—	—	—	—	—
(2-d) Domestic skilled labour	150	175	180	245	—	—	—	—	—
(2-e) Unskilled labour.	400	350	210	40	—	—	—	—	—
(3) Working capital	—	—	—	—	950	1,100	1,950	—	—
(3-a) Foreign exchange	—	—	—	—	650	650	700	—	—
(3-b) Domestic materials	—	—	—	—	300	450	1,250	—	—
(4) Operating costs	—	—	—	—	12,105	17,113	17,113	17,113	—
(4-a) Foreign exchange (materials)	—	—	—	—	7,242	10,854	10,854	10,854	—
(4-b) Foreign personnel	—	—	—	—	1,390	1,500	1,500	1,500	—
(4-c) Domestic skilled labour	—	—	—	—	1,390	1,500	1,500	1,500	—
(4-d) Unskilled labour.	—	—	—	—	70	80	80	80	—
(4-e) Domestic materials	—	—	—	—	2,013	3,179	3,179	3,179	—
(5) Repatriated profits (foreign exchange) ...	—	—	—	—	912	3,521	3,096	2,850	—
(6) Repatriated equity (foreign exchange) ...	—	—	—	—	—	—	—	—	9,200
(7) Reclaimed working capital	—	—	—	—	—	—	—	—	4,000
(7-a) Foreign exchange	—	—	—	—	—	—	—	—	2,000
(7-b) Domestic materials	—	—	—	—	—	—	—	—	2,000
Cash transfers									
(8) Land payment	250	—	—	—	—	—	—	—	—
(9) Duty on imported materials	—	—	—	—	960	1,625	1,625	1,625	—
(10) Corporate tax	—	—	—	—	—	—	—	2,443	—
(11) Tariff on import substitutes	—	—	—	—	2,760	4,600	4,600	4,600	—

imported commodities is simply a transfer of cash from the private firm to the Government and does not reflect any use of Palavian resources and thus should not be counted as a cost to the project. The case of depreciation is somewhat different. It is not even a transfer item, since it is merely a device to account for the fact that the fixed capital will not last for ever. We have

also seen in table 20.7 that repairs and small replacements of fixed capital are not provided from the depreciation funds, but are a separate cost item (items (17) and (18)). From this we conclude that the annual depreciation figure of 0.720 million guildas does not involve any cost to Palavia but is merely a fund that accumulates over the years.

Item (5) of table 20.13 consists of repatriated profits (i.e. 50 per cent of item (8) in table 20.8). This is a net loss in foreign exchange to Palavia and must be regarded as a cost due to the project. Item (6) of table 20.13 consists of the repatriated equity (worth 9.2 million guildas) in year 24. Once again, this is a cost to Palavia in the form of foreign exchange. Finally, item (7) gives the working capital, consisting of raw materials and goods in process, that will be available to Palavia at the end of the project (year 24). This item should thus be regarded as resources provided by the project in year 24.

We now come to the items under the heading "Cash transfers" in table 20.13. Item (8) is the payment for land, which we have already discussed. Item (9) consists of item (5) in table 20.11 and represents the duty that the private firm must pay to the Government for the import of production and packaging materials for the plant. Item (10) of table 20.13 is the same as item (6) of table 20.8 and represents the corporate profit tax, which also is a cash transfer from the private firm to the Government. Finally, item (11) in table 20.13 is the same as the total in table 20.3, and gives the profile of the tariffs on the import of the chemicals for which the products of the plant substitute. One might be surprised that this should figure as a cash transfer, but actually it should be so, and for the following reason: On the completion of the plant, imports of inorganic chemicals will be reduced by the amounts that the plant produces. Hence, the Government will lose the tariffs on the imports that have now ceased. But it was stated before that the products of the plant will be sold to domestic purchasers at the price they were paying before. It follows that the owners of the plant will collect the equivalent of the tariffs that the Government loses. So the tariff figures (item (11) of table 20.13) do, in the final analysis, represent a cash transfer from the Government to the private sector.

As in the previous case study, we proceed to evaluate the net aggregate-consumption benefits to Palavia due to the project in successive stages of approximation. The first step is to assume that market prices adequately reflect social opportunity costs and, therefore, the ultimate consumption benefits and costs involved. On this basis the aggregate-consumption benefits due to the project consist of items (1) and (7) in table 20.13.[79] They represent real gains to the Palavian economy as a whole and would not have come about in the absence of the project. Analogously, items (2), (3), (4), (5) and (6) correspond to costs borne by the Palavian economy due to the project and reflect resources that could have been used elsewhere in the economy in the absence of the project. These items, therefore, measure the sacrifice of consump-

---

[79] From here on all item references are to table 20.13 unless otherwise stated.

tion possibilities that Palavia sustains. The market value of the net aggregate-consumption benefits in any one year of the project is, therefore, given by

$$MC = (1) - (2) - (3) - (4) - (5) - (6) + (7) \qquad (20.1)$$

We now proceed to the second approximation by assuming tacitly that the only resources that require price adjustment are foreign exchange, skilled labour and unskilled labour. All other resources are assumed to be correctly priced by the competitive market mechanism.

As to foreign exchange, we assume that the guilda is overvalued. The official exchange rate is maintained by quantitative import controls and export subsidies. The opportunity cost of foreign exchange relative to its official price will be denoted by $(1 + \Phi)$, where Φ represents the foreign exchange premium, which is positive in Palavia and is expected to remain constant over the lifetime of the project.

Skilled labour, which is fully employed in Palavia, is recognized to be underpaid. That is, the marginal skilled worker contributes more to aggregate-consumption benefits than is reflected by the wage he commands. The opportunity cost of skilled labour—relative to the existing wage—will be denoted by $(1 + \varkappa)$, that is, $\varkappa$ represents the (positive) social premium on the market wage of skilled labour and is assumed to remain constant over the lifetime of the project.

Finally, we come to unskilled labour, which is assumed to be surplus in Palavia. The case of unskilled labour is, therefore, opposite to that of foreign exchange and skilled labour. The opportunity cost of unskilled labour —relative to the market wage rate—will be denoted by $(1 + \delta)$, where λ represents the (negative) social premium on unskilled labour.

It was mentioned that foreign personnel will be paid in domestic currency, but will be allowed (in line with the policy of the Government) to expatriate any part of their salary. We denote by δ the fraction of the salary to foreign personnel that will be spent in Palavia, that is, $(1 - \delta)$ is the fraction of the salary that is removed from Palavia. We assume that δ will remain constant throughout.

We now express the net aggregate-consumption benefits in a given year of the project—after incorporating the opportunity cost premiums—as

$$SC = MC + \Phi F + \lambda L + \varkappa W \qquad (20.2)$$

where

$$F = (1) - (2\text{-a}) - (1 - \delta)(2\text{-c}) - (3\text{-a}) - (4\text{-a}) - (1 - \delta)(4\text{-b}) - $$
$$- (5) - (6) + (7\text{-a}) \qquad (20.2\text{a})$$
$$L = -(2\text{-e}) - (4\text{-d}) \qquad (20.2\text{b})$$
$$W = -(2\text{-d}) - (4\text{-c}) \qquad (20.2\text{c})$$

The second approximation, SC, is obtained by adding three terms to the first approximation, MC. The first term, ΦF, corrects MC for the opportunity cost of foreign exchange by multiplying the net foreign exchange component

of benefits and costs, F, by the (positive) foreign exchange premium. The second term, λL, corrects MC for the opportunity cost of unskilled labour by multiplying the net unskilled labour component, L, by the (negative) labour premium, λ. The third term, χW, does the same for skilled labour with its (positive) premium, χ.

We now come to the third and final correction to the net aggregate-consumption benefits due to the project. This correction takes into account that the social value of funds devoted to investment exceeds the social value of the same funds devoted to consumption. This feature has arisen in Palavia owing to the inability of the Government to use its fiscal and monetary powers to bring about the rate of investment it deems optimal for the country as a whole (see chapters 6 and 14). To evaluate the indirect future benefits (and costs) of the project, we shall have to assess the net effect on the mix of consumption and investment in the economy due to the project. To do this it is necessary to distinguish all the benefits and cost flows that make up SC, as well as the accompanying cash transfers, according to the group that gains or loses, and to estimate the respective marginal savings propensities of each group.

For this purpose, three broad groups of gainers and losers have been distinguished with regard to the present project: (*a*) unskilled labour, L; (*b*) the Government, G; and (*c*) the private sector in Palavia, P. Each of the benefits and cost flows that enter into SC, as defined in equation (20.2) can be identified with one of these three groups. We proceed to do this now, and begin with P. The private sector owns and operates the plant and sells the output to domestic purchasers at the price they were paying in the absence of the project. It follows that both (1) and (11) are direct benefits that are captured by P. Similarly, items (2) to (6) are costs borne by P. Item (7), reclaimed working capital, belongs to P and therefore is a benefit captured by P. Next, items (8), (9) and (10) represent cash transfers from P to G, and hence are costs borne by P. It is assumed that domestic skilled labour employed in the project has been drawn away from the rest of the private sector in Palavia. It follows that the extra opportunity cost, χW, is borne by P, that is, P loses χW.[80]

Since the Government controls the foreign exchange market in Palavia, it effectively bears the cost of the foreign exchange premium associated with all imports. As a result of this project the Government no longer loses the foreign exchange premium, $\Phi(1)$, on the imported chemicals for which the project substitutes. Hence, $\Phi(1)$ represents a benefit due to the project that is

---

[80] A word of explanation may be required for this last point, since, by our assumptions, skilled labour simply moves from one private-sector project to another private-sector project. It might, then, be thought that χW will vanish, but this is not so. We are assuming that skilled domestic labour is paid a salary lower than its opportunity cost. The extra benefit that P makes owing to this feature is already reflected in the value of the output of our given project. So it is entirely correct that we take into account the loss that P sustains somewhere else because these workers have migrated from these other projects to the given one.

captured by G. Similarly, G captures Φ(7-a), since the availability of the foreign exchange component of the working capital in year 24 will prevent G from losing the foreign exchange premium that would have resulted from an equivalent amount of additional imports of the resources involved in item (7-a). Analogously, G loses Φ(2-a), $\Phi(1-\delta)$ (2-c), Φ(3-a), Φ(4-a), $\Phi(1-\delta)$ (4-b), Φ(5) and Φ(6). If we turn to the cash transfer items, it is clear that G gains (8), (9) and (10) and loses (11).[81]

It remains now to consider the (negative) costs included in SC, which are represented by the unskilled labour premium, λL, defined in equation (20.2b). This premium corresponds to the margin by which the total project wage bill for unskilled labour exceeds the amount necessary to attract unskilled workers to the project. This margin corresponds exactly to the net extra income received by unskilled labour on account of the project. That is, the (negative) costs $-\lambda [(2\text{-e}) + (4\text{-d})]$ accrue to L.

The distribution by group of the second approximation to net aggregate-consumption benefits can now be summarized as follows:

$$SC = SC^P + SC^G + SC^L \tag{20.3}$$

where

$$SC^P = MC + (11) - (8) - (9) - (10) + \varkappa W \tag{20.3a}$$
$$SC^G = \Phi F - (11) + (8) + (9) + (10) \tag{20.3b}$$
$$SC^L = + \lambda L \tag{20.3c}$$

SC^P, SC^G and SC^L represent the value of net consumption benefits flowing to P, G and L, respectively. To arrive at the final social value of net aggregate-consumption benefits, C, it is necessary to correct SC^P, SC^G and SC^L according to the proportions in which each is divided between consumption and investment. Thus, if the average unskilled worker saves a proportion s_L of his marginal gains, the social value of the net consumption benefits flowing to unskilled labour is

$$C^L = [(1 - s_L) + s_L \, P^{\text{inv}}] \, SC^L$$

where P^{inv} is the shadow price of investment (see equation A.6.12). Similarly, if s_G and s_P are the marginal propensities to save of G and P, respectively, then the social value of net consumption benefits flowing to G and P are, respectively,

$$C^G = [(1 - s_G) + s_G \, P^{\text{inv}}] \, SC^G$$
$$C^P = [(1 - s_P) + s_P \, P^{\text{inv}}] \, SC^P$$

We may now write the third and final approximation to the value of net aggregate-consumption benefits, C, to Palavia in any given year as the sum of the social value of net benefits flowing to each distinct group (see equation 6.7), i.e.

$$C = C^G + C^P + C^L$$

---

[81] See section 16.5.

A variety of parameters have been introduced in the discussion of this case study. In principle, each of these parameters is a function of time, and the appropriate values may, therefore, change according to the year in which the benefits and costs are measured. To simplify the calculations, however, it is assumed that the value of each parameter remains constant over the lifetime of the project. In table 20.14, each parameter is listed with the corresponding numerical value that is assumed to be appropriate to the economy of Palavia.

TABLE 20.14   VALUES OF CENTRAL PARAMETERS

(1) Foreign exchange premium	Φ	$= +0.2$
(2) Unskilled labour premium	λ	$= -1.0$
(3) Domestic skilled labour premium	χ	$= +1.0$
(4) Marginal rate of return to investment	q	$= 0.20$
(5) Social rate of discount	i	$= 0.08; 0.12; 0.16$
(6) Associated shadow price of investment[a]	p^{inv}	$= 4; 2; 1.33$
(7) Marginal rate of reinvestment out of profits	s	$= 0.20$
(8) Marginal propensities to save:		
(a) Government	s_G	$= 1.0$
(b) Private sector	s_P	$= 0.5$
(c) Unskilled labour..................................	s_L	$= 0.0$
(9) Proportion of foreign personnel salary spent in Palavia ...	δ	$= 0.5$

[a] The shadow price of investment, p^{inv}, is evaluated according to formula 14.16 (see chapter 14), so that:

$$p^{inv}_{i = 0.08} = \frac{(1-s)\,q}{i - sq} = \frac{(1 - 0.2) \times 0.2}{0.08 - 0.2 \times 0.2} = 4.$$

Given the values of all these parameters (table 20.14) and given all the relevant flows (items) over time in table 20.13, it is now possible to compute the net aggregate-consumption benefits in each year of the project by substituting into the appropriate equations in this chapter. However, since all the relevant parameters are assumed constant, it is not necessary to make separate calculations for each year of the project. Instead, all the time flows in table 20.13 can be converted into their equivalent present values by discounting back to year 0 at the social rate of discount, and the present value of each flow item can then be substituted into the equations given earlier to compute the total contribution of the project to the aggregate-consumption objective. Table 20.15 lists the present values in year 0 of each of the flows (items) of table 20.13, discounted at the social rate of discount of 8 per cent, 12 per cent and 61 per cent. Using these present values, the present value of net aggregate-consumption benefits due to the project is shown in successive stages of approximation in table 20.16.

Considering the 8 per cent social discount rate, we find that the present value of MC, the first approximation, is $+13.468$ million guildas. The second approximation, SC, turns out to be of the same order of magnitude, $+14.702$ million guildas. This may seem surprising, since the project is a net foreign exchange earner ($F = +59.767$ million guildas). But, in fact, the premium on foreign exchange is small ($\Phi = 0.2$), and the amount of domestic skilled labour

TABLE 20.15   PRESENT VALUES IN YEAR 0 OF ITEMS IN TABLE 20.13

(Thousand guildas)

Item	Social rate of discount		
	8%	*12%*	*16%*
(1) Output (foreign exchange)	172,491	116,486	75,330
(2) Construction costs	4,434	4,223	4,036
(2-a) Foreign exchange (materials)	754	676	609
(2-b) Domestic materials	1,424	1,391	1,360
(2-c) Foreign personnel	660	624	592
(2-d) Domestic skilled labour	660	624	592
(2-e) Unskilled labour	936	908	883
(3) Working capital	2,676	2,217	1,847
(3-a) Foreign exchange	1,361	1,137	955
(3-b) Domestic materials	1,315	1,080	892
(4) Operating costs	129,695	87,838	62,196
(4-a) Foreign exchange (materials)	81,941	55,435	39,208
(4-b) Foreign personnel	11,610	7,908	5,633
(4-c) Domestic skilled labour	11,610	7,908	5,633
(4-d) Unskilled labour	615	419	298
(4-e) Domestic materials	23,919	16,168	11,424
(5) Repatriated profits	21,397	14,432	10,169
(6) Repatriated equity	1,451	607	258
(7) Reclaimed working capital	630	264	112
(7-a) Foreign exchange	315	132	56
(7-b) Domestic materials	315	132	56
(8) Land payment	250	250	250
(9) Duty on imported materials	12,178	8,220	5,801
(10) Corporate tax	14,041	8,817	5,760
(11) Tariff on import substitutes	34,500	23,297	16,446

TABLE 20.16   PRESENT VALUE OF NET AGGREGATE-CONSUMPTION BENEFITS OF PLANT IN YEAR 0

(Thousand guildas)

Item	Equation No.	Social rate of discount		
		8%	*12%*	*16%*
MC	(20.1)	+13,468	+ 7,443	− 3,064
F	(20.2a)	+59,767	+40,065	+21,075
L	(20.2b)	− 1,551	− 1,327	− 1,181
W	(20.2c)	−12,270	− 8,532	− 6,225
SC	(20.3)	+14,702	+ 8,351	− 3,893
SC^P	(20.3a)	+ 9,229	+ 5,021	− 4,654
SC^G	(20.3b)	+ 3,922	+ 2,003	− 420
SC^L	(20.3c)	+ 1,551	+ 1,327	+ 1,181
C	(20.4)	+40,312	+12,865	− 4,823

used in this project is large ($W = -12.270$ million guildas). Moreover, the premium on skilled labour is high in Palavia ($\varkappa = +1.0$). Thus, the extra foreign exchange benefits of the project roughly cancel out the extra cost of domestic skilled labour, so that SC is not much different from MC.

The final approximation, C, is, however, much larger than SC, being $+40.312$ million guildas. This is due to the high social value of investment relative to consumption ($P^{inv} = 4$) and to the very favourable over-all effect of the project on the rate of investment elsewhere in Palavia. The two groups with the highest propensities to save, G and P, make net gains due to the project ($SC^G = +3.922$ million guildas and $SC^P = +9.229$ million guildas). The result is that when all things are considered, the net aggregate-consumption benefits due to the project amount to $+40.312$ million guildas.

Unlike the project in Sarania, this project has no regional impact, since it is located near the capital in the most advanced region of the country. Its implementation will, therefore, contribute to the goals of the plan that have already been incorporated into the aggregate-consumption objective. These include increased employment, laying the foundation of a modern industrial estate, savings in foreign exchange, higher capital investment etc. Therefore, the project should be accepted or rejected only on the basis of its contributions to the aggregate-consumption objective.

As can be seen from table 20.16, the present value of the aggregate-consumption objective is positive at a 12 per cent discount rate, but negative at a 16 per cent discount rate.[82] The "switching value" for the social rate of discount for this project is approximately 15 per cent.[83] If the social rate of discount is judged to be less than this, the project should be accepted.

APPENDIX TO CHAPTERS 19 AND 20

The two case studies we have analysed so far have been taken from actual feasibility reports, but the financial arrangements have been altered to introduce the kinds of features we thought should be explored. The national parameters have been chosen with a view to showing the orders of magnitude that are likely to be involved in actual countries. For these reasons we have preferred to place the two projects in the mythical countries of Sarania and Palavia.

In this appendix we comment on some of the steps that were followed in the evaluation of the two projects. We restrict our comments to the objective of increasing net aggregate-consumption benefits. These comments are not meant to be substitutes for the text, but they may illuminate the rationale behind some of the procedures that we pursued. We do this even at the risk of repetition.

In evaluating a project whose feasibility report is complete, the correct procedure is to go directly to the core of the matter and see what changes in the economy the project will bring about. The banality of this prescription

---

[82] Considering that hoped-for rates of growth seldom exceed 8 per cent, it is hard to imagine a social discount rate of 16 per cent.

[83] This "switching value", with only one subjective parameter, i.e. the social discount rate, is a parallel concept to the "internal rate of return" for commercial profitability.

is matched only by the convenience it provides. The first question the project evaluator should inquire into is the resources the project under review will make available to the economy and the resources of the economy it will use up.

Both the projects that we studied produced import substitutes. Clearly, then, the resources provided by the projects are precisely the resources that are released because of import substitution. In other words, the projects provided Sarania and Palavia with foreign exchange. This much is probably quite straightforward. But when it came to evaluating the indirect benefits (e.g. housing) of the projects, matters became somewhat more complex (and consequently our procedure somewhat arbitrary!). In the pulp and paper mill for Sarania we needed to assess the benefits due to housing. The problem was to discover the willingness to pay for them. But this was impossible to ascertain, since the feasibility report did not give any information about the demand for housing (e.g. rents etc.) in the province of Sarakand. We found it therefore necessary to impute to housing and welfare the over-all social rate of return to investment in Sarania. This is not strictly a correct procedure; but little damage was done to the evaluation by this step, since the housing benefits were, in any case, rather small.

Assessing the resources of the economy that the project will consume must be done carefully. The correct procedure is to inquire into the alternative use of the resources that the project will require. In the case of the chemical plant in Palavia we found that the private firm was to pay a certain sum to the Government for the use of the land on which the plant was to be built. The payment itself is of no consequence at this point. What is of importance is the resources that Palavia was deprived of as a result of the project. We assumed for convenience that the piece of land was not going to have any alternative use. That is why "land" did not figure in the actual investment outlay of the project (table 20.13). But suppose that this piece of land produced annually a net 100,000 guildas worth of some agricultural product and suppose that this market price reflected accurately the willingness to pay for the net agricultural output. Clearly, then, the annual figure of 100,000 guildas should be imputed as a cost to the project, since Palavia will be deprived of this net benefit of 100,000 guildas once the project is under way.

The method of financing a project is of great importance in the assessment of project costs. We found that the pulp and paper project for Sarania was being financed partly by a loan from the World Bank. We assumed that this loan was untied, i.e. the loan would be available to Sarania irrespective of whether the pulp and paper mill was initiated. We therefore found it appropriate to impute the loan itself as a cost incurred by the mill, the reason being that the rest of the Saranian economy would be deprived of the loan if the mill were constructed. As a result we did not regard the loan repayment as a cost due to the project, since the repayment would, in any case, have to be made (under the same terms) whether or not the pulp and paper mill was embarked upon. It is instructive to note that if the project evaluator in Sarania were to study a second project competing for the same World Bank loan, this same

loan would be regarded as a cost item incurred by this second project, but once again the repayment would not be regarded as a cost. The principle followed here is the one that we have stressed throughout these Guidelines, namely, to ascertain whether the resources required by a project have an opportunity cost and, if so, what this opportunity cost is.

Matters are somewhat different if an external loan for financing a project is tied to the project, i.e. the loan would not be available in the absence of the project. Neither of the projects that we have studied involved a tied external loan, but the chemical plant in Palavia was financed partly by foreign equity, and in many respects they both have similar economic features. We made the entirely plausible assumption that this foreign equity would not be available to Palavia in the absence of the chemical plant. It followed that the use of the foreign equity by the project involved no cost to the Palavian economy. However, the repatriation of the dividends or the return of the foreign equity to the foreign shareholders involves a cost to the Palavian economy and thus should be imputed as a cost (in foreign exchange) incurred by the project, since in the absence of this project such repatriations would not have occurred.

Corporate taxes and tariffs on imported operating materials, both of which featured in the Palavian case study, do not involve the use of any resources of Palavia. Consequently, although they are important "cost" items for a private firm, they are not costs to the Palavian economy. But they are important in the final approximation to the net aggregate-consumption benefits due to the project simply because they involve the transfer of funds between two groups with different savings propensities and thereby influence the consumption-investment mix due to the project. If the rate of corporate taxation had been higher in Palavia, there would have been two effects on the economic outcome of the project: (1) Net profits, and hence dividends, would have been smaller and therefore less funds would have been repatriated, thereby improving the character of the project from the point of view of Palavia; (2) there would have been a greater transfer of cash from the private sector to the Government, and since it was assumed that the Government has a higher propensity to save than the private sector in Palavia, the fraction of the net benefits of the project reinvested would have been larger, thereby increasing the social benefits of the project once again. Questions of efficiency, incentives and encouragement to foreign capital apart, the Government's fiscal policy has an important immediate impact on the mix of consumption and investment in the economy.

We now come to the question of employment, the last issue that we shall discuss in this appendix. Here we are discussing only the national objective of increasing net aggregate-consumption benefits; hence, we do not give a project extra credit for providing people with jobs. We want to discuss the reasons for treating skilled and unskilled labour differently.

Unskilled labour figured prominently in the Saranian project (the present value of wages to unskilled labour came to about 28 million creons). We assumed that Sarania possesses unemployed unskilled labour, i.e. the direct

opportunity cost of the marginal unskilled worker is strictly zero. This was an extreme assumption, but nothing in principle was lost by making it. If the Government of Sarania had informed us that the direct opportunity cost of the marginal unskilled worker was not zero but, say, $\frac{1}{4}$ of the industrial wage rate, the appropriate thing would have been to put λ (the negative premium on unskilled labour) equal to $-\frac{3}{4}$ and proceed with the analysis in exactly the same way as in the case study. Analytically, the important assumption was not that $\lambda = -1$ (as in both the case studies) but the assumption that λ is less than zero.[84] That is, unskilled labour made a definite gain in being employed in the industrial projects. That is why we singled out unskilled labour as a separate group, whose savings propensity mattered. And it did matter in a very important way in the Saranian project. For although the direct opportunity cost was assumed to be zero, the indirect opportunity cost of unskilled labour was very high (because unskilled labour was assumed to save nothing and the shadow price of investment in Sarania was high). In fact, it was so high that the project failed to increase net aggregate-consumption benefits even though the present value of the net benefits to unskilled labour was over 29 million creons and the present values of the net disbenefits to the Government and the private sector in Sarania amounted to only 7 million creons and 4 million creons, respectively.

Skilled labour was handled differently in both the projects. We assumed that skilled labour is fully employed in both Sarania and Palavia but that it is underpaid, i.e. its wage bill underestimates its productivity. Thus, when a project employs a skilled worker he is removed from some other project, and the economy sustains a loss equal to his productivity (his opportunity cost). If we assume that this skilled worker gets paid roughly what he was getting paid in his previous employment, we cannot suggest that his new employment gives him any extra benefits. That is why in both the Saranian and the Palavian projects we did not single out skilled workers as a separate group receiving any positive (or negative) net benefits due to the projects. But if the industrial wage rate underestimates the opportunity cost of the marginal skilled worker, his departure from one project to a new one causes his previous employers to lose the excess of his opportunity cost over his wage rate. We assumed in both the case studies that domestic skilled workers required by the two projects were previously employed in the private sector. Hence, in both instances we assumed that the private sector bore the loss of this excess (i.e. the premium on skilled labour). This loss was particularly heavy for the Palavian project (about 12 million guildas in present value at a 10 per cent discount rate). If it is thought that the industrial wage rate of a marginal skilled worker does reflect his opportunity cost (i.e. $\chi = 0$) in Palavia, we cannot say that his previous employers lose anything by his departure. They lose his productivity, but they do not have to pay his wages, and so they come out even. If it is observed, as it sometimes is, that even the marginal skilled worker is unemployed, the treatment of the skilled worker should be the same as that of the unskilled

---

[84] See in particular, chapter 15, section 15.2.

worker, since his employment in a project implies that he receives a net (positive) benefit. (His savings propensity is likely to be higher, and so he ought to be considered in a separate group.) But not much should be read into the unemployment of skilled workers, if it is indeed observed. In project evaluation we are necessarily peering into the long run, and the unemployment of skilled workers is often a result of short-run imbalances.

The approach that we pursued in the case studies consisted in evaluating the present value of a project, using first the market prices of the goods and services involved in the project. We then proceeded to make a sequence of corrections to this first approximation wherever we felt that the market prices did not reflect adequately the social costs and benefits involved in the use or provision of the goods and services. The "ideal" is to obtain finally the present-value figure that involves only the correct estimates of the shadow prices. But presumably this ideal will never be achieved. Price estimates are often badly conceived; quantity estimates are more often than not biased guesses; possible bottlenecks are often totally ignored, and so on. It then becomes pertinent to ask how many corrections to the first approximation of the present value are really worth making. What was the point, the reader may ask, in correcting for the repatriation of the salaries of expatriates of the Palavia project when one can surmise that the future cost items were cavalierly estimated? The question would be well taken since, after all, salaries to expatriates amounted to very little of the project cost. Our defence is that in the case studies we did not wish to pronounce on which corrections are worth making and which ones are not. What we wished to demonstrate was the way the argument would have to run if it is deemed worth while to pursue a particular correction. Ultimately, project evaluation is as much an art as a systematic pursuit of a well-defined procedure. One can believe that the evaluator would be better employed in improving the quantity and price estimates of future outputs and inputs than in assessing the fraction of foreign personnel salary that is repatriated. But to determine which corrections are worth carrying out is, in the final analysis, a matter of judgement, which the project evaluator has to resolve for himself when confronted with actual feasibility studies.

Chapter 21

SOCIAL BENEFIT-COST ANALYSIS
OF THE MANAGUA WATER PROJECT

21.1 INTRODUCTION

The Managua project has been proposed by the Ministry of Irrigation of the mythical country of Galivia as part of a broad scheme for the development of water resources in the western region of the country. This region is a primitive agricultural region, with a minimum of industry. One of the principal obstacles to the economic and social development of the region is the irregular distribution of water. Rainfall in most areas is inadequate for profitable cultivation. However, the rivers in the region could provide sufficient water to irrigate a substantial portion of the dry land.

The Managua project is located in the province of Mendalva. It is designed to divert water from the Rio Casqueya to irrigate an area of 40,000 hectares in the Secotuan valley. The predominant climate in this valley is hot and dry, and the vegetation is typical of arid zones. Owing to the lack of water, there is currently very little productive activity in the valley. Given the requisite irrigation, however, the soil would permit very profitable farming. At present, the land is covered by wild vegetation.

The project involves the construction of a group of basic works for the storage, conduction and distribution of the waters of the Rio Casqueya. It includes provision for surface flow-off, drainage and service roads, as well as the necessary earth moving and land clearing in the area. The project also includes activities directed towards the social betterment of the inhabitants of the area. There are too few farmers in the Secotuan valley to accomplish the goals of the project. Hence, it is necessary to promote the settlement of the land area to be irrigated and to establish satisfactory living conditions for the farmers of the region. The social welfare programme recommended is considered indispensable to the success of the proposed agricultural production programme.

The Managua project will be administered and operated by the Mendalvan Water Authority (MWA), a public corporation formed in 1960 by the Ministry of Irrigation to promote the development of water resources in the entire western region of Galivia.

21.2 OBJECTIVES

The Managua project was designed to achieve a variety of objectives the Galivian Government considered important in judging the merits of alternative investment programmes. These objectives include the following:

(1) Increased economic and social productivity and increased consumption of goods and services;
(2) Accelerated economic and social development of the region of Mendalva in which the project is carried out;
(3) Distribution of benefits to the greatest number of inhabitants, and in particular to the small farmers of the area;
(4) Generation of new occupational activities;
(5) Better housing and sanitary conditions;
(6) Production of exportable goods and services, and the minimizing of imports.

21.3 THE CONSTRUCTION OF THE PROJECT WORKS

The core of the project is the construction of the Managua dam at the narrows of the Rio Casqueya, 75 river kilometres from the sea. The dam is of the earth-fill type the dimensions of which are: height, 40 m; length, 2,730 m; and width, 10 m at the top and 176 m at the base. The total capacity of the reservoir created by the dam will be 607 million m³.

The main canal of the irrigation system will conduct water from the reservoir to the Secotuan valley. This canal will be 58 km long and will carry the full project discharge of 50 m³ per second. A pair of major lateral canais will then branch off to delineate the southern and western limits of irrigation of the region. The distribution system includes a series of small canals with a total length of 295 km. These canals will be trapezoidal in cross section and lined with concrete to reduce conduction loss. The drainage system will have a total length of 385 km and will be constructed by means of straightening and widening the beds of the streams that cross the Secotuan valley. A road system, whose total length will be 235 km, will service the irrigated region, so that every parcel of land will have access to a trunk road. Finally, substantial tracts of land will have to be cleared for future cultivation. The total irrigable area of 40,000 hectares includes most of the best soil in the Secotuan valley.

In addition to these basic construction works, the project calls for a variety of social improvement works. Nine centres are to be constructed throughout the region to be irrigated in which the population that will benefit by the project will be concentrated. One of these centres will have the public services required of an urban locality, and the remaining eight will be formed as villages with rural characteristics. The urban centre will require a substantial investment for ground levelling, access roads, street paving, water piping, sewerage, electrification, dwellings and offices and other municipal facilities. The eight villages will not require a heavy investment in urbanization. However, provision has been made for the construction of functional and hygienic

housing for all the small farmers to be settled in the valley, as well as a series of basic utilities, including drinking water supply, health centres, electrification and school buildings.

The construction of the project works is expected to be carried out within a four-year period, at a total cost of 484 billion pesetas. In table 21.1, the

TABLE 21.1 DISTRIBUTION OF TOTAL PROJECT CAPITAL COSTS OVER TIME
(Million pesetas)

Item	Year				Total
	1	*2*	*3*	*4*	
Basic construction works					
(1) Managua dam	42	42	56	—	140
(2) Main canals	22	28	69	18	137
(3) Distribution system	—	—	16	35	51
(4) Drainage system	—	—	20	51	71
(5) Roadways	—	—	3	7	10
(6) Land clearing	—	—	3	27	30
Social improvement works					
(7) Housing for farmers	—	—	7	7	14
(8) Basic rural utilities	—	—	7	7	14
(9) Urban centre	—	5	7	—	12
Others					
(10) Compensation	—	5	—	—	5
Total	64	80	188	152	484

TABLE 21.2 DISTRIBUTION OF PROJECT CAPITAL COSTS BY RESOURCE CATEGORY
(Per cent)

Item	Machinery	Skilled labour	Unskilled labour	Cement	Iron and steel	Other materials
Basic construction works						
(1) Managua dam	50	10	30	3	—	7
(2) Main canals	25	10	35	15	5	10
(3) Distribution system ..	20	10	45	10	3	12
(4) Drainage system	45	10	40	—	—	5
(5) Roadways	35	10	35	5	2	13
(6) Land clearing	45	10	45	—	—	—
Social improvement works						
(7) Housing for farmers ..	—	5	65	10	—	20
(8) Basic rural utilities ...	15	15	40	5	5	20
(9) Urban centre	10	10	50	5	5	20
Others						
(10) Compensation	—	—	—	—	—	—

BREAKDOWN OF MACHINERY COSTS	Per cent
Depreciation of equipment	30
Semi-skilled operating labour	20
Fuels, oils, grease etc.	25
Spare parts, components, miscellaneous items	25

capital costs of the project are divided into their major components and
distributed over the envisaged four-year construction period. Table 21.2 further
subdivides the capital cost of each component into several broad input
categories. It is assumed that the percentage distribution of expenditures among
resource categories will remain roughly the same for each year of construction.

21.4 THE AGRICULTURAL PRODUCTION-COST MIX

Land ownership

The land area relevant to the project includes both the 40,000 hectares
to be irrigated in the Secotuan valley and the 6,800 hectares that will be covered
by the reservoir created by the dam. The current distribution of landholdings
in the total 46,800 hectares is highly unbalanced. As table 21.3 shows, over
90 per cent of the farmers hold less than half of the land, and less than
2 per cent of the farmers hold close to 40 per cent of the land.

TABLE 21.3   DISTRIBUTION OF LANDHOLDINGS IN THE PROJECT REGION

Size of holding	Area (ha)	Per cent	Farmers (no.)	Per cent	Average holding (ha)
Now					
Less than 10 ha	19,961	42.9	1,907	91.7	10.5
10 to 100 ha	8,724	18.8	135	6.5	64.5
More than 100 ha	17,791	38.3	38	1.8	468.0
Total	46,476	100.0	2,080	100.0	22.3
With project					
10 ha	35,790	89.5	3,579	96.4	10.0
10 to 50 ha	4,210	10.5	134	3.6	31.4
Total	40,000	100.0	3,713	100.0	10.8

In view of the Government's interest in spreading the project benefits to
the greatest possible number of farmers, the distribution of the newly irrigated
land is to be carried out so that a substantial degree of equalization of holdings
will be achieved. All the farmers now holding land in the area to be irrigated,
as well as those affected by the construction of the reservoir, are to be furnished
with parcels of a minimum of 10 hectares and a maximum of 50 hectares,
depending on the size of their present landholdings. The remaining land in the
irrigable area is to be withdrawn from the present owners and distributed
in 10-hectare parcels among small landholders now living in adjacent regions.
Table 21.3 also shows the resulting distribution of land ownership for the
40,000 hectares to be irrigated by the project.

Crop distribution and production

Because of the lack of water, only 360 of the 40,000 hectares of land to be
irrigated and 1,090 of the 6,800 hectares where the reservoir is to be located are

currently under cultivation. All the cultivated land is farmed seasonally, and the principal crops are beans, corn, sesame and sorghum. The first part of table 21.4 gives the present figures on crop distribution and average annual production.

In formulating a cropping pattern to take effect after the completion of the project works, the planners sought to balance the availability of water and the regional demand for different crops on the one hand with the dual objectives of maximizing over-all economic benefits and raising the living standards of as many of the local farmers as possible on the other. The second part of table 21.4 gives the resulting crop distribution. The suggested distribution is adapted in particular to the predominance of small holdings, which will be the future pattern of land ownership. It is assumed that cultivation will begin in the fifth year of the project, immediately after the construction of the works is completed. All the crops are intended for domestic consumption, with the exception of the tomatoes, which are destined for export to the United States.

The figures on expected future yields, prices and value of output given in table 21.4 reflect the situation anticipated after the project is in full swing and the farmers have fully mastered the new techniques required for cultivation. It is expected that these conditions will prevail only after an initial learning period of 5 years. In the first year of cultivation (year 5), yields are anticipated to reach only half their ultimate level. In each of the following years, yields

TABLE 21.4 PRESENT AND FUTURE CROP DISTRIBUTION AND PRODUCTION

Crop	(1) Area (ha)	(2) Yield (ton/ha)	(3) Production (tons) = (1) × (2)	(4) Price (Ps/ton)	(5) Value of production (thousand Ps) = (3) × (4)	(6) Unit value of production (Ps/ha) = (5) / (1)
Present						
Beans	300	0.72	216	910	196	657
Corn	600	1.27	762	600	456	762
Sesame	400	0.60	240	1,270	305	763
Sorghum	150	1.62	243	380	93	620
Total	1,450	—	—	—	1,050	726
Future						
Beans	2,000	1.32	2,640	1,310	3,460	1,730
Corn	4,000	3.30	13,200	780	10,300	2,580
Sesame	4,000	1.10	4,400	1,450	6,400	1,600
Sorghum	3,000	3.53	10,590	540	5,720	1,910
Alfalfa	4,000	11.00	44,000	330	14,520	3,630
Safflower	3,000	2.20	6,600	940	6,200	2,070
Soybeans	9,000	2.20	19,800	1,370	27,140	3,010
Tomatoes	2,000	11.00	22,000	1,450[a]	32,000	16,000
Other vegetables	2,000	—	—	—	7,400	3,700
Wheat	4,000	3.30	13,200	580	7,660	1,920
Other crops	3,000	—	—	—	10,800	3,600
Total	40,000	—	—	—	131,600	3,290

[a] Official peseta equivalent of dollar export price.

are projected to rise by 10 per cent of their ultimate level until the maximum is reached by year 10. For the rest of the project life, yields are assumed to remain at this maximum.

Individual costs of production

Table 21.4 brings out clearly the increase in yields and the new variety of agricultural products that will be made possible through irrigation in the Secotuan valley. At the same time, the costs of cultivation will rise as more farm equipment, more material inputs and more intensive labour are required for the irrigated land. Table 21.5 gives the unit production cost per hectare for each crop, present and future. This unit cost includes all expenditures for labour, material input, depreciation or rental of equipment, interest on credit, and also the imputed value of family labour; it excludes any charges made for irrigation water or for land rent. Table 21.5 also lists for the area devoted to each crop the total cost of production, the total value of the produce (from table 21.4) and the surplus remaining after deducting cost from value of output. The last column of the table calculates the unit surplus obtained from each crop; it will be observed that the new crops introduced with irrigation generally provide a much larger surplus per hectare than the old crops, with or without irrigation.

Just as the figures on yields and production in table 21.4 represent the situation anticipated for year 10 (5 years after the basic project works have been completed) so the cost figures of table 21.5 correspond to the ultimate

TABLE 21.5   PRESENT AND FUTURE FARMER COSTS OF CULTIVATION

Crop	(1) Area (ha)	(2) Unit cost (Ps/ha)	(3) Cost (thousand Ps) = (1) × (2)	(4) Value of produce (thousand Ps)	(5) Surplus (thousand Ps) = (4) — (3)	(6) Unit surplus (Ps/ha) = (5) / (1)
Present						
Beans	300	285	85	196	112	374
Corn	600	268	160	456	298	497
Sesame	400	237	95	305	211	522
Sorghum	150	196	30	93	64	427
Total or average	1,450	256	370	1,050	680	470
Future						
Beans	2,000	1,250	2,500	3,460	960	480
Corn	4,000	800	3,200	10,300	7,100	1,780
Sesame	4,000	1,040	4,160	6,400	2,240	560
Sorghum	3,000	730	2,190	5,720	3,530	1,180
Alfalfa	4,000	1,870	7,480	14,520	7,040	1,760
Safflower	3,000	890	2,670	6,200	3,530	1,180
Soybeans	9,000	1,040	9,360	27,140	17,780	1,970
Tomatoes	2,000	8,000	16,000	32,000	16,000	8,000
Other vegetables	2,000	1,600	3,200	7,400	4,200	2,100
Wheat	4,000	960	3,840	7,660	3,820	960
Other crops	3,000	1,200	3,600	10,800	7,200	2,400
Total or average	40,000	1,450	58,200	131,600	73,400	1,840

input levels that will be required for the full yields. In the first few years, inputs as well as yields are expected to be below their final levels. For convenience, the same adjustment is made with respect to anticipated costs as to returns for each crop from year 5 to year 9: 50 per cent in year 5, 60 per cent in year 6, 70 per cent in year 7 etc.

TABLE 21.6 APPROXIMATE BREAKDOWN OF FUTURE FARMER COSTS OF CULTIVATION

Item	Per cent
(1) Family (unskilled) labour	30
(2) Hired labour	10
(3) Machinery and equipment and spare parts	15[a]
(4) Fuel and grease requirements for machinery	5
(5) Chemical fertilizers	18
(6) Pesticides, fungicides etc.	5
(7) Seeds	5
(8) Fodder	10
(9) Interest on credit	2[b]
Total	100

[a] Charges for rental paid to Ministry of Agriculture.
[b] Charges for credit paid to Ministry of Agriculture.

Table 21.6 presents a rough percentage breakdown of the total production cost to the farmer (exclusive of irrigation fees) as projected for future cultivation on the irrigated land. Unfortunately, this information was not available for each crop, and hence the average figures must be applied to all the crops under consideration. Forty per cent of total costs represents (unskilled) labour inputs, evaluated at the going market wage rate; on the average, the farming families will themselves provide three fourths of the labour. The remaining 60 per cent of total costs covers current and capital goods inputs, as well as an allowance for interest on agricultural credit. The Ministry of Agriculture of the Galivian Government will provide farm equipment and agricultural credit as part of the over-all project. The cost to the farmer of the equipment represents a charge for rental of government-owned machinery, which is calculated to cover amortization with interest at a rate of 8 per cent over the useful life of each machine. The 2 per cent allowance for interest represents payments made to the Ministry of Agriculture for the supply of credit to finance approximately 50 per cent of the cost of production, for an average period of six months each year at the same interest rate of 8 per cent.

21.5 THE OPERATION OF THE PROJECT

Once the basic project works have been completed, it will be the responsibility of the MWA to operate, maintain and repair the works over their expected useful life of 50 years. Furthermore, the Ministry of Agriculture of the Galivian Government will provide the farm machinery and equipment necessary for the cultivation of the newly irrigated land; it will provide for the

financing of the crops from sowing to harvest time; and it will also provide agricultural extension services in order to familiarize the farmers with the required new methods of cultivation.

Table 21.7 presents the expected annual costs of operation, including maintenance and repair, of the works, as well as a breakdown of these operating costs into their major components. To help defray the operating costs, as well as part of the capital costs of the project, the cultivators will be required to make annual payments to the MWA for the use of irrigation water at a rate of 500 pesetas per hectare. (This payment is not included in the costs of cultivation listed in tables 21.5 and 21.6.) It will be observed from table 21.5 that the average unit surplus for all the irrigated crops is 1,840 pesetas per hectare; hence, the farmer has every incentive to make profitable use of the water, and there can be no doubt about his capacity to pay the irrigation fee.

TABLE 21.7   PROJECT ANNUAL OPERATING COSTS

Item	Per cent	Million pesetas
(1) Skilled labour	20.0	0.8
(2) Unskilled labour	40.0	1.6
(3) Machinery[a]	15.0	0.6
(4) Cement	7.5	0.3
(5) Other materials	17.5	0.7
Total	100.0	4.0

[a] Percentage breakdown same as in table 21.2.

The cost of the machinery and equipment required for the agricultural programme was estimated at an average of 1,500 pesetas per hectare, or a total investment of 60 million pesetas. Since the intensity of cultivation—as well as the associated costs—is expected to rise gradually from 50 per cent to 100 per cent of its ultimate level during the initial years of the programme, the Ministry of Agriculture will undertake to purchase 30 million pesetas' worth of equipment for the first year (5) and add an extra 6 million pesetas' worth in each of the five subsequent years. The average life of the equipment, taking into account the need for both spare parts and complete replacement, is estimated at approximately 10 years. Hence, the ministry must expect an average recurring expenditure on the equipment of 10 per cent of its total value each year. For simplicity of calculation, these replacement expenditures are assumed to begin in year 10—as soon as the complete stock of equipment is built up—and to continue at a constant rate for the duration of the project. As noted earlier, the ministry will charge the farmers an annual rental fee for the equipment used at a rate that will cover amortization with interest at 8 per cent over the average equipment life of 10 years. Evaluated as a percentage of the total costs of cultivation, this fee amounts to the 15 per cent shown in table 21.6.

The supply of credit to the farmers is handled in the same way as the provision of equipment, except that there is, of course, no problem of replace-

ment or amortization. Credit needs are estimated (from table 21.6) at a rate of 53 per cent of the costs of production; this covers the cost of all inputs other than family labour, which is assumed to require no advance credit, and farm equipment, which is separately financed. From table 21.5, it will be seen that the total annual cost of cultivation of the 40,000 hectares of irrigated land amounts to 58.2 million pesetas of which 53 per cent equals roughly 30 million. Since credit is needed for an average period of only 6 months, a revolving fund of working capital of 15 million pesetas would be adequate to finance the costs of cultivation. It is assumed that the Ministry of Agriculture will build up such a fund in line with the credit needs of the farmers: 7.5 million pesetas in year 5 and an additional 1.5 million in each subsequent year until the final level of 15 million pesetas is reached in year 10. The farmers will be charged interest at a rate of 8 per cent on the credit extended for 6 months; this is roughly equivalent to an annual interest rate of 4 per cent, which, applied to 53 per cent of total costs, results in the interest payments of 2 per cent shown in table 21.6

The provision of agricultural extension services to the farmers of the Secotuan valley will be made as part of the country-wide extension programme administered by the Ministry of Agriculture. It is estimated that during the first six years of cultivation—from year 5 to year 10—an intensive educational effort will have to be made to teach the farmers how best to cultivate the newly irrigated land. This effort will call for approximately one extension worker for every 20 holdings of land, or every 200 hectares. As a result, 200 extension workers will be needed each year for 6 years, at an average annual salary equivalent to 15,000 pesetas in domestic currency, and the annual cost to the Ministry of Agriculture will amount to 3 million pesetas. After the initial extension effort is completed and yields reach their expected maximum levels, the need for extension workers will be correspondingly reduced. For the remaining years of the project's useful life, the ministry plans to allocate only 600,000 pesetas annually to cover the services of a total of 40 extension workers at an average rate of one per 1,000 hectares. Table 21.8 gives the total costs incurred by the Ministry of Agriculture in connexion with the operation of the agricultural programme of the Managua project.

TABLE 21.8 PROGRAMME COSTS INCURRED BY MINISTRY OF AGRICULTURE
(Million pesetas)

Year	Farm machinery and equipment	Agricultural credit	Agricultural extension service	Total
5	30.0	7.5	3.0	40.5
6	6.0	1.5	3.0	10.5
7	6.0	1.5	3.0	10.5
8	6.0	1.5	3.0	10.5
9	6.0	1.5	3.0	10.5
10	6.0	1.5	3.0	10.5
11—54	6.0	—	0.6	6.6

21.6 FINANCIAL ASPECTS OF THE PROJECT

The Managua project involves directly two separate branches of the Galivian Government: the Mendalvan Water Authority (MWA), under the Ministry of Irrigation, and the Ministry of Agriculture. The MWA incurs all the expenditures in connexion with the construction and operation of the project works, and it receives the payments the farmers make for the use of the water provided. The Ministry of Agriculture incurs the costs of the farm equipment, agricultural credit and extension services made available to the farmers under the agricultural programme; it receives rental payments for the equipment and interest on the credit.

To finance the capital costs of the project, the MWA will apply for loans from the World Bank and from the Galivian Government. It is proposed that the foreign exchange component of the investment, which amounts to $14.3 million, or 143 million pesetas at the official exchange rate, be financed by the World Bank and that the remaining 341 million pesetas be covered by funds borrowed from the Central Treasury. The World Bank loan is to be amortized over a 20-year period following completion of the project works, with an effective rate of interest of 7 per cent on the due balance. The Treasury will allow a 30-year term for amortization, with an interest rate of 5 per cent on the due balance. In view of the nature and objectives of the project, it is expected that both the World Bank and the Treasury will grant a period of grace during the time of construction and charge no interest until the new programme of agricultural production is underway.

The MWA incurs the operating costs of the project at an average annual rate of 4 million pesetas during the period of operation of the project works, i.e. from years 5 to 54. The repayment of the construction loans is made to the World Bank over the 20-year period from year 5 through year 24, and to the Treasury over the 30-year period from year 5 to year 34. Assuming that equal annual instalments are to be paid over the full term of amortization of each loan, the annual value of these payments can be calculated from annuity tables as follows:

World Bank loan (million pesetas)

143 at 7% over 20 years
= 143 × 0.0944 annually
= 13.5 annually.

Treasury loan (million pesetas)

341 at 5% over 30 years
= 341 × 0.0651 annually
= 22.2 annually.

As against these annual payments, the MWA will receive annual irrigation fees from the farmers at a rate of 500 pesetas per hectare, or a total of 20 million pesetas per year.

Table 21.9 shows the gross cash payments and receipts of the MWA for each year of the project. During the first four years the outlays on the construction of the works are exactly matched by the loans from the World Bank and the Central Treasury. From years 5 to 34, the loan repayment instalments and the costs of operation of the project exceed the receipts from irrigation fees, so that there is a net cash outflow from the MWA. During the last 20 years, irrigation fees exceed operating costs, and the MWA registers net profits.

A similar balance sheet can be drawn up for the Ministry of Agriculture. The Ministry incurs programme expenditures as shown in table 21.8 and receives payments for the equipment and agricultural credit from the farmers. These payments were evaluated as a percentage of the total annual farmer costs of cultivation (excluding irrigation fees) at 15 per cent and 2 per cent, respectively. Thus, the annual receipts for rental of equipment rise from 4.36 to 8.73 million pesetas from year 5 to year 10, and the corresponding interest receipts for the credit rise from 0.58 to 1.16 million pesetas. All the cash flows affecting the Ministry of Agriculture are listed for each year in table 21.10. There is a substantial net cash outflow in year 5, due to the purchase of farm equipment, and continued net outflows until year 10, after which the receipts from farmers catch up with the annual outlays.

While the MWA and the Ministry of Agriculture incur most of the costs of the project, the farmers to be settled in the irrigated area are the chief beneficiaries. Table 21.11 presents a cash flow account for the farmers as a group, in parallel to tables 21.9 and 21.10. Farmer payments include the irrigation fees paid to the MWA, the rental and interest charges paid to the Ministry of Agriculture, and the remaining costs of cultivation listed in table 21.6. With the exception of the irrigation fees, these costs are expected to rise

TABLE 21.9   MENDALVAN WATER AUTHORITY ACCOUNT
(Million pesetas)

Item	Year						
	1	*2*	*3*	*4*	*5—24*	*25—34*	*35—54*
Payments							
(1) Construction costs	64.0	80.0	188.0	152.0	—	—	—
(2) Operating costs	—	—	—	—	4.0	4.0	4.0
(3) World Bank loan	—	—	—	—	13.5	—	—
(4) Treasury loan	—	—	—	—	22.2	22.2	—
Total	64.0	80.0	188.0	152.0	39.7	26.2	4.0
Receipts							
(5) World Bank loan	22.3	24.5	54.0	42.4	—	—	—
(6) Treasury loan	41.7	55.5	134.0	109.6	—	—	—
(7) Irrigation fees	—	—	—	—	20.0	20.0	20.0
Total	64.0	80.0	188.0	152.0	20.0	20.0	20.0
Net cash inflow	—	—	—	—	—17.7	—6.2	+16.0

TABLE 21.10   MINISTRY OF AGRICULTURE ACCOUNT
(Million pesetas)

Item	Year						
	5	6	7	8	9	10	11—54
Payments							
(1) Farm equipment	30.00	6.00	6.00	6.00	6.00	6.00	6.00
(2) Working capital	7.50	1.50	1.50	1.50	1.50	1.50	—
(3) Extension workers	3.00	3.00	3.00	3.00	3.00	3.00	0.60
Total	40.50	10.50	10.50	10.50	10.50	10.50	6.60
Receipts							
(4) Rental and interest on equipment	4.36	5.23	6.10	6.97	7.85	8.73	8.73
(5) Interest on credit	0.58	0.70	0.81	0.93	1.04	1.16	1.16
Total	4.94	5.93	6.91	7.90	8.89	9.89	9.89
Net cash inflow	−35.56	−4.57	−3.59	−2.60	−1.61	−0.61	+3.29

TABLE 21.11   FARMER ACCOUNT
(Million pesetas)

Item	Year					
	5	6	7	8	9	10—54
Payments						
(1) Irrigation fees	20.00	20.00	20.00	20.00	20.00	20.00
(2) Rental and interest on equipment	4.36	5.23	6.10	6.97	7.85	8.73
(3) Interest on credit	0.58	0.70	0.81	0.93	1.04	1.16
(4) Other cultivation costs	24.16	28.99	33.83	38.66	43.49	48.31
Total	49.10	54.92	60.74	66.56	72.38	78.20
Receipts						
(5) Value of agricultural production ..	65.80	78.96	92.12	105.28	118.44	131.60
Net cash inflow	16.70	24.04	31.38	38.72	46.06	53.40

in equal linear increments from year 5 to their maximum level in years 10 to 54. Farmer receipts for the sale of their agricultural output are expected to rise in the same manner and to remain well above costs. Thus, farmer net profits rise from an annual rate of 16.7 million pesetas to 53.4 million pesetas by year 10 of the project.

21.7 EVALUATION OF THE PROJECT

The technical feasibility of the Managua project has been assured by Messrs. Ramón y Román, S.A., the engineering firm assigned by the Ministry of Irrigation to design the works. The report of the firm appeared as a separate technical study and is not included in this publication. It remains now to consider the economic feasibility of the project in order to evaluate its over-all

merit. A preliminary evaluation was carried out by Sr. Esteban A. Nilgram, Deputy Managing Director of the MWA, and was submitted as part of the Project Report to the Galivian Central Budget Bureau. Before taking any action, the Budget Bureau decided to undertake its own analysis of the project and delegated this task to a working group under the direction of Dr. T. Emilio Blancabeza, a senior staff economist. After studying the report, Dr. Blancabeza suggested an alternative approach to the evaluation of the project and appended his comments and results to the report.

Sr. Nilgram's analysis

It is proposed to appraise the economic feasibility and desirability of the Managua project by comparing total benefits with total costs and by examining the computed over-all benefit-cost ratio in the context of the general nature and objectives of the project. The main problems are to determine which are the relevant benefits and costs and to put these benefits and costs on a comparable basis so that a meaningful ratio can be computed.

The costs of the project works include capital costs for construction and current costs for operation. Although the capital expenditures are made during the first four years of the project, these costs are met entirely by the loans from the World Bank and the Central Treasury. Hence, from the point of view of the MWA, the costs are the interest and amortization payments that must be made to repay these loans. The loan repayments and the annual operating expenses incurred by the MWA thus represent the relevant costs of the project works; they are distributed over years 5—54 as shown in table 21.9.

The costs the Ministry of Agriculture incurs for the accompanying agricultural programme do not represent net costs for the project as a whole. The expenditures on farm equipment and working capital are repaid by the farmers on the terms noted in section 21.6, and the payment of salaries to agricultural extension workers is not really a net drain on the Ministry's budget, since these workers are likely just to be transferred from elsewhere in the country. In any case, the project will be the responsibility of the MWA, and it is the benefits and costs as viewed by the MWA that are of interest for the evaluation of the project. Whether the Ministry of Agriculture chooses to assist the farmers on the project-irrigated land is a decision that is outside the scope of the MWA and therefore of the project itself.

The economic benefits of the project are measured by the value of the irrigation water the project provides. It is recognized that the actual irrigation fees the cultivators pay to the MWA do not adequately reflect the value of the water, since even after paying their fees the cultivators will be substantially better off than before. To determine the real value of the water, it is proposed to compare the net surplus of the farmers under the currently prevailing crop system with their anticipated net surplus under the future crop plan for the affected area. The net surplus must be measured by subtracting from the value of agricultural production all costs other than fees for irrigation water, so that

the benefits directly attributable to the water may be isolated. This net surplus corresponds exactly to the concept of surplus defined in table 21.5, and hence the figures from that table may be used in the calculation of the project benefits.

From table 21.5, it will be observed that the total annual surplus of production value over production cost is equal to 680,000 pesetas at present, and that this surplus is expected to rise to 73.4 million pesetas after the project is completed. However, this maximum level of surplus will not be attained until year 10; in the first five years of cultivation—from year 5 through year 9—there will be shortfalls of 50 per cent, 40 per cent, 30 per cent, 20 per cent and 10 per cent, respectively. Thus, the corresponding surplus figures rise by equal linear increments of 7.34 million pesetas from 36.7 million pesetas in year 5 to 73.4 million pesetas in year 10.

The time flows of benefits and costs relevant to the evaluation of the project may now be summarized as in table 21.12. Benefits are measured by the difference between farmer surplus before and after the project, and costs are equal to the sum of investment loan repayments and operating costs. The project is clearly very desirable, because only in year 5 do total costs exceed total benefits; from year 6 on, benefits exceed costs by increasing margins.

To compute the benefit-cost ratio, it is proposed to calculate the equivalent annual values of the relevant flows shown in table 21.12. The farmer surplus before irrigation and the operating costs of the project present no problem, since the annual flows remain constant over the 50-year period in question. To account for the shortfalls from years 5 to 9 in the farmer surplus after

TABLE 21.12   SUMMARY OF BENEFITS AND COSTS (A)

(Million pesetas)

Item	Year							
	5	6	7	8	9	10—24	25—34	35—54
Benefits								
(1) Farmer surplus with project	36.70	44.04	51.38	58.72	66.06	73.40	73.40	73.40
(2) Farmer surplus without project (—)	—0.68	—0.68	—0.68	—0.68	—0.68	—0.68	—0.68	—0.68
Total	36.02	43.36	50.70	58.04	65.38	72.72	72.72	72.72
Costs								
(3) World Bank loan repayment .	13.50	13.50	13.50	13.50	13.50	13.50	—	—
(4) Treasury loan repayment	22.20	22.20	22.20	22.20	22.20	22.20	22.20	—
(5) Operating costs .	4.00	4.00	4.00	4.00	4.00	4.00	4.00	4.00
Total	39.70	39.70	39.70	39.70	39.70	39.70	26.20	4.00
Total benefits minus costs	+3.68	+3.66	+11.00	+18.34	+25.68	+33.02	+46.52	+68.72

irrigation, the following correction (in million pesetas) is made on the ultimate average annual value of farmer surplus (73.4 million pesetas):

Total shortfall $= (0.5 + 0.4 + 0.3 + 0.2 + 0.1) \times 73.4 =$
$= 1.5 \times 73.4$

Total surplus over project
useful life $= (50 - 1.5) \times 73.4$

Average annual surplus $= (50 - 1.5) / (50) \times 73.4 =$
$= 0.97 \times 73.4 = 71.2$

To convert the loan repayments, which are spread over 20 and 30 years, into equivalent annual payments over 50 years, the annual World Bank payments are multiplied by 20/50 and the annual Treasury payments by 30/50, with the following results (in million pesetas):

Annual equivalent World Bank repayments $= 2/5 \times 13.5 = 5.4$
Annual equivalent Treasury repayments $= 3/5 \times 22.2 = 13.32$

Using the equivalent annualized flows, it is now possible to compute the over-all benefit-cost ratio as follows:

	Million pesetas
Farmer surplus with project:	71.20
Farmer surplus without project:	— 0.68
Benefits	70.52
World Bank loan repayment:	5.40
Treasury loan repayment:	13.32
Operating costs:	4.00
Costs	22.72

$$\text{Benefit-cost ratio} = \frac{70.52}{22.72} = \underline{3.1}$$

The benefit-cost ratio for the Managua project thus turns out to be 3.1, a high value, which further attests to the desirability of the project. Apart from its immediate economic appeal, the project can be strongly recommended because of the many additional social and economic benefits that are not reflected in the benefit-cost ratio. These extra benefits include:

(1) The provision of profitable employment to many small farmers with limited incomes;
(2) The promotion of a better geographical distribution of population and more diversified agricultural production by settling an almost deserted area;
(3) The extension of basic social services to the people who will live in the Secotuan valley;
(4) The expansion of agricultural production, which will stimulate the general rate of economic development in the province of Mendalva.

For all these reasons, it is believed that the Managua project will make an important contribution both to the development of the national economy and to the welfare of the Galivian people.

Dr. Blancabeza's analysis

The analysis of Sr. Nilgram appears to suffer from several serious defects, both procedural and conceptual. As to procedure, Sr. Nilgram fails in his computations to recognize the role of time—the fact that benefits in early years are more valuable than benefits in later years. The methods used to annualize benefits and costs in effect imply that all benefits and costs are of equal value whether they occur in year 5 or year 54; exactly the same benefit-cost ratio would have been obtained by summing all the flows over the 50-year period. To clear up the confusion caused by Sr. Nilgram's insistence on computing equivalent annual values, it is recommended that a discount rate be introduced to reflect the general preference for present over future benefits. Using this rate, all benefits and costs should be discounted back to a given year, and the total value of benefits and costs as of that year should be compared for the purpose of evaluating the project.

The problem then is to choose an appropriate rate of discount. It was first suggested that this rate should reflect the ability of the Government to raise funds by borrowing, and therefore the current market rate of interest of 6 per cent on long-term government bonds should be used. It was later countered, however, that the marginal rate of return on investment in the private sector, estimated at 15 per cent, was the relevant figure, since public-sector projects should at least meet private-sector standards. After considerable discussion, a consensus was finally reached on a compromise figure of 10 per cent.

Using this rate, each of the five time streams shown in table 21.12 can be discounted back to year 0 (the present year) to yield the following total present values:

	Million pesetas
Farmer surplus with project:	436.0
Farmer surplus without project:	— 4.6
Benefits	431.4
World Bank loan repayment:	85.8
Treasury loan repayment:	156.7
Operating costs:	27.1
Costs	269.6

On this basis, the benefit-cost ratio turns out to be

$$\frac{431.4}{269.6} = 1.60$$

which is substantially less than the figure determined by Sr. Nilgram. The difference reflects the fact that the total value of benefits minus costs (as

shown in table 21.12) is lower in earlier than in later years, and the earlier years with a positive discount rate are the more important.

Apart from Sr. Nilgram's procedural mistakes, his general approach to the evaluation of the project reflects too limited a conception of the national welfare. Although he may feel, as deputy managing director of the MWA, that his primary responsibility is to this organization, the commitment of public funds to investment in an undertaking such as the Managua project calls for scrutiny in the light of the national responsibility of the Central Government. Thus, the expenditures of the Ministry of Agriculture on a project under the authority of the Ministry of Irrigation cannot be dismissed as irrelevant, for they, too, represent costs to the Galivian Government. Furthermore, all the costs to the MWA must be examined to determine to what extent they correspond to costs at the central government level. In accordance with these principles, several further adjustments are required for an adequate evaluation of the project.

First of all, it is suggested that the capital costs of the project be measured by the actual outlays on construction rather than by the loan repayments of the MWA. Whatever the obligations of the MWA, the Central Treasury will be required to find funds to pay for the domestic construction costs of the project in years 1 to 4. All subsequent loan repayments from the MWA to the Treasury simply represent accounting transfers from one agency of the Government to another, and therefore no real economic significance can be attached to them. As for the foreign exchange component of the construction costs, the issue is more complex. If the World Bank made loans purely on the merit of individual projects, the foreign exchange costs of construction of the Managua project would properly be equated with the required loan repayments. But it is felt that, by and large, an informal quota system applies to World Bank loans to Galivia, so that a similar foreign exchange loan could be expected for an alternative project if—and only if—the Managua project were withdrawn. Under these circumstances, the Galivian Government can count on the availability of this foreign exchange in years 1 to 4, and the cost of using it for the Managua project should be measured by the loss involved in not using it elsewhere.

A second adjustment must be made to include the costs the Ministry of Agriculture incurs in connexion with the agricultural programme of the project. These costs include all the payments listed in table 21.10. To avoid double-counting, it is also necessary to subtract the receipts from the farmers for equipment and credit, since these have been included as farmer costs in calculating the farmer surplus. Just as the irrigation fees paid by the farmers to the MWA represent simply transfer payments and are not relevant to the evaluation of the water benefits, so the rental and interest charges paid to the Ministry of Agriculture are cash transfers that do not necessarily measure the real costs of equipment and credit. These costs are properly measured by the original outlays by the Ministry; these outlays are hence to be added to the costs of construction and operation of the project works, and the farmer payments must be subtracted to obtain a net value.

On the benefit side of the ledger, the method for assessing the value of the irrigation water is accepted as proposed by Sr. Nilgram. It is worth noting that the value of the water—measured in this way—clearly depends on the provision of agricultural assistance from the Ministry of Agriculture, and it is therefore essential to include the costs of this assistance in evaluating the project as a whole. Apart from the benefits to the farmer arising from the sale of agricultural output, additional benefits are derived from the housing and social services provided by the "social improvement works" of the project. Since the costs of these works are charged to the project, the corresponding benefits should also be included. It is estimated that the annual value of these benefits, realized from year 5 through year 54, is equal to 7 per cent of the total capital investment of 40 million pesetas, which comes to 2.8 million pesetas per year.

Taking into account all these modifications, the benefits and costs of the project may now be summarized as in table 21.13. By comparison with table 21.12, total costs are now much more concentrated in the early years of the project, and the excess of benefits over costs is higher in the later years. It is no longer obvious that the project is desirable—that will depend on the relative importance of the early versus the later years, i.e. on the discount rate.

Using the discount rate of 10 per cent suggested above, each of the time streams shown in table 21.13 can be converted to its present value in year 0 as follows:

Million pesetas

Farmer surplus with project:	436.3
Farmer surplus without project:	— 4.6
Housing and social services:	19.0
Benefits	450.7
Construction of project works:	369.3
Operation of project works:	27.1
Agricultural assistance:	77.9
Net of farmer payments:	— 58.8
Costs	415.5

The benefit-cost ratio is thus $\dfrac{450.7}{415.5} = \underline{1.08}$,

which is lower than the earlier value of 1.60 largely because—at a discount rate of 10 per cent—it is more expensive to pay for construction outlays as they are incurred than to finance them with loans at rates of interest of 5 per cent and 7 per cent.

While the benefit-cost ratio is an indicator of the relative margin of benefits over costs, it tells nothing about the absolute size of the gains from the project. It is quite possible that a large project with a low benefit-cost ratio would provide greater net benefits than a small project with a high benefit-cost ratio,

TABLE 21.13 SUMMARY OF BENEFITS AND COSTS (B)

(Million pesetas)

Item	Year										
	1	2	3	4	5	6	7	8	9	10	11—54
Benefits											
(1) Farmer surplus with project	—	—	—	—	36.70	44.04	51.38	58.72	66.06	73.40	73.40
(2) Farmer surplus without project (—)	—	—	—	—	−0.68	−0.68	−0.68	−0.68	−0.68	−0.68	−0.68
(3) Housing and social services	—	—	—	—	2.80	2.80	2.80	2.80	2.80	2.80	2.80
Total	—	—	—	—	38.82	46.16	53.50	60.84	68.18	75.52	75.52
Costs											
(4) Construction of project works	64.00	80.00	188.00	152.00	—	—	—	—	—	—	—
(5) Operation of project works	—	—	—	—	4.00	4.00	4.00	4.00	4.00	4.00	4.00
(6) Agricultural assistance	—	—	—	—	40.50	10.50	10.50	10.50	10.50	10.50	6.60
(7) Net of farmer payments (—)	—	—	—	—	−4.94	−5.93	−6.91	−7.90	−8.89	−9.89	−9.89
Total	64.00	80.00	188.00	152.00	39.56	8.57	7.59	6.60	5.61	4.61	0.71
Total benefits minus costs	−64.00	−80.00	−188.00	−152.00	−0.74	+37.59	+45.91	+54.24	+62.57	+70.91	+74.81

so that, if the two are mutually exclusive, the first might be preferred. Given this ambiguity, it is proposed that attention be paid also to the net present value (PV) of the project, defined as the difference between the present value of benefits and costs. Thus, we derive

$$\text{PV (million pesetas)} = 450.7 - 415.5 = 35.2$$

from the figures that yielded a benefit-cost ratio of 1.08: the Managua project results in a net gain to Galivia worth 35.2 million pesetas at the present time.

The benefit-cost ratio of 1.08 is much lower than the value of 3.1 originally calculated by Sr. Nilgram; it corresponds to a present value of net benefits of only 35.2 million pesetas, as compared with a total commitment of 415.5 million pesetas. These figures suggest that the project will make only a marginal contribution to the economic welfare of the country. However, in view of the significant social and economic benefits which, as Sr. Nilgram observed, cannot be reflected adequately in the benefit-cost computations, the Managua project is still strongly recommended for approval.

21.8 THE SOCIAL BENEFIT-COST ANALYSIS

Before proceeding to the social benefit-cost analysis of the Managua project, it will be useful to comment briefly on the evaluations described in section 21.7. Sr. Nilgram's initial evaluation was criticized by Dr. Blancabeza, who suggested several adjustments and presented an alternative evaluation. Dr. Blancabeza correctly pointed out that the Managua project should be evaluated in terms of benefits and costs to the Galivian people as a whole, and he properly insisted on the recognition of society's preference for present over future gains. While Dr. Blancabeza's analysis represents a substantial improvement over Sr. Nilgram's effort, it still raises many problems it does not solve satisfactorily.

The first problem relates to the concept of national welfare. Unless planners are given some notion of what national welfare means, it is impossible for them to evaluate the net contribution—benefits minus costs—of any given project to this national welfare. The meaning of national welfare is generally articulated in the objectives set by the national Government, which should in turn reflect the best interests of the people to whom the Government is responsible. Some of the principal objectives of the Galivian Government were set out in section 21.2. In addition to promoting the economic growth of the country as a whole and higher consumption levels, the Government has a special concern for the economic development of the Mendalvan region and the social welfare of its inhabitants as well as for the alleviation of balance-of-payments problems.

In his evaluation, Dr. Blancabeza considered explicitly only the over-all economic benefits and costs. The distribution of the benefits and the costs, the social implications of the project and its effect on the balance of payments were all omitted from the calculations. The importance of these additional considera-

tions, however, emerges clearly from Dr. Blancabeza's recommendation. In spite of a very low value for the benefit-cost ratio, approval of the project was urged on the grounds that the project contributed significantly to the economic and social development of a poor region of the country. Thus, the numerical benefit-cost ratio calculated purely on the basis of contributions to the over-all economic growth of Galivia proved to be of only limited relevance and was ultimately obscured by other considerations. In principle, it would clearly be most desirable to give quantitative expression to all the relevant government objectives and to incorporate them into a generalized benefit-cost analysis for greater usefulness in decision making.[85]

A second general problem raised in the analysis of Dr. Blancabeza concerns the evaluation of resources from a national point of view. Dr. Blancabeza correctly stressed that the value of a resource should be measured with reference to the alternative possibilities for its use; an input into a project costs the economy whatever benefits it would have enjoyed by using that input elsewhere. Thus, Dr. Blancabeza measured the capital costs of the project in terms of construction outlays rather than loan repayments, because he felt that the relevant alternative to using the bank and government loans for the project was not the liquidation of the debt, but the use of the same funds for other purposes.

The logic of resource evaluation according to opportunity cost (value in alternative use) raises further problems with which Dr. Blancabeza did not deal. It becomes necessary to evaluate each input—as well as the output—of a project according to its opportunity cost and to recognize that the opportunity cost may differ from the actual market price of a product. Such differences can arise for a variety of reasons, including the imperfect functioning of the market system, the inadequacy of even a perfectly functioning market system, and the political and institutional constraints that prevent the Government from correcting what it considers to be a misallocation of resources. Examples of market price deviations from true (social) opportunity cost are plentiful, particularly in undeveloped economies. If the national currency is pegged at an officially fixed exchange rate with foreign currencies, and if this rate is maintained by import and export controls, the opportunity cost of foreign exchange is very likely to be above the official rate of exchange.[86] If there is a significant degree of unemployment in the country, the opportunity cost of unskilled labour may well be below the market wage.[87] If the rate of saving and investment in an economy is lower than the rate the nation as a whole would judge optimal, the opportunity cost of investment is higher than market prices would indicate.[88]

In all the examples mentioned, the relevant opportunity cost is a "social" cost in the sense that it corresponds to national rather than private or other more limited objectives. The problem of evaluation arises because social

---

[85] See in particular, chapters 3 and 9.
[86] See chapters 9 and 16.
[87] See chapters 6 and 15.
[88] See chapters 6 and 14.

preferences, as articulated in national objectives, may not be properly transmitted by the market system into the pricing of goods and services. In such cases, the evaluation of projects from a national point of view calls for the adjustment of market prices to reflect the underlying social opportunity costs. While in practice it is not possible to adjust every price involved in the evaluation of a project, it is important to make corrections for major and evident discrepancies. Thus, in addition to incorporating explicitly the many and varied government objectives into benefit-cost analysis, it is necessary at a tactical level to recognize that market prices may be imperfect measuring rods and to correct such prices wherever possible to reflect the relevant opportunity costs.

Dr. Blancabeza also raised a few additional issues, primarily tactical issues. What is the appropriate rate of discount to be used in evaluating public projects? And what is the appropriate criterion: the benefit-cost ratio or the net present value of the project? Provided that alternative opportunities have been properly accounted for in terms of the social opportunity costs discussed above, the rate of discount applied in comparing contributions to a given national objective at different points in time should reflect the intertemporal time preferences held by the Government—as proxy for the people—with respect to that objective.[89] The market rate of interest, or the rate of return on investment in the private sector, is not appropriate in this context, for the alternative uses of investment funds are already accounted for in the estimation of the opportunity cost of investment. If, in addition to the proper use of social opportunity costs, the quantitative calculations reflect the multiplicity of national objectives, it behoves the Government to undertake all projects for which the net present value of (social) benefits is positive, irrespective of the magnitude of the benefit-cost ratio.

In conclusion, it is apparent that a complete evaluation of the Managua project calls for a detailed application of social benefit-cost analysis going well beyond the effort of Dr. Blancabeza. In the next section we evaluate the Managua project from the social point of view.

21.9 OBJECTIVES

The evaluation of a project according to social benefit-cost criteria begins with an explicit statement of the relevant social objectives. With reference to the Managua project, various objectives of the Galivian Government were listed in section 21.2. These objectives may be restated as follows:

(1) Increased aggregate consumption—the raising of the average standard of living in Galivia as a whole;

(2) Redistribution of income to the region of Mendalva—the promotion of regional as opposed to national economic welfare;

(3) Redistribution of income to small farmers—the distribution of benefits to the greatest number of beneficiaries;

---

[89] See in particular chapter 13.

(4) The creation of new employment opportunities;

(5) The provision of basic social welfare facilities;

(6) The reduction of pressures on the balance of payments.

The first three objectives are clearly quite distinct, and the project's net contribution to each of them must be assessed separately. The last three objectives may or may not be subsumed by the first. Thus, more employment opportunities may be desired primarily for the contribution that a larger working force could make to national income and hence to consumption. Only if additional employment is considered desirable for its own sake should it be regarded as a separate objective.[90] Social welfare facilities should be treated as a separate objective only if the Government wishes to give more weight to such facilities than would the Galivian people in their capacity as consumers. Finally, a separate objective of improvement in the balance of payments is justified only if the Government's concern goes beyond the promotion of aggregate consumption through an optimal policy of foreign trade.[91] In all likelihood, the last three items do not so much represent separable objectives as observations on the limited ability of market prices—the wage rate, the price of social services and the foreign exchange rate—to reflect true social benefits and costs with respect to the aggregate-consumption objective. Thus, in the analysis to follow, explicit consideration will be limited to the first three stated objectives: aggregate consumption, regional (Mendalvan) redistribution, and group (small farmer) redistribution.

The analysis proceeds by evaluating separately the net contribution of the Managua project to each of these three objectives, and subsequently combining the contributions with weights reflecting the relative importance the Galivian Government attributes to each objective.

21.10 Basic data requirements

The information base required for social benefit-cost analysis is substantially greater than that required for the cruder methods of evaluation used in the original Managua project report. On the one hand, more detail is required in the description of the benefits and costs of a project, so that items can be distinguished according to the contributions they make to different objectives and according to the need for adjustment of market prices. On the other hand, additional information is required at the national level regarding the relative weights given to alternative objectives and regarding several parameters used in the adjustment of market prices to reflect social opportunity costs. This latter information is common to the evaluation of all projects and must be provided by government authorities.

A basic core of essential data at the project level was presented in tables 21.1 through 21.8, although much of the detail was not used in the earlier

---

[90] See the detailed discussion in chapter 8.

[91] See chapters 9 and 16.

TABLE 21.14 CONSTRUCTION COSTS BY YEAR AND INPUT

(Million pesetas)

Item	*Year* 1	2	3	4	*Total*
Input					
(1) Machinery	26.5	28.5	61.6	50.1	166.7
(1-a) Depreciation	8.0	8.6	18.5	15.0	50.1
(1-b) Labour	5.3	5.7	12.3	10.1	33.4
(1-c) Fuel	6.6	7.1	15.4	12.5	41.6
(1-d) Parts	6.6	7.1	15.4	12.5	41.6
(2) Skilled labour	6.4	7.5	18.8	15.2	47.9
(3) Unskilled labour	20.3	24.9	69.4	64.4	179.0
(4) Cement	4.5	5.7	15.2	7.6	33.0
(5) Iron and steel	1.1	1.7	4.7	2.4	9.9
(6) Other materials	5.2	6.7	18.3	12.3	42.5
(7) Compensation for land	—	5.0	—	—	5.0
Total	64.0	80.0	188.0	152.0	484.0
Resource					
(8) Unskilled labour	20.3	24.9	69.4	64.4	179.0
(9) Skilled labour	11.7	13.2	31.1	25.3	81.3
(10) Domestic materials	9.7	12.4	33.5	19.9	75.5
(11) Foreign exchange	22.3	24.5	54.0	42.4	143.2
Cash transfers					
(12) Compensation to landowners	—	5.0	—	—	5.0

evaluations. These data have been recompiled and presented in a more useful format in tables 21.14 through 21.18. Table 21.14 presents the costs of construction of the project works, divided according to year and input, but summed over all the elements of the works listed in tables 21.1 and 21.2. Table 21.15 gives a parallel breakdown of the costs of operation and maintenance of the project works; these costs are assumed to remain constant throughout the useful life of the project. Tables 21.16 and 21.17 list the costs of agricultural production borne by the cultivators and by the Ministry of Agriculture, respectively, and also include detail on input categories by year. Farmer costs—other than irrigation fees—rise in equal linear increments from one half to their full level by year 10; government costs show a different trend. Finally, table 21.18 gives a similar picture of the time pattern of project benefits. Agricultural production rises with costs from year 5 to year 10; the forgone benefits of agricultural production before the project are constant throughout; and the annual value of housing and social services also remains in constant proportion to the corresponding original fixed investment.

In addition to the underlying figures described in the preceding paragraph, each table also includes a regrouping of inputs and outputs according to the resource category to which each belongs. A few of the benefit and cost flows do not correspond to real resource flows, and these are separated out as cash transfers.

In the analysis to follow, it will be necessary to distinguish between imported and domestically supplied material inputs and between different types of labour; it will also be necessary to distinguish export earnings from

TABLE 21.15 OPERATING COSTS BY YEAR AND INPUT
(Million pesetas)

	Year	
	5 $\longrightarrow$	54
Input		
(1) Machinery		0.60
(1-a) Depreciation	0.18	
(1-b) Labour	0.12	
(1-c) Fuel	0.15	
(1-d) Parts	0.15	
(2) Skilled labour		0.80
(3) Unskilled labour		1.60
(4) Cement		0.30
(5) Other materials		0.70
Total		4.00
Resource		
(6) Unskilled labour		1.60
(7) Skilled labour		0.92
(8) Domestic materials		1.00
(9) Foreign exchange		0.48

TABLE 21.16   FARMER COSTS OF CULTIVATION BY YEAR AND INPUT

(Million pesetas)

			Year			
	5	6	7	8	9	10—54
Input						
(1) Cultivating labour	11.64	13.97	16.30	18.63	20.95	23.28
(1-a) Family	8.73	10.48	12.22	13.97	15.71	17.46
(1-b) Hired	2.91	3.49	4.08	4.66	5.24	5.82
(2) Fodder	2.91	3.49	4.08	4.66	5.24	5.82
(3) Seeds	1.46	1.75	2.04	2.33	2.62	2.91
(4) Chemical fertilizers	5.24	6.29	7.34	8.38	9.44	10.48
(5) Pesticides etc.	1.46	1.75	2.04	2.33	2.62	2.91
(6) Fuel and grease	1.45	1.74	2.03	2.33	2.62	2.91
(7) Equipment and parts	4.36	5.23	6.10	6.97	7.85	8.73
(8) Agricultural credit	0.58	0.70	0.81	0.93	1.04	1.16
(9) Irrigation water	20.00	20.00	20.00	20.00	20.00	20.00
Total	49.10	54.92	60.74	66.56	72.38	78.20
Resource						
(10) Unskilled labour	11.64	13.97	16.30	18.63	20.95	23.28
(11) Domestic materials	4.37	5.24	6.12	6.99	7.86	8.73
(12) Foreign exchange	8.15	9.78	11.41	13.04	14.68	16.30
Cash transfers						
(13) Rental and interest payments	4.94	5.93	6.91	7.90	8.89	9.89
(14) Irrigation fees	20.00	20.00	20.00	20.00	20.00	20.00

TABLE 21.17   MINISTRY OF AGRICULTURE COSTS BY YEAR AND INPUT
(Million pesetas)

				Year			
	5	6	7	8	9	10	11—54
Input							
(1) Equipment and parts	30.0	6.0	6.0	6.0	6.0	6.0	6.0
(2) Working capital	7.5	1.5	1.5	1.5	1.5	1.5	—
(3) Extension workers	3.0	3.0	3.0	3.0	3.0	3.0	0.6
Total	40.5	10.5	10.5	10.5	10.5	10.5	6.6
Resource							
(4) Skilled labour	3.0	0.6	0.6	0.6	0.6	0.6	0.6
(5) Domestic materials	7.5	1.5	1.5	1.5	1.5	1.5	—
(6) Foreign exchange	30.0	6.0	6.0	6.0	6.0	6.0	6.0

TABLE 21.18   PROJECT BENEFITS BY YEAR AND OUTPUT
(Million pesetas)

			Year			
	5	6	7	8	9	10—54
Agricultural output						
Beans	1.73	2.08	2.42	2.77	3.11	3.46
Corn	5.15	6.18	7.21	8.24	9.27	10.30
Sesame	3.20	3.84	4.48	5.12	5.76	6.40
Sorghum	2.86	3.43	4.00	4.58	5.15	5.72
Alfalfa	7.26	8.71	10.16	11.62	13.07	14.52
Safflower	3.10	3.72	4.34	4.96	5.58	6.20
Soybeans	13.57	16.28	19.00	21.71	24.43	27.14
Tomatoes	16.00	19.20	22.40	25.60	28.80	32.00
Other vegetables	3.70	4.44	5.18	5.92	6.66	7.40
Wheat	3.83	4.60	5.36	6.13	6.89	7.66
Other crops	5.40	6.48	7.56	8.64	9.72	10.80
Total	65.80	78.96	92.11	105.29	118.44	131.60
Housing and social services .	2.80	2.80	2.80	2.80	2.80	2.80
Agricultural income forgone	−0.68	−0.68	−0.68	−0.68	−0.68	−0.68
Resource						
Domestic earnings	49.80	59.76	69.72	79.68	89.64	99.60
Foreign exchange	16.00	19.20	22.40	25.60	28.80	32.00
Non-market	2.80	2.80	2.80	2.80	2.80	2.80
Domestic losses	−0.68	−0.68	−0.68	−0.68	−0.68	−0.68

domestic sales. Thus, the resource categories used for grouping the resource flows are as follows: unskilled labour, skilled labour, domestic inputs (outputs) and foreign exchange inputs (outputs). Machinery and parts, iron and steel, fuel, chemical fertilizers and pesticides are all currently imported into Galivia; and it will be assumed (for convenience of computation) that they will continue to be imported throughout the life of the project. All other material inputs are

produced domestically. On the benefit side, the tomato crop is exported and earns foreign exchange, while all other crops are sold on the domestic market. Skilled workers—engineers, technicians, managers etc.—are already distinguished as such in the tables. For the purpose of the analysis, semi-skilled machinery operators and agricultural extension workers will also be classified as skilled workers. The remaining labour inputs—including all farm labourers—are assumed to be unskilled.

Table 21.19 provides a comprehensive summary of all the flows brought about by the Managua project that will be required in the analysis to follow. The benefit flows are measured by the sales value of agricultural output, and the (imputed) value of housing and social services, each of which corresponds to a real benefit to Galivia. The cost flows are measured by the outlays on construction, operation and cultivation, which correspond directly to the use of resources. Hence, land compensation, irrigation fees and rental and interest payments are listed separately under cash transfers. Agricultural income forgone was listed in table 21.18 as a negative item under benefits, but it may also be considered a proxy for the real cost of land use, and it is thus listed in table 21.19 as a positive item under costs. The value of each of the principal benefit and cost flows is subdivided, wherever applicable, according to the shares attributable to each of the resource categories distinguished in tables 21.14 through 21.18. All the values shown in table 21.19, like the figures in the earlier tables, are based on prevailing market prices. For imported inputs and exported outputs, the peseta value is obtained by applying the official exchange rate (10 pesetas to a dollar) to the foreign currency involved.

In addition to the project-level data summarized in table 21.19, values are required for a set of parameters that serve to place the Managua project in the national context in which it must be evaluated. These parameters will be defined, since they are required in the measurement of benefits and costs and in the reconciliation of multiple objectives during later stages of the analysis.

21.11 THE AGGREGATE-CONSUMPTION OBJECTIVE

The evaluation of the net aggregate-consumption benefits of the Managua project is most clearly carried out in successive stages of approximation. The first, and most straightforward, step is to assess the benefits and costs under the assumption that market prices adequately represent social opportunity costs and, hence, the ultimate consumption benefits and costs involved. On this basis, the consumption benefits of the project include items (1) and (2) in table 21.19, and the consumption costs include items (3), (4), (5), (6) and (7).

Items (1) and (2) correspond to real gains for the Galivian economy as a whole, which would not have come about in the absence of the project. Analogously, items (3) through (6) represent payments for resources that could have been used elsewhere, were it not for the project, and that therefore measure the sacrifice of consumption possibilities that the Galivian economy sustains because of the project. Item (7) measures directly the consumption

TABLE 21.19 BENEFIT, COST AND TRANSFER FLOWS BY YEAR (AT MARKET PRICES)

(*Million pesetas*)

							Year				
	1	*2*	*3*	*4*	*5*	*6*	*7*	*8*	*9*	*10*	*11–54*
Benefits											
(1) Agricultural output	—	—	—	—	65.80	78.96	92.12	105.28	118.44	131.60	131.60
(1-D) Domestic currency	—	—	—	—	49.80	59.76	69.72	79.68	89.64	99.60	99.60
(1-F) Foreign exchange	—	—	—	—	16.00	19.20	22.40	25.60	28.80	32.00	32.00
(2) Housing and social services	—	—	—	—	2.80	2.80	2.80	2.80	2.80	2.80	2.80
Costs											
(3) Construction costs	64.00	75.00	188.00	152.00							
(3-L) Unskilled labour	20.30	24.90	69.40	64.40							
(3-S) Skilled labour	11.70	13.20	31.10	25.30							
(3-D) Domestic materials	9.70	12.40	33.50	19.90							
(3-F) Foreign exchange	22.30	24.50	54.00	42.40							
(4) Operating costs	—	—	—	—	4.00	4.00	4.00	4.00	4.00	4.00	4.00
(4-L) Unskilled labour	—	—	—	—	1.60	1.60	1.60	1.60	1.60	1.60	1.60
(4-S) Skilled labour	—	—	—	—	0.92	0.92	0.92	0.92	0.92	0.92	0.92
(4-D) Domestic materials	—	—	—	—	1.00	1.00	1.00	1.00	1.00	1.00	1.00
(4-F) Foreign exchange	—	—	—	—	0.48	0.48	0.48	0.48	0.48	0.48	0.48
(5) Farmer agricultural costs	—	—	—	—	24.16	28.99	33.73	38.66	43.49	48.31	48.31
(5-DF) Family (unskilled) labour	—	—	—	—	8.73	10.48	12.22	13.97	15.71	17.46	17.46
(5-LH) Hired (unskilled) labour	—	—	—	—	2.91	3.49	4.08	4.66	5.24	5.82	5.82
(5-D) Domestic materials	—	—	—	—	4.37	5.24	6.12	6.99	7.86	8.73	8.73
(5-F) Foreign exchange	—	—	—	—	8.15	9.78	11.41	13.04	14.68	16.30	16.30
(6) Ministry agricultural costs	—	—	—	—	40.50	10.50	10.50	10.50	10.50	10.50	6.60
(6-S) Extension workers	—	—	—	—	3.00	3.00	3.00	3.00	3.00	3.00	0.60
(6-D) Working capital	—	—	—	—	7.50	1.50	1.50	1.50	1.50	1.50	—
(6-F) Foreign exchange	—	—	—	—	30.00	6.00	6.00	6.00	6.00	6.00	6.00
(7) Agricultural income forgone	—	—	—	—	0.68	0.68	0.68	0.68	0.68	0.68	0.68
Transfers											
(8) Compensation to landowners	—	5.00	—	—	—	—	—	—	—	—	—
(9) Irrigation fees	—	—	—	—	20.00	20.00	20.00	20.00	20.00	20.00	20.00
(10) Rental and interest payments	—	—	—	—	4.94	5.93	6.91	7.90	8.89	9.89	9.89

sacrifice involved in adopting new methods of cultivating the previously farmed land. The last three items, (8)—(10), do not enter into the aggregate-consumption calculations, for they represent gains to one group of people that are exactly offset by losses to others, and hence have no net effect on the aggregate welfare.

The market value of net aggregate-consumption benefits in any given year of the project may thus be defined as follows:

$$MC = (1) + (2) - (3) - (4) - (5) - (6) - (7) \qquad (21.1)$$

MC represents the first approximation to the net aggregate-consumption benefits of the project. The second approximation involves the adjustment of the market prices of specific resources wherever these prices do not reflect the real contribution of the resources to the aggregate-consumption objective—i.e. their "social opportunity cost". As noted earlier, such discrepancies can occur for a variety of reasons and in a variety of ways. In the evaluation of the Managua project, two major resources are singled out for price adjustment: foreign exchange and unskilled labour. In addition, it is observed that agricultural extension workers contribute more to national output than is measured by their wage. It is tacitly assumed that all the project's remaining inputs and outputs are correctly priced by the competitive market mechanism— i.e. there is no rationing (at artificially low prices) or unemployment (at artificially high prices) of any other factors, goods or services.

As for the foreign exchange position, it is noted that heavy pressure on the Galivian balance of payments has resulted in strict quantitative import controls and export subsidies to maintain the dollar value of the peseta. As a result, it is clear to all concerned that a dollar of foreign exchange is worth substantially more than 10 pesetas—its value at the official exchange rate. In the analysis to follow, the opportunity cost of foreign exchange relative to its official market price will be denoted by $(1 + \varPhi)$; $\varPhi$ represents the foreign exchange premium, which is currently positive in Galivia, but may decline over time.[92]

The situation of unskilled labour in Galivia is opposite to that of foreign exchange; while foreign exchange is effectively rationed at a price well below its opportunity cost, unskilled labour is found in surplus, and the market wage exceeds the opportunity cost of employing additional workers. The opportunity cost of unskilled labour—relative to the going market wage—will be denoted by $(1 + \lambda)$; λ represents the unskilled labour premium, which is likely to be negative in the Mendalvan region and especially as far as the rurally oriented Managua project is concerned.[93]

Although skilled workers in general are assumed to be fully employed in Galivia at wages that reflect their social opportunity cost, agricultural extension workers in particular are regarded as underpaid by the Ministry of Agriculture. The social value of an extension worker is measured by the contribution his services make to aggregate-consumption benefits for Galivia, via improved

---

[92] See chapter 16.
[93] See chapters 6 and 15.

agricultural production techniques. Since farmers in many parts of the country urgently need instruction, the marginal extension worker is in a position to contribute much more than the wage he commands. In parallel with Φ and λ, λ^E is defined as the social premium on the market wage of an agricultural extension worker; λ^E is expected to remain positive in Galivia for a long time.

It is now possible to express the net aggregate-consumption benefits of the Managua project, after incorporating the opportunity cost premiums, as

$$SC = (1) + \Phi (1\text{-}F) + (2) - (3) - \lambda (3\text{-}L) - \Phi (3\text{-}F) -$$
$$- (4) - \lambda (4\text{-}L) - \Phi (4\text{-}F) - (5) - \lambda (5\text{-}L^F) -$$
$$- \lambda (5\text{-}L^H) - \Phi (5\text{-}F) - (6) - \lambda^E (6\text{-}S) - \Phi (6\text{-}F) - (7) \qquad (21.2)$$

Rearranging the terms, equation (21.2) may also be written as follows:

$$SC = MC + \Phi FE + \lambda L + \lambda^E E \qquad (21.2^*)$$
$$\text{where } FE = (1\text{-}F) - (3\text{-}F) - (4\text{-}F) - (5\text{-}F) - (6\text{-}F) \qquad (21.2a)$$
$$L = - (3\text{-}L) - (4\text{-}L) - (5\text{-}L^F) - (5\text{-}L^H) \qquad (21.2b)$$
$$E = - (6\text{-}S) \qquad (21.2c)$$

The second approximation, SC, is obtained by adding three terms to the first approximation, MC. The first term corrects MC for the opportunity cost of foreign exchange by multiplying the net foreign exchange component of benefits and costs, FE, by the (positive) foreign exchange premium, Φ. The second term corrects MC for the opportunity cost of unskilled labour by multiplying the net unskilled labour component, L, by the (negative) labour premium, λ; and the third term does the same for agricultural extension workers with their (positive) premium, λ^E.

The third and final approximation to the net aggregate-consumption benefits of the project takes into account the adjustments necessary when the social value of funds devoted to investment exceeds the social value of the same funds devoted to consumption. This possibility has arisen because the limitations of the Galivian Government's fiscal and monetary powers have prevented it from bringing about the rate of investment which, in its capacity as representative of the Galivian people, it deems optimal for the country as a whole. The Government has not been in a position to raise savings—and investment—to the point where the marginal rate of return on investment, q, is equal to the social rate of discount, i, which reflects the intertemporal time preferences of the nation.

The opportunity cost of investment, P^{inv}, is defined as the ratio of the social value of investment to the social value of consumption, where "social value" is understood to mean the value of the relevant time stream of aggregate-consumption benefits discounted back to the present at the social rate of discount.[94] The value of P^{inv} can be determined according to the following formula:[95]

$$P^{inv} = \frac{(1 - s) q}{i - sq} \qquad (21.3)$$

---

[94] See chapters 6 and 14.
[95] See equation (14.16) in chapter 14.

where i and q are defined as above; s is the economy-wide marginal rate of reinvestment of profits, expressed as a fraction of total profits; and all three parameters are assumed to remain constant over time.

Once it is recognized that P^{inv} does not equal 1, it becomes essential to evaluate the net effect of the project on the mix of consumption and investment in the economy. We have discussed this at length in chapter 6. To evaluate the net effect of the project on the rate of investment, it is necessary to distinguish all the benefit and cost flows that make up SC, as well as the accompanying cash transfers, according to the group that gains or loses, and to estimate the respective marginal consumption and saving propensities of each group.

For this purpose, four broad groups of gainers and losers have been distinguished with respect to the Managua project: farmers, F; unskilled workers, L; the Government, G; and the taxed public, T. G includes all branches of the Galivian Government—the MWA, the Ministry of Agriculture etc., for they all operate under a common budget. Each of the benefit and cost flows that enter into SC, as defined in equation (21.2), can be identified with one of these four groups. The market value of agricultural production (1) accrues to F, whether the crops are sold on the market or retained for home consumption. The extra value of foreign exchange earned by tomato exports $\Phi(1\text{-}F)$ accrues to G, for the Galivian Government is assumed to pay farmers for their foreign exchange earnings at the official exchange rate, and thereby to capture for its own use the excess value of the foreign exchange. The benefits of housing and social services (2) are gained by F.

The identification of the group that pays for construction costs (3) depends on the manner in which these costs are financed, in particular, from whom the corresponding resources are ultimately diverted. If the construction costs of the project are paid out of government revenues without any corresponding receipts, then G is the loser. However, if the Government finances the cost of construction through additional taxation or borrowing, then the holders of taxed or borrowed funds are the losers. Part of the cost of the Managua project is financed by a World Bank loan and the rest by the Galivian Government. It is assumed that the bank loan would have been available to the Government on the same terms in the absence of the project; hence, G pays for the foreign exchange component (3-F), which it could have used on an alternative project. In addition to the market value of the foreign exchange component, G also loses the extra opportunity cost represented by $\Phi(3\text{-}F)$. It is assumed that the domestic currency funds provided out of the Galivian budget are raised by general taxation (or, equivalently, that in the absence of the project, taxes would have been reduced). The effect is that resources are diverted away from the taxed public, and the construction cost components (3-S), (3-D) and (3-L) are paid for by T.

The costs of operating the project works (4), and the costs of the farm equipment (6-F) and working capital (6-D) provided by the Ministry of Agriculture are all paid for by G; and the additional opportunity costs due

to the foreign exchange components $\Phi(4\text{-}F)$ and $\Phi(6\text{-}F)$ are also sustained by G. In the case of the agricultural extension services, whose total value is measured by $[1 + \lambda^E](6\text{-}S)$, the loss is borne by those farmers (F) from whom the extension workers are drawn away by the Ministry for assignment to the Managua project. The costs of agricultural production paid by the cultivators (5) and the value of net agricultural income forgone (7) are losses to F. However, the extra opportunity cost of foreign exchange $\Phi(5\text{-}F)$ is borne by G, since the Galivian Government is in effect subsidizing the use of imported inputs in agriculture by making them available to the farmer at the official exchange rate. It remains only to consider the (negative) costs included in SC, which are represented by the unskilled labour premiums λL, as defined in equation (21.2). These premiums correspond to the margin by which the total project wage bill for unskilled labour, including farm labour, exceeds the amount necessary to attract the unskilled workers to the project, i.e. their earnings in alternative employment plus the costs of transfer. This margin corresponds exactly to the net extra income received by the unskilled labour on account of the project, so that the (negative) costs $\lambda[(4\text{-}L)+(5\text{-}L^H)+(6\text{-}L)]$ accrue to L, and the remaining (negative) costs $\lambda(5\text{-}L^F)$ go to farm labour belonging to F.

Although the cash transfer items, (8), (9) and (10), are not relevant to the evaluation of aggregate benefits and costs, they are certainly relevant to the distribution of these benefits and costs. Hence, they too must be considered here in assessing the allocation of net benefits among the four groups—F, L, G and T. Item (8) represents a gain to the landowners among F and an equal loss to G. Items (9) and (10) represent costs to F and corresponding benefits to G. Since these items enter both as benefits and costs, the sum total of net benefits to the four groups remains equal to the total net benefits, SC.

The distribution of second approximation net consumption benefits, SC, by group can now be summarized as follows:

$$SC = SC^F + SC^L + SC^G + SC^T \tag{21.4}$$
$$SC^F = (1) + (2) - (5) - (6\text{-}S) - (7) + (8) - (9) - (10) - \lambda(5\text{-}L^F) -$$
$$- \lambda^E(6\text{-}S) \tag{21.4a}$$
$$SC^L = -\lambda[(3\text{-}L) + (4\text{-}L) + (5\text{-}L^H)] \tag{21.4b}$$
$$SC^G = -(3\text{-}F) - (4) - (6\text{-}D) - (6\text{-}F) - (8) + (9) + (10) + \Phi(FE) \tag{21.4c}$$
$$SC^T = -(3\text{-}L) - (3\text{-}S) - (3\text{-}D) \tag{21.4d}$$

where SC^F, SC^L, SC^G and SC^T represent the value of net consumption benefits flowing to F, L, G and T, respectively. To arrive at the final social value of net aggregate-consumption benefits, C, it is necessary to correct SC^F, SC^L, SC^G and SC^T according to the proportions in which each is divided between consumption and investment. Thus, if the average farmer saves a proportion S^F of his marginal gains, the social value of the net consumption benefits flowing to farmers is

$$C^F = [S^F P^{\text{inv}} + (1\text{-}S^F)] SC^F \tag{21.5a}$$

Similarly, the social value of net consumption benefits flowing to unskilled workers, to the Government and to the taxed public can be expressed as follows:[96]

$$C^L = [S^L \, P^{\text{inv}} + (1\text{-}S^L)] \, SC^L \qquad (21.5b)$$
$$C^G = [S^G \, P^{\text{inv}} + (1\text{-}S^G)] \, SC^G \qquad (21.5c)$$
$$C^T = [S^T \, P^{\text{inv}} + (1\text{-}S^T)] \, SC^T \qquad (21.5d)$$

We may now write the third and final approximation to the value of net aggregate-consumption benefits, C, to Galivia as a whole in any given year as the sum of the social value of net benefits flowing to each group:

$$C = C^F + C^L + C^G + C^T \qquad (21.5)$$

Using equations (21.5a) through (21.5d), equation (21.5) may be rewritten as follows:

$$C = SC + (P^{\text{inv}} - 1) \, [S^F \, SC^F + S^L \, SC^L + S^G \, SC^G + S^T \, SC^T] \qquad (21.5^*)$$

Thus, the final approximation, C, is equal to the second approximation, SC, corrected by a term that multiplies the total marginal savings out of net project consumption benefits by the excess of the social value of investment over the social value of consumption $(P^{\text{inv}} - 1)$.

21.12 THE REGIONAL-REDISTRIBUTION OBJECTIVE

The second national objective to be considered in the evaluation of the Managua project is the objective of redistributing benefits to the underdeveloped Mendalvan region of the country. It is now necessary to review the benefits and costs of the project to assess their net effect on the welfare of Mendalva. Some of the benefit and cost flows shown in table 21.19 are relevant to Mendalvan welfare, and others are not; the relevant items may affect the redistribution objective in a different way from the way they affect the aggregate-consumption objective.

The market value of agricultural production (1) clearly represents a direct benefit to Mendalva, since the earnings flow to the farmers of the region. The extra value of the foreign exchange component $(1\text{-}F)$, however, does not result in a benefit for the region, since it is captured by the Central Government. Clearly, the value of housing and social services (2) is also included among the direct benefits to Mendalva.

Among the cost flows, only the agricultural production costs of the farmers (5) and the net agricultural income forgone (7) represent losses to Mendalva. But to the extent that farmer costs result in net gains to other inhabitants of Mendalva, a compensating benefit is involved. Payments to the Government and payments for imported inputs clearly go out of Mendalva and represent pure losses to the region. Payments for domestic inputs produced in Mendalva, e.g. fodder and seeds, as well as wages paid (in cash or in kind)

---

[96] See equation A6.12 in the appendix to chapter 6.

to inhabitants of Mendalva would appear not to represent net costs to the region. This, however, requires more careful attention. When the farmer buys fodder and seeds in Mendalva, the total supply of these materials available in the region is reduced, or the flow into the region must be increased, or the production within the region must be stepped up. Whichever the case, there is indeed a net cost to Mendalva unless otherwise idle Mendalvan resources are put to use. Thus, the likelihood is that farmer payments for domestic materials do represent costs to the region, just as do payments to the Government and payments for imported inputs.

The situation in regard to wage payments, on the other hand, is different. When workers are put to work in Mendalva, there is no corresponding reduction in the regional labour force, because it can safely be assumed that there will be a corresponding marginal immigration of labour into the region. Thus, it is most likely that—in contrast to payments for material inputs—wage payments will remain within the region and result in benefits for inhabitants of Mendalva. Accordingly, the wage component of farmer production costs, $(5\text{-}L^F)$ plus $(5\text{-}L^H)$, must be added in as a compensating benefit to the regional cost of (5). By the same token, the wage payments made by the MWA for the construction and operation of the project and the payments made by the Ministry of Agriculture to extension workers also result in net benefits to Mendalva. These wage payments are made to both skilled and unskilled workers and are covered by items (3-L), (3-S), (4-L), (4-S) and (6-S).

Just as the cash transfer items, (8), (9) and (10), had to be taken into account in evaluating the allocation of net benefits among groups, so they must be considered in assessing the distribution of net benefits to the Mendalvan region. Item (8) enters as a benefit to Mendalva, while items (9) and (10) clearly represent costs to the region. The total value of net aggregate-consumption benefits redistributed to the Mendalvan region in any given year can now be expressed as follows:

$$DR^M = (1) + (2) + (3\text{-}L) + (3\text{-}S) + (4\text{-}L) + (4\text{-}S) - (5) + (5\text{-}L^F) + \\ + (5\text{-}L^H) + (6\text{-}S) - (7) + (8) - (9) - (10) \qquad (21.6)$$

Unlike the first approximation to net aggregate-consumption benefits, MC, DR^M does not have to be corrected for the social opportunity costs of foreign exchange, unskilled labour and investment vis-à-vis consumption. What is an opportunity cost with respect to the aggregate consumption of the whole country is not necessarily an opportunity cost for a particular region. Thus, although Galivia as a whole forgoes benefits equal to the opportunity cost of foreign exchange when imported inputs are used in the Managua project, the loss of benefits to the Mendalvan farmer when he pays for imported fertilizers is simply the market cost that he gives up. The loss due to the extra social value of the foreign exchange used is spread over the whole country, and its effect on Mendalva can be regarded as negligible. For similar reasons, the benefits to Mendalva of employing unskilled labour are not limited to the excess of the market wage over the amount actually necessary to attract the

labour; the latter represents a cost to the country as a whole, but not to the Mendalvan region. Finally, if investment is valued higher than the equivalent current consumption in calculating aggregate-consumption benefits, this is because the increased consumption flow provided by investment is a gain to the country as a whole. The fraction of the gain that reaches Mendalva may for practical purposes be ignored.

There does remain, however, one important adjustment of DR^M that must be made to assess the total net consumption benefits distributed to Mendalva by the project. Whether the direct benefits measured by DR^M are consumed or invested, a part of them will be respent within the Mendalvan region; to the extent that they result in a net transfer of wage and profit earnings from elsewhere in Galivia to Mendalva or activate otherwise idle Mendalvan resources, they will result in a new round of benefits to the region. This was discussed in detail in chapter 7. There it was shown that if γ represents the proportion of marginal benefits to Mendalvans which, when respent, results in additional benefits to the region, then the total value of net regional-consumption benefits in any given year is given by:[97]

$$R^M = \frac{DR^M}{1 - \gamma} \tag{21.7}$$

21.13 The group-redistribution objective

The third national objective to be considered in the evaluation of the Managua project is the objective of redistributing benefits to small farmers.

To evaluate the net effect of the project on the welfare of small farmers, it is necessary to compare their economic position before and after the construction of the project. As shown in table 21.3, there are at present 1,907 small farm units (defined as holdings of less than 10 hectares) in the Secotuan valley area, and this number will rise to 3,579 when the project is completed. Not all of the 3,579 units, however, will belong to the original class of small farmers, since some of these 10-hectare units are to be formed by paring down larger holdings of the farmers who own land in the irrigated area. Apart from the 1,907 small units, there are at present 173 units of over 10 hectares. Of these, 134 are expected to remain over 10 hectares, and the remaining 39 will be cut down to 10 hectares. Thus, of the total of 3,579 10-hectare units to be located on the irrigated land, 1,907 will belong to the original small holders, 1,633 will belong to small farmers relocated from the surrounding area, and 39 will belong to farmers with previously larger holdings.

According to table 21.3, the 1,907 small farmers cultivate at present 42.9 per cent of the land area to be taken over by the project. It will be assumed that they earn likewise 42.9 per cent of the annual net agricultural income resulting from current cultivation. No figures are available on the current earnings of the 1,633 small farmers to be relocated from adjacent areas, but

---

[97] See equation (7.2).

it may be reasonable to assume that their holdings are so small and the land so marginal that their sacrifice of current farm income is negligible. Thus, the net agricultural income forgone by small farmers because of the project may be estimated as 0.429 (7), where (7) refers to the total value of net agricultural income forgone as given in table 21.19.

After the project is under way, the 3,540 small farmers will hold 35,400 of the 40,000 cultivated hectares, or 88.5 per cent of the total cultivated area. As before, it may be assumed that they receive the same percentage of the total market value of agricultural production and incur the same percentage of cultivating costs, so that their net farm earnings amount to 0.885 [(1) — (5) — (9) — (10)]. The same percentage of imputed family wages also accrues to the small farmers as a group: 0.885 $(5-L^F)$. With respect to the housing and social service benefits (2), it is more appropriate to assume that they will be enjoyed by small farmers according to their fraction in numbers rather than in acreage. Thus, the relevant value of benefits becomes 3,540/3,713 (2) = 0.954 (2). Finally, it is clear that the gains from land compensation (8) go to large rather than small farmers and must not be included among benefits to small farmers.

The total value of net consumption benefits provided by the Managua project to small farmers can now be expressed as

$$R^{SF} = 0.885 [(1) — (5) + (5-L^F) — (9) — (10)] + 0.954 (2) — 0.429 (7) \quad (21.8)$$

For reasons analogous to those given in analysing the regional-redistribution benefits, there is no need to correct R^{SF} for the failure of market prices to reflect social opportunity costs; such corrections are relevant only to the aggregate-consumption objective. In the case of benefits to small farmers, there is also no reason to consider indirect benefits of the kind included with the calculation of regional benefits, since the expenditures of small farmers are very unlikely to return additional benefits in successive rounds of spending.

21.14 THE EVALUATION OF THE PROJECT

In the course of the three previous sections, dealing with the three principal objectives of the Galivian Government vis-à-vis the Managua project, various parameters were defined for which values are required to evaluate the project. In principle, each of these parameters is a function of time, and the appropriate values may therefore change according to the year in which the benefits and costs are being measured. To simplify the computations, however, it will be assumed for the purposes of illustration that the value of each parameter remains constant over the entire lifetime of the project. In table 21.20, each parameter is listed with the corresponding numerical value that is assumed to be appropriate to the Galivian economy and, where applicable, to the circumstances of the project.

Foreign exchange is assumed to be worth twice its value at the official exchange rate ($\Phi = +1.0$). Given the rural setting of the project, the nature

of the work—farming and construction—and the overpopulation and backwardness of the Mendalvan region, it may not be unreasonable to regard the opportunity cost of unskilled labour as equal to zero ($\lambda = -1.0$). In contrast, the opportunity cost of agricultural extension workers is assumed to be twice the market wage ($\lambda^E = +1.0$). Given the social rate of discount, which is meant to reflect the collective preference of the nation for present over future consumption,[98] the social value of investment relative to the social value of consumption[99] can be derived from equation 21.3. Since the social discount rate is to be treated as an unknown within a limited range, we have chosen values of 5 per cent, 7.5 per cent and 10 per cent. The corresponding shadow prices of investment (P^{inv}) are, therefore, 16, 4.57 and 2.67. As for propensities to save (resulting in investment), farmers are assumed to consume 90 per cent of their earnings ($S^F = 0.1$), while unskilled workers consume all their wages ($S^L = 0.0$). The Galivian Government, in view of the high value of investment, is ready to devote all available funds to that purpose ($S^G = 1.0$). The marginal propensity to save of the taxed public depends on who pays for marginal increases in taxation. It is likely that corporations and high-income brackets will be most affected, so that the corresponding marginal propensity to save is very high ($S^T = 0.8$). Finally, the marginal propensity to respend within Mendalva is assumed to be 20 per cent ($\gamma = 0.2$).

Given the values of the parameters (1) through (9) in table 21.20 and given all the relevant flows over time in table 21.19, it is now possible to calculate

TABLE 21.20 VALUES OF GENERAL PARAMETERS

(1) Foreign exchange premium	Φ	$= +1.0$
(2) Unskilled labour premium	λ	$= -1.0$
(3) Extension worker premium	λ^E	$= +1.0$
(4) Marginal rate of return on investment in private sector	q	$= 0.20$
(5) Marginal rate of reinvestment of profits	s	$= 0.20$
(6) Social rate of discount	i	$= 0.05; 0.075; 0.10$
(7) Associated social price of investment	P^{inv}	$= 16.00; 4.57; 2.67$
(8) Marginal propensities to save:		
(8-a) Farmers	S^F	$= 0.2$
(8-b) Unskilled workers	S^L	$= 0.0$
(8-c) Government	S^G	$= 1.0$
(8-d) Taxed public	S^T	$= 0.8$
(9) Marginal propensity to (re-)spend in Mendalva	γ	$= 0.2$
(10) Rates of discount on objectives:		
(10-a) Aggregate consumption	i^C	$= 0.10$
(10-b) Redistribution to Mendalva	i^{R^M}	$= 0.10$
(10-c) Redistribution to small farmers	$i^{R^{SF}}$	$= 0.10$
(11) Weights on objectives:		
(11-a) Aggregate consumption	Θ^C	$= 1.00$
(11-b) Redistribution to Mendalva	Θ^{R^M}	$= 0.25$
(11-c) Redistribution to small farmers	$\Theta^{R^{SF}}$	$= 0.50$

[98] See chapters 12 and 13 for detailed discussions of this value parameter.

[99] It should be remembered that we are using the social value of consumption as a *numéraire*.

the contributions made by the project to each of the three objectives in each year of the project by substituting into the appropriate equations derived in sections 21.11, 21.12, 21.13. To calculate the total contribution to each objective, all that is needed in addition is a set of weights to put the contributions in different years on a comparable basis. Table 21.21 lists the present value in year 0 of each of the flows of table 21.19, discounted at the rates of 5 per cent, 7.5 per cent and 10 per cent. The results are obtained as shown in table 21.22.

The present value of net aggregate-consumption benefits is shown in successive stages of approximation. Using market prices and a social discount rate of 10 per cent, the present value, MC, turns out to be positive but comparatively low, at a level of 39.3 million pesetas. This figure corresponds very closely to the value computed by Dr. Blancabeza in section 21.7. Using

TABLE 21.21 PRESENT VALUE OF FLOWS IN YEAR 0
(Million pesetas)

		Social rate of discount		
		5%	*7.5%*	*10%*
Benefits				
(1)	Agricultural output	1,829.0	1,152.0	782.0
(1-D)	Domestic currency	1,384.0	871.5	591.8
(1-F)	Foreign exchange	445.0	280.5	190.2
(2)	Housing and social services	42.1	27.2	19.0
Costs				
(3)	Construction costs	416.2	389.7	365.2
(3-L)	Unskilled labour	154.9	144.5	135.2
(3-S)	Skilled labour	70.7	66.4	62.3
(3-D)	Domestic materials	65.9	61.6	57.6
(3-F)	Foreign exchange	124.7	117.2	110.1
(4)	Operating costs	60.1	38.8	27.1
(4-L)	Unskilled labour	24.1	15.5	10.8
(4-S)	Skilled labour	13.8	8.9	6.2
(4-D)	Domestic materials	15.0	9.7	6.8
(4-F)	Foreign exchange	7.2	4.7	3.3
(5)	Farmer agricultural costs	671.4	423.6	286.9
(5-L^F)	Family (unskilled) labour	242.6	153.0	103.7
(5-L^H)	Hired (unskilled) labour	80.9	51.0	34.6
(5-D)	Domestic materials	121.4	76.6	51.8
(5-F)	Foreign exchange	226.5	143.0	96.8
(6)	Ministry agricultural costs	141.5	101.8	77.9
(6-S)	Extension workers	18.1	14.3	11.9
(6-D)	Working capital	10.9	9.5	8.2
(6-F)	Foreign exchange	112.5	78.0	57.8
(7)	Agricultural income forgone	10.2	6.6	4.6
Transfers				
(8)	Compensation to landowners	4.5	4.3	4.1
(9)	Irrigation fees	300.5	194.2	135.4
(10)	Rental and interest payments	137.5	86.7	58.8

TABLE 21.22　PRESENT VALUE OF NET BENEFITS OF THE MANAGUA PROJECT IN YEAR 0
(Million pesetas)

Item	Equation number	Social rate of discount		
		5%	7.5%	10%
Aggregate consumption				
MC	(21.1)	+ 571.7	+ 218.7	+ 39.3
FE	(21.2a)	− 25.9	− 62.4	− 77.8
L	(21.2b)	− 502.5	− 364.0	−284.3
E	(21.2c)	− 18.1	− 14.3	− 11.9
SC	(21.2)	+1,030.2	+ 506.0	+233.9
SC^F	(21.4a)	+ 962.4	+ 596.8	+399.3
SC^L	(21.4b)	+ 259.9	+ 211.0	+180.6
SC^G	(21.4c)	+ 99.4	− 29.3	− 90.9
SC^T	(21.4d)	− 291.5	− 272.5	−255.1
C	(21.5)	+ 466.8	− 163.8	−276.2
Redistribution to Mendalva				
R^M	(21.7)	+1,701.4	+1,157.5	+855.1
Redistribution to small farmers				
R^{SF}	(21.8)	+ 887.3	+ 554.5	+374.1

also a 10 per cent rate of discount, Dr. Blancabeza arrived at a figure of
35.2 million pesetas, which he labelled the net present value of the project
as a whole. The slight difference between the two figures arises because
Dr. Blancabeza (incorrectly) included compensation payments to landowners
—with a present value of 4.1 million pesetas—as an element of construction costs.

The second approximation, SC, suggests a substantially greater project
contribution to the aggregate-consumption objective. The (positive) foreign
exchange and extension worker premiums, applied to negative net benefits,
reduce the value given by MC; but the (negative) unskilled labour premium,
applied to the total market wage bill of unskilled labour, raises the value of net
benefits by a much greater amount. The 284.3 million pesetas originally charged
to the project as unskilled labour costs are replaced by the corresponding social
opportunity cost of zero, and SC becomes equal to 233.9 million pesetas.[100]

The final approximation, C, however, indicates that the Managua project
actually makes a decidedly negative contribution to the aggregate-consumption
objective. This is due to the high social value of investment relative to consumption and to the unfavourable over-all effect of the project on the rate of investment elsewhere in the Galivian economy. The two groups with the highest
propensity to invest, the Galivian Government and the (marginally) taxed
public, suffer net losses on account of the project. Funds raised to finance the
project carry a high opportunity cost, for they would have been invested largely
on alternative projects. On the other hand, the chief beneficiaries of the project,
the farmers and unskilled workers, consume most of their benefits and add

---

[100] All numbers quoted here refer to those obtained with a 10 per cent social rate of
discount.

little to investment in the economy. The result is that, when all things are considered, the net aggregate-consumption benefits of the Managua project amount to minus 276.2 million pesetas at a 10 per cent discount.[101]

As against this negative contribution to aggregate consumption, the project does make substantially positive contributions to both redistribution objectives. The Mendalvan region and the small farmers of the Secotuan valley do not pay the high price of drawing funds away from investment elsewhere in Galivia, but they do reap most of the benefits of the Managua investment itself. According to table 21.22, the present value of net benefits—direct and indirect—to Mendalva is equal to 855.1 million pesetas, and the corresponding figure for the small farmers is 374.1 million pesetas. It is clear that on aggregate-consumption grounds alone, the Managua project is not justified at a social discount rate of 10 per cent.[102] It is worth undertaking only if the Galivian Government places a sufficient weight on redistribution of welfare to the Mendalvan region and to the small farmers so that the combined net present value of all benefits is positive.

Figure 35, the graph associated with table 21.22, shows what combination of weights will make the project acceptable. As the weight for regional-income distribution increases, the region of acceptance, which is to the left and above the appropriate curve, increases; thus, the project is acceptable, i.e. it yields a positive present value of aggregate benefits (at the highest possible social discount rates and the lowest possible weights for distribution to low-income farmers).

The final decision as to whether the project is or is not acceptable clearly depends on what values the Government gives to the three "value judgement" parameters for this and other potential projects.

21.15 A FEW QUALIFICATIONS

The evaluation carried out in section 21.14 was designed to answer a yes-or-no question: Should the Managua project be undertaken? This approach is valid only if there are no specific variants, or mutually exclusive alternatives, to the project as formulated in the report and if the national parameters are all judged to be given to the project evaluator.[103] In this event, the only relevant alternative to the project is the general alternative of investing the same funds elsewhere in the economy, and this has been taken into account in the analysis. If, however, there exists the possibility of varying or replacing the project with an otherwise excluded alternative, it is necessary to inquire into the possibility of obtaining additional net benefits. Thus, even though the Managua project in its present form yields a significantly positive net present value, it should not

---

[101] At 7.5 per cent discount rate the net aggregate-consumption benefits are —163.8 million, while at 5 per cent they are +466.8 million.

[102] On aggregate-consumption grounds alone the project is justifiable only if the social discount rate is below 6.3 per cent.

[103] See, in particular, chapter 12.

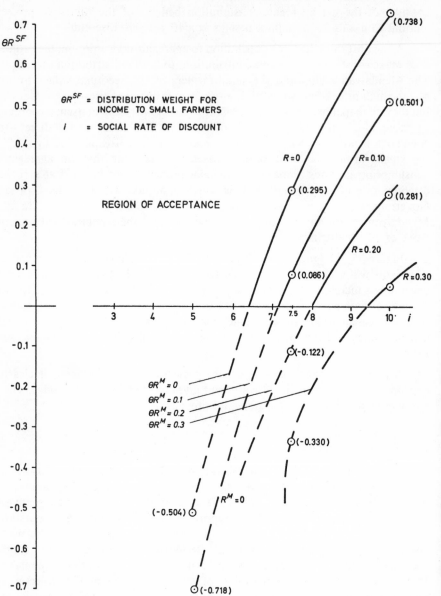

Figure 35   Switching values for Managua project

be undertaken if it prevents the undertaking of an alternative project with an even greater total net present value. Such a possibility might arise in several ways.

First of all, it might well be possible to make marginal adjustments in the method of construction or operation of the project or in the related agricultural production programme, which would result in a higher net present value than

yielded by the project in its proposed form. Unless the engineers who designed, and the officials who formulated, the project were continuously aware of the appropriate methods for evaluating alternative possibilities, it is more than likely that there would still be scope for improvement when the project reached the decision makers. To anticipate this likelihood, it would be useful to present the project not as a single package, but as a manageable array of alternatives from among which the decision makers could choose the most favourable according to the accepted method of evaluation. In any case, it would be necessary to ask whether adjustments in the nature or scope of the Managua project could raise its net present value.

An additional—and potentially important—adjustment of the project concerns neither its nature nor its scope, but its timing. If the project is begun in 1975, this excludes the possibility of starting it at any later date. Provided all benefits and costs are dependent only on the age of the project itself, it would clearly be worth undertaking right away or not at all, for the longer it is put off, the lower the discounted present value of the net benefits. However, if some of the benefits or costs are affected by the calendar date on which they occur, and if net benefits are expected to increase with time, a higher present value may be realized if the project is delayed. This alternative must also be considered when the project is evaluated.

Apart from asking about possible adjustments in the project itself, the decision makers must compare the Managua project with wholly different projects that it excludes. If, for example, there is an alternative use for the water resources of the Rio Casqueya, such a possibility must be explored before the Managua project pre-empts it. Similarly, if there are alternative ways of supplying the Secotuan valley with irrigation water, e.g. via a network of tube wells, this possibility must also be compared with the Managua project in terms of its net contribution to national objectives.

In sum, the positive net present value obtained in the evaluation of the Managua project indicates that there is a national gain to be realized by under-taking a water-resource project in the Rio Casqueya–Secotuan valley area. But until all the relevant alternatives have been explored, it cannot be concluded that the Managua project should be undertaken in the precise form in which it was originally proposed.

21.16 ALTERING THE AGRICULTURAL PROGRAMME

As stressed in section 21.15, it is important to consider various alternative possibilities before proceeding with the Managua project as proposed. In this section, the effect of altering the suggested agricultural programme by changing the pattern of land ownership and crop distribution will be considered. The pattern of land ownership proposed is characterized by a vast number of small 10-hectare holdings covering almost 90 per cent of the irrigated land, and the remaining 10 per cent is divided among holdings no greater than 50 hectares

(see table 21.3). The crop distribution corresponding to this system of land tenure emphasizes diversity and self-sufficiency, and includes both low and high profit-yielding crops in roughly equal measure (see table 21.4).

To study the range of alternatives, it will now be hypothesized that the 40,000 hectares of newly irrigated land are divided into 400 large holdings of 100 hectares each. On such large holdings, it is presumed that a greater proportion of the land can be devoted to the cultivation of the commercially most profitable crops. Table 21.23 presents figures for an alternative distribution of crops based on 100-hectare holdings, consistent with the constraints imposed by the availability of irrigation water and the requirements of on-farm consumption. A comparison of table 21.23 with table 21.4 shows that the production of high-profit-yielding tomatoes has been stepped up the most radically. More acreage is also devoted to corn, alfalfa, soybeans and other vegetables, while the cultivation of low-yielding beans, sesame and wheat has been cut to a minimum.

As a result of the changes in cropping pattern, the total value of annual agricultural production is almost doubled—from 131.60 to 252.56 million pesetas—while the total annual farmer costs (exclusive of irrigation fees) are also doubled—from 58.20 to 116.48 million pesetas—and the surplus rises from 73.40 to 136.08 million pesetas. As before, it will be assumed that in the initial years 5 to 10 the annual value of agricultural production and costs rises from one half to its full level in equal linear increments. Government-supplied farm equipment and agricultural credit are assumed to rise in the same proportion as farmer costs, but irrigation fees remain as before, since there has been no change in the costs of construction or operation of the project works. It will also be assumed that only half as many extension workers are required as before. The change in cropping pattern is much more drastic and calls for a more intensive education in new techniques; but there are now far fewer farmers to teach, and this permits a considerable saving.

The evaluation of the project in the light of the revised agricultural programme may now proceed by comparison with the earlier computations. Table 21.24 lists the present values in year 0, under the new assumptions, of each of the benefit, cost and transfer flows distinguished in table 21.19, discounted at the alternative rates of 5 per cent, 7.5 per cent and 10 per cent. The flows whose values differ from the corresponding figures in table 21.21 are identified by an asterisk in table 21.24. The market value of the crops (1) is raised by a factor of 1.919, while the foreign exchange component (1-F) due to the tomato exports is raised by a factor of 5.0. The domestic currency component (1-D) simply represents the difference between the two. Neither the costs of construction (3) or of operation (4) of the project works nor the agricultural income forgone by farmers (7), the land-compensation payments (8) or the irrigation fees (9) are affected by the changed agricultural programme. All the other items under (5), (6) and (10), which relate to the costs of agricultural production, are increased in the same proportion, with the exception of the extension-worker costs (6-S), which are cut in half.

TABLE 21.23 ALTERNATIVE CROP DISTRIBUTION FOR LARGE HOLDINGS: COSTS AND VALUE OF PRODUCTION

Crop	(1) Area (ha)	(2) Unit value of production (Ps/ha)	(3) = (1) (2) Value of production (thousand Ps) = (1) × (2)	(4) Unit cost (Ps/ha)	(5) = (1) (4) Cost (thousand Ps) = (1) × (4)	(6) Unit surplus (Ps/ha)	(7) = (1) (6) Surplus (thousand Ps) = (1) × (6)
Beans	500	1,730	870	1,250	630	480	240
Corn	5,000	2,580	12,900	800	4,000	1,780	8,900
Sesame	—	1,600	—	1,040	—	560	—
Sorghum	1,000	1,910	1,910	730	730	1,180	1,180
Alfalfa	5,000	3,630	18,150	1,870	9,350	1,760	8,800
Safflower	1,000	2,070	2,070	890	890	1,180	1,180
Soybeans	10,000	3,010	30,100	1,040	10,400	1,970	19,700
Tomatoes	10,000	16,000	160,000	8,000	80,000	8,000	80,000
Other vegetables	4,000	3,700	14,800	1,600	6,400	2,100	8,400
Wheat	500	1,920	960	960	480	960	480
Other crops	3,000	3,600	10,800	1,200	3,600	2,400	7,200
Total or average (B)	40,000	6,310	252,560	2,910	116,480	3,400	136,080
Previous total (A)	40,000	3,290	131,600	1,450	58,200	1,840	73,400
Ratio or average (B) / (A)	1.000	1.919	1.919	2.001	2.001	1.854	1.854

TABLE 21.24   PRESENT VALUE OF FLOWS IN YEAR 0 UNDER ALTERNATIVE AGRICULTURAL
                          PROGRAMME

		Social rate of discount		
		5%	7.5%	10%
Benefits				
(1)[a]	Agricultural output	3,509.9	2,210.7	1,500.7
(1-*D*)[a]	Domestic currency	1,284.9	808.2	549.7
(1-*F*)[a]	Foreign exchange	2,225.0	1,402.5	951.0
(2)	Housing and social services	42.1	27.2	19.0
Costs				
(3)	Construction costs	416.2	389.7	365.2
(3-*L*)	Unskilled labour	154.9	144.5	135.2
(3-*S*)	Skilled labour	70.7	66.4	62.3
(3-*D*)	Domestic materials	65.9	61.6	57.6
(3-*F*)	Foreign exchange	124.7	117.2	110.1
(4)	Operating costs	60.1	38.8	27.1
(4-*L*)	Unskilled labour	24.1	15.5	10.8
(4-*S*)	Skilled labour	13.8	8.9	6.2
(4-*D*)	Domestic materials	15.0	9.7	6.8
(4-*F*)	Foreign exchange	7.2	4.7	3.3
(5)[a]	Farmer agricultural costs	1,343.5	847.6	574.1
(5-*L^F*)[a]	Family (unskilled) labour	485.5	306.1	207.5
(5-*L^H*)[a]	Hired (unskilled) labour	161.9	102.0	69.2
(5-*D*)[a]	Domestic materials	242.9	153.3	103.7
(5-*F*)[a]	Foreign exchange	453.2	286.2	193.7
(6)[a]	Ministry agricultural costs	256.0	182.1	137.9
(6-*S*)[a]	Extension workers	9.1	7.1	5.9
(6-*D*)[a]	Working capital	21.8	19.0	16.4
(6-*F*)[a]	Foreign exchange	225.1	156.0	115.6
(7)	Agricultural income forgone	10.2	6.6	4.6
Transfers				
(8)	Compensation to landowners	4.5	4.3	4.1
(9)	Irrigation fees	300.5	194.2	135.4
(10)[a]	Rental and interest payments	275.1	173.5	117.7

[a] Values differ from corresponding figures in table 21.21.

Table 21.25 lists the numerical results obtained under the new assumptions for the total net present value, *PV*, of the project, the net contribution obtained with respect to each major objective, *C*, R^M and R^{SF}, and the various approximations and component elements of *C*. The values with respect to the aggregate-consumption and regional-redistribution objectives were calculated on the basis of the formulae derived earlier in sections 21.11 and 21.12. The value for R^{SF} is based on the corresponding formula (21.8) derived in section 21.13, except that the relevant small farmer percentages of 88.5 and 95.4 are reduced to zero under the new programme, so that $R^{SF} = -0.429$ (7).

It is clear from the results shown in table 21.26 that the present values of both the aggregate-consumption objective and the regional-distribution objective are substantially higher for the new alternative programme. In fact, from the graph of switching values between the two programmes (figure 36,

graph associated with table 21.27), it can be seen that even at a social discount rate of 10 per cent and a regional-distribution weight of zero, the Government must place a weight of over 6 for distribution to small farmers before they would logically and consistently choose the project as originally designed rather than the alternative. This is equivalent to saying that it is worth sacrificing 6 pesetas of aggregate consumption just to increase small-farmer income by one peseta, a highly improbable situation. If the social discount rate is less

TABLE 21.25   PRESENT VALUE OF NET BENEFITS OF THE ALTERNATIVE AGRICULTURAL PROGRAMME IN YEAR 0

(Million pesetas)

Item	Equation number	Social rate of discount		
		5%	7.5%	10%
Aggregate consumption				
MC	(21.1)	+ 1,466.0	+ 773.1	+ 410.8
FE	(21.2a)	+ 1,414.8	+ 838.4	+ 528.3
L	(21.2b)	— 826.4	— 568.1	— 422.7
E	(21.2c)	— 9.1	— 7.1	— 5.9
SC	(21.2)	+ 3,698.1	+ 2,172.5	+ 1,355.9
SC^F	(21.4a)	+ 2,094.5	+ 1,312.2	+ 887.7
SC^L	(21.4b)	+ 340.9	+ 262.0	+ 215.2
SC^G	(21.4c)	+ 1,554.2	+ 870.8	+ 508.1
SC^T	(21.4d)	— 291.5	— 272.5	— 255.1
C	(21.5)	+ 26,660.1	+ 4,971.5	+ 2,011.6
Redistribution to Mendalva				
R^M	(21.7)	+ 3,184.0	+ 2,088.5	+ 1,486.3
Redistribution to small farmers				
R^{SF}	(21.8*)	— 4.4	— 2.8	— 2.0

TABLE 21.26   DIFFERENCES IN PRESENT VALUES BETWEEN ORIGINAL AND ALTERNATIVE PROGRAMME

	Social rate of discount		
	5%	7.5%	10%
C	+ 26,193.3	+ 5,138.3	+ 2,287.8
R^M	+ 1,482.6	+ 931.6	+ 631.2
R^{SF}	— 882.9	— 551.3	— 373.9

TABLE 21.27   SWITCHING VALUES OF ΘR^{SF} BETWEEN ORIGINAL AND ALTERNATIVE PROGRAMMES

	Social rate of discount		
	5%	7.5%	10%
$\Theta R^M = 0.0$	29.7	9.3	6.1
$= 1.0$	31.3	11.0	7.8
$= 2.0$	33.0	12.7	9.5
$= 3.0$	34.7	14.4	11.2

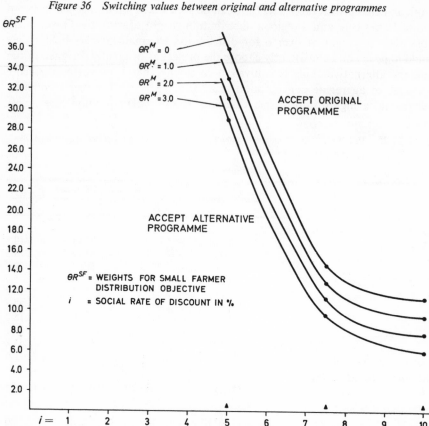

Figure 36   Switching values between original and alternative programmes

than 10 per cent or the regional-distribution weight is positive, the switching value of the small-farmer-distribution weight is much higher.

It is quite conceivable, however, that the Government cannot afford for political reasons to turn all the newly irrigated farm land over to a few cultivators with 100 hectares each. Among other things, this would involve the ejection of a majority of the small farmers who currently hold land in the affected area. In the interests of political realism—if not elementary social justice—the Government's interest in large farm units may have to be confined to the surplus area remaining after all the original landholders have been provided with a share of the newly irrigated land. Under these circumstances, the following distribution of landholdings might be envisaged:

Size of holding	Area (ha)	Per cent	Farmers (no.)	Per cent	Average holding (no.)
Less than 10 ha	19,961	49.9	1,907	88.5	10.5
10 to 100 ha	8,724	21.8	135	6.3	64.5
More than 100 ha	11,315	28.3	113	5.2	100.1
Total	40,000		2,155		18.7

As can be seen by comparison with table 21.3, this distribution assures to all farmers holding less than 100 hectares of land the same area that they held before irrigation, and it breaks up the remaining parcels greater than 100 hectares into equal 100-hectare units. (One hundred hectares may be regarded as the maximum irrigated land allowed by law to a single farming unit.) Under this system of tenure, the 1,907 small farmers may be assumed to cultivate their 49.9 per cent of the land according to the cropping pattern envisaged under the first (small-unit) agricultural programme, and the remaining 248 larger landholders may be assumed to cultivate their 50.1 per cent of the land according to the second (large-unit) agricultural programme.

The effect of such a compromise on the net present value of the project is very easy to calculate: it amounts in every respect to an almost 50—50 split between the outcomes of the two polar cases. Ignoring the minor differences arising because the original programme included a few medium-sized holdings in addition to the small-farm units, the results are summarized in table 21.28 (assuming the same values as before for the key parameters). Since the difference in the values of all the objectives between the original programme and this new, politically feasible programme are exactly one half of the differences between the original and first alternative programme, the switching values of the national weights for choosing between the two programmes will be the same. Thus, unless the weight given to small-farmer income is more than six times the weight given to increase in national income, the Government should revise the agricultural programme to the extent that it is politically possible to increase large farm units. The net present value of the project is now reduced but still exceeds the original value by a substantial margin. The net reduction in present value of the aggregate-consumption benefits of between 13,096 and 1,144 million pesetas, depending on the actual social discount rate, from 5 per cent to 10 per cent, respectively, which is caused by the need to maintain the land ownership of existing farmers with units less than 100 hectares, is a measure of the value of this politico-social constraint and the importance attached to it (if it is respected) by the Galivian Government.

TABLE 21.28 SUMMARY OF RESULTS OF POLITICALLY FEASIBLE MIXED PROGRAMME (HALF WAY BETWEEN ORIGINAL AND ALTERNATIVE PROGRAMMES)

	Social rate of discount		
	5%	7.5%	10%
C	+13,563.5	+2,403.9	+ 867.7
R^M	+ 2,442.7	+1,623.0	+1,170.7
R^{SF}	+ 441.5	+ 275.9	+ 186.0

Chapter 22

FIBREBOARD PLANT IN OASIS

22.1 BACKGROUND

Oasis, as the name suggests, is a relatively small country in a region with a warm and dry climate. Although it is primarily a peasant, agricultural country, its nascent industrial sector has been expanding for some years. It has few natural resources. Because it has no readily exploitable raw materials to export, it is encountering the normal difficulties with its foreign exchange, and these are expected to increase throughout the early stages of its industrialization programme. Oasis, therefore, has a strong desire to exploit to the utmost the resources it does possess.

One of the major products of Oasis is dates. These are harvested by individual farmers and sent to the co-operative packaging plants from where a large percentage is exported. Since a domestic source of wood is lacking, imported fibreboard is used for crating.

A proposed new national industry will produce fibreboard from waste products of the date trees.

22.2 MARKET AND PRICES

Currently, date producers use 10,000 tons of fibreboard for packaging materials. In addition, fibreboard can be used as a substitute for wood in the production of doors and furniture. If all doors were to be made from fibreboard, 2,500 tons would be required for this purpose. Owing to the growth of urban areas, demand is expected to increase at the rate of 10 per cent per year.

The furniture industry is still in its infancy in Oasis. It is anticipated that as the result of an aggressive educational and sales campaign the demand for fibreboard in this industry will rise to 1,000 tons per year. This expectation is based on the fact that fibreboard products will cost 30 to 50 per cent less than alternative wood products. In addition, a good potential exists for expanding the use of fibreboard through the introduction of special finishing processes to make it more attractive for general household and office use. Other possible uses are for construction and maintenance materials.

On the basis of the market studies for each of the end products mentioned above, it has been estimated that the total domestic demand for fibreboard can reach about 15,000 tons per year by the time the plant begins to operate at full capacity.

Fibreboard is currently imported at a c.i.f. price of 78 aras per ton.[104] The present 10 per cent import duty brings the wholesale price up to 85.8 aras per ton. The domestic product of approximately the same quality will be sold at a wholesale price of 90 aras per ton. It is anticipated that if the Government gives a manufacturing licence to the company it will also increase the import duty to 25 per cent. This will make the price of imported fibreboard 97.5 aras per ton, thereby ensuring a switch of consumption to the domestic manufacturer as long as the quality is adequate. Domestic consumers will thus have to pay an additional 4.2 aras per ton. This small increase in domestic price is not expected to slow substantially the growth of domestic demand.

Since costs of transportation from the manufacturing plant to major consumers will be equal to those from the importers' warehouses, they will have no effect on the relative cost of imported domestic production and will, therefore, be ignored in the following analysis.

Other countries within the region currently import about 20,000 tons of fibreboard per year. It is expected that Oasis will be able to capture up to 30 per cent of this market. However, probable differences in quality between the domestic and the European product will require a lower selling price for the Oasis fibreboard in the international market. The net export price (ex factory) will be a conservative 60 aras per ton. It is anticipated that the Government will give a 50 per cent subsidy to the factory in order to make up the difference between the domestic and the export price. This analysis will attempt to determine whether this subsidy is justifiable.

22.3 TECHNOLOGY AND RAW MATERIALS

The most acceptable bid to supply international machinery was based on a "dry" process technology that has been used for a number of years in Europe, although with other raw material inputs. The bid envisages a plant of 70 tons per day working on three shifts. On the basis of 300 working days per year the plant will produce 21,000 tons of fibreboard per year at full capacity. The technical feasibility study was based on large-scale technical tests of the palm stems to ensure their suitability and included water-treatment facilities and fire-protection equipment as essential parts of the project. This technical feasibility study was examined by UNIDO experts and found to be technically sound, accurate and complete when the appropriate equipment performance guarantees are given by the equipment suppliers.

According to the technical study, only the fruit stems have the appropriate chemical and physical properties to allow for economical production of fibre-

---

[104] 1 ara = $1.40 at the current official exchange rate.

board. Most of the stems are picked with the dates and discarded or burned at the packing stations after the fruit has been removed. There are from 8 to 12 stems per tree, yielding a total of 4 to 6 kg. A 21,000-ton-capacity plant will require 38,000 tons of stems, or stems from 7.6 million palm trees. Since it is likely that only 75 per cent of the available stems will be collected for transport to the factory, it is estimated that a region containing 10 million palm trees will be needed to meet the input requirements for full-capacity operation. It has been recommended that these stems be purchased at a price of 7 aras per ton directly from the packing stations.

22.4 LOCATION

The plant will be located in one of the least industrialized regions of the country. Although this choice will entail considerable expense in training both the skilled and unskilled workers, who, for the most part, will have had no previous industry experience, it will add a large number of new jobs to a region which has surplus labour. No additional housing facilities are anticipated for the local labour force.

Seven-and-a-half million palm trees, sufficient to supply 75 per cent of the date stems needed for full-capacity operation, are within 40 km of the plant. The rest will have to be obtained from adjacent districts, at an average transportation distance of 90 km. Transport costs will, of course, reflect the additional cost as the plant reaches full capacity.

22.5 INVESTMENT

The total investment will be 4.298 million aras, of which 3.286 million aras will be in direct foreign exchange, mainly for equipment and machinery. The remaining cost represents items that are purchased locally. There are no taxes on imported capital equipment. The facilities will be constructed over a three-year period. The costs are broken down by commodity and year in table 22.1A.

Inventory accumulation, although generally considered part of the capital costs, is counted separately, since the costs are borne in the fourth through seventh years as production is brought to full capacity. Table 22.1B gives the working capital requirements.

22.6 OPERATION

The plant will begin operation during the fourth year. Production is expected to start at only 25 per cent of capacity and will continue to expand until it reaches full capacity after four years. This will allow sufficient time to solve technical problems as they arise and to train the labour force adequately on the job. Although this may appear to be a long break-in period, one must remember that a large percentage of the output will be exported. Success in selling on the export market will be determined almost exclusively by the competitive quality of the product. Table 22.2 gives output and income from sales.

TABLE 22.1A   INVESTMENT COSTS: PHYSICAL EXPENDITURE BY YEAR
(Thousand aras)

Item	Year 1		Year 2		Year 3	
	Direct domestic currency	Foreign exchange	Direct domestic currency	Foreign exchange	Direct domestic currency	Foreign exchange
(1) Civil engineering works	200	64	200	64	—	—
(2) Machinery, utilities and spare parts ...	—	—	2	1,213	—	1,460
(3) Erection works	—	—	80	70	80	70
(4) Consulting engineers	80	50	80	50	80	50
(5) Training	20	—	20	—	20	—
(6) Contingencies .	50	65	50	65	50	65
Total investment ..	350	179	432	1,462	230	1,645

TABLE 22.1B   NET ADDITIONS TO WORKING CAPITAL
(Thousand aras)

Item	Year			
	4	5	6	7
(1) Raw materials—palm stems (one month) ...	7.5	7.5	7.5	7.5
(2) Inventory (in process and sales)	15.0	15.0	15.0	15.0
(3) Supplies—imported (three months)	11.0	11.0	11.0	11.0

TABLE 22.2   OPERATING OUTPUT AND INCOME
(Thousand aras)

Item	Year			
	4	5	6	7—17
(1) Output				
(1-a) In tons	5,250.0	10,500.0	15,750.0	21,000.0
(1-b) Domestic consumption (tons)	5,250.0	10,500.0	15,750.0	15,750.0
(1-c) For export (tons)	—	—	—	5,250.0
(1-d) In m²	157.5	315.0	462.5	630.0
(2) Earnings				
(2-a) Domestic (at 90 aras/ton)	472.5	945.0	1,417.5	1,417.5
(2-b) Foreign exchange (at 60 aras/ton)	—	—	—	315.0
(3) Potential subsidy for exports (50%)	—	—	—	162.5
(4) Total income including subsidy	472.5	945.0	1,417.5	1,895.0
(5) Foreign exchange				
(5-a) From import savings at c.i.f. import price 78 aras/ton	409.5	819.0	1,228.5	1,228.5
(5-b) From exports at f.o.b. export price 60 aras/ton	—	—	—	315.0
(5-c) Total	409.5	819.0	1,228.5	1,543.5

Table 22.3 gives a breakdown of the operating costs. It should be noted that costs do not rise linearly with output. Most initial costs are higher than 25 per cent of full-capacity costs. This reflects the cost of training new workers and of achieving a more efficient operation through experience.

Transportation costs (4) have been divided between imports and domestic materials. This reflects the fact that (4-b) is directly imported by the domestic supplier. The cost of (4-b) is not large enough to make it necessary to take into account the import taxes and tariffs, which are transfers to the Government, not real costs to the economy. The same comments apply to item (5), power and fuel, although here it was found that the Government does not tax the imports for this sector of the economy. Item (6), supplies, refers to all the basic chemicals needed for the manufacturing operation. Basic industrial raw materials are imported duty-free into Oasis.

22.7 THE "TERMINAL" YEAR

The technical feasibility study estimated that, with proper maintenance, the major equipment will last for 14 years. For the purpose of this analysis

TABLE 22.3   OPERATING COSTS: FLOW OF PHYSICAL EXPENDITURES BY YEAR
(Thousand aras)

Item	Year			
	4	*5*	*6*	*7—17*
(1) Direct labour				
(1-a) Unskilled	30.0	40.0	50.0	60.0
(1-b) Skilled	30.0	40.0	50.0	60.0
(2) Supervision (skilled labour) ...	24.0	24.0	30.0	36.0
(3) Direct raw materials				
(palm stems)	67.0	134.0	201.0	268.0
(4) Transport of direct raw materials				
(4-a) Domestic materials	2.1	4.2	6.3	12.6
(4-b) Imported materials	4.9	9.8	14.7	29.4
(4-c) Unskilled labour	1.0	2.0	3.0	6.0
(5) Power and fuel				
(5-a) Domestic	30.0	60.0	90.0	120.0
(5-b) Imports	15.0	30.0	45.0	60.0
(6) Supplies (imported)	40.0	80.0	120.0	160.0
(7) Maintenance and repair				
(7-a) Skilled labour	20.0	22.0	24.0	28.0
(7-b) Domestic materials	13.0	15.0	17.0	20.0
(7-c) Imported materials	20.0	24.0	26.0	30.0
(8) Administration				
(8-a) Professional staff ...·....	32.0	32.0	32.0	32.0
(8-b) Unskilled labour	8.0	8.0	8.0	8.0
(8-c) Materials (domestic)	5.0	5.0	5.0	5.0
(9) Other (sales and product development staff—				
professionals)	15.0	30.0	45.0	60.0

it is assumed that this is also the life expectancy of the plant and facilities. A decision on reinvestment in plant and machinery including a decision on future capacity will have to be taken at that time. What is necessary is an evaluation of the net value of the plant and equipment at the end of year 17, when the new investment decision must be made. Table 22.4 gives this terminal value.

It should be noted that buildings and equipment are valued at their actual scrap value, that is, the price that the corporation could expect to obtain if they were to sell them and go out of business. The inventory and working capital are valued at cost, assuming that purchases of inputs would decrease during the last year of actual operation if the operation were to be shut down.

Items (4) and (5), business intangibles and business know-how, need explanation. Both intangibles and business know-how represent items that will have no value if the operation ceases. The buildings will be far more valuable if they continue to be used for the same purpose than if they are used for some new, unrelated purpose. The machinery will be worth more if it does not have to be dismantled and transported somewhere else or sold completely as scrap. It is far more valuable in use even after the cost of major repairs has been accounted for than it would be as scrap metal. Thus, the item "intangibles" represents the value of physical assets to a going concern above what these assets would be worth if they were sold to another user. It is a case where the whole is greater than the sum of its parts. Our estimate is that these intangibles have a value equal to the actual scrap value of the plant and equipment.

Business know-how represents the valuable (and probably costly) experience that management has gained during the first 14 years of operating the project. Although it is difficult to determine the exact value of this

TABLE 22.4   TERMINAL VALUES OF NON-CASH ASSETS
(Thousand aras)

Item	
(1) Buildings, scrap value	225 (approximately 25% of original cost)
(2) Machinery, utilities and spare parts	275 (approximately 25% of original cost)
(3) Inventory and working capital, scrap value	175
	Subtotal: 675
(4) Business intangibles[a]	500
(5) Know-how[b]	400
	Subtotal: 900

EXPECTED VALUE AT TERMINAL PERIOD[c]

$$675 \times 20\% + (675 + 900)\,80\% = 1{,}395$$

[a] Plant and equipment value above scrap value if production continues.
[b] Value of management and worker experience if production continues.
[c] See section 22.7 for detailed discussion of this table.

experience, a reasonable minimum estimate might be the equivalent of the costs for the original consulting engineers plus the training costs.[105]

In view of the general experience of both developing and developed countries, we feel that it is reasonable to assume an 80 per cent probability that the operation will continue after year 18. Using basic probability theory one can determine the expected value of the terminal capital, as is done in table 22.4. This terminal capital value plus the cash assets is equal to the value of the stockholders' equity in year 18.

22.8 FINANCIAL ASPECTS

The project will be a wholly domestically owned corporation. It is expected that the stock will be fully subscribed by the private sector of the economy. The total equity capital subscription will be 2 million aras, 600,000 of which will be forthcoming at the beginning of year 1, and 1.4 million at the beginning of year 2.

The suppliers of the machinery and equipment have offered a 1.6 million loan on the 2.67 million aras' worth of equipment purchased. This loan will carry an interest of 6 per cent and will be repayable in five yearly instalments starting with the first year of operation of the facilities. Payment will, of course, be subject to the fulfilment of the equipment specification guarantees. If the equipment does not meet specification guarantees, a formula has been devised for suspending payments of principal and interest during the time necessary for making the adjustments.

The Industrial Development Bank of Oasis (IDBO) will give a long-term loan of 1.1 million aras at 8 per cent interest for the rest of the investment capital. IDBO has also promised a reserve loan of 300,000 aras to ensure that the corporation will not be threatened with insolvency if, through unforeseen circumstances, costs are higher than expected during the first five years of the project. The repayment of the principal and interest will be in six yearly instalments starting with year 7.

With the above information, the total cash flow picture can be derived as shown in table 22.5.

22.9 COMMERCIAL PROFITABILITY

On the basis of table 22.5, which is self-explanatory, we are now in a position to decide whether the project will be commercially profitable. Thus, we are in a position to determine whether the first basic assumption is justified: that private individuals within the country will in fact be willing to put their

---

[105] For those who object, and rightly so, to the use of "guestimates" for this very nebulous concept, we may point out that the process of discounting over 18 years will reduce the size of this figure by over 80 per cent at a 10 per cent discount rate and by over 90 per cent at a 16 per cent discount rate, thus making any errors of estimation small relative to other potential errors in the estimation of future prices, demand, productivity etc.

money into this project. The only information that an individual needs for this purpose is the cash flow associated with the equity investors.[106] This cash flow can be obtained from table 22.5. Item (1-d), equity (payments investors make to the corporation) and item (4-a), dividends (benefits to investors) plus cumulative cash reserves (items 5-c) in year 18, and the net terminal value of cash and non-cash assets [from table 22.6, item (10)].

The cash flow is:

						End value
Years:	(1)	(2)	(3)—(5)	(6)—(8)	(9)—(11)	(12)—(17)	(beginning year 18)
Cash flow:	—600	—1,400	0	200	400	600	3,604.3
(1,000 aras)							

The present value of this cash flow, discounted at 13 per cent, is $+67,200$ aras; discounted at 16 per cent it is $—405,600$ aras. The internal rate of return is approximately 13 per cent. Obviously, the project is profitable from a private point of view. Whether it is profitable enough to draw investors will, of course, be determined by what alternative investments are available in the private sector.

22.10 TREATMENT OF DEPRECIATION ALLOWANCES

The most casual observer will undoubtedly note that by the end of the project's life the total permissible depreciation allowance is much greater than the cumulative reserves of the company. In fact, it is even greater than the net value of the company's assets (i.e. cumulative reserves plus scrap value) in the last year of the project. The reason that the real increase in cash reserves is not sufficient to cover the costs of replacing worn-out machinery is quite clear. The designers of the project are convinced that it is more important to pay substantial dividends to stockholders, thus attracting the initial investors, than it is to accumulate funds for new investment. Thus, the promoters are well aware that if the corporation can pay its debts, pay substantial dividends, and still have capital assets considerably higher than the original equity capital at the end of the project's life, they will have little difficulty in raising new funds for the additional investment needed to rejuvenate the plant and equipment. Surely they will have less difficulty than they had in raising the money on the original, untried and therefore highly risky project. If the operation goes as planned, it will be able to sustain itself and grow if the market potential for such growth exists at the time the renewal decision is made. *Only an exceptionally profitable project can be expected to repay all its loans, pay substantial dividends and also finance its reinvestment programme exclusively through internal resources.*

22.11 CONSOLIDATED ACCOUNTS FOR NATIONAL BENEFIT-COST ANALYSIS

In order to move from the commercial profitability calculation to the national economic profitability calculation, it will be convenient to consolidate

---

[106] The question of risk is not one the project evaluator can bring in here. The private investor generally makes his own personal interpretation on this question.

TA**
(1

Item	1	2	3	4	5	6
(1) Income	600	2,120.0	1,580.0	872.5	945.0	1,417.5
(1-a) Domestic sales	—	—	—	472.5	945.0	1,417.5
(1-b) Foreign sales	—	—	—	—	—	—
(1-c) Subsidy on foreign sales	—	—	—	—	—	—
(1-d) Equity	600	1,400.0	—	—	—	—
(1-e) Equipment credit ...	—	720.0	880.0	—	—	—
(1-f) Long-term loan— Domestic Development Bank ..	—	—	700.0	400.0	—	—
(2) Expenditures	529	1,894.0	1,875.0	390.5	593.5	800.5
(2-a) Investment plus operating expenses...	529	1,894.0	1,875.0	401.2	383.4	364.2
(2-b) Loan repayments						
(i) Supplier's credit: principal	—	—	—	308.6	308.6	308.6
interest	—	—	—	92.6	74.8	55.6
(ii) Domestic bank loan: principal	—	—	—	—	—	—
interest	—	—	—	—	—	—
(3) Operating cash flow	71	226.0	—295.0	80.8	—31.9	252.8
(4) Disbursements						
(4-a) Dividends	—	—	—	—	—	200.0
(4-b) Taxes[a]	—	—	—	—	—	—
(4-c) Depreciation	—	—	—	295.0	295.0	295.0
(5) Real cash balance						
(5-a) Interest[b]	—	1.6	4.9	1.0	5.0	3.7
(5-b) Additions to cash balances after taxes ..	71	226.0	—295.0	80.8	—31.9	52.8
(5-c) Cumulative cash in the bank	71	298.6	18.5	100.3	73.4	132.9

[a] Taxes: 30% of taxable income; there is ten-year tax starting from the first year of operation.
[b] Interest computed at 5% of the previous year's cumulative surplus in the bank, including depreciation funds a

LOW

Year								
9	10	11	12	13	14	15	16	17
1,895.0	1,895.0	1,895.0	1,895.0	1,895.0	1,895.0	1,895.0	1,895.0	1,895.0
1,417.5	1,417.5	1,417.5	1,417.5	1,417.5	1,417.5	1,417.5	1,417.5	1,417.5
315.0	315.0	315.0	315.0	315.0	315.0	315.0	315.0	315.0
162.5	162.5	162.5	162.5	162.5	162.5	162.5	162.5	162.5
—	—	—	—	—	—	—	—	—
—	—	—	—	—	—	—	—	—
—	—	—	—	—	—	—	—	—
995.0	995.0	995.0	995.0	995.0	995.0	995.0	995.0	995.0
296.6	278.6	260.7	242.9	—	—	—	—	—
—	—	—	—	—	—	—	—	—
—	—	—	—	—	—	—	—	—
224.7	224.7	224.7	224.7	—	—	—	—	—
71.9	53.9	36.0	18.0	—	—	—	—	—
603.4	621.3	139.3	157.1	900.0	900.0	900.0	900.0	900.0
400.0	400.0	400.0	600.0	600.0	600.0	600.0	600.0	600.0
—	—	—	—	—	203.6	206.1	208.8	211.5
295.0	295.0	295.0	295.0	295.0	295.0	295.0	295.0	295.0
9.6	20.3	32.4	45.9	51.0	73.6	82.1	90.9	100.0
203.4	221.3	239.3	57.1	300.0	96.4	93.9	91.2	88.5
405.0	646.6	918.3	1,020.3	1,472.7	1,642.7	1,818.7	2,000.8	2,189.3

TABLE 22.6 CONSOLIDATED ACCOUN

(T

Item	1	2	3	4	5
(1) Output					
(1-a) At domestic prices (not including government subsidy)	—	—	—	472.5	945.0
(1-b) At foreign exchange earning and saving prices	—	—	—	409.5	819.0
(2) Human resource inputs	200	280	190	160	198
(2-a) Unskilled labour	50	60	20	39	50
(2-b) Trained labour	20	20	20	30	40
(2-c) Skilled labour	50	120	70	44	46
(2-d) Professionals	80	80	80	47	62
(3) Material resource inputs	329	1,614	1,685	230.5	395.5
(3-a) Palm stems	—	—	—	74.5	141.5
(3-b) Directly imported inputs	179	1,462	1,645	90.9	154.8
(3-c) Other domestic inputs	150	152	40	65.1	99.2
(3-d) Adjusted actual domestic inputs	120	122	30	47.3	74.2
(3-e) Indirect import component	30	30	10	17.8	25.0
(3-f) Direct plus indirect imports: (3-b) + (3-e)	209	1,492	1,655	108.7	179.7
(4) Foreign loan (supplier's credit)	—	720	880	—401.2	—383.4
(5) Government transfers					
(5-a) Tariffs (loss)	—	—	—	41.0	81.9
(5-b) Subsidy (loss)	—	—	—	—	—
(5-c) Taxes (gain)	—	—	—	—	—
(6) Bank transfers					
(6-a) Loan and repayments	—	—	—700	—400.0	—
(6-b) Deposits	71	226	—295	80.8	—31.9
(6-c) Repayments	—	—	—	—	—
(7) Investors' transfers					
(7-a) Equity	—600	—1,400	—	—	—
(7-b) Dividends	—	—	—	—	—
(8) Low-income-group transfers (Increase in costs of fibreboard for date packing, 4.2 aras per ton) (loss)	—	—	—	22.1	42.0
(9) Private-sector transfers (Increase in costs of fibreboard, 4.2 aras per ton) (loss)	—	—	—	—	2.1
(10) Terminal values					
(10-a) Scrap value	—	—	—	—	—
(10-b) Cash reserves	—	—	—	—	—

BENEFIT-COST ANALYSIS

	Year										End of project
8	9	10	11	12	13	14	15	16	17	
,732.5	1,732.5	1,732.5	1,732.5	1,732.5	1,732.5	1,732.5	1,732.5	1,732.5	1,732.5	—
,543.5	1,543.5	1,543.5	1,543.5	1,543.5	1,543.5	1,543.5	1,543.5	1,543.5	1,543.5	—
290	290	290	290	290	290	290	290	290	290	—
74	74	74	74	74	74	74	74	74	74	—
60	60	60	60	60	60	60	60	60	60	—
64	64	64	64	64	64	64	64	64	64	—
92	92	92	92	92	92	92	92	92	92	—
705.0	705.0	705.0	705.0	705.0	705.0	705.0	705.0	705.0	705.0	—
268.0	268.0	268.0	268.0	268.0	268.0	268.0	268.0	268.0	268.0	—
279.4	279.4	279.4	279.4	279.4	279.4	279.4	279.4	279.4	279.4	—
157.6	157.6	157.6	157.6	157.6	157.6	157.6	157.6	157.6	157.6	—
117.6	117.6	117.6	117.6	117.6	117.6	117.6	117.6	117.6	117.6	—
40.0	40.0	40.0	40.0	40.0	40.0	40.0	40.0	40.0	40.0	—
319.4	319.4	319.4	319.4	319.4	319.4	319.4	319.4	319.4	319.4	—
–327.3	—	—	—	—	—	—	—	—	—	—
122.9	122.9	122.9	122.9	122.9	122.9	122.9	122.9	122.9	122.9	—
162.5	162.5	162.5	162.5	162.5	162.5	162.5	162.5	162.5	162.5	—
—	—	—	—	—	—	203.6	206.1	208.8	211.5	—
314.6	296.6	278.6	260.7	242.9	—	—	—	—	—	—
58.1	203.4	221.4	239.3	57.1	300.1	96.4	93.9	91.2	88.5	—
—	—	—	—	—	—	—	—	—	—	2,189.3
—	—	—	—	—	—	—	—	—	—	—
200.0	400.0	400.0	400.0	600.0	600.0	600.0	600.0	600.0	600.0	—
42.0	42.0	42.0	42.0	42.0	42.0	42.0	42.0	42.0	42.0	—
24.2	24.2	24.2	24.2	24.2	24.2	24.2	24.2	24.2	24.2	—
—	—	—	—	—	—	—	—	—	—	1,415.0
—	—	—	—	—	—	—	—	—	—	2,189.3

the information from tables 22.1 through 22.5 into categories that will be of importance in the following analysis. This is done in table 22.6. A short explanation of the arrangement of this table may help to clarify some of the data needed for a national profitability analysis.

Item (1), output, is divided into (1-a), sales at real domestic prices, and (1-b), the opportunity cost of output in terms of foreign exchange saved through not importing the fibreboard (at c.i.f. prices) plus the foreign exchange actually earned on exporting surplus fibreboard (at f.o.b. prices). In the national profitability analysis only the second set of figures will be used, since they represent the real income that Oasis derives from the project.[107]

Item (2), human resources, is divided into unskilled labour; trained labour; skilled labour; and professionals, which include white-collar technicians and management. As will become apparent in the analysis, each of these groups has its own pattern of consumption and saving and therefore must be treated separately.

Item (3), material resource inputs, is divided into palm stems, directly imported inputs and other domestic inputs. Domestic inputs, other than palm stems, are subdivided into an indirect import component and an adjusted, actual domestically produced component. The reasoning behind this additional division is that direct information from the project itself shows only which items are purchased from domestic producers and which are directly imported. However, it is known that imports account for a large share of the raw materials and intermediate goods that go into the manufacture of these domestically produced goods. Although the evaluator did not have a reliable input/output matrix to work with, he was able to trace the foreign requirement for the production of the major domestic inputs during the construction stage (civil engineering works and associated contingencies). This study showed that the indirect foreign exchange requirements were approximately 20 per cent of these inputs. Likewise, a careful study of the major components of domestic materials used in the operating phase showed that the imports associated with the domestic manufacture of these goods are of an even larger magnitude. Our estimate is that indirect imports account for 30 per cent of the cost of domestic materials.

Thus, the foreign exchange used by the project is much higher than that shown by the direct import component alone. When foreign exchange savings and earnings are one of the objectives of the project, the total use of this foreign exchange must be estimated so that the contribution of the project to this objective is not overvalued. Item (3-f) gives the total consumption of foreign exchange by the project.

Item (4) is the supplier's credit. The loan and associated repayment contract is the "real time" foreign exchange cost of the imported machinery.

---

[107] It may be noted, however, that the market price of the product will have an impact on the project through its effect on the redistribution of income: thus, the identity (1-a) = = (1-b) + (5-a) + 8 + 9.

As such, it represents the actual time pattern of the transfer of resources associated with the purchase of machinery for this project.[108] Notice that this loan will yield a positive contribution to the national welfare so long as the interest rate paid is less than the social discount rate.

Items (5) through (9) show the impact of this project on the redistribution of income within Oasis. Five groups have been distinguished here because each has a different saving and consumption pattern. Each of these groups will be explained later. It may be noted that the corporation that will run the project is not included in these five groups. This is because the income from the project will go to the equity holders. Hence, the total income and disbursements of the corporation will be equal. Thus:

$$(1\text{-a}) - (2) - (3) + (4) + (5\text{-b}) - (5\text{-c}) - (6\text{-a}) - (6\text{-b}) - (6\text{-c}) =$$
$$= + (7\text{-a}) + (7\text{-b}) + (10\text{-b})$$

22.12 NATIONAL BENEFIT-COST ANALYSIS

To simplify the calculations and to have eventually a single measure of the worth of the project, one must be able to add together the benefits and costs of each year. This is done by weighting each year through a discount rate[109] so that each item can be consolidated into a single figure, called the discounted present value. Table 22.7 gives the present values of each item discounted at 10 per cent, 13 per cent and 16 per cent. All numbered items on the following pages will refer to this table. The values of all parameters used will be found in table 22.8.

As in the previous case studies, we proceed to evaluate the net aggregate-consumption benefits to Oasis due to the project in successive stages of approximation. The first step is to assume that market prices adequately reflect social opportunity costs and, therefore, the net aggregate-consumption benefits involved. This is equivalent to a national commercial profitability calculation. Thus, the first estimate of the net aggregate-consumption benefits due to the project consists of output (1-a) plus terminal value of non-cash assets (10-a) plus the value of the foreign loan minus labour costs (2) and material outputs. Thus the first estimate is:

$$\text{NCP}[110] = (1\text{-a}) + (10\text{-a}) + (4) - (2) - (3)[111] \qquad (22.1)$$

The next stage is to re-evaluate the inputs and outputs in terms of their real opportunity costs to the country. This is done in three steps. The first

---

[108] Putting the loan as a benefit is equivalent to subtracting the value of the loan from imported materials (3-b).

[109] See chapters 11, 12 and 13.

[110] NCP = national commercial profitability.

[111] The numerical values of all equations are given in table 22.9 for discount rates of 10 per cent, 13 per cent and 16 per cent.

TABLE 22.7　PRESENT VALUE IN YEAR 1 OF DISCOUNTED CASH FLOWS OF ITEMS IN TABLE 22.6

(Thousand aras)

Item	10%	13%	16%
(1) Output			
(1-a) At domestic prices	8,867.8	7,024.6	5,645.1
(1-b) At foreign exchange earning and saving prices	7,854.5	6,217.3	4,993.0
(2) Human resource inputs	2,187.0	1,855.5	1,603.4
(2-a) Unskilled labour	520.9	438.0	375.3
(2-b) Trained labour	377.6	311.1	260.8
(2-c) Skilled labour	573.1	496.6	437.9
(2-d) Professionals	715.4	609.8	529.4
(3) Material resource inputs	6,840.2	5,973.9	5,304.5
(3-a) Palm stems	1,367.9	1,082.4	869.5
(3-b) Directly imported inputs	4,080.5	3,725.2	3,438.7
(3-c) Other domestic inputs	1,492.0	1,239.8	1,050.2
(3-d) Real adjusted domestic inputs	884.4	752.2	652.2
(3-e) Indirect import component	419.3	343.9	287.4
(3-f) Direct plus indirect imports	4,588.0	4,139.3	3,782.8
(4) Foreign loan (supplier's credit)	229.2	310.4	374.7
(5) Government transfers			
(5-a) Tariffs (loss)	658.6	524.7	424.1
(5-b) Subsidy (loss)	655.3	501.6	388.9
(5-c) Taxes (gain)	209.3	142.0	97.5
(6) Bank transfers (gain)			
(6-a) Loan and repayments	−87.3	−187.4	−258.5
(6-b) Deposits	618.3	493.1	401.6
(6-c) Repayments	447.3	308.7	203.6
(7) Investors			
(7-a) Equity	−1,872.6	−1,839.0	−1,806.8
(7-b) Dividends	1,857.8	1,398.0	1,066.4
(8) Low-income group transfers[a]	240.6	193.5	157.4
(9) Private-sector transfers[b]	114.1	89.1	70.6
(10) Terminal values for year 18			
(10-a) Scrap value	308.5	199.5	131.6
(10-b) Cash reserves	477.3	308.7	203.6
(11) T: Benefits from training labour	111.1	53.6	24.3

[a] Increase in costs of fibreboard for date packing, 4.2 aras per ton (loss).
[b] Increase in costs of fibreboard for general use 4.2 aras per ton (loss).

step is to evaluate the foreign exchange savings and losses. The second step is to re-evaluate the labour resources used so that their price reflects their real opportunity costs. The third step is to evaluate the real cost of all other material inputs for which one feels that the market does not represent the true opportunity cost (in this case, the palm stems and labour training).

The output of this project will be a substitution for imports. As discussed in chapter 4, it is necessary to revalue the output in terms of its opportunity cost in foreign exchange, since foreign exchange is the real output of any import-substitution project. The first "social calculation", SC_1, will then be

TABLE 22.8 TABLE OF NATIONAL PARAMETERS

(1) Foreign exchange premium	Φ	$= +0.30$
(2) Premium for palm stems	Θ	$= -1.00$
(3) Unskilled labour premium	λ	$= -0.75$
(4) Previously skilled labour premium	χ	$= +0.50$
(5) Social rate of return on private investment	r	$= 0.25$
(6) Marginal rate of reinvestment out of profits	s	$= 0.30$
(7) Social rate of discount	i	$= 0.10, 0.13, 0.16$
(8) Shadow price of investment	p^{inv}	$= 7.00, 3.18, 2.06$
(9) Marginal propensity to save:		
(a) Bank	S_B	$= 1.00$
(b) Government	S_G	$= 0.90$
(c) Investors		
equity (capital)	S_E	$= 1.00$
dividends (income)	S_D	$= 0.30$
(d) Skilled and unskilled labour and agricultural sector	S_L	$= 0.05$
(e) Rest of the private sector	S_P	$= 0.20$
(10) Premium for redistribution of income to region	γ	$= 0.10$
(11) Premium for redistribution of income to low-income groups	a	$= 0.10$
(12) Marginal propensity to spend income in region	δ	$= 0.20$
(13) Marginal tax rate on new imports	ζ	$= 0.20$
(14) Ratio of unskilled to skilled labour wage rates	σ	$= 0.40$

a substitution of foreign exchange costs and benefits at the official exchange rate for the benefits previously associated with domestic materials as follows:[112]

$$SC_1 = (1\text{-}b) + (10\text{-}a) + (4) - [(2) + (3\text{-}a) + (3\text{-}d) + (3\text{-}f)] \qquad (22.2)$$

The Central Government has informed the project evaluator that foreign exchange is overvalued at its current market rate. The official rate is maintained by both quantitative import controls and high tariffs. The opportunity cost of foreign exchange relative to the official price is denoted by $1 + \Phi$, where Φ[113] represents the foreign exchange premium, which is expected to remain constant over the lifetime of the project. The correction for the social value of foreign exchange above its market price is made by multiplying the foreign exchange components of the inputs and outputs of the project by Φ, where the foreign exchange component is:

$$FE = (1\text{-}b) + (4) - (3\text{-}f) \qquad (22.3)$$

Project evaluators are aware that there is considerable underemployment of unskilled labour in Oasis. After having studied the region in which the

---

[112] It should be noted that no attempt was made to revalue the terminal assets in terms of their foreign exchange component. This could have been done for such obvious items as the inventory of finished-goods and spare parts.

The project evaluators have not done this only because they think that the benefit-cost ratio of increase in accuracy of their final results to the increase in effort necessary does not justify it. This is one of the many instances where theoretical completeness is not justified in terms of the magnitude of the potential difference in results.

[113] The value of this national parameter, along with all the other national parameters, can be found in table 22.8.

factory is to be established, they have estimated that the opportunity cost of employing unskilled labour is approximately 25 per cent of the real wage bill, W_U, that would be paid.[114] This opportunity cost of unskilled labour relative to the wage rate is denoted by $(1 + \lambda)$, where λ represents the social premium for the use of unskilled labour.[115]

Skilled labour is fully employed in Oasis and, in fact, the need for it exceeds its supply at its current wage. The reasons for this, fully discussed in chapter 5, are based on the institutional wage structure in Oasis. Since the marginal skilled worker contributes more to the aggregate-consumption benefits of the society than his monetary wage indicates, the opportunity cost of skilled labour relative to its wage bill, W_S, is $(1 + \chi)W_S$, where χ is the social premium above the market wage rate.[116]

The labour trained on the job was originally unskilled labour. Thus, its opportunity cost to the country as a whole must be the same as that of untrained labour. It is known that the wage rate for unskilled labour is only a fraction, σ, of that for skilled labour. Thus, the wage bill of these trained workers, W_T, if they had not been trained would have been $\sigma(W_T)$, and their real opportunity cost is $\sigma(W_T)(1 + \lambda)$.

For lack of information to the contrary, the project evaluators have assumed that professionals are paid their real opportunity cost. Therefore, no correction is needed to the cost of this input. The real costs of labour are therefore:

$$SC_L = (1 + \lambda)W_U + (1 + \chi)W_S + \sigma(1 + \lambda)W_T + W_P.$$

Since the original estimate of costs based on market prices was

$$MC_L = W_U + W_S + W_T + W_P,$$

the change in cost of labour for the new estimate based on opportunity cost is:

$$L = SC_L - MC_L = \lambda W_U + \chi W_S + [\sigma(1 + \lambda) - 1]W_T \qquad (22.4)$$

where: $W_U = -$ (2-a);
$\quad\quad\quad W_S = -$ (2-c);
$\quad\quad\quad W_T = -$ (2-b).

In Oasis, the market prices represent the best estimate of the real opportunity cost for all the domestic material inputs except the palm stems. As mentioned earlier, the palm stems have no alternative use (they are currently being burned as rubbish). The opportunity cost relative to its market price is $(1 + \Theta)$. The correction for the opportunity cost of this input will, therefore, be ΘM, where

$$M = -\text{(3-a)} \qquad (22.5)$$

---

[114] That is, the marginal output of labour in its current activities is only 25 per cent of the wage that the new enterprise will pay. For full discussion of this question, see sections 5.5 and 7.2.

[115] λ is negative because unskilled labour has a social cost of less than its real wage. $\lambda = -0.75$; thus $1 + \lambda = 0.25$ as indicated in table 22.8.

[116] χ is a parallel concept to λ, but is positive, since the real cost of skilled labour in the economy is greater than its wage rate.

Thus, the total correction for the market prices of inputs and outputs is:

$$SC_2 = SC_1 + \Phi(FE) + L + \Theta M \qquad (22.6)$$

As can be seen from table 22.9, this project is basically one of import substitution and uses resources that would otherwise be idle. Thus, the national economic benefits will increase when one uses the imputed prices for direct inputs and outputs. But this is only part of the total picture. Stopping here would give as inaccurate a result as using only commercial profitability as a guide.

22.13 NATIONAL BENEFITS FROM THE TRAINING OF LABOUR

One of the important aspects of this project is the training of labour for industrial employment. The meaning of this type of indirect benefit is fully discussed in section 6.1. To evaluate the contribution to the national economy from this creation of "human capital", the project evaluator must first determine its source and magnitude. The contribution can be divided into the primary value of the labour, while employed on the project, and the secondary value, after it leaves the project. While the labour remains on the project, the project will automatically absorb the benefits of the difference between labour's productivity and its wage; and the difference between the opportunity cost of the workers before they were trained and the wage they will get has already been taken into account in the preceding section. However, after the terminal year the economy will have the additional pool of skilled

TABLE 22.9   NUMERICAL VALUE OF EQUATIONS IN TEXT

Equations	Social rate of discount		
	10%	13%	16%
(1) NCP = (1-a) + (10-a) + (4) — (2) — (3)	855.6	13.8	—552.9
(2) SC_1 = (1-b) + (10-a) + (4) — [(2) + (3-a) + (3-d) + + (3-f)]	—157.8	—793.5	—1,205.0
(3) FE = (1-b) + (4) — (3-f)........................	3,495.7	2,388.4	1,584.9
(4) L = $\lambda W_U + \chi W_S + [\sigma(1 + \lambda) - 1] W_T$ where $W_U = -(2\text{-a})$; $W_S = -(2\text{-c})$; $W_T = -(2\text{-b})$	444.0	856.8	735.2
(5) M = — (3-a)	—1,367.9	—1,082.4	—869.5
(6) SC_2 = $SC_1 + \Phi(FE) + L + \Theta M$.................	2,702.8	1,862.2	875.2
(7) SC_3 = $SC_2 + [1 + \chi - \sigma(1 + \lambda)] T$	2,858.3	1,937.2	909.2
(8) SC_G = (5-c) — (5-b) — (5-a) + ζ (FE)	—405.5	—406.6	—398.5
(9) SC_B = (6-a) + (6-b) — (6-c)	53.7	—3.0	—60.5
(10) SC_L = (3-a) — (8) — λ (2-a) + + [1 — (1 + λ) σ] [(2-b) + T]	1,957.8	1,545.6	1,250.2
(11) SC_E = (7-a) + (10-a) + (10-b) + (6-c)	—609.5	—1,022.1	—1,268.0
(12) SC_D = (7-b)	1,857.8	1,398.0	1,066.4
(13) SC_P = — (9) — χ (2-c) + χ (T) + [Φ — ζ] (FE)	4.5	424.8	319.0
(14) TS = $S_G SC_G + S_B SC_B + S_L SC_L + S_E SC_E$ + + $S_D SC_D + S_P SC_P$	—264.7	—734.1	—1,281.2
(15) C = $SC_3 + (P^{inv} - 1)(TS)$	628.7	336.9	—448.9

labour that has been trained.[117] The value of this pool of skilled labour must be added to the national benefits created by the project. Thus, the additional value to the economy will be the discounted sum of the difference between the opportunity cost of this skilled labour if it had not been trained and its marginal product now that it is trained. Its opportunity cost, as calculated in section 22.14, will be $\sigma(1 + \lambda)$ times its wage bill, while its marginal productivity will be the same as other trained labour, that is, $(1 + \chi)$ times its wage bill. Assuming that the real wages paid to trained labour remain at 60,000 aras per year and that, on the average, the trained workers will work an additional 20 years, the total wage bill is:

$$T = \sum_{t=18}^{t=37} \frac{60,000}{(1 + i)^t} \text{ (See item (11), table 22.7 for quantitative values.)}$$

Including this external benefit, the next approximation to the net social benefits of the project is:[118]

$$SC_3 = SC_2 + [1 + \chi - \sigma(1 + \lambda)] T \tag{22.7}$$

22.14 CORRECTIONS FOR THE SOCIAL VALUE OF INVESTMENT

The final correction to be applied to the net aggregate-consumption benefits stemming from the project is designed to account for the fact that the social value of funds devoted to investment exceeds the social value of the same funds devoted to consumption. This feature has arisen in Oasis because the Government is unable to bring about the rate of investment it deems optimal for the country as a whole through the use of its normal fiscal and monetary powers.[119] Thus, the social rate of discount of future consumption benefits is lower than the social opportunity rate of return. To evaluate the indirect future benefits (and costs) of the project, the project evaluator will have to assess the net change in the consumption-investment mix in the economy due to the project. To do this, it is necessary to distinguish all the benefit and cost flows, as well as the accompanying cash transfers, according to the group that gains or loses, and to estimate the respective marginal savings propensities of each group.[120] For this purpose five broad

---

[117] We have assumed for simplicity's sake that all the trained labour will remain on the job for the life of the project. We know of no way to take account of the possible effect of the departure of trained workers during the life of the project.

[118] The assumption used here is that the real productivity of skilled workers will remain constant over the next 40 years. We will admit that this is a highly implausible assumption. It is, in fact, much less justifiable than the assumption that the opportunity cost of unskilled workers will remain constant in real terms or as a constant percentage of the wages of skilled workers. One could, alternatively, assume that productivity increased by 50 per cent over the period. One would make a rough estimate $[(1 + \chi)(1.5) - \sigma(1 + \lambda)] T$. Our purpose here, however, has been to make a minimum estimation of this benefit. It should be noted that the assumption about the relationship between real wages and real productivity (or opportunity cost) of skilled labour will not affect the residual value of this human capital in trained labour, although it will influence the distribution of the benefits.

[119] See chapter 6 for further discussion of this point.

[120] These marginal savings propensities are national parameters needed for national profitability calculations. Their values for Oasis are found in table 22.8.

groups of gainers and losers have been distinguished with regard to the present project. They are: (a) the Government; (b) the Development Bank; (c) the low-income group—the agricultural sector and unskilled labour; (d) the private investors; and (e) the rest of the private economy.

The Government gains the taxes the enterprise pays (5-c) and loses the subsidy it must pay the enterprise for exporting the fibreboard (5-b); in addition, it loses the income from tariffs on the fibreboard no longer imported. At first glance one might think that this income loss will be equal to the total loss in revenue from the no-longer-imported fibreboard. However, this would be a gross exaggeration of the actual loss, since the foreign exchange that is not used for importing fibreboard will surely be used for importing other goods, the duty on which will be a revenue for the Government. In fact, the Government might even increase its income if the tariff on the new imports is higher than the tariff on the goods no longer imported. In the previous case studies this problem was handled by dividing it into two parts. The loss of tariffs on the goods no longer imported was counted as a cost for the Government, while the total increase in available foreign exchange was counted as a direct benefit to the Government. In Oasis, the Government is not free to do as it pleases with the additional foreign exchange, which will be distributed throughout the economy in much the same proportions as it is now being distributed.[121]

For this reason, the Government will gain only the tariffs that it collects on the imports made possible by the net additions to the available foreign exchange.[122] The present value of this net change in government income is the net increase in foreign exchange $(1\text{-}b) + (4) - (3\text{-}d)$ multiplied by the marginal tax rate on new imports, ζ,[123] minus the decrease in tariff caused by import substitution of fibreboard (5-a). Thus, the total change in the present value of government income is:

$$SC_G = (5\text{-}c) - (5\text{-}b) - (5\text{-}a) + \zeta \, (FE) \qquad (22.8)$$

The Development Bank loses investable funds when it makes the loan to the corporation and gains the funds back when the loan is repaid (6-a). It also gains the cash deposited by the corporation (6-b), losing it when it is withdrawn in year 18 (6-c). The present value of the bank's investable resources is:

$$SC_B = (6\text{-}a) + (6\text{-}b) - (6\text{-}c) \qquad (22.9)$$

The agricultural sector, one part of the low-income group, loses from the increase in cost of the fibreboard needed for packing the dates (8). This loss can be directly identified with the agricultural sector, since the packaging plants are run as a producer co-operative. The loss is equal to the difference

---

[121] Although this policy could be changed in the future, there appears to be no indication of such a change at the present moment.

[122] However, the economy as a whole will have a higher real income because of the increased availability of foreign exchange.

[123] ζ is one of the central parameters supplied by the Ministry of Planning.

between the wholesale price of the domestically produced fibreboard of 90 aras per ton and the previous wholesale price of 85.8 aras per ton (which includes a 10 per cent tariff). To offset these costs, agriculture gains the total income from the sale of the palm stems (3-a), while unskilled workers, including trained workers who were originally unskilled, the other part of the low-income group, gain the income equal to the difference between opportunity cost (marginal output) in their previous occupation and their factory wages. The trained workers also gain the value of their higher wages for their entire working lives. As was shown in sections 22.13 and 22.17, this is:

$$SC_L = (3\text{-a}) - (8) - \lambda\,(2\text{-a}) + [1 - (1 + \lambda)\,\sigma]\,[(2\text{-b}) + T] \quad (22.10)$$

The treatment of income of investors (equity holders) is somewhat complicated by the fact that this group treats its capital differently from its income. In particular, it has been found that these private investors will invest their equity capital in another project if this project is not undertaken. In a similar manner they will maintain their capital intact after the terminal year by reinvesting it. However, they will treat the dividend income from their investments as part of their total spendable income, spending a large portion of it. Since one is trying to determine how total investment and consumption will change because of the project, the present value of equity must be treated independently of the present value of dividends.

$$SC_E = (7\text{-a}) + (10\text{-a}) + (10\text{-b}) + (6\text{-c}) \qquad (22.11)$$

$$SC_D = (7\text{-b}) \qquad (22.12)$$

The private sector loses a sum equal to the increase in cost of the fibre-board it buys (9). It also loses the services of skilled workers whose marginal product is $[1 + \varkappa]\,(2\text{-c})$, but since it no longer has to pay their wages the net loss is only (2-c). In a similar fashion, it gains from the increase in skilled labour due to training, $\varkappa(T)$, which will be available to the country as a whole after the terminal year of the project.

The additional foreign exchange available to the country represents a real income of Φ above its market cost. The institutional organization of the foreign exchange market in Oasis is such that gain not captured by the Government through tariffs is distributed to the private sector of the economy through the increase in imports that it allows. Thus, the difference between the premium value of foreign exchange and the marginal tax rate goes to the private sector. The change in the present value of the private sector's income is:

$$SC_P = - (9) - \varkappa\,(2\text{-c}) + \varkappa\,(T) + [\Phi - \zeta]\,(FE) \qquad (22.13)$$

Multiplying the income change of each group by the group's national propensity to save, we obtain the total sum of the present value of future changes in savings (and investment), which is:

$$TS = S_G\,SC_G + S_B\,SC_B + S_L\,SC_L + S_E\,SC_E + S_D\,SC_D + \\ + S_P\,SC_P \qquad (22.14)$$

and the final approximation for the net contribution to the aggregate-consumption objective is:

$$C = SC_3 + (P^{inv} - 1)\, TS \qquad (22.15)$$

where P^{inv} is the social value of investment so that $(P^{inv} - 1)$ is the difference between the social value of investment and the social value of consumption.[124]

It should not be surprising to note that the value of the sum of equations 22.8 through 22.13 is equal to the value of equation 22.7. Thus, the direct consumption benefits as seen for the project as a whole are equal to the sum of the benefits to each group in the society. For this reason, one can use the alternative formulation for C, the total direct and indirect benefits of the project, as:

$$C = SC_G\,[1 - S_G + S_G\, P^{inv}] + SC_B\,[1 - S_B + S_B\, P^{inv}] + \ldots +$$

or $\quad C = \sum_x SC_x\,[1 - S_x + S_x\, P^{inv}]$

where $x = G, B, L, E, D, P,$ $\qquad\qquad\qquad\qquad\qquad$ (22.16)

as has been done in previous case studies. In fact, one could eliminate equations 22.1 through 22.8 and calculate directly the total benefits to each group using only equations 22.9 through 22.14 and equation 22.16.

So far the project evaluator has taken into account the need for additional foreign exchange earnings and savings, the desire to use available domestic resources wherever possible, the value of increasing labour force skills through training, the value of increasing government income, the cost of losses of government income, and the need for increasing total savings and investment. All these goals have been included in the calculation of the present value of the total net aggregate-consumption benefits of the project. The present value of the net aggregate-consumption benefits of the project will, of course, depend on the social rate of discount used. With a social discount rate of 10 per cent, 13 per cent and 16 per cent, the present value of the net aggregate-consumption benefits is 628.7, 336.9 and —448.9 thousand aras, respectively.

Does this mean that the project should be rejected if the second discount rate decided upon by the policy makers is higher than 14 per cent? (Remember, the social discount rate is a value judgement. See chapter 15.) The answer is "not necessarily", since in addition to the goal of maximizing the aggregate-consumption objective, the policy makers also wish to increase income to the lower-income groups in the poorer regions. Thus, the project evaluator must also take into account this second objective in evaluating the project.

22.15 INCOME-DISTRIBUTION CRITERIA

It must be remembered that the Government has other goals besides the ones outlined above. It also wishes to improve the distribution of income, especially to the low-income groups in the lowest-income regions. Since this

---

[124] For a further explanation of the social value of investment, see sections 6.3.

project creates employment for low-income groups in a low-income region, and also uses otherwise wasted resources belonging to these low-income groups, it is clear that an inclusion of this criterion in the calculation will increase the social national economic profitability of the project.

To assess the contribution of this project to the income-distribution objective, we must determine what income flows go to these groups. The two groups important here are the agricultural sector and the unskilled workers. The increase in their income has already been calculated; it is

$$R = SC_L$$

Social rate of discount (%)		Thousand aras
10	=	1,957.8
13	=	1,545.6
16	=	1,250.2

Since the policy-makers have not determined exactly what the weight on redistribution of income should be, we will calculate the two value-judgement weights that will allow the project to just be acceptable, i.e. the present value equal to zero. These are called switching values of the parameters. The following table and graph (fig. 37) summarize this information.

Figure 37   Switching values graph

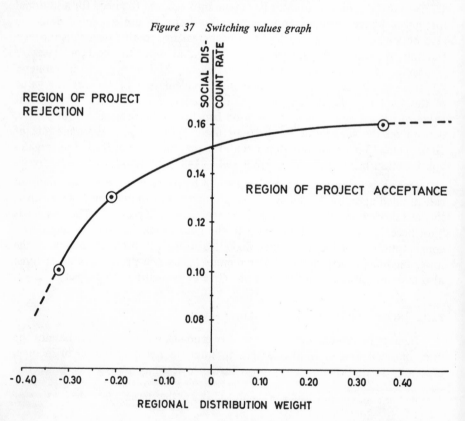

Switching values

Social rate of discount (%)	Present value of aggregate-consumption objective (thousand aras)	PV of redistribution objective (thousand aras)	Switching value of redistribution weight (%)
10	628.7	1,957.8	−31.8
13	336.9	1,545.6	−21.8
16	−448.9	1,250.2	35.9

As can be seen from the graph, the project should be accepted when the combination of weights are to the left and above the switching line. It should be rejected when the weights are to the right and below.

22.16 FINAL REMARKS ON PRIVATE-SECTOR PROJECTS

Since the project is a private-sector project, its profitability will in the last analysis determine whether the project will be undertaken. If the private sector does not consider it to be sufficiently profitable, it might be in the national interest to take measures to stimulate more interest in it. The reader may wish to re-do this exercise assuming a 10 per cent government subsidy on sales and higher dividend payments, or a 10 per cent subsidy on total investment with a concomitant reduction in equity capital.

Two ways of doing this come to mind immediately. One way would be for the development bank to allow a longer loan, thus reducing the total equity that need be raised and increasing the profits through "investors' leverage".[125] Alternatively, the Government could agree to pay a subsidy of 5 per cent on all sales, thus greatly increasing profits. Either alternative will, however, create certain transfer costs, i.e. costs of transferring income from very high savers and investors (banks or Government) to lower savers (private investors). The calculation of the new commercial profitability and social costs of either of the above suggestions will be left to the reader who wishes to test his understanding of the subject.

---

[125] Leverage is a function of the difference between the internal rate of return and the interest paid on a loan. For example, if a project costs 100 and returns 110 the next year, its return is 10 per cent; if one can borrow 50 at 8 per cent interest, one will invest 50 and get back 56 after paying the principle and interest, yielding a return of 12 per cent; if one can borrow 90 at 8 per cent, one will invest 10 and get back 12.8, yielding a return of 20 per cent.

9130